Praise for *21st Century Business Icons*

Whether you are wanting to learn more about today's successful business icons or pick up tips and ideas to enhance your own practice, Sally Percy's book is an interesting and inspiring read. AUDREY TANG, CHARTERED PSYCHOLOGIST AND LEADERSHIP DEVELOPMENT TRAINER

Sally Percy writes with insight about established icons and about emerging leaders. I found something new and interesting in every chapter, and found the chapter summaries very powerful. It's a book I'll be referring to time and time again. ROGER DELVES, PROFESSOR OF PRACTICE FOR LEADERSHIP AND MANAGEMENT, HULT INTERNATIONAL BUSINESS SCHOOL

Such an insightful book and a must-read for anyone in business or thinking of starting one. Motivating and inspiring – and a book to come back to again and again! MARTINA DOHERTY, BUSINESS PSYCHOLOGIST AND LEADERSHIP COACH

If you are looking for a dose of inspiration to guide the next steps in your career, look no further. Sally Percy's gift for storytelling shines through her 21 profiles of some of the world's most impactful entrepreneurs. JOHN MULLINS, ASSOCIATE PROFESSOR, LONDON BUSINESS SCHOOL

This is a must-read for anybody who aspires to a senior leadership role. It certainly won't be one of those business books you buy but never quite get round to reading! MARK SIMMONDS, CREATIVITY EXPERT CHAMPION

If you want to know how today's most influential business bosses got to the top, look no further than this book. Sally's knack of getting quickly to the heart of a story makes it a real page-turner, and it's a fascinating source of insight about the personal journeys of leaders. PATRICK WOODMAN, EDITOR OF *DIALOGUE* MAGAZINE AND FREELANCE CONSULTING EDITOR

Through inspiring stories and thoughtful analysis, this book teaches us valuable lessons from modern leaders. Whether you want to be a leader yourself or just love reading about business, this book helps us understand the qualities and sacrifices that drive success. RAMEEZ KALEEM, FOUNDER AND MANAGING DIRECTOR, 3R STRATEGY

Sally Percy provides a unique insight into the philosophies, mindsets, behaviours and backgrounds of some of the most successful leaders of our time. This book will become the sought-after text for anyone who is trying to make sense of what it means to be a leader during these tough and challenging, yet hugely exciting, times. DAVID LIDDLE, FOUNDING PRESIDENT, PEOPLE AND CULTURE ASSOCIATION, AND CEO, TCM

A gem of a book, written with the sparkle and insight that characterizes Sally Percy's renowned coverage of leadership and business. A great learning lesson in leadership. MATT SYMONDS, DIRECTOR, FORTUNA ADMISSIONS, AND EDITOR-IN-CHIEF, BLUESKY THINKING

21st Century Business Icons

The leaders who are changing our world

Sally Percy

KoganPage

First published in Great Britain and the United States in 2023 by Kogan Page

2nd Floor, 45 Gee Street
London
EC1V 3RS
United Kingdom
www.koganpage.com

8 W 38th Street, Suite 902
New York, NY 10018
USA

4737/23 Ansari Road
Daryaganj
New Delhi 110002
India

© Sally Percy, 2023

ISBNs
Hardback   978 1 3986 1134 4
Paperback   978 1 3986 1132 0
Ebook   978 1 3986 1133 7

British Library Cataloguing-in-Publication Data
A CIP record for this book is available from the British Library.

Library of Congress Cataloging-in-Publication Data
Names: Percy, Sally, author.
Title: 21st century business icons: the leaders who are changing our world / Sally Percy.
Other titles: Twenty-first century business icons
Description: London; New York, NY: Kogan Page, 2023. | Includes bibliographical references and index.
Identifiers: LCCN 2023017441 (print) | LCCN 2023017442 (ebook) | ISBN 9781398611320 (paperback) | ISBN 9781398611344 (hardback) | ISBN 9781398611337 (ebook)
Subjects: LCSH: Businesspeople–Case studies. | Success in business–Case studies. | Leadership–Case studies. | Entrepreneurship–Case studies.
Classification: LCC HC29 .P47 2023 (print) | LCC HC29 (ebook) | DDC 338.092/2–dc23/eng/20230413
LC record available at https://lccn.loc.gov/2023017441
LC ebook record available at https://lccn.loc.gov/2023017442

Typeset by Hong Kong FIVE Workshop, Hong Kong
Print production managed by Jellyfish
Printed and bound by CPI Group (UK) Ltd, Croydon CR0 4YY

CONTENTS

Introduction 1

PART ONE
Leadership icons of today 7

1 Mary Barra (General Motors) 9

2 Jeff Bezos (Amazon) 19

3 Sara Blakely (Spanx) 33

4 Rosalind Brewer (Walgreens Boots Alliance) 46

5 Brian Chesky, Joe Gebbia and Nathan Blecharczyk
   (Airbnb) 58

6 Yvon Chouinard (Patagonia) 70

7 Jimmy Donaldson (MrBeast) 86

8 Sir James Dyson (Dyson) 97

9 Kiran Mazumdar-Shaw (Biocon) 112

10 Elon Musk (SpaceX, Tesla and Twitter) 123

11 Satoshi Nakamoto (Bitcoin) 141

12 Melanie Perkins (Canva) 159

13 Zhang Ruimin (Haier Group) 170

14 Uğur Şahin and Özlem Türeci (BioNTech) 181

15 Whitney Wolfe Herd (Bumble) 191

16 Mark Zuckerberg (Meta Platforms) 203

PART TWO
The next generation 219

17 Lucrezia Bisignani (Kukua) 221

18 Mette Lykke (Too Good To Go) 230

19 Nthabiseng Mosia (Easy Solar) 242

20 Akindele Phillips (Farmcrowdy) 251

21 Andrea Thomaz (Diligent Robotics) 259

Conclusion 269

About the author 272

Introduction

Where there is no vision, the people perish.
PROVERBS 29:18

Leadership is an enormously important activity, not least because it has underpinned human survival and prosperity over time. Effective leaders do not just set a vision for people to work towards. They also help us to organize ourselves so that we have a realistic chance of achieving our most pressing goals. Furthermore, effective leaders build trust in the overall mission by acting with fairness and integrity. And they inspire and motivate us to keep going, even in the most challenging circumstances. Finally, by being frankly unreasonable on occasions, they encourage us to aim higher and push harder, improving the outcomes for all.

We can only enjoy the world we have today because of the leaders of the past. These leaders include well-known religious figures, warriors, monarchs, politicians, writers, philosophers, scientists and businesspeople. The list of leaders who have helped to shape our society is extensive. In fact, if you were to ask a group of people to suggest a famous leader from history who has positively influenced the modern world, you would probably be bombarded with a vast array of names, ranging from Jesus Christ and Julius Caesar through to William Shakespeare, Henry Ford and Nelson Mandela. The overwhelming majority would be men.

Yet it is not just the male leaders from the history books who have played an instrumental role in building our society. In every age, there have also been many more leaders whose deeds have gone unreported, if not unnoticed, but who still made an important difference in their own way. These are the people who led their communities on a day-to-day basis, who helped and served others, who rallied their friends and relatives behind an important cause, and who sometimes even sacrificed their own lives for the greater good. Notably, these people were just as likely to be women as they were to be men.

The truth is that leaders are not simply people who hold more senior job titles than we do, or those we read about in books or on the internet. Regardless of what we do, or where we live, or how many people report into us, each of us is a leader in our own way. That's because every one of us is someone who takes decisions, someone who influences to get results, and someone who touches the lives of others, often with lasting consequences.

But while everyone is capable of leadership, leadership is nevertheless a very broad concept that exists at different levels and in different contexts, with considerable variation in terms of the complexity, politics and responsibility involved. Leading a country is not the same as leading a community group, for example. Leading a multinational business with tens of thousands of employees is not the same as running a corner shop. So, it's natural that anyone who is interested in becoming a better leader would want to learn from those leaders who are operating in an apparently more challenging context than their own so that they can reflect on, and refine, their leadership practice.

Today's leaders must navigate an incredibly wide range of macro issues, from geopolitical tensions, economic uncertainty and rapid technological change through to some notable workplace trends such as 'quiet quitting', largescale skills shortages and widespread remote working. At the same time, expectations are evolving around what a 'good leader' looks like. Increasingly, there is recognition that a good leader is not necessarily an outgoing 'charismatic' person, who has an innate ability to 'rally the troops'. Quiet, introverted leaders can often be just as effective at uniting their team behind a vision, with powerful results.

Leadership in business

This book looks at leadership specifically in the context of business. In particular, it examines some of the most successful people in business today, both male and female, across a range of markets. The first section of the book focuses on 16 individual leaders and leadership teams. These people are already very well known within the business community and many are household names. Most – but not all – of them are so successful that they are already billionaires.

So, does being a billionaire mean that someone is a good leader? Many would argue that is not necessarily the case. Nevertheless, the scale of their success would suggest that they are doing something right, and that we can learn from them in some way. By reading their stories, we can glean some insights into the behaviours and characteristics that underpin phenomenal success. The conclusion to this book highlights some of the common themes to emerge.

The second section of the book features five business leaders who are not household names, but who are impressive pioneers in their fields. They represent the new generation of leaders who often have a strong social and environmental focus. While they have much in common with the entrepreneurs profiled in Part One, their ideas on leadership also reflect the changing trends and expectations of our time.

In total, across the two sections, there are 21 individual leaders or leadership teams. Together they represent 21 leaders for the 21st century. To be selected for this book, they needed to be alive at the time of writing, have an ongoing connection with their business, and be changing, or have already changed, the world in some way.

When selecting a relatively small number of people to appear in a book such as this, the challenging question is often who to leave out, rather than who to include. But with the world evolving at speed, and perspectives around leadership evolving accordingly, it seemed logical that this book should include a diverse range of leaders, with a broad range of perspectives. For that reason, it includes people who are not widely recognized by the general public while leaving out some well-known business leaders who enjoyed a high profile in the not-so-distant past.

Similarly, it is important to explore the leadership approaches of those people who would not necessarily be regarded as traditional 'leaders', but who are still making a major cultural impact on our world. These individuals include the mysterious bitcoin founder Satoshi Nakamoto and Jimmy Donaldson, who is better known by his YouTube persona MrBeast. Inevitably, when making this selection, I was also influenced by my own cultural reference points, including being a native English speaker, based in a western economy.

As a journalist, I have written about leadership and management for many years, both as editor of the official journal of the UK's Institute of Leadership and as a leadership contributor to Forbes.com. I have also written a previous book, *Reach the Top in Finance*, looking specifically at the attributes of those who rise to the highest echelons of the finance profession. The topic of what makes good leadership and management never ceases to fascinate me and I think it's crucial both to the future of business and the future of our world more broadly. I believe we can learn a huge amount from reading the stories of some of the world's most successful business leaders and studying their approaches and philosophies.

In this book, I have largely focused on the positive aspects of the leaders that I have profiled for two reasons. The first is that the book is intended to be inspirational and to highlight the achievements of a small number of people who have had – in my view – a disproportionately positive impact on the world. The second is that the amount of negative information available on leaders varies greatly. While we are all flawed, the flaws of certain leaders are far more widely discussed than the flaws of others. To be fair to all, therefore, this book does not overly dwell on flaws.

Although we might all be leaders to a greater or lesser degree, the fact remains that at its highest levels, business leadership is an extremely demanding role. It requires huge amounts of energy, patience and resilience, and the people who do it will have often made major sacrifices on their path to success. This book examines the leadership lessons we can learn from these 21st-century business icons – the leaders who are changing our world.

PART ONE

Leadership icons of today

Which 21st-century business icons are having the greatest impact on our world today? That's a huge question – to which there is no definitive answer. If 10 different people were asked that same question, they would probably come up with 10 very different lists of leaders – although there would likely be some overlap in terms of the people they would cite. The people who feature in this section are my own list of impactful leaders. Some of them are obvious choices – others less so. But they are all hugely successful businesspeople who more than warrant their place on the list. In this section, you will read about some outstanding men and women, drawn from different markets around the world, who each bring their own unique perspective to the practice of leadership. As you read their stories, I hope you find something inspiring in each of them. I know that I have.

CHAPTER ONE

Mary Barra

General Motors

Leadership philosophy
'DON'T CONFUSE PROGRESS WITH WINNING.'[1]

Once the world's largest motor vehicle manufacturer, General Motors owns many of the best-known car marques in the US. These include Buick, Cadillac, Chevrolet and Pontiac. The business, which was founded in 1908, is based in Detroit, the largest city in the midwestern US state of Michigan. General Motors was valued at around $50 billion as of January 2023[2] and employs more than 150,000 people worldwide.

Mary Barra became CEO of General Motors in January 2014 (and later also its chair in 2016). She is the first woman to have led one of the big three carmakers in the US – with the other two being Stellantis (formerly Chrysler) and Ford Motor Company. Her appointment followed a tumultuous period in the company's history as General Motors had been badly affected by a dramatic fall-off in car sales during the financial crisis of 2008–10. In 2009, the US government saved General Motors from bankruptcy, spending around $50 billion in exchange for a 61 per cent equity stake. It had sold all its shares in the company by the end of 2013, however, just before Barra stepped up to the top job.[3]

Barra has worked at General Motors for her entire career, having joined the Pontiac Motor Division as an 18-year-old line inspector back in 1980. She credits her early experience of being involved with the physical vehicle production process for giving her a vital understanding of how the automobile business works.[4] At the time she was also studying electrical engineering with what was then known as the General Motors Institute or GMI (it's now known as Kettering University). GMI, which was operated by General Motors between 1926 and 1982, produced a steady pipeline of engineering and managerial talent for the carmaker over the years. Nevertheless, Barra was the first GMI graduate to become CEO of General Motors.[5]

In 1985, Barra graduated from GMI with a Bachelor of Science degree. Five years later, she also earned an MBA from the Stanford Graduate School of Business. As she climbed the ranks of General Motors, Barra held several executive and staff positions, including manager of the Detroit-Hamtramck Assembly, a car-making plant straddling the two cities of Detroit and Hamtramck; vice president of global manufacturing engineering; and vice president of global human resources. Prior to becoming CEO, she served in senior product development roles, leading teams responsible for the design, engineering and quality of General Motors vehicle launches globally.[6]

Safety first

Immediately after taking over as CEO, Barra was thrust into a major controversy known as the ignition switch crisis. During February and March 2014, General Motors had to recall 2.6 million small cars due to a faulty ignition switch, which could inadvertently shut down a car's engine and disable its power steering and airbags while driving. In total, 124 people died in accidents caused by the faulty switch while another 275 were injured.[7]

In 2014, Barra testified to Congress over the company's lengthy delay in issuing the recall, which should have happened at least a decade previously. She attributed the delay to a 'pattern of incompetence and neglect'.[8] Barra sincerely apologized to everyone who had been affected by the recall, but especially the family and friends of those who had died or suffered injuries. She won much respect for her open, honest and human approach to dealing with the crisis.

Determined to ensure that a similar tragedy did not occur again, Barra launched the 'Speak up for Safety' programme to encourage employees to report concerns with vehicle safety and come up with ideas for making vehicles safer. She said that General Motors 'must embrace a culture where safety and quality come first' and called for the company's employees to raise safety concerns 'quickly and forcefully'.[9] In doing so, she effectively ushered in an era of massive cultural change for General Motors, moving the company away from a culture that was associated with cutting costs and ignoring problems to one that prized accountability, collaboration and honesty while prioritizing customers and their safety.

Today, Barra is driving the transformation of General Motors from being a traditional manufacturer of internal combustion engine vehicles to a technology-focused maker of electric vehicles. Despite its reputation for producing gas-guzzling trucks and SUVs, General Motors has committed to selling only zero-emissions vehicles by 2035. With this goal in mind, the company has made the Detroit-Hamtramck Assembly its first, fully dedicated electric vehicle assembly plant and rebadged it as 'Factory ZERO'. It also has an autonomous vehicle subsidiary called Cruise, which has launched a fleet of all-electric, self-driving taxis in San Francisco. Barra took her first drive in one of the company's driverless cars in January 2022, describing the trip as 'nothing short of incredible'.[10]

Taking General Motors into an all-electric future is a major undertaking for Barra, who has admitted that a major concern is getting the transformation achieved quickly enough, given the number of start-ups and tech companies that are jostling to enter the industry.[11] The company's future growth depends on its capacity to produce electric vehicles and build a competitive advantage in associated areas such as batteries and software.

Barra is a strong advocate of diversity and inclusion, recognizing that different thinking styles are crucial to long-term, sustainable business success. In 2020, she announced that General Motors intended to become 'the most inclusive company in the world'. The company aims to achieve this ambitious objective by attracting and retaining a diverse workforce and providing its employees with development opportunities to support their professional growth.[12] Barra is a founding member of General Motors' Inclusion Advisory Board, set up in the same year.[13]

Time named Barra on its list of the 100 Most Influential People of 2021, with the magazine describing her as an 'agent of change' who empowers others. What's more, it is not only within her own industry that she is helping to drive change. Barra is a signatory of the OneTen coalition, an alliance of leading chief executives and their companies that aims to create one million jobs for black talent.[14] In January 2022, Barra embarked on a two-year term as chair of the prestigious Business Roundtable, an association of CEOs from America's leading companies. She is the first-ever woman to have held the role.

Secrets to success

Barra's success in the male-dominated auto industry has resulted in her becoming one of the world's most closely observed female executives. But if she feels this pressure, she doesn't let it show. She has credited her mother with bringing her up to believe in her right to have a seat at the table[15] and has also said that being a woman has been an advantage, as well as a disadvantage, during the course of her career.[16]

Barra believes in working hard and doing your best. She also argues that everyone has room to improve, which is why she thinks it is important to welcome feedback from others. In addition, Barra embraces the concept of servant leadership – a leadership philosophy where the leader sees their goal as being to serve their people and prioritize their growth, wellbeing and empowerment. As such, she makes a point of supporting other people to be successful while providing constructive feedback, helping with decision making, and offering analysis when things have gone wrong.[17]

When she was General Motors' vice president of global human resources, Barra famously reduced the company's lengthy dress code to two simple words: 'Dress appropriately'. This is indicative of her leadership style – keep things simple and empower other people to be responsible for making their own decisions.[18]

In the past, General Motors has suffered from being too slow to adapt to market changes. As a leader, Barra is careful to avoid complacency, however. She likes to keep looking ahead and anticipating the next change to come over the horizon. That's why she's so strongly committed to General Motors' all-electric future. She knows that the transformation is necessary if the company is not only to survive, but to prosper for decades down the line.

In her work, Barra tries to focus her time on where she can make the greatest impact, in terms of moving her company forward. She tries to avoid unnecessary distractions and instead ensures that she has the right people and strategy in place.[19] In fact, Barra is very clear about where her strategic priorities lie as chair and CEO of General Motors – in guiding her company to help build a better planet. A statement on General Motors' website says that under her leadership, it envisions a world with 'zero crashes, to save lives; zero emissions, so future generations can inherit a healthier planet; and zero congestion, so customers get back a precious commodity – time'.[20]

Barra has a reputation for being an authentic, unostentatious leader who is good at building strong relationships with other people. She is seen as an inspiration by many other leaders thanks to her quietly confident approach, her obvious compassion and humility, and her unflinching determination to wrestle with the big issues facing her company, her industry and the world. Furthermore, she has shown that women can succeed in a male-dominated industry, and has paved the way for more women to reach the highest levels of business.

LEADERSHIP LESSONS FROM MARY BARRA

- **Be a servant leader**. See it as your role to empower everyone in your team to perform to the best of their abilities.

- **Know your business inside out**. The more you know, the better grasp you will have of the fundamentals of your business.

- **Solicit the opinions of other people**. Don't be afraid to ask for help and advice. No single leader can expect to have all the answers.

- **Don't run away from a problem**. Far better to tackle it face-on, being honest about what the problem is and what you are doing to address it.

- **Look over the horizon to see what changes are coming down the line**. Then you can support your organization to prepare for them.

Notes

1   LaReau, J (2022) GM CEO Mary Barra's rare, behind-the-scenes interview: Who she relies on in 'lonely job', *Deloitte Free Press*, 3 June, https://eu.freep.com/in-depth/money/cars/general-motors/2022/06/03/gm-ceo-mary-barra-reveals-personal-details-rare-interview/9705679002 (archived at perma.cc/D8NF-WC9M)

2   Yahoo! Finance (2023) General Motors Company (GM), https://finance.yahoo.com/quote/GM (archived at perma.cc/A4NM-UD7S)

3   CNBC (2014) US government says it lost $11.2B on GM bailout, 30 April, https://www.cnbc.com/2014/04/30/us-government-says-it-lost-112b-on-gm-bailout.html (archived at perma.cc/67D9-2DZW)

4   Jiang, S (2022) General Motors CEO Mary Barra shares her leadership journey, visions for the future, *The Michigan Daily*, 13 April, www.michigandaily.com/news/general-motors-ceo-mary-barra-shares-her-leadership-journey-visions-for-the-future (archived at perma.cc/Q56H-A7RL)

5   Automotive News (2014) Barra is first GMI graduate to be auto CEO, 17 March, https://www.autonews.com/article/20140317/OEM02/303179962/barra-is-first-gmi-graduate-to-be-auto-ceo (archived at perma.cc/T7E4-QV8D)

6   General Motors (2022) Mary T. Barra Chair and Chief Executive Officer, https://www.gm.com/company/leadership.detail.html/Pages/bios/global/en/corporate-officers/Mary-Barra (archived at perma.cc/Y9KE-YD87)

7 Isidore, C (2015) Death toll for GM ignition switch: 124, CNNMoney, 10 December, https://money.cnn.com/2015/12/10/news/companies/gm-recall-ignition-switch-death-toll/index.html (archived at perma.cc/N65P-YQ62)

8 Rushe, D (2014) GM chief Mary Barra: 'Pattern of incompetence' caused fatal recall delay, *The Guardian*, 5 June, www.theguardian.com/business/2014/jun/05/gm-mary-barra-fatal-recall-incompetence-neglect (archived at perma.cc/45GM-DAEX)

9 General Motors (2014) GM creates Speak Up For Safety program for employees, 10 April, https://news.gm.com/newsroom.detail.html/Pages/news/us/en/2014/Apr/0410-speakup.html (archived at perma.cc/338V-ARAP)

10 Barra, M (2022) GM CEO Mary Barra takes her first driverless ride [LinkedIn] www.linkedin.com/posts/mary-barra_gm-ceo-mary-barra-takes-her-first-driverless-activity-6938274651076775936-HaQA/?trk=public_profile_like_view&originalSubdomain=uk (archived at perma.cc/2AR2-ZN3G)

11 LaReau, J (2022) GM CEO Mary Barra's rare, behind-the-scenes interview: Who she relies on in 'lonely job', *Deloitte Free Press*, 3 June, https://eu.freep.com/in-depth/money/cars/general-motors/2022/06/03/gm-ceo-mary-barra-reveals-personal-details-rare-interview/9705679002 (archived at perma.cc/D8NF-WC9M)

12 General Motors (2022) Diversity, Equity & Inclusion, www.gmsustainability.com/priorities/developing-talented-people/diversity-equity-and-inclusion.html (archived at perma.cc/VB7L-635X)

13 Hall, K (2020) GM names members of new Inclusion Advisory Board, The Detroit News, https://eu.detroitnews.com/story/business/autos/general-motors/2020/06/22/gm-names-members-newly-formed-inclusion-advisory-board/3236091001 (archived at perma.cc/LXF4-WA4U)

14 Rometty, G (2021) Mary Barra, *Time*, 15 September, https://time.com/collection/100-most-influential-people-2021/6095976/mary-barra/ (archived at perma.cc/5XHG-UWGY)

15 LaReau, J (2022) GM CEO Mary Barra's rare, behind-the-scenes interview: Who she relies on in 'lonely job', *Deloitte Free Press*, 3 June, https://eu.freep.com/in-depth/money/cars/general-motors/2022/06/03/

gm-ceo-mary-barra-reveals-personal-details-rare-interview/
9705679002 (archived at perma.cc/D8NF-WC9M)

16 The Wharton School (2018) GM CEO Marry Barra discusses career,
    management, and diversity, 9 April, www.wharton.upenn.edu/
    story/8-insights-leadership-gm-ceo-mary-barra-wharton-people-
    analytics-conference (archived at perma.cc/E4NG-EVZH)

17 The Wharton School (2018) GM CEO Marry Barra discusses career,
    management, and diversity, 9 April, www.wharton.upenn.edu/story/
    8-insights-leadership-gm-ceo-mary-barra-wharton-people-analytics-
    conference (archived at perma.cc/E4NG-EVZH)

18 Feloni, R (2015) GM CEO Mary Barra explains how shrinking the
    dress code to 2 words reflects her mission for the company, *Business
    Insider*, 27 March, www.businessinsider.com/gm-ceo-mary-barra-on-
    changing-gms-dress-code-2015-3?IR=T (archived at perma.cc/
    B9EC-CK7U)

19 The Wharton School (2018) GM CEO Marry Barra discusses career,
    management, and diversity, 9 April, www.wharton.upenn.edu/
    story/8-insights-leadership-gm-ceo-mary-barra-wharton-people-
    analytics-conference (archived at perma.cc/E4NG-EVZH)

20 General Motors (2022) Diversity, Equity & Inclusion, www.
    gmsustainability.com/priorities/developing-talented-people/diversity-
    equity-and-inclusion.html (archived at perma.cc/VB7L-635X)

CHAPTER TWO

Jeff Bezos

Amazon

Leadership philosophy
'THE WAY YOU EARN TRUST, THE WAY YOU DEVELOP A
REPUTATION, IS BY DOING HARD THINGS WELL OVER AND OVER.'[1]

As the world's biggest online retailer, Amazon scarcely needs an introduction. Nicknamed the 'everything store', Amazon sells a vast range of products from books and toys through to electronics, groceries and power tools. It offers hundreds of millions of products to hundreds of millions of customers worldwide. Amazon operates in 21 countries, including the US, Germany and the UK, but ships to more than 200 countries and territories. The company employs around 1.5 million people globally.

Jeff Bezos, the visionary behind Amazon, was born in Albuquerque, New Mexico, in 1964. His mother, Jackie, was just 17 when he was born and only stayed briefly married to his biological father. When her son was four, she remarried – this time to a Cuban immigrant called Miguel Bezos, known as Mike. Mike Bezos later adopted the child, who took his last name and thought of him as his real father. Later Bezos said that growing up with his mother contributed to his 'unbelievable grit'.[2]

Bezos grew up in Texas and Florida. A gifted child, he excelled at school and later studied electrical engineering and computer science at Ivy League university Princeton.[3] He was working for hedge fund D E Shaw & Co in New York when he read about the internet and discovered that it was experiencing exponential growth.

Seeing a huge opportunity, Bezos was determined to seize it before anyone else got there before him. So, in 1994, he quit his job, moved close to the technology hub of Seattle with his then-wife MacKenzie, and launched Amazon, initially as an online bookstore. While his dream was to create an online store that sold everything, it seemed sensible to test his hypothesis about the internet with one product. So, he chose books – partly because he was a voracious reader (he's a big fan of science fiction) and partly because they were non-perishable commodities that could be bought from large wholesalers. As a web-based retailer, he could also display far more titles than a bricks-and-mortar store.[4]

To begin with, the fledgling business operated from the converted garage of the couple's house and was largely funded by Bezos, his parents and interest-free loans. He warned his parents there was a 70 per cent chance that they would lose all their money.[5] (In fact, as a result of their shrewd investment, the couple are now thought to be billionaires.[6])

In the early days of the internet, website listings tended to be alphabetical. So, Bezos called his business Amazon after poring over the 'A' section of the dictionary and deciding that what he hoped would eventually become the world's largest bookstore should be named after the world's largest river by water flow.[7]

From zero to a trillion

The Amazon website officially went live on 16 July 1995 and the company took off rapidly, confirming Bezos's faith in the internet was more than justified. Within its first week, Amazon took in $12,000 of orders.[8] In 1996, it notched up $16 million in sales.[9] Less than two years after its launch – on 15 May 1997 – Amazon completed a successful IPO, raising $54 million and giving the company a market value of $438 million.[10] Its revenues for that year soared to $147.8 million.[11]

Bezos – as CEO – outlined the core principles of Amazon's decision-making approach in what is now regarded as a legendary letter to shareholders. The letter, first printed in the company's 1997 annual report, has been reprinted in every annual report since. In it, Bezos emphasized Amazon's prioritization of long-term growth above short-term profits, the company's commitment to making 'bold rather than timid investment decisions', and its preoccupation with 'hiring and retaining versatile and talented employees'. The letter also vowed that the company would 'continue to focus relentlessly on our customers', saying it would even 'obsess' over them.[12]

It is these principles – combined with the energetic leadership of Bezos himself – that have underpinned Amazon's enduring success in the decades since its IPO. It survived the bursting of the Dotcom Bubble (a crash in the value of technology stocks) in 2000, despite racking up a net loss of $1.4 billion that same year.[13] In 2001, it recorded its first quarterly profit – a modest $5 million.[14] By 2021, however, it was notching up profits in excess of $33 billion per year.[15] In 2003, Bezos was involved in a helicopter crash in Texas, which could have drastically changed the trajectory of the Amazon story, but fortunately he escaped with only minor injuries.[16]

Over the years, Amazon has progressively expanded its product lines to live up to its founder's vision of being the 'everything store'. It has also transformed the shopping behaviours of the markets where it operates and, thanks to the convenience it offers, helped to transform how we live, work and consume content. Among its most pioneering inventions are cloud computing operation Amazon Web Services, e-reader Kindle, paid subscription and expedited shipping service Amazon Prime, smart speaker device Amazon Echo, and voice-enabled virtual assistant Amazon Alexa. From its early days, Bezos has believed strongly in the power of user-generated reviews to 'help customers make purchase decisions'.[17]

Amazon generates a large part of its revenue from the commission and fees paid by third-party sellers that use its e-commerce platform – Amazon Marketplace – to sell and market their goods. In the second quarter of 2022, for example, 57 per cent of units sold on Amazon were provided by third-party sellers.[18]

During the Covid-19 pandemic of 2020–22, Amazon ramped up its operations, hiring additional staff to meet the demands of customers confined to their homes as a result of national lockdowns.[19] During this time, the company wrestled with supply chain issues and faced intense public scrutiny over accusations that it failed to keep its warehouse staff safe from the virus. Nevertheless, the pandemic helped to establish the retailer as an 'essential service' and it emerged from the crisis even stronger than ever.[20]

Bezos has described Amazon as having 'a heartfelt passion for invention'.[21] Certainly the company stands out for its relentless commitment to innovation. It consistently reinvents itself and fearlessly disrupts established industries. As well as being a retailer and a technology company, it now distributes downloadable and streaming content through Amazon Prime Video, Amazon Music, audiobook service Audible and video live streaming service Twitch. It also publishes books through Amazon Publishing and produces film and television content through Amazon Studios. In 2022, it acquired legendary film production company Metro-Goldwyn-Mayer for $8.5 billion, with the aim of bringing more than 4,000 films and 17,000 TV shows to Prime Video.[22]

Amazon entered the mobility-as-a-service industry when it bought Zoox, a developer of self-driving robo-taxis, in 2020.[23] Perhaps unexpectedly for an online business, it has even ventured into the world of bricks-and-mortar retail by purchasing the Whole Foods supermarket chain and launching the Amazon Go cashier-less convenience stores.

As the powerhouse of online retail, Amazon has been described as one of the most influential and cultural forces in the world.[24] In January 2023, its valuation was $975 billion, making it the fifth most valuable company on the planet.[25] At the time of writing, Bezos was ranked the world's fourth richest person, according to the Bloomberg Billionaires Index, with a net worth of $117 billion.[26] In July 2021, he stood down as Amazon's CEO so that he could focus on other interests, but he remains the company's executive chairman.[27]

A billionaire's passions

So, what other interests does Bezos have? Amazon has been a phenomenal success and, you might have thought, an all-consuming project for its founder. Nevertheless, it turns out that he has numerous other passions – with space probably foremost among these.

Bezos has been fascinated by space ever since he watched US astronaut Neil Armstrong become the first person to walk on the Moon in July 1969. This fascination led to him founding spaceship company Blue Origin in 2000, with the aim of helping to create an extra-terrestrial economy. Bezos has a vision of millions of people living and working in space and all heavy industry being moved off Earth.[28] In July 2021, he flew to space for the first time, taking a trip of around 11 minutes on a Blue Origin rocket.[29]

Space is not Bezos's only passion project, however. In 2013, he bought prominent daily newspaper *The Washington Post* after deciding that it had 'an incredibly important role to play' in US democracy.[30] He also oversees a couple of philanthropic endeavours. In 2018, he launched the Bezos Day One Fund, which focuses on tackling homelessness and funding preschools in low-income communities.[31] Then, in 2020, he founded the Bezos Earth Fund, committing $10 billion to be disbursed as grants to organizations that are fighting climate change and protecting nature.[32]

But perhaps the most ambitious and intriguing of all his interests is his apparent quest for eternal life. Bezos has reportedly invested in a biotechnology start-up called Altos Labs, which is trying to work out how to reverse the ageing process.[33]

Secrets to success

Undoubtedly, Bezos is a highly intelligent man. But there are countless other intelligent people who have enjoyed only a fraction of his success. So, what makes him different? Bezos's impressive achievements can be attributed to his bold outlook, his immense intellectual curiosity, and his willingness to take risks and learn from mistakes. He believes avidly in the power of experimentation and focuses firmly on the long term. In fact, he was an advocate of long-term value creation before it was fashionable, telling Amazon's shareholders in the 1997 annual report: 'We believe that a fundamental measure of our success will be the shareholder value we create over the *long term*.'[34]

As a leader, Bezos is known for his strong work ethic and exacting standards. He drives people hard to achieve his vision, causing both Amazon and Blue Origin to be accused of having toxic work cultures.[35,36] He has openly said that he doesn't like the term 'work–life balance', preferring the term 'work–life harmony' since he believes that happiness at work increases happiness at home, and vice versa.[37] In his first letter to Amazon shareholders, Bezos said: 'It's not easy to work here (when I interview people, I tell them, "You can work long, hard, or smart, but at Amazon.com you can't choose two out of three"), but we are working to build something important, something that matters to our customers, something that we can all tell our grandchildren about. Such things aren't meant to be easy.'[38]

While building Amazon, Bezos was adamant that hiring the brightest and the best would drive the company's success. As a result, he was always looking to lift hiring standards. He said: 'Every time we hire someone, he or she should raise the bar for the next hire, so that the overall talent pool is always improving.'[39] He also recognized that small teams tend to be more agile and productive. So, in the early days of the company, he introduced the so-called two-pizza rule – every internal team should be small enough that it could be fed by two pizzas.[40]

Bezos is renowned for his dislike of slide presentations, believing they undermine the power of storytelling. Amazon staff were therefore asked to pitch their ideas in the form of six-page documents known as 'narratives'. The memos were supposed to be written with clarity (to force clarity of thinking) and sometimes incorporated proposed press releases.[41]

Bezos takes a highly methodical approach to decision making. At the point when he was deciding whether to walk away from his well-paid job at the hedge fund in order to launch Amazon, he used what he called his 'regret minimization framework'. This meant imagining how he would feel when he reached the age of 80 and thought back on the decision. 'I want to have minimized the number of regrets I have,' he says. 'I knew that when I was 80, I was not going to regret having tried this. I was not going to regret trying to participate in this thing called the internet... but I knew the one thing I might regret is not ever having tried.'[42]

In the past, Bezos has reproved organizations for taking a 'one-size-fits-all' approach to decision making. He believes there are fundamentally two types of decisions that need to be made and decision-making approaches should therefore be tailored to the nature of the decision. Type 1 decisions are consequential and irreversible or nearly irreversible. He says these decisions must be made 'methodically, carefully, slowly, with great deliberation and consultation'. In contrast, Type 2 decisions – decisions that are easily changeable and reversible – 'can and should be made quickly by high-judgement individuals or small groups'. The issue, he argues, is that large organizations have a tendency to use the 'heavy-weight Type 1 decision-making *process* on most decisions, including many Type 2 decisions'. This, in turn, leads to 'slowness, unthoughtful risk aversion, failure to experiment sufficiently, and consequently diminished intervention'.[43]

Failure is something that Bezos embraces, as he sees it as an inevitable part of invention and risk-taking. He admits that Amazon has 'made billions of dollars of failures'.[44] Nevertheless, he believes that most decisions should 'probably be made with around 70 per cent of the information you wish you had'. If you wait for 90 per cent of the information, he says, 'in most cases, you're probably being slow'.[45]

A larger-than-life personality, Bezos has been criticized for having a short temper and an adversarial communication style. Over the years, he's delivered some harsh rebukes to employees, as noted by journalist Brad Stone, author of *The Everything Store*, a history of Amazon. These rebukes, relayed by Amazon veterans, include: 'Are you lazy or just incompetent?' and 'I trust you to run world-class operations and this is another example of how you are letting me down.'[46] On the flip side, however, Bezos is recognized for having a great sense of humour and famed for his booming laugh. In fact, so famed is his laugh that there is even a video compilation on YouTube dedicated to his best laughs ever.[47]

LEADERSHIP LESSONS FROM JEFF BEZOS

- **Think big**. Don't limit your ambitions. You will achieve incredible things when you set unrealistic goals.

- **Take a long-term perspective**. Be willing to experiment, invent, take risks and sacrifice short-term profits to secure great outcomes.

- **Be intellectually curious**. Read voraciously. Follow new and emerging trends. Ask yourself what could be done differently in order to create a transformational product or service.

- **Obsess over the customer**. You may have the best product, the best processes and the best people, but your business is still nothing without your customers.
- **Aim to be the best you can be**. High standards underpin individual success.

Notes

1   Bezos, J and Isaacson, W (2021) *Invent & Wander*, Public Affairs and Harvard Business Review Press, United States, p 221

2   Bezos, J and Isaacson, W (2021) *Invent & Wander*, Public Affairs and Harvard Business Review Press, United States, p 6

3   Deutschman, A (2004) Inside the mind of Jeff Bezos, *Fast Company*, August, www.fastcompany.com/50541/inside-mind-jeff-bezos-4 (archived at perma.cc/754L-ETZW)

4   Bezos, J and Isaacson, W (2021) *Invent & Wander*, Public Affairs and Harvard Business Review Press, United States, pp 4–9

5   Stone, B (2013) *The Everything Store*, Penguin, United States, p 48

6   Lipchick, S (2022) Meet Jeff Bezos' billionaire parents, Jacklyn and Miguel 'Mike' Bezos, SCMP, www.scmp.com/magazines/style/celebrity/article/3188951/meet-jeff-bezos-billionaire-parents-jacklyn-and-miguel (archived at perma.cc/ER29-2Z49)

7   Stone, B (2013) *The Everything Store*, Penguin, United States, p 51

8   Stone, B (2013) *The Everything Store*, Penguin, United States, p 56

9   Stone, B (2013) *The Everything Store*, Penguin, United States, p 76

10 Wilhelm, A (2017) A look back in IPO: Amazon's 1997 move, *TechCrunch+*, 28 June, https://techcrunch.com/2017/06/28/a-look-back-at-amazons-1997-ipo (archived at perma.cc/G3H6-4JAM)

11 Bezos, J (1998) Letter to Shareholders, https://ir.aboutamazon.com/annual-reports-proxies-and-shareholder-letters/default.aspx (archived at perma.cc/Q4XM-WXR6)

12 Bezos, J (1998) Letter to Shareholders, https://ir.aboutamazon.com/annual-reports-proxies-and-shareholder-letters/default.aspx (archived at perma.cc/Q4XM-WXR6)

13 Amazon (2001) Annual Report, p 32

14 Hansell, S (2002) A surprise from Amazon: Its first profit, *The New York Times*, 23 January, https://www.nytimes.com/2002/01/23/business/technology-a-surprise-from-amazon-its-first-profit.html (archived at perma.cc/VX45-D9AG)

15 Statista (2022) Quarterly value of Amazon third-party seller services 2017–22, www.statista.com/statistics/1240236/amazon-third-party-seller-services-value/ (archived at perma.cc/99G3-MANM)

16 CNN.com/Technology (2003) Amazon's Bezos hurt in helicopter crash, 13 March, https://edition.cnn.com/2003/TECH/biztech/03/13/bezos.hurt.reut/index.html (archived at perma.cc/B6RX-GNBQ)

17 Stone, B (2022) *The Everything Store*, Penguin, United States, p 54

18 Statista (2022) Annual net income of Amazon.com from 2004 to 2021, www.statista.com/statistics/266288/annual-et-income-of-amazoncom (archived at perma.cc/BN68-2GCD)

19 Amazon (2020) Amazon's actions to help employees, communities, and customers affected by COVID-19, 13 May, www.aboutamazon.eu/news/working-at-amazon/amazons-actions-to-help-employees-communities-and-customers-affected-by-covid-19 (archived at perma.cc/FH4L-KZKS)

20 Palmer, A (2020) How Amazon managed the coronavirus and came out stronger, CNBC, 29 September, www.cnbc.com/2020/09/29/how-amazon-managed-the-coronavirus-crisis-and-came-out-stronger.html (archived at perma.cc/E6LD-NTVM)

21 Bezos, J and Isaacson, W (2021) *Invent & Wander*, Public Affairs and Harvard Business Review Press, United States, 122

22 Malik, A (2017) Amazon completes $8.5 billion acquisition of MGM, 17 March, techcrunch.com/2022/03/17/amazon-completes-its-8-5-billion-acquisition-of-mgm (archived at perma.cc/XAF8-BAPT)

23 Palmer, A (2020) Amazon Zoox unveils self-driving robotaxi, CNBC, 14 December, www.cnbc.com/2020/12/14/amazons-self-driving-company-zoox-unveils-autonomous-robotaxi.html (archived at perma.cc/Q7FV-S964)

24 Frontline (2020) Amazon Empire: The rise and reign of Jeff Bezos, www.pbs.org/wgbh/frontline/documentary/amazon-empire (archived at perma.cc/98C2-GUYS)

25 CompaniesMarketCap.com (2022) Market capitalization of Amazon (AMZN), https://companiesmarketcap.com/amazon/marketcap (archived at perma.cc/U92L-5PUG)

26 Bloomberg Billionaires Index (2022) Bloomberg, www.bloomberg.com/billionaires (archived at perma.cc/LKE8-Z85Z)

27 Palmer, A (2021) Jeff Bezos to formally step down as Amazon CEO on July 5, Andy Jassy to take over, CNBC, 26 May, www.cnbc.com/2021/05/26/jeff-bezos-to-formally-step-down-as-amazon-ceo-on-july-5.html (archived at perma.cc/A6S5-RU44)

28 Clifford, C (2018) Jeff Bezos dreams of a world with a trillion people living in space, CNBC, 1 May, www.cnbc.com/2018/05/01/jeff-bezos-dreams-of-a-world-with-a-trillion-people-living-in-space.html (archived at perma.cc/Q67C-M99D)

29 Koren, M (2021) Jeff Bezos knows who paid for him to go to space, *The Atlantic*, 20 July, www.theatlantic.com/science/archive/2021/07/jeff-bezos-blue-origin-successful-flight/619484/ (archived at perma.cc/79E3-EUP7)

30 Bezos, J and Isaacson, W (2021) *Invent & Wander*, Public Affairs and Harvard Business Review Press, United States, p 20

31 Bezos Day One Fund, www.bezosdayonefund.org (archived at perma.cc/N5CL-YY8T)

32 Bezos Earth Fund, www.bezosearthfund.org (archived at perma.cc/UFS5-QQ6G)

33 Regalado, A (2021) Meet Altos Labs, Silicon Valley's latest wild bet on living forever, *MIT Technology Review*, 4 September, www.technologyreview.com/2021/09/04/1034364/altos-labs-silicon-valleys-jeff-bezos-milner-bet-living-forever (archived at perma.cc/P95C-R9F7)

34 Bezos, J (1998) Letter to Shareholders, https://ir.aboutamazon.com/annual-reports-proxies-and-shareholder-letters/default.aspx (archived at perma.cc/Q4XM-WXR6)

35 Head Topics (2020) Amazon has a sexist and 'toxic' culture, some employees say, *Business Insider*, 3 October, https://headtopics.com/us/amazon-has-a-sexist-and-toxic-culture-some-employees-say-business-insider-16040131 (archived at perma.cc/BWW2-5WRU)

36 Bateman, T and AP (2021) Jeff Bezos' Blue Origin has a 'toxic culture of sexism and safety failings, allege former employees', *Euronews*, 1 October, www.euronews.com/next/2021/10/01/jeff-bezos-blue-origin-has-a-toxic-culture-of-sexism-and-safety-failings-allege-former-emp (archived at perma.cc/YD7F-XZMJ)

37 Bezos, J and Isaacson, W (2021) *Invent & Wander*, Public Affairs and Harvard Business Review Press, United States, 223

38 Bezos, J (1998) Letter to Shareholders, https://ir.aboutamazon.com/annual-reports-proxies-and-shareholder-letters/default.aspx (archived at perma.cc/Q4XM-WXR6)

39 Stone, B (2013) *The Everything Store*, Penguin, United States, p 61

40 Hern, A (2018) The two-pizza rule and the secret of Amazon's success, *The Guardian*, 24 April, www.theguardian.com/technology/2018/apr/24/the-two-pizza-rule-and-the-secret-of-amazons-success (archived at perma.cc/4RKS-K3BX)

41 Bezos, J and Isaacson, W (2021) *Invent & Wander*, Public Affairs and Harvard Business Review Press, United States, p 23

42 Bezos, J and Isaacson, W (2021) *Invent & Wander*, Public Affairs and Harvard Business Review Press, United States, p 9

43 Bezos, J and Isaacson, W (2021) *Invent & Wander*, Public Affairs and Harvard Business Review Press, United States, p 143

44 Bezos, J and Isaacson, W (2021) *Invent & Wander*, Public Affairs and Harvard Business Review Press, United States, p 260

45 Bezos, J and Isaacson, W (2021) *Invent & Wander*, Public Affairs and Harvard Business Review Press, United States, p 150

46 Stone, B (2013) *The Everything Store*, Penguin, United States, p 223

47 YouTube (2015) Jeff Bezos BEST laughs compilation EVER!!!! (Online video) www.youtube.com/watch?v=lZ_DyimkS54 (archived at perma.cc/6RSY-REG4)

CHAPTER THREE

Sara Blakely

Spanx

Leadership philosophy
'CARE THE MOST.'[1]

Spanx is a US clothing company that is on a mission to solve our 'wardrobe woes'. It is famous for producing slimming 'shapewear' – a range of attractively designed underwear that helps to give women the appearance of a flatter tummy, hips, or bottom. Additionally, it sells a wide range of other clothing including bras, jackets, jeans, leggings and maternity wear, as well as an active range including swimwear.

Spanx describes itself as being 'for women, by women' and it is focused on producing comfortable clothing that enables women to look and feel great. Men aren't entirely neglected, however, since the brand has also developed an underwear range for them. While Spanx is based in Atlanta, the capital city of the southern US state of Georgia, the brand is found in more than 50 countries around the world. Its mission is to make the world a better place 'one butt at a time'.[2]

The Spanx story began back in 1998 when 27-year-old Sara Blakely was getting ready for a party. Realizing that she didn't have the right undergarment to provide a smooth look under cream trousers, she picked up a pair of scissors and cut the feet off a pair of tights with a control top. She wore the cut-off tights as an undergarment beneath her trousers, but they repeatedly rolled up during the night. It was this frustration that set her on a mission to create an 'undergarment that didn't exist'.[3]

At the time, Blakely was working as a door-to-door fax machine salesperson in Florida. She had grown up in the state and originally wanted to become a lawyer, but twice failed her law school admission tests. After leaving Florida State University with a degree in legal communications, she briefly worked at Disney World before taking on the fax machine sales role with office supply company Danka, now part of Japanese printer giant Ricoh.

Blakely found selling fax machines very demoralizing and would sometimes lose her nerve when she walked into an office, leading her to turn around and walk straight back out again with the excuse that she had come to the wrong place. But that didn't stop her becoming Danka's national sales trainer at the age of 25. Nevertheless, she didn't envisage spending the rest of her career selling fax machines. 'I was really determined to create a better life for myself,' she revealed in a podcast interview with radio group NPR in 2016.[4]

Using $5,000 in savings that she had earned from her job, Blakely started her brand, founding Spanx in 2000. To begin with, she continued in her sales role with Danka and relocated to Atlanta. But she worked on her new idea at night and at weekends, keeping it as secret as possible in case anyone tried to discourage her or cause her to lose confidence in her project.

It took a lot of persistence and numerous visits to male-run hosiery manufacturing plants in the state of North Carolina before Blakely was able to persuade a manufacturer to make a prototype for her. That manufacturer happened to have three daughters who loved her concept of footless, body-shaping tights (or 'pantyhose' as they are known in the US). She patented the product and came up with the name Spanx, after initially playing with the word 'Spanks'. She had read that made-up words tend to perform better for products than real words. She also liked the fact that Spanx sounded naughty, fun and a little bit risky. 'The name was just right,' she said in the NPR podcast interview. 'My product was all about the rear end, and it's about making the rear end look better and no panty lines.'[5]

Once she had her product, Blakely's next challenge was to find people to buy it. She managed to secure an appointment with a buyer for upmarket department store Neiman Marcus and flew to Dallas to showcase her product. She took with her the same pair of cream trousers that had originally inspired her to invent Spanx and wore them in front of the buyer – once wearing Spanx and once without. The buyer was so impressed that she put in an order for Spanx and trialled the product in seven stores.[6]

The hard work didn't end there, however. Blakely paid her friends to buy Spanx from the seven stores where

Neiman Marcus was selling the product, to encourage the retailer to order more. She also travelled to the stores herself to promote the product – alongside a giant 'before and after' image of her wearing the cream trousers – and artfully managed to put Spanx in stands close to the tills. A major breakthrough came when she had the bright idea of sending Spanx to talk show star Oprah Winfrey, who picked them for her 'Favorite Things' list in 2000. (Today, Winfrey is an investor in Spanx, as is Hollywood actor Reese Witherspoon.)

Soon Blakely was shipping Spanx to women across the world from her apartment. Then she made another unconventional decision – to start selling Spanx on the shopping channel QVC. People warned her that was a sure-fire way to kill her brand, but she ended up selling 8,000 pairs of Spanx in five minutes of airtime. Within a couple of years, the company was making millions, with its fame spreading by word of mouth.[7] In fact, Spanx did not spend any money on advertising for its first 16 years in existence.[8]

By 2012, Spanx was turning over $250 million in annual sales and Wall Street analysts were valuing the company at $1 billion. The same year, Blakely, then 41, appeared on the cover of *Forbes*, after the magazine proclaimed her to be the world's youngest self-made female billionaire at the time.[9] She was also named in *Time* magazine's annual list of the 100 most influential people in the world.

As the years have passed, Spanx has faced greater competition from other shapewear brands, including Honeylove and reality star Kim Kardashian's line, Skims. Meanwhile, the Covid-19 pandemic proved to be a challenging period for the business due to the dramatic fall in the number of parties and weddings, which led to reduced demand for shaping garments that are often worn beneath formal attire. By summer 2020, *Forbes* had reduced its estimated valuation of Spanx to $540 million, nearly half its valuation of eight years earlier.[10]

In 2021, Blakely sold a majority stake in Spanx to private equity giant Blackstone in a deal that valued the company at $1.2 billion. She believed that the additional resources Blackstone could provide would help her pioneering legacy brand to compete more successfully in an increasingly crowded marketplace. Blakely remains executive chair and a significant shareholder in the business.[11] In an Instagram post, she said: 'With all my heart I love this brand. With all my heart I will continue to love this brand.' She added that she would 'continue to help the business fulfil its greatest potential, as well as continue to fulfil my greatest passion – elevating women.'[12]

As well as her business brand, Blakely has invested in growing her personal brand over the years, including through television appearances. She appeared in Richard Branson's reality show, *The Rebel Billionaire*, which aired in 2004. In the show, 16 contestants competed on a series of business tasks, as well as daredevil challenges, to prove that they were most qualified to take over from Branson as president of his conglomerate, Virgin Group. Blakely came second, losing in the final to Shawn Nelson, founder of US furniture company LoveSac. Branson said the only reason he didn't give her the top prize was because she was already so successful. He did, however, write her a personal cheque to start up a foundation.[13]

In 2006, Blakely founded the Spanx by Sara Blakely Foundation, which aims to make the world a better place by supporting women through entrepreneurship, education and the arts. One of the foundation's icons is Blakely's 'lucky red backpack', which she took to the meeting where she initially succeeded in selling Spanx to Neiman Marcus. During the Covid-19 pandemic, she launched The Red Backpack Fund, giving donations of $5,000 each to 1,000 female business owners in the US, to help them withstand the pressures of the pandemic.[14]

As well as appearing on *The Rebel Billionaire*, Blakely has featured as a judge on the ABC television competition *American Inventor* and appeared on *Shark Tank*, a show where aspiring entrepreneurs around the world pitch their business models to a panel of investors. Additionally, she appeared in the television drama *Billions* in a very brief cameo, as herself.

Blakely's current net worth is estimated at $1.2 billion.[15] The mother of four has, however, signed the Giving Pledge founded by Bill and Melinda Gates and Warren Buffett. As a result, she has committed to giving away half her wealth to empower women.[16] Along with her husband, fellow entrepreneur Jesse Itzler, Blakely has a minority stake in the Atlanta Hawks professional basketball team.

Secrets to success

In the Instagram post that she published at the time of the Blackstone sale, Blakely said that caring about what you do is vital if you want to start a successful business. 'Never underestimate what you can do if you truly care the most,' she said. She pointed out that when she started out, she had no background in business and knew no one in the clothing industry, but because she 'cared the most' she had the courage to launch her own company. 'At the time, men were making women's undergarments and I decided to advocate for women through product,' she explained. 'I thought, somebody needs to speak up who's actually wearing the product... might as well be me.'[17]

Blakely's determination to achieve in life is linked to some tragedies she experienced as a teenager. Her best friend was run over by a car, right in front of her. The same year, her parents' marriage ended and soon afterwards both her prom dates died. She told *Forbes* in 2012 that witnessing death at the age of 16 had given her a sense of urgency about life. 'The thought of my mortality – I think about it a lot. I find it motivating. It can be any time that your number's up.'[18]

Given the early sadness she experienced, it is no surprise that Blakely views mindset as the single biggest asset for any entrepreneur. In fact, she believes that entrepreneurs should work continually on developing a positive mindset and using visualization techniques to envisage success. When she was still a teenager her father gave her cassettes by the late motivational speaker Dr Wayne Dyer on the topic of how to be a 'no-limit' person. Listening to these cassettes helped her to understand that she's in control of how she thinks and that she can use a positive mindset to propel herself forward.

Having a positive mindset can be particularly useful for entrepreneurs when they find themselves taking a leap into the unknown. 'What you don't know will be your greatest asset if you let it,' Blakely argues. 'When you don't know how it's supposed to be done, there's the innovation, there's the magic.'

Blakely believes it's important for leaders to focus on the 'why' behind what they're doing because that's what customers connect with. Customers are interested in the problem that the product is solving, rather than the product itself. While a big part of Blakely's 'why' was to solve the problem of visible panty lines, she also wanted to push herself as hard as she could on behalf of other women in the world who don't have the same opportunities as she does.

Blakely advises would-be entrepreneurs to free themselves up from worrying about what other people think. She intentionally embarrasses herself because she sees failures and embarrassments as ways to connect with other people. Growing up, her father encouraged both her and her brother to fail and he would ask her what she had failed at that week. By doing that, she says he reframed her definition of failure, so it became less about the outcome and more about not trying.

From a leadership perspective, Blakely makes a point of prioritizing and delegating to others so that she can focus on the business and personal issues that matter to her most. 'Invest the time in hiring your weaknesses,' she has said. 'If you put the right people in place in certain areas, then it will free you up to be able to prioritize your time.'[19]

As someone who has not only founded a brand but effectively reinvented a clothing category, Blakely is rightly respected as an innovator and pioneer. She values being an innovator and, for that reason, doesn't get too caught up in what her competition is doing. As she puts it: 'There's innovators, and there's imitators. I'd far rather be an innovator. It's harder, it requires more work. But it's so much more rewarding.'

Blakely comes across as bright, bubbly and fun, and as someone who doesn't take herself too seriously. She's an enthusiastic model for her company's products, even allowing herself to be filmed wearing her shapewear so that she can showcase its capacity to transform women's body shapes. Thanks to her warm, approachable nature, she has also got a distinctive 'girl next door' appeal that boosts her brand. With her marketing strategies, she always tried to talk to the consumer 'the way I would talk to my friends at dinner'.

Having the ability to make someone laugh is a very powerful tool in business, according to Blakely. She used to do some stand-up comedy prior to starting Spanx and has said that she used humour as her secret weapon when growing her business. If people can't be funny, her advice for connecting with others is to be vulnerable instead.[20]

Blakely is known for having a very positive relationship with money. She has said: 'Money is fun to make, fun to spend and fun to give away.'[21] The joy she takes in giving money away was clear when she gifted all her employees $10,000 each, along with first-class plane tickets to anywhere in the world, as an act of appreciation following Blackstone's majority purchase of Spanx. 'I wanted them to have an experience,' she said. 'My motto in life is, the more you experience in life, the more you have to offer others.'[22]

LEADERSHIP LESSONS FROM SARA BLAKELY

- **Care the most about what you're doing**. If you care more than anyone else, you will outperform others who are trying to do the same thing.

- **Keep your best ideas secret at first**. If you share your ideas too early, there is a risk that well-intentioned people might criticize or question them, causing you to lose confidence or even give up.

- **Know when to bring in extra help and resources**. Sometimes you will need outside support to take a business to the next level.

- **Work on your mindset**. If you have a positive mindset and visualize yourself succeeding at your goals, you greatly increase your chances of getting what you want.

- **Don't procrastinate**. Life is short and you don't know how much time you have left to do what you want to do. So, get on with doing it now.

Notes

1 NPR (2016) How a pitch in a Neiman Marcus ladies room changed Sara Blakely's life [podcast transcript] 12 September, www.npr.org/transcripts/493312213 (archived at perma.cc/VQ8J-JPDT)

2 SPANX (2022) About us, https://spanx.com/pages/about-us (archived at perma.cc/99HX-9SLD)

3 Haverstock, E (2021) Sara Blakely is a billionaire (again) after selling a majority of Spanx to Blackstone, *Forbes*, 20 October, www.forbes.com/sites/elizahaverstock/2021/10/20/sara-blakely-is-a-billionaire-

again-after-selling-a-majority-of-spanx-to-blackstone (archived at perma.cc/SZ76-XVPR)

4 NPR (2016) How a pitch in a Neiman Marcus ladies room changed Sara Blakely's life [podcast transcript] 12 September, www.npr.org/transcripts/493312213 (archived at perma.cc/VQ8J-JPDT)

5 NPR (2016) How a pitch in a Neiman Marcus ladies room changed Sara Blakely's life [podcast transcript] 12 September, www.npr.org/transcripts/493312213 (archived at perma.cc/VQ8J-JPDT)

6 NPR (2016) How a pitch in a Neiman Marcus ladies room changed Sara Blakely's life [podcast transcript] 12 September, www.npr.org/transcripts/493312213 (archived at perma.cc/VQ8J-JPDT)

7 NPR (2016) How a pitch in a Neiman Marcus ladies room changed Sara Blakely's life [podcast transcript] 12 September, www.npr.org/transcripts/493312213 (archived at perma.cc/VQ8J-JPDT)

8 Forbes (2021) Spanx founder Sara Blakely shares secrets to building a billion-dollar business, #Next1000 Summit (Online video) www.youtube.com/watch?v=0K-TQcV-Xoo (archived at perma.cc/WV2R-LMA4)

9 Haverstock, E (2021) Sara Blakely is a billionaire (again) after selling a majority of Spanx to Blackstone, *Forbes*, 20 October, www.forbes.com/sites/elizahaverstock/2021/10/20/sara-blakely-is-a-billionaire-again-after-selling-a-majority-of-spanx-to-blackstone (archived at perma.cc/SZ76-XVPR)

10 Haverstock, E (2021) Sara Blakely is a billionaire (again) after selling a majority of Spanx to Blackstone, *Forbes*, 20 October, www.forbes.com/sites/elizahaverstock/2021/10/20/sara-blakely-is-a-billionaire-again-after-selling-a-majority-of-spanx-to-blackstone (archived at perma.cc/SZ76-XVPR)

11 Haverstock, E (2021) Sara Blakely is a billionaire (again) after selling a majority of Spanx to Blackstone, *Forbes*, 20 October, www.forbes.com/sites/elizahaverstock/2021/10/20/sara-blakely-is-a-billionaire-again-after-selling-a-majority-of-spanx-to-blackstone (archived at perma.cc/SZ76-XVPR)

12 Blakely, S (2021) Today marks a HUGE milestone for @spanx and for me personally... [Instagram] 20 October, www.instagram.com/p/CVQQX0gAUGw (archived at perma.cc/R855-RJHX)

13 O'Connor, C (2012) Undercover billionaire: Sara Blakely joins the rich list thanks to Spanx, *Forbes*, 7 March. www.forbes.com/sites/clareoconnor/2012/03/07/undercover-billionaire-sara-blakely-joins-the-rich-list-thanks-to-spanx/?sh=718d7b4cd736 (archived at perma.cc/ZE3E-2TCG)

14 Jackson, E (2020) Coronavirus: Spanx founder giving $5 million to women-run businesses, *The Business Journals*, 6 April, www.bizjournals.com/bizwomen/news/latest-news/2020/04/coronavirus-spanx-founder-giving-5-million-to.html?page=all (archived at perma.cc/98UF-AYGX)

15 CEO Today (2021) How Spanx founder Sara Blakely created a billion-dollar brand, www.ceotodaymagazine.com/2021/10/how-spanx-founder-sara-blakely-created-a-billion-dollar-brand (archived at perma.cc/K3XY-66N4)

16 Blakely, S (2013) My Giving Pledge, www.spanxfoundation.com/giving-pledge (archived at perma.cc/2726-2GWH)

17 Blakely, S (2021) Today marks a HUGE milestone for @spanx and for me personally... [Instagram] 20 October, www.instagram.com/p/CVQQX0gAUGw (archived at perma.cc/R855-RJHX)

18 O'Connor, C (2012) Undercover billionaire: Sara Blakely joins the rich list thanks to Spanx, *Forbes*, 7 March, www.forbes.com/sites/clareoconnor/2012/03/07/undercover-billionaire-sara-blakely-joins-the-rich-list-thanks-to-spanx/?sh=718d7b4cd736 (archived at perma.cc/ZE3E-2TCG)

19 Howes, L (2020) Multi-billionaires explain their steps to success & happiness, Sara Blakely & Jesse Itzler (Online video) www.youtube.com/watch?v=Ueh7W0xGac0 (archived at perma.cc/8EZZ-7J6N)

20 Forbes (2021) Spanx founder Sara Blakely shares secrets to building a billion-dollar business, #Next1000 Summit (Online video) www.youtube.com/watch?v=0K-TQcV-Xoo (archived at perma.cc/WV2R-LMA4)

21 O'Connor, C (2012) Undercover billionaire: Sara Blakely joins the rich list thanks to Spanx, *Forbes*, 7 March, www.forbes.com/sites/clareoconnor/2012/03/07/undercover-billionaire-sara-blakely-joins-the-rich-list-thanks-to-spanx/?sh=718d7b4cd736 (archived at perma.cc/ZE3E-2TCG)

22 Forbes (2021) Spanx founder Sara Blakely shares secrets to building a billion-dollar business, #Next1000 Summit (Online video) www.youtube.com/watch?v=0K-TQcV-Xoo (archived at perma.cc/ WV2R-LMA4)

CHAPTER FOUR

Rosalind Brewer

Walgreens Boots Alliance

Leadership philosophy
'WE BELONG HERE. GET USED TO US.'[1]

U S-based retail pharmacy chain Walgreens Boots Alliance is one of the biggest and best-known companies in the United States. It employs more than 325,000 people and has approximately 13,000 stores in the US, Europe and Latin America. In 2022, it recorded sales of $132.7 billion. More than a century old, it serves millions of patients and customers every day.[2]

At the helm of this behemoth is Rosalind (Roz) Brewer, who took over as CEO in March 2021, amid the throes of the Covid-19 pandemic. Brewer, in her early sixties, is one of very few black women to have led a Fortune 500 company – at the time of writing, there have only been four.[3] She is also one of the most preeminent business leaders in the US, ranked #7 on the *Fortune* 2022 list of the 50 Most Powerful Women in Business[4] and #13 on the *Forbes* 2022 list of The World's 100 Most Powerful Women.[5]

Brewer's ascent to the top of the corporate world is down to her focused determination, willingness to take risks, commitment to learning, and passion for developing people, as well as the sacrifices she's made along the way. She told *Harvard Business Review* in 2021 that she had worked 'very hard to get where I am'.[6] In another interview, with the Economic Club of Chicago, she admitted that earlier in her career she probably averaged between four and five hours sleep per night.[7]

Growing up in Detroit as the youngest of five children, Brewer learned to assert herself at an early age. 'I knew how to really fight for that last piece of bread on the table,' she revealed in a Stanford Graduate School of Business podcast recorded a few months after her appointment to the Walgreens role, adding that being the youngest 'taught me how to… take care of myself.' Occasionally her attempts to get her voice heard landed her in trouble, however. She was suspended from school in third grade for trying to teach her teacher a shortcut to a maths problem.[8]

Brewer's parents both worked in the automotive industry and neither finished high school, but they wanted their children to have better educations than they did and therefore set high expectations for their achievement. This explains why all five ended up going to college – although Brewer was the only one to attend college outside the family's home state of Michigan.

Brewer herself studied chemistry at the private Spelman College in Atlanta, a liberal arts and science college that focuses on educating women of African descent. Her time at Spelman was a defining experience for her because it enabled her to hone her critical thinking skills. It also put her in an environment of 'women who look like me, but came from different walks of life'. Tragically, her father died of cancer when she was in her last year of college, six weeks before graduation.[9]

From chemist to CEO

Brewer began her career as an organic chemist with personal care company Kimberly-Clark. Intrigued by business, she moved into administration and management roles and rose up the ranks. Eventually she served as Kimberly-Clark's group president of global manufacturing and operations. In 2006, she joined retail giant Walmart as a vice president, accepting a lower-grade role because she wanted to 'learn retail'.[10] There she rapidly established herself and held several executive roles.

In 2012, Brewer made headlines when she became president and CEO of Sam's Club, the chain of membership-only retail warehouse clubs owned and operated by Walmart and named after Walmart founder Sam Walton. She was the first woman and the first African American to hold the role.[11]

Under her leadership, Sam's Club pioneered some major digital innovations. These included a drive-thru club pickup service, which allows customers to order items online and pick them up at the store, as well as a scan-and-go programme that enables customers to skip checkout lines and pay for items via a digital app.[12]

While she was at Sam's Club, Brewer became embroiled in a major controversy after discussing diversity in an interview with news channel CNN. She commented on her experiences of attending a meeting with suppliers where 'the entire other side of the table was all Caucasian males'. The comments, which she herself believed to be fairly innocuous, were cited as evidence that she discriminated against white men and were widely shared on right-wing websites.[13]

Despite having the full support of Walmart's president and CEO, Doug McMillon, Brewer received death threats and had to have security around her home.[14] 'It was scary and it was a reminder that we aren't as far as I thought we were,' she said in a later interview. 'And it reminded me that there's hate; it reminded me that I am different.'[15]

In early 2017, Brewer left Sam's Club in search of a new challenge. That challenge was to be group president and chief operating officer (COO) of international coffeehouse chain Starbucks – a role she assumed in October of that year.[16] At Starbucks, she helped to innovate new business models, including pick-up-only stores where customers collected their coffees through a drive-thru window.[17]

Significantly, Brewer was COO at the time two young black men were arrested on suspicion of trespassing at a Starbucks store in Philadelphia in April 2018. The pair, who had been waiting to attend a business meeting, had not ordered anything to eat or drink, leading the store manager to call the police. When footage of the arrests was published on social media, it sparked outcry and resulted in the hashtag #BoycottStarbucks trending on Twitter.[18] Starbucks promptly apologized, with CEO Kevin Johnson saying that the circumstances surrounding the incident 'led to a reprehensible outcome'.[19]

For Brewer, the incident 'was deeply personal' as the two young black men in question were around the same age as her own son and she believed that the same thing could have happened to him. 'I knew also that this happened on my watch, and I had to take control of the situation,' she later said. 'It was a time for me to step up and admit that we had done something probably that needed correcting. Our policies were not updated. Our store manager acted too early, too soon.' In response to the event, Starbucks closed all 8,000 of its US coffee shops for one afternoon to provide racial bias training to all its staff.[20]

Nearly three years later, Brewer became CEO of Walgreen Boots Alliance at a momentous time. The company was about to embark on a large-scale vaccine rollout that would help to turn the tide of the Covid-19 pandemic. By August 2021, it had administered 29 million Covid vaccinations across the United States.[21]

Brewer's rationale for leaving Starbucks – a company that she had very much enjoyed working for – was that she wanted a role where she could 'have impact, make change happen, lead something that would leave an impression on people's lives'. She told NBC's *Today* show in May 2021: 'As I've seen people get their first shot and they've looked back at our pharmacist and they are crying... I know I've made the right decision and this is the right place for me to be.'[22]

Secrets to success

Today Brewer holds one of the biggest jobs in business, but she believes she's benefited from doing smaller jobs during her career. In the Stanford podcast, she said: 'Quite honestly there were times in my career where I was given the unfortunate work to do. And I always had to do some of the toughest, dirtiest jobs... but it gave me a chance to learn and I try and put it to work every day and look at it as a blessing that I got some of the smaller jobs, the unfortunate positions.'[23]

She also believes that her background as a chemist has been a good foundation for a career in business. Speaking to the *Today* show, she said: 'When you're a scientist, you're curious, you ask a lot of questions. You're analytic. So, you look at data and that translates into business and some of the best business leaders are those who really challenge the status quo.'[24]

Whenever she starts a new role, Brewer is clear about 'my role, what my intent is, and how do I bring together my toolbox'.[25] Authenticity is also very important to her. She told *Harvard Business Review* that she learned early on in her career that she wanted to bring her whole self to work.

A tireless champion of diversity, Brewer believes that one of the advantages of her role is that she has an opportunity to teach and train others. When she's been told that she's a token who has only advanced because of her race, or she's not as smart as she thinks she is, she's found the remarks painful but also energizing because 'I feel as if I'm going to teach a couple of lessons'.

As a black woman, Brewer finds she still has to explain who she is, even in situations where she's with other senior figures. 'It's just amazing to me that sometimes I have to tell people who I am,' she says. 'We are still so underrepresented in so many different places. I feel like I'm on a mission to help people understand we're here to stay.'[26]

Self-development has been crucial to Brewer's success in life. A self-confessed life-long learner,[27] she 'studies like mad' whenever she takes on a new role. She says: 'I constantly read, learn and train. I've been that person who has to self-develop and I've taken on that responsibility.'[28]

As a senior leader, Brewer sees hiring other people as the most important part of her job. 'I look, first of all, for diversity of thought when I'm building a team,' she says. 'And a lot of times that comes with diversity of race and gender.' When recruiting people into executive positions, she also looks for 'what's inside the person', explaining 'these jobs are tough, they're hard. And, at some point, their inner is going to become their outer experience'.[29]

Brewer has compared being CEO with being the conductor of an orchestra – someone who brings together the many different talents within her team to create the best possible performance. She believes in building trusting relationships with people, in an environment of psychological safety. 'I stand up for them, I fight for them,' she has said. 'They know I'm not gonna blame them, they know I'm gonna dig into the details with them.'[30] Brewer is also a great advocate of agile teams, consisting of people from different disciplines, who get together to think about how to solve the company's biggest problems.[31]

Throughout her career, Brewer has undoubtedly received advice from many people. Nevertheless, she says the best advice she ever got came from her late father, who instilled in her the importance of personal integrity. He told her 'to manage who I was, and the impression I left with people'.[32] She herself has left a lasting impression, by proving that a black woman can become one of the world's leading businesspeople.

LEADERSHIP LESSONS FROM ROSALIND BREWER

- **Prioritize diversity and inclusion**. Having a diverse range of people in the room will mean you have more robust conversations about the business and reach solutions faster.

- **Be prepared to roll up your sleeves and get your hands dirty**. When you work on the front line, you will get a good idea about what is – and isn't – working within your organization.

- **Create an environment of psychological safety**. This is an environment where people feel able to speak up and make mistakes without fearing possible negative consequences.

- **Don't expect your career to follow a consistently upwards trajectory**. Sometimes you need to step back or sideways to get ahead. In the right circumstances, an apparent demotion or a lateral move can be a valuable learning experience.

- **Keep learning throughout your career**. The more you learn, the more you grow, and the more you grow, the more successful you will be.

Notes

1   Walker, R (2021) How Detroit native Rosalind 'Roz' Brewer is breaking barriers, *ClickOnDetroit*, 5 May, www.clickondetroit.com/news/local/2021/05/05/how-detroit-native-rosalind-roz-brewer-is-breaking-barriers (archived at perma.cc/Z8M9-C4BT)

2   Walgreens Boots Alliance (2022) Annual Report, https://s1.q4cdn.com/343380161/files/doc_financials/2022/ar/WBA-2022-Annual-Report.pdf (archived at perma.cc/9B8C-WZJY)

3   Kowitt, B (2021) Roz Brewer on what it feels like to be 1 of 2 Black female CEOs in the Fortune 500, *Fortune*, 4 October, https://fortune.com/longform/roz-brewer-ceo-walgreens-boots-alliance-interview-fortune-500-black-female-ceos/ (archived at perma.cc/CWK2-RRF6)

4   Fortune (2022) The 50 Most Powerful Women, https://fortune.com/most-powerful-women (archived at perma.cc/SS4D-HFXT)

5   Forbes, M, McGrath, M, Jones, N and Burho, E (eds) (2022) The World's 100 Most Powerful Women, *Forbes*, 6 December, https://www.forbes.com/lists/power-women/?sh=667f9ed25a95 (archived at perma.cc/V8FB-NK9C)

6   *Harvard Business Review* (2021) Walgreens CEO Roz Brewer to leaders: Put your phones away and listen to employees (Online video) 9 December, www.youtube.com/watch?v=Rk1y7Yahtic (archived at perma.cc/D9JD-WCHC)

7   The Economic Club of Chicago (2022) Roz Brewer, CEO, Walgreens Boots Alliance (Online video) 17 February, https://www.youtube.com/watch?v=nQY0FKIoOl4 (archived at perma.cc/5M2S-8RWU)

8   Stanford Graduate School of Business (2021) Rosalind Brewer: Find your voice and don't be silent (Podcast), 23 June, https://www.gsb.stanford.edu/insights/rosalind-brewer-find-your-voice-dont-be-silent (archived at perma.cc/4383-E3W3)

9   Stanford Graduate School of Business (2021) Rosalind Brewer: Find your voice and don't be silent (Podcast), 23 June, https://www.gsb.stanford.edu/insights/rosalind-brewer-find-your-voice-dont-be-silent (archived at perma.cc/4383-E3W3)

10 *Harvard Business Review* (2021) Walgreens CEO Roz Brewer to leaders: Put your phones away and listen to employees (Online video)

9 December, www.youtube.com/watch?v=Rk1y7Yahtic (archived at perma.cc/D9JD-WCHC)

11   Alcorn, C (2021) Rosalind Brewer officially takes the helm at Walgreens, becoming the only Black woman Fortune 500 CEO, CNN, 15 March, https://edition.cnn.com/2021/03/15/business/rosalind-brewer-walgreens/index.html (archived at perma.cc/6RUR-WMFX)

12   Neiswanger, R (2017) Brewer to retire as CEO at Sam's, *Arkansas Democrat Gazette*, 7 January, www.arkansasonline.com/news/2017/jan/07/brewer-to-retire-as-ceo-at-sam-s-201701/?f=business (archived at perma.cc/3FCN-X4JM)

13   Peterson, H (2015) People are calling Sam's Club CEO 'racist' after she gave an interview about diversity, *Business Insider*, 14 December, www.businessinsider.com/sams-club-ceo-accused-of-racism-after-cnn-interview-2015-12?r=US&IR=T (archived at perma.cc/7XYL-WNWA)

14   Alcorn, C (2021) Rosalind Brewer officially takes the helm at Walgreens, becoming the only Black woman Fortune 500 CEO, CNN, 15 March, https://edition.cnn.com/2021/03/15/business/rosalind-brewer-walgreens/index.html (archived at perma.cc/6RUR-WMFX)

15   *Today* (2021) Watch Hoda's full interview with Rosalind Brewer, the newest CEO of Walgreens (Online video) 5 May, www.youtube.com/watch?v=2t35ETrJygo (archived at perma.cc/D2WM-6AXT)

16   Starbucks (2017) Starbucks names Rosalind Brewer Group President and Chief Operating Officer, https://stories.starbucks.com/press/2017/starbucks-names-rosalind-brewer-group-president-and-chief-operating-officer (archived at perma.cc/BC48-NRCY)

17   Stanford Graduate School of Business (2021) Rosalind Brewer: Find your voice and don't be silent (Podcast), 23 June, https://www.gsb.stanford.edu/insights/rosalind-brewer-find-your-voice-dont-be-silent (archived at perma.cc/4383-E3W3)

18   Stevens, M (2018) Starbucks CEO apologizes after arrests of 2 black men, *The New York Times*, 15 April, www.nytimes.com/2018/04/15/us/starbucks-philadelphia-black-men-arrest.html (archived at perma.cc/H7NV-QEXY)

19   Starbucks (2018) Starbucks CEO. Reprehensible outcome in Philadelphia incident (14 April), https://stories.starbucks.com/press/2018/starbucks-ceo-reprehensible-outcome-in-philadelphia-incident (archived at perma.cc/SDH5-6ULV)

20   Stewart, E (2018) Starbucks says everyone's a customer after
      Philadelphia bias incident, *Vox*, 19 May, www.vox.com/
      identities/2018/5/19/17372164/starbucks-incident-bias-bathroom-
      policy-philadelphia (archived at perma.cc/T5QR-FK8Z)

21   Walgreens (2021) Walgreens surpasses 29 million COVID-19
      vaccinations administered, implements new policies to continue to lead
      against pandemic, 4 August, https://news.walgreens.com/press-center/
      news/pharmacy-and-healthcare/walgreens-suprasses-29-million-covid-
      19-vaccinations-delivered-implements-new-policies-to-continue-to-
      lead-fight-against-pandemic.htm (archived at perma.cc/4BHP-84P6)

22   *Today* (2021) Watch Hoda's full interview with Rosalind Brewer, the
      newest CEO of Walgreens (Online video) 5 May, www.youtube.com/
      watch?v=2t35ETrJygo (archived at perma.cc/D2WM-6AXT)

23   Stanford Graduate School of Business (2021) Rosalind Brewer: Find
      your voice and don't be silent (Podcast), 23 June, https://www.gsb.
      stanford.edu/insights/rosalind-brewer-find-your-voice-dont-be-silent
      (archived at perma.cc/4383-E3W3)

24   *Today* (2021) Watch Hoda's full interview with Rosalind Brewer, the
      newest CEO of Walgreens (Online video) 5 May, www.youtube.com/
      watch?v=2t35ETrJygo (archived at perma.cc/D2WM-6AXT)

25   *Harvard Business Review* (2021) Walgreens CEO Roz Brewer to
      leaders: Put your phones away and listen to employees (Online video)
      9 December, www.youtube.com/watch?v=Rk1y7Yahtic (archived at
      perma.cc/D9JD-WCHC)

26   *Today* (2021) Watch Hoda's full interview with Rosalind Brewer, the
      newest CEO of Walgreens (Online video) 5 May, www.youtube.com/
      watch?v=2t35ETrJygo (archived at perma.cc/D2WM-6AXT)

27   CNBC (2018) Starbucks COO Rosalind Brewer: 'It's amazing to bring
      my head and heart to work' (Online video) 7 May, www.cnbc.com/
      video/2018/05/07/rosalind-brewer-its-amazing-to-bring-my-head-and-
      heart-to-work.html (archived at perma.cc/DVQ2-2N2Y)

28   *Today* (2021) Watch Hoda's full interview with Rosalind Brewer, the
      newest CEO of Walgreens (Online video) 5 May, www.youtube.com/
      watch?v=2t35ETrJygo (archived at perma.cc/D2WM-6AXT)

29 *Today* (2021) Watch Hoda's full interview with Rosalind Brewer, the newest CEO of Walgreens (Online video) 5 May, www.youtube.com/watch?v=2t35ETrJygo (archived at perma.cc/D2WM-6AXT)

30 Stanford Graduate School of Business (2021) Rosalind Brewer: Find your voice and don't be silent (Podcast), 23 June, https://www.gsb.stanford.edu/insights/rosalind-brewer-find-your-voice-dont-be-silent (archived at perma.cc/4383-E3W3)

31 The Economic Club of Chicago (2022) Roz Brewer, CEO, Walgreens Boots Alliance (Online video) 17 February, https://www.youtube.com/watch?v=nQY0FKIoOl4 (archived at perma.cc/5M2S-8RWU)

32 The Economic Club of Chicago (2022) Roz Brewer, CEO, Walgreens Boots Alliance (Online video) 17 February, https://www.youtube.com/watch?v=nQY0FKIoOl4 (archived at perma.cc/5M2S-8RWU)

CHAPTER FIVE

Brian Chesky, Joe Gebbia and Nathan Blecharczyk

Airbnb

Leadership philosophy
'IF YOU BREAK THE CULTURE, YOU BREAK THE MACHINE THAT CREATES YOUR PRODUCTS.'[1]

Airbnb is the world's leading home-sharing platform, with more than six million active listings. It operates in over 220 countries and regions and more than 100,000 cities worldwide. To date, over one billion guests have stayed in Airbnb accommodation, welcomed by more than four million hosts.[2] The website offers a wealth of accommodation to suit all tastes – from city apartments to lakefront cabins, from island retreats to historic homes, from shepherd's huts to houseboats. And the driver behind this hugely successful business model is the simple idea of empowering people to make money by renting out their spare rooms.

Airbnb's story began back in 2007, when Brian Chesky and Joe Gebbia were agonizing about how they were going to pay their rent. The pair were then unemployed 26-year-old graduates of the Rhode Island School of Design. To cover their rent, they decided to rent out three air mattresses in their San Francisco apartment during a big design conference, throwing in breakfast as well. They created a basic website and appealed to design blogs and the conference organizers to help promote the slightly whacky-sounding service, which they called AirBed & Breakfast. Fortunately, the design blogs and organizers agreed to support them and the two would-be entrepreneurs soon booked in their first three guests, all professional designers. Flush with the success of their venture, the pair decided to start a company. To help, they brought in Nathan Blecharczyk, a talented coder and a former roommate of Gebbia's.[3]

Initially their business idea was to supply additional accommodation for sold-out conferences, but gradually the trio broadened their vision. They started to envisage AirBed & Breakfast as a website where people could book rooms in other people's houses just as easily as they could book a room in a hotel. This website would need to be underpinned by a payment system and have the capability to feature customer reviews.[4]

At first, the young entrepreneurs struggled to secure funding as investors found the concept both risky and odd. Nevertheless, the trio kept pushing their idea and were increasingly successful at securing media coverage. One of their early stunts, which gathered a fair amount of attention, was to create fictitious brands of breakfast cereals – Obama O's and Cap'n McCain's – named after the then-presidential contenders Barack Obama and John McCain. They sent the branded cereal boxes out to reporters, who loved the gimmick, and the resultant press coverage helped them sell enough cereals to keep the business afloat.

Significantly, their foray into branded cereals resulted in the trio being accepted for the prestigious Y Combinator start-up accelerator, which has also helped to launch file-hosting service Dropbox and digital currency platform Coinbase, among other well-known tech companies. Admission to Y Combinator brought the co-founders $20,000 in seed funding in exchange for giving up a 6 per cent stake in the company, plus access to a wealth of connections, knowledge and support.[5]

After joining Y Combinator, the co-founders made some important tweaks to their business model. In those days, most of their hosts were in New York so they went door-to-door in the city, signing people up. They encouraged hosts to display professional photos on their listings by offering to send a professional photographer free of charge. In fact, it was Chesky who took the photos. They also amended the rules of the business. They dropped the requirement that hosts rent out an air mattress even if they could offer a bed, along with the stipulation that guests should receive breakfast. They also allowed hosts to rent out an entire residence – not just a spare room. And they rebranded the business Airbnb.[6]

In 2009, the fledgling business took a major leap forward when it secured a $585,000 investment from Sequoia, a venture capital firm that had previously funded Apple, Google and Oracle. This funding, combined with an additional $30,000 investment from another source, valued the company at $2.4 million. After that, Airbnb took off. By August 2009, the weekly volume of bookings on Airbnb had reached almost $100,000, generating weekly revenue of $10,000. At this point, the three founders – who were working 18 hours a day, seven days a week – realized that they needed to take on employees. By summer 2010 the company had a staff of around 25.[7] Further funding rounds followed, and in July 2012, Airbnb was valued at $1.2 billion, giving it the exclusive status of a unicorn – a privately held company worth at least $1 billion.[8]

Challenges and opportunities

Next came several years of rapid expansion, with Airbnb enjoying consistent, year-on-year growth until 2020. The platform's popularity was boosted by its fast, well-designed, user-friendly website and the simplicity of the concept. Hosts can make money from renting out unused space, while guests have their pick of a range of exciting – and often unusual – accommodation options. Airbnb, meanwhile, earns its money from booking fees paid by both hosts and guests. The company offers guest identity verification, reservation screening (to block any bookings likely to have been made by disruptive parties) and a commitment to cover the costs of damage made by guests to the host's home and belongings – currently up to $3 million.[9]

To further enhance its proposition, Airbnb launched its 'Experiences' concept in 2016. Airbnb Experiences are memorable activities designed by local hosts that enable travellers to connect with local craftspeople and other experts. The experiences cover a wide range of activities, with pottery making, horse riding and water sports being just a few examples.

Much of Airbnb's brand appeal lies in its hippyish origins and its commitment to building a 'community' of hosts and guests. It has always been careful to position itself as a company that exists to make the world a better place, rather than purely to make money out of hospitality and travel. Airbnb's mission is to 'create a world where anyone can belong anywhere'.

Despite its well-meaning philosophy, Airbnb has become caught up in various controversies over the years. In particular, the company has come under fire for worsening the housing crisis that already existed in some of the world's most densely populated urban areas. This is because it effectively removes some properties from the long-term rental market, with the resultant shortage of accommodation serving to drive up the rent of those properties that remain. Hosting on Airbnb is now illegal or restricted in numerous cities and countries, including Barcelona, London, New York and Japan.[10]

Airbnb has also needed to respond purposefully to other controversies. These included hosts having their homes damaged by partying guests and hosts discriminating against guests on racial grounds. Additionally, there have been instances of guests dying in Airbnb rentals, which have raised issues around safety. In 2022, for example, three Americans died after suffering carbon monoxide poisoning in their Airbnb rental in Mexico City.[11]

When the Covid-19 pandemic broke out in 2020, Airbnb faced a huge challenge. The imposition of lockdowns and travel restrictions by governments dramatically reduced people's need for short-term accommodation, impacting the company's business model. Even when restrictions eased, both guests and hosts were worried about the safety implications of using Airbnb. Bookings plummeted and the company's revenue for the year was down 29.7 per cent on 2019.[12] In response to the crisis, the company laid off around a quarter of its workforce in May 2020.[13]

Nevertheless, Airbnb quickly bounced back. Despite the difficult trading conditions, and the revelation that it had also suffered a major data breach, the company pressed ahead with a planned IPO (initial public offering). Its listing on the NASDAQ stock exchange in December 2020 was the biggest US IPO of 2020, valuing the company at more than $100 billion.[14] In 2021, Airbnb's revenues recovered sharply, hitting almost $6 billion – around 20 per cent higher than in 2019, before Covid struck.

Airbnb aims to be a socially responsible organization – in line with its stance that it is a community and not just a company. Between 2016 and 2020 the company removed 1.3 million people from its platform for 'declining to treat others without judgement or bias'. It also launched Project Lighthouse in the US, an initiative to tackle discrimination when hosting or booking on Airbnb.[15]

Every year thousands of people around the world lose their homes due to conflict or natural disaster – an issue that Airbnb wants to help address. In 2017, it launched Open Homes, a platform that helped refugees to find temporary shelter. That initiative has since evolved into Airbnb.org, a non-profit organization with its own board of directors that includes Airbnb co-founder Gebbia. Airbnb.org allows hosts on Airbnb to provide free and discounted stays to people around the world who have been impacted by emergencies. In August 2022, Airbnb. org announced that, with the support of Airbnb hosts, it had been able to offer short-term accommodation to over 100,000 refugees who had fled the war in Ukraine.[16]

Airbnb continually reassesses whether the operations of its business remain in line with its values. In November 2022, Chesky expressed concerns about the inflated costs of accommodation on the site, after the average price per night had soared by more than 40 per cent since 2019. He admitted that he wanted Airbnb to become more affordable and was trying to increase room supply. He even listed his own home on the platform, with vetted guests able to stay at the property while he's there without having to pay a fee. As well as generating publicity, Chesky said his decision to list his house was an attempt to stay 'in touch'.[17]

Airbnb was not the first online platform to list accommodation, but it has become the most successful, largely through its clever execution of the concept. What's more, it has managed to totally disrupt the hospitality industry by drawing on the optimism, and the fundamental faith in the goodness of human nature, that have been integral to the brand and the culture of the business from the very start.

As Chesky himself has said: 'Airbnb is rooted in the fundamental idea that people are good.'[18]

Secrets to success

Undoubtedly, the collaboration between the three co-founders has been instrumental to Airbnb's phenomenal success. Each brought different attributes and strengths to the business, enabling them to effectively complement one another. What they shared was a passion for their business, a strong work ethic and a commitment to building and preserving the company's authentic, creative, entrepreneurial and humane culture over time.

Airbnb's chief executive, Chesky, is a keen learner, an avid note taker and a voracious reader, who believes in sharing knowledge with others. An extremely curious person, he has studied the careers of other business leaders such as Walt Disney and Steve Jobs. As Airbnb took off, he also actively sought out support from expert mentors, including LinkedIn co-founder Reid Hoffman and Meta's Mark Zuckerberg. While he has access to the kinds of mentors that most leaders only dream of, he believes that everyone can find good mentors, regardless of what level they're at in their organization.[19]

Chesky is regarded as a great visionary by those who work with him. He is always thinking ahead, reflecting on what needs to happen next. He is also an idealist who believes ardently in the company's mission. Back in 2010, he decided that to improve the company's service he needed to experience it for himself – what's popularly known in

Silicon Valley as 'eating your own dog food'. Accordingly, he spent several years living in different types of Airbnb accommodation.[20]

If Chesky is the visionary, then Gebbia is the innovator who has been coming up with inventive solutions to problems ever since his childhood. As a student, he created cushions that would sit comfortably on top of the hard stools in his art school.[21] In fact, Gebbia is so full of ideas that in July 2022 he announced he would be stepping down from an operating role in the company to pursue other interests and passions, including parenthood, documentary making and philanthropy.[22]

As chief strategy officer, Blecharczyk drives many of Airbnb's key strategic initiatives, especially those that involve public policy, product, data, and the company's long-term stakeholder interests. A graduate in computer science from Harvard, Blecharczyk's technical expertise was critical to Airbnb's success as an online platform. He's also helped to keep the business grounded as it's grown through his analytical, methodical and calm approach.[23] Together with his wife, Blecharczyk is an active Airbnb host who has welcomed hundreds of guests.[24]

Today, Chesky, Gebbia and Blecharczyk are all billionaires. Nevertheless, they have publicly committed to the idea of community by signing The Giving Pledge – a promise made by the world's wealthiest people to give the majority of their wealth to charitable causes.

LEADERSHIP LESSONS FROM BRIAN CHESKY, JOE GEBBIA AND NATHAN BLECHARCZYK

- **Find collaborators who complement you and share your vision**. By working as part of a team, you will likely achieve far more than if you work solely on your own.

- **Focus on building a healthy culture**. Culture sustains organizations through difficult times and acts as the foundation for innovation.

- **Eat your own dog food**. The best way to understand how your customers or users experience your product is to try it out for yourself.

- **Embrace crazy ideas**. Often the craziest ideas turn out to be the most successful.

- **Seek out mentors**. Whatever industry you're in, whatever level you're at, you will be able to find a mentor who can help you to progress.

Notes

1 Chesky, B (2014) Don't fuck up the culture, *Medium*, 20 April, https://medium.com/@bchesky/dont-fuck-up-the-culture-597cde9ee9d4 (archived at perma.cc/79J8-A3G2)

2 Airbnb (2022) About us, https://news.airbnb.com/about-us (archived at perma.cc/3NX4-3T3C)

3 Gallagher, L (2017) *The Airbnb Story*, Virgin Books, United Kingdom, pp 1–11

4 Gallagher, L (2017) *The Airbnb Story*, Virgin Books, United Kingdom, p 16

5   Gallagher, L (2017) *The Airbnb Story*, Virgin Books, United Kingdom, pp 20–25

6   Gallagher, L (2017) *The Airbnb Story*, Virgin Books, United Kingdom, pp 27–28

7   Gallagher, L (2017) *The Airbnb Story*, Virgin Books, United Kingdom, pp 30–37

8   Gallagher, L (2017) *The Airbnb Story*, Virgin Books, United Kingdom, p 47

9   Airbnb (2022) Airbnb it easily with Airbnb Setup, https://www.airbnb.co.uk/host/homes (archived at perma.cc/U23E-P9G4)

10 Zuo, S (2019) Top cities (and countries) where Airbnb is illegal or restricted, passive Airbnb, www.passiveairbnb.com/top-cities-and-countries-where-airbnb-is-illegal-or-restricted (archived at perma.cc/YU7X-8NA5)

11 Blanco, A (2022) Three Americans found dead inside Mexico city Airbnb from carbon monoxide poisoning, *The Independent*, 9 November, www.independent.co.uk/news/world/americas/carbon-monoxide-poisoning-mexico-city-americans-b2221702.html (archived at perma.cc/EP6M-4EJ4)

12 Macrotrends (2022) Airbnb Revenue 2018–2022, https://www.macrotrends.net/stocks/charts/ABNB/airbnb/revenue (archived at perma.cc/2GSL-Y6NQ)

13 Yurieff, K (2020) Airbnb is laying off 25% of its employees, CNN, 5 May, https://edition.cnn.com/2020/05/05/tech/airbnb-layoffs/index.html (archived at perma.cc/8VC8-TYXD)

14 Hussain, NZ and Franklin, J (2020) Airbnb surges past $100 billion in biggest U.S. IPO of 2020, *Reuters*, 10 December, www.reuters.com/article/airbnb-ipo-idUSKBN28K261 (archived at perma.cc/2NT5-323P)

15 Airbnb (2020) A new way we're fighting discrimination on Airbnb, 15 June, www.airbnb.co.uk/resources/hosting-homes/a/a-new-way-were-fighting-discrimination-on-airbnb-201 (archived at perma.cc/ZEE8-RR9J)

16 Airbnb (2022) 100,000 people fleeing Ukraine have found stays through Airbnb.org, 31 August, https://news.airbnb.com/100000-people-fleeing-ukraine-found-temporary-stays-through-airbnb-org (archived at perma.cc/9GTH-PFP6)

17   Lee, D (2022) Airbnb makes renewed push to boost supply as rental rates soar, *Financial Times*, 16 November, www.ft.com/content/40f3b66a-1ac5-48ed-a488-9b884fc5c06d (archived at perma.cc/5GJF-SVWG)

18   Hussain, NZ and Franklin, J (2020) Airbnb surges past $100 billion in biggest U.S. IPO of 2020, *Reuters*, 10 December, www.reuters.com/article/airbnb-ipo-idUSKBN28K261 (archived at perma.cc/2NT5-323P)

19   Gallagher, L (2017) *The Airbnb Story*, Virgin Books, United Kingdom, pp 164–68

20   Fairweather, A (2013) Meet Brian Chesky, the homeless entrepreneur, *Tech Central*, 14 March, https://techcentral.co.za/meet-brian-chesky-the-homeless-entrepreneur/187552 (archived at perma.cc/2BLL-743C)

21   Hunter, B (2018) Airbnb's co-founder has been innovating ever since he was a kid, *FEE*, 14 May, https://fee.org/articles/airbnbs-co-founder-has-been-innovating-since-he-was-a-kid (archived at perma.cc/VEF4-NVNL)

22   Wiggers, K (2022) Airbnb co-founder Joe Gebbia steps back from leadership role, *TechCrunch*, 21 July, https://techcrunch.com/2022/07/21/airbnb-co-founder-joe-gebbia-steps-back-from-leadership-role (archived at perma.cc/58KH-9NP9)

23   Gallagher, L (2017) *The Airbnb Story*, Virgin Books, United Kingdom, pp 180–81

24   Airbnb (2022) Nathan Blecharczyk, https://news.airbnb.com/about-us/leadership/nathan-blecharczyk (archived at perma.cc/29KD-KRW9)

CHAPTER SIX

Yvon Chouinard

Patagonia

Leadership philosophy
'I AM DEAD SERIOUS ABOUT SAVING THIS PLANET.'[1]

Patagonia is a California-based designer of outdoor clothing and equipment for a range of 'silent sports' including climbing, surfing, skiing and fly fishing. It sells its products globally through its own retail stores, as well as through mail order, e-commerce and dealers. Since it believes strongly in reducing consumption to help preserve the planet, it offers a free repair service for almost all its products.

Alongside its clothing range, Patagonia has a books division, and produces films on environmental and sport-related topics. It also has a food business called Patagonia Provisions, which sells responsibly sourced food. Patagonia's values are to build the best products while causing no unnecessary harm, using business to protect nature, and developing new ways to do things.[2]

After half a century in existence, the enduring power of Patagonia's brand owes much to its revolutionary founder, Yvon Chouinard. Chouinard was born in November 1938 in Lewiston, a city in the north-eastern US state of Maine, to a French-speaking household. His parents, who were French Canadians from Québec, later moved west to the Californian city of Burbank, taking their family with them. Unfortunately, Chouinard struggled at school, initially because he couldn't speak English, but also because he had no interest in most of the subjects. As a result, he ended up being branded a troublemaker.

The young Chouinard did enjoy sports, however. As a teenager, he also became involved with the South California Falconry Club, where he learned how to train falcons and hawks for hunting. During his time with the club, he learned how to climb – igniting what was to become a lifelong passion. When he graduated from high school in 1956, he attended community college for two years while working part-time for his brother, who ran a private detective business (its main client was the US billionaire businessman and film producer Howard Hughes). He spent his spare time climbing and surfing.

In 1957, Chouinard bought a used coal-fired forge from a junkyard, along with an anvil, some tongs and a hammer, and began to teach himself blacksmithing. He wanted to make his own climbing hardware, including carabiners (shackles) and pitons (metal spikes that are driven into climbing surfaces using a hammer, to protect climbers in case they fall). For the next few years, he made climbing equipment during the winter months and spent the summer climbing in the mountains. He earned a little money by selling equipment from the back of his car, but it was scarcely enough to live on. So, to survive on his meagre income, he ate cat food from dented tins and captured and ate ground squirrels. At ease in the natural world, he regarded himself as a rebel against consumer culture, someone who regarded corporations as 'the source of all evil'.[3]

Already it was clear that Chouinard was a man who would not necessarily conform with society's rules. In 1962, he and a friend were arrested for riding on a freight train after returning from a climbing trip and the pair spent 18 days in jail. Soon afterwards he was drafted into the US army and was sent to Korea where he 'caused nothing but trouble by "forgetting" to salute officers, looking slovenly, going on hunger strikes, and generally acting unbalanced'.[4]

Once he was discharged from military service, Chouinard split up with his first wife – whom he had hastily married before leaving for Korea – and moved to Ventura on California's southern coast, where he could be close to some of the state's best surf breaks. With demand for his equipment growing, he went into partnership with a couple of businesspeople called Tom and Doreen Frost. They worked as partners for nine years, seeing the business not as an end in itself but rather as a means to pay for climbing trips. Nevertheless, by 1970, their company, Chouinard Equipment, had become the largest supplier of climbing hardware in the United States.

At that time, Chouinard made his first significant environmental decision. Conscious that pitons were responsible for disfiguring the rock in areas of outstanding natural beauty, such as California's Yosemite Valley, he moved away from pitons towards the production of aluminium chocks that could be wedged into cracks by hand.

Patagonia is born

Another important decision that Chouinard made was to move into clothing. During a climbing trip to Scotland in 1970, he bought himself a rugby shirt and started to wear it while climbing back home. After his friends asked where they could get one, he ordered more rugby shirts from England, New Zealand and Argentina. He believed that selling clothing would help to support the hardware business, which was only marginally profitable.

By 1972, the company was operating its own retail store, selling rugby shirts, rain cagoules, gloves and backpacks among other items. As the clothing line took off, it was clear that it needed its own name. Since the clothing was intended for outdoor use in tough conditions, it seemed appropriate to name it after the mountainous region of Patagonia at the southernmost tip of South America. In 1973, the Patagonia brand was officially founded, with its distinctive label of jagged peaks based on the Mount Fitz Roy skyline.

But, a year later, crisis struck. In 1974, the company contracted a garment factory in Hong Kong to produce thousands of rugby shirts, but the shipments arrived late and the quality of the clothes was terrible. The rugby shirts had to be disposed of for less than cost price, creating severe cashflow problems for the business. Chouinard's second wife, Malinda, had now joined the company, but the financial pressures were so great that, in December 1975, the Chouinards' partnership with the Frosts came to an end. After that, Chouinard and his wife became the sole owners of both the tool and the clothing businesses.

The couple managed to save their businesses with the help of a revolving credit line from the bank. They also had the support of Kris McDivitt Tompkins, who took over as general manager in 1979 and stayed as general manager and CEO for 13 years. She played a crucial role in shaping the evolution of the company since Chouinard himself was a reluctant businessman. In fact, so reluctant was he that for a long time he even avoided thinking of himself as a businessman at all, preferring to regard himself as a climber, a surfer, a kayaker, a skier and a blacksmith.

When Chouinard did finally accept that he was, in fact, a businessman, he resolved that he was going to be a businessman on his own terms. He was determined that work would be enjoyable on a day-to-day basis and that he and his staff would come to work 'on the balls of our feet and go up the stairs two steps at a time'.[5] With this approach to leadership and management, he proved to be way ahead of his time.

Having survived its cashflow crisis, Patagonia began to focus on producing technical clothing for mountaineers – clothing such as pile jackets and thermal underwear. Sales grew rapidly during the 1980s and by 1990, the company – now called Patagonia Inc – was turning over $100 million and expanding internationally. But Chouinard was beginning to have concerns about the sustainability of its growth given the deterioration he saw in the natural environment when he travelled. So, he resolved to provide financial support to environmental organizations that were working to protect and restore the natural habitat. The company began recycling all its paper waste in 1984 and its catalogue became the first in the United States to use recycled paper.[6]

Because of Chouinard's commitment to environmentalism, Patagonia has been donating to non-profit environmental groups since the early 1980s. In 1986, it committed to giving 10 per cent of its profits. Then, in 1996, it committed to giving 1 per cent of its sales, meaning it had to give money to environmental causes regardless of whether it made a profit or not. It sees the donation as a self-imposed 'earth tax' – the price it pays for existing on the planet, using its resources and contributing to the environmental crisis through its activities. The individuals and organizations that Patagonia supports tend to be grass-roots environmental activists who are fighting to save the natural world, often with minimal resources.[7] In 2002, Chouinard co-founded 1% for the Planet, a global alliance of businesses that pledge to donate at least 1 per cent of their sales towards active efforts to protect and restore the natural environment.[8]

The late 1980s brought fresh business challenges after Chouinard Equipment, Patagonia's sister firm, was targeted by several lawsuits. In the end, Chouinard Equipment filed for Chapter 11 bankruptcy and was bought out by its employees, leaving Chouinard and his wife to focus on

Patagonia. But Patagonia itself was plunged into crisis in 1991, when recession limited its growth to 20 per cent rather than the 40 per cent it had planned for and – importantly – hired for. On 31 July 1991, the company laid off 120 employees – 20 per cent of its workforce. Chouinard has described that day as 'certainly the single darkest day of the company's history'.

But this sad event also proved to be an opportunity for Patagonia to rethink its priorities and clarify its values. After much soul-searching about what it stood for, the company adopted a set of environmentally based values. Chouinard recognized that if Patagonia was to survive, it had to make all its decisions as though it would be in business for 100 years, growing only at a rate that it could sustain for that long.[9]

One of the most significant decisions that Patagonia made to its operations was to switch all its cotton styles to organically grown cotton from 1996. It has also limited its growth to organic growth – the amount by which its customers believe it should grow by each year. And it has measured its success not by sales figures or profits but by the environmental threats it has averted, such as old forests that have not been cut down and toxic pesticides that have never been sprayed.[10]

Although Patagonia has attracted the attention of numerous potential purchasers who have an ambition to grow the company and take it public, it has remained privately held. This has allowed it to focus on its bottom line of doing good.[11] Thanks to a groundbreaking decision taken by Chouinard and his family, there is no chance of it becoming a public company at any time in the future, either.

In 2022, Chouinard made headlines when he, his wife and his two adult children transferred their ownership of Patagonia (by then valued at about $3 billion) to a specially designed trust and non-profit organization. Through its new legal structure, Patagonia will continue acting as a for-profit company, while channelling its future profits towards protecting nature, supporting the community, and fighting the environmental crisis.[12] Although it will remain privately owned, Patagonia is no longer owned by the Chouinards. Nevertheless, the family will guide the trust.[13]

'Earth is now our only shareholder,' Patagonia declared in a statement. The legal structure is designed to ensure that the company is not sold or taken public, which could lead to a change in its values. It is also intended to let the company act as an example to its peers – by proving, as a for-profit business, that capitalism can work for the planet. Rather than 'going public', it is 'going purpose'. As Chouinard himself explained: 'Instead of extracting value from nature and transforming it into wealth, we are using the wealth Patagonia creates to protect the source.'[14]

It will be interesting to see how this decision by Chouinard and his family will play out in the long run. Will Patagonia continue to succeed, influencing and inspiring a whole new generation of environmentally and socially responsible companies? Or will it lose its way without the vision and guiding passion of its founder? Regardless of how the future pans out, we can be sure of one thing, however: the Patagonia test case will certainly be closely studied by business schools.

To this day, Chouinard remains uncomfortable with the idea that he is an ultra-successful businessman. He refers to himself as a 'dirtbag' (a term used to describe a poor climber or outdoor person who lives cheaply)[15] and leads a modest lifestyle, shunning most of the outward trappings of wealth. In 2017, he was horrified to find himself named as a billionaire by *Forbes* and added to its list of the world's richest people. Later he told *The New York Times* that the article 'really pissed me off', saying: 'I don't have $1 billion in the bank. I don't drive Lexuses.'[16]

Despite – or perhaps because of – his own environmental efforts, Chouinard admits to being 'a total pessimist' about the fate of the natural world. This is due to the environmental destruction he's witnessed over the years and the lack of will within society to tackle 'the impending doom'. Ultimately, he believes, the human species may, in fact, have 'run its course'.[17]

Secrets to success

Unconventional and outspoken, Chouinard is a radical firebrand who is trying to transform the way we think about business. As a pioneer of sustainable capitalism, he believes that economic growth should not exceed the capacity of the natural world to support that growth. To preserve the planet, he also argues that we need to address the issue of consumerism by encouraging people to buy only what they need rather than what they desire. It is these principles, so sincerely held by Chouinard, which underpin the strength of the Patagonia brand.

Chouinard believes that Patagonia's bottom line is not the amount of profit it generates but the amount of good that it can accomplish over a single year. Nevertheless, he understands that a company needs to be profitable to stay in business and to set an example to other companies. His view is that profit is what happens when a company does other things right. Meanwhile his attitude to growth challenges one of the fundamental tenets of capitalism today: that rapid – and fundamentally unsustainable – growth is always a good thing. Patagonia aims to grow at a 'natural rate' – serving customers who genuinely need its clothing rather than creating an artificial market of people who desire it as a fashion item. Patagonia is a member of B Lab, a non-profit organization working to build a community of companies called B Corps that are committed to improving their social and environmental practices. It is itself a B Corp.[18]

Chouinard's autobiography, *Let My People Go Surfing*, outlines the philosophies that underpin Patagonia's ongoing success. The brand aims to make high-quality, useful products and it expects its clothes to be the best of their kind. To ensure that its products are indeed best in class, Patagonia designers must ask themselves several fundamental questions. These include: Is it functional? Is it multifunctional (i.e. can it be used for more than one activity, such as climbing AND skiing)? Is it durable and can it stand up to prolonged, hard use? Is it repairable? Is it as simple as possible? Is it easy to care for and clean? Is it beautiful? Does it cause any unnecessary harm?[19]

Patagonia works with a small number of high-quality suppliers and contractors, and has long-term relationships with them, using its leverage as a customer to improve working conditions, as well as product quality. It does thorough homework before using a new fabric or supplier. What's more, it is constantly looking to improve its business processes and is not afraid to borrow ideas from other companies and cultures.[20]

Importantly, Patagonia's own culture still reflects the origins of Chouinard Equipment – a workplace populated by climbers who enjoyed working with their friends and who didn't adhere to traditional corporate values. When it recruits today, the company seeks out employees who are also customers – people who enjoy the outdoors and buy the Patagonia brand. But it also hires people with other passions – whether that's singing, writing or environmental activism. It values diversity of background – believing that this encourages flexible thinking and an openness to new ways of doing things. It also takes its time when hiring, to make sure it finds the people who will best fit. To maintain its culture, it hires from within as much as possible and invests in training its staff.[21]

Chouinard describes his own management style as MBA (management by absence). Over the years, he spent a lot of time out in the world, away from the office, gathering ideas. So, while he and his wife Malinda were always closely involved with Patagonia's operations, they always had a CEO as well. There is no such thing as a one-size-fits-all CEO, Chouinard believes. CEOs with different backgrounds and skills are needed for different business situations. He also argues that effective CEOs do not immediately hire a consultant when an issue arises; instead, they will first try to solve the problem themselves.[22]

Chouinard strongly believes that work should be fun and a means for people to pursue their passions. He doesn't see why it needs to be a constraint on people's lives. This explains why Patagonia has a flexitime policy called 'Let My People Go Surfing', which employees can take advantage of to go surfing, climbing or simply meet their children when they get home from school. Patagonia is also strongly committed to supporting working parents, seeing this as a great way to attract and retain motivated staff. Hence the company provides onsite childcare, as well as afterschool clubs.[23]

Chouinard's experience of doing risky sports has taught him to know his limits. He believes that people and businesses should both know their strengths and weaknesses and live within their means.[24] Nevertheless, he realizes that it is important to take calculated risks in business, saying that sometimes you can't afford to wait until you have all the answers before you act, or you risk losing first-mover advantage.[25]

Probably more than anything else, Chouinard is known for being a fervent environmentalist who uses his platform to advocate for greater action on issues such as climate change, deforestation, soil degradation and water usage. Nevertheless, he is no hypocrite. He knows that regardless of Patagonia doing everything it can to reduce its harm, it is, by the nature of its business, still part of the problem. The garment industry is associated with water pollution, soil degradation and high carbon emissions, as well as major social issues such as modern slavery. Chouinard fully acknowledges that Patagonia will never make a totally sustainable product that doesn't damage the world in some way.[26]

Despite having lived through an era of rapid technological development, Chouinard is not technologically savvy. He owns neither a computer nor a cellphone[27] and once mistook the office air conditioner for a new IBM system.[28] While he embraces change, he believes in the old-fashioned values of restraint, quality and simplicity, saying: 'I believe the mastering of any endeavour is to work toward simplicity; replace complex technology with knowledge.' Choosing to live more simply, he adds, won't be an impoverished life 'but one richer in all the ways that really matter'.[29]

LEADERSHIP LESSONS FROM YVON CHOUINARD

- **Ask yourself some hard questions about your organization's impact on the planet**. Is it growing in a sustainable way or pursuing growth merely for growth's own sake? What harm is it causing through its growth? Use the answers to these questions to inform your business strategy.

- **Be an independent and unconventional thinker**. You don't have to do something the same way that others do it, just because they do it that way.

- **Make work fun**. If people enjoy coming to your workplace, they will work hard and care about what they do.

- **Use your platform to be an advocate for the issues that you passionately believe in**. Each of us has the power to make a genuine difference in the world.

- **Embrace the simple life**. Only buy what you need rather than what you desire. Through your example, you can influence others.

Notes

1   Patagonia (2022) Patagonia's Next Chapter: Earth is now our only shareholder, 14 September, www.patagoniaworks.com/press/2022/9/14/patagonias-next-chapter-earth-is-now-our-only-shareholder (archived at perma.cc/3SZW-49MU)

2   Patagonia (2023) Core Values, https://eu.patagonia.com/gb/en/core-values (archived at perma.cc/GG5A-5BBN)

3   Chouinard, Y (2016) *Let My People Go Surfing*, Patagonia/Penguin, United States, pp 4–13

4   Chouinard, Y (2016) *Let My People Go Surfing*, Patagonia/Penguin, United States, p 17

5   Chouinard, Y (2016) *Let My People Go Surfing*, Patagonia/Penguin, United States, p 38

6   Chouinard, Y (2016) *Let My People Go Surfing*, Patagonia/Penguin, United States, pp 38–57

7   Chouinard, Y (2016) *Let My People Go Surfing*, Patagonia/Penguin, United States, p 207

8   1% for the Planet (2023) About Us, https://onepercentfortheplanet.org/en/about (archived at perma.cc/465Q-N8BD)

9   Chouinard, Y (2016) *Let My People Go Surfing*, Patagonia/Penguin, United States, pp 57–66

10 Chouinard, Y (2016) *Let My People Go Surfing*, Patagonia/Penguin, United States, p 70

11 Chouinard, Y (2016) *Let My People Go Surfing*, Patagonia/Penguin, United States, p 155

12 McCormick, E (2022) Patagonia's billionaire owner gives away company to fight climate crisis, 15 September, www.theguardian.com/us-news/2022/sep/14/patagonias-billionaire-owner-gives-away-company-to-fight-climate-crisis-yvon-chouinard (archived at perma.cc/3DNC-NPY3)

13 *Suston* (2022) Patagonia: 'Earth is now our only shareholder', 19 September, https://sustonmagazine.com/2022/09/19/patagonia-earth-is-now-our-only-shareholder (archived at perma.cc/XH9F-FDKR)

14 Patagonia (2022) Patagonia's Next Chapter: Earth is now our only shareholder, 14 September. www.patagoniaworks.com/press/ 2022/9/14/patagonias-next-chapter-earth-is-now-our-only-shareholder (archived at perma.cc/3SZW-49MU)

15 Neate, R (2022) Yvon Chouinard – the 'existential dirtbag' who founded and gifted Patagonia, *The Guardian*, 15 September, www. theguardian.com/global/2022/sep/15/yvon-chouinard-the-existential-dirtbag-who-founded-and-gifted-patagonia (archived at perma.cc/ UUQ2-JU9L)

16 Gelles, D (2022) Billionaire no more: Patagonia founder gives away the company, *The New York Times*, 14 September, www.nytimes. com/2022/09/14/climate/patagonia-climate-philanthropy-chouinard. html (archived at perma.cc/FLM9-3EQR)

17 Chouinard, Y (2016) *Let My People Go Surfing*, Patagonia/Penguin, United States, p 175

18 Chouinard, Y (2016) *Let My People Go Surfing*, Patagonia/Penguin, United States, pp 151–52

19 Chouinard, Y (2016) *Let My People Go Surfing*, Patagonia/Penguin, United States, pp 77–95

20 Chouinard, Y (2016) *Let My People Go Surfing*, Patagonia/Penguin, United States, pp 111–19

21 Chouinard, Y (2016) *Let My People Go Surfing*, Patagonia/Penguin, United States, pp 157–65

22 Chouinard, Y (2016) *Let My People Go Surfing*, Patagonia/Penguin, United States, pp 167–73

23 Chouinard, Y (2016) *Let My People Go Surfing*, Patagonia/Penguin, United States, pp 157–65

24 Chouinard, Y (2016) *Let My People Go Surfing*, Patagonia/Penguin, United States, p 66

25 Chouinard, Y (2016) *Let My People Go Surfing*, Patagonia/Penguin, United States, p 48

26 Chouinard, Y (2016) *Let My People Go Surfing*, Patagonia/Penguin, United States, pp 175–230

27 Gelles, D (2022) Billionaire no more: Patagonia founder gives away the company, *The New York Times*, 14 September, www.nytimes.com/ 2022/09/14/climate/patagonia-climate-philanthropy-chouinard.html (archived at perma.cc/FLM9-3EQR)

28 Chouinard, Y (2016) *Let My People Go Surfing*, Patagonia/Penguin, United States, p 57

29 Chouinard, Y (2016) *Let My People Go Surfing*, Patagonia/Penguin, United States, p 231

CHAPTER SEVEN

Jimmy Donaldson

Mrbeast

Leadership philosophy
'MY OVERARCHING GOAL IN LIFE IS TO MAKE A LOT OF MONEY
AND THEN, BEFORE I DIE, GIVE IT AWAY.'[1]

Mrbeast is an American YouTube personality known for devising entertaining philanthropic and endurance stunts that have earned him millions of fans from around the world. Videos on his YouTube channel show him giving away large sums of money (between $10,000 and $1 million) to people who succeed at an array of imaginative challenges, such as being the last to leave a revolving door or staying in a circle painted on a field for 100 days. In addition to his challenges, he is famous for carrying out random acts of largesse, such as giving a waitress or a pizza deliveryman a $10,000 tip.[2] On one occasion, he started up his own bank to give away money for free.[3] On another, he sold a house for $1.[4] As of January 2023, MrBeast's YouTube channel – @MrBeast – had more than 125 million subscribers globally, making him one of the five most popular channels on the platform.[5] He is the most-followed individual on YouTube, popular with both adults and children, and his videos have attracted billions of views.

The real-life individual behind the larger-than-life persona of MrBeast is Jimmy Donaldson, a fresh-faced member of Generation Z. Born in May 1998, Donaldson is the younger son of a single mother who worked in the military. As a child, he moved around a lot and spent many evenings on his own since his mother worked night shifts. He first posted videos to YouTube as a 13-year-old in 2012, using the handle 'MrBeast6000'. His early efforts were comedic tutorials of online games, including Minecraft.[6] In 2016, he dropped out of East Carolina University to become a full-time creator, devising stunts such as wrapping himself in toilet paper and food wrap. His mother, not wanting to encourage him, told him to move out of the house.[7] In a tweet published in 2019, Donaldson defended his mother's action, explaining that she loved him and had only wanted him to be a success.[8] Ironically, of course, he has turned out to be far more successful than she probably ever dreamed.

When Donaldson landed his first brand deal in 2017 – securing $10,000 – he went outside and gave the money to a homeless person, with the gesture filmed on camera. The video went viral. This led him to adopt his now trademark influencing strategy of giving away cash. Later, he said that it 'felt good' to 'take 10 grand and light it on fire and make 20 grand'.[9]

Over time, Donaldson's stunts have become progressively more ambitious. His outlandish – but carefully planned – endeavours include counting to 100,000 (a feat that took him 40 hours),[10] spinning a fidget spinner for 24 hours,[11] being buried alive in a coffin,[12] spending 50 hours in solitary confinement,[13] and camping out in the midst of Antarctic blizzards,[14] naturally with a camera to keep him company every time. While Donaldson is the frontman of the act, MrBeast is very much a team effort, with much of the entertainment arising from the way he interacts with his crew. This crew initially included four of his childhood friends (Chris Tyson, Chandler Hallow, Garrett Ronalds and Jake Franklin), who quickly became social media stars in their own right. Since then, the crew has grown to 30.[15]

As well as having a positive social impact, the MrBeast platform has been harnessed to promote environmentalism. In 2019, MrBeast launched a fundraising campaign for US-based non-profit the Arbor Day Foundation. The campaign, called #TeamTrees, aimed to fund the planting of 20 million trees by the end of the year. Donaldson achieved the target despite describing it as his biggest project ever.[16]

Donaldson makes his videos in a secret 100-acre compound in the US state of North Carolina, spending millions of dollars on each one that he produces. As well as his primary YouTube channel, MrBeast, Donaldson now has several other YouTube channels (including MrBeast Gaming and Beast Reacts). His channels earn Donaldson's studio millions of dollars in revenue from advertising, as well as sponsored content.[17] It is these valuable brand deals that enable him to give so much money away.

Donaldson's choice of YouTube as his preferred channel for content creation is instrumental to his success. YouTube is the world's second most visited website after Google, with more than 2.6 billion monthly users.[18] Through the YouTube platform he is able to reach a vast international audience that enjoys his distinctive brand of stunt philanthropy and endurance challenges.

More recently, Donaldson has branched out from the online world of YouTube into the offline worlds of restaurants and confectionery. He started a delivery-only burger chain, MrBeast Burger, as a joint venture in 2020, and it quickly became the fastest-growing restaurant brand in the United States. In 2022, Donaldson launched his own chocolate brand, Feastables, made with organic cacao. Inspired by the character of Willy Wonka in Roald Dahl's children's book, *Charlie and the Chocolate Factory*, he even created his own faux chocolate factory, with gummy bears hanging off tree branches and a real chocolate river. To promote the chocolate, he invited 10 fans who had found a golden ticket in his Feastable bars to come to the factory and enter a competition to win $500,000 and a new car.[19]

MrBeast is fundamentally a positive, feel-good brand. Nevertheless, Donaldson's 'nice guy' image took a hit in 2021 when some of his past employees told *The New York Times* that he made unreasonable demands and created a hostile work environment. They also criticized him for being a perfectionist and for changing his demeanour when the cameras were not around. Previously Donaldson had attracted controversy over homophobic tweets he posted as a teenager and that he subsequently took down.[20] Donaldson's representative did not comment on the accusations about workplace conditions, but said the content creator had now matured into someone who did not use homophobic rhetoric. Donaldson also came under fire in 2021 for promoting and investing in a cryptocurrency scheme in which his fans lost money.[21]

Donaldson is often referred to as 'YouTube's biggest philanthropist' although he has occasionally faced a backlash for his efforts. In 2023, he paid for 1,000 people with severe cataracts to receive eye surgery so that they could see again. But he incurred criticism after posting a video of patients getting their bandages removed following the surgery. His critics argued that he was exploiting vulnerable people for the purposes of generating content. In response to this criticism, Donaldson promised to give away all his money before he dies.[22]

Despite these controversies, Donaldson's star continues to rise, and it's clear that his career still has a long way to go. *Forbes* named him on its 30 Under 30 North America list for 2023, with the provocative headline: '*Could MrBeast Be The First YouTuber Billionaire?*' The magazine described him as the 'world's top-earning creator' and estimated his worth at $500 million.[23]

Secrets to success

As he's proved, Donaldson is far more than just a bunch of whacky ideas, a goofy smile and a towering height (he is six foot, four inches tall). Not only is he a creative genius, he is also an astute businessman who is acutely conscious of the opportunities to monetize the MrBeast brand through channels such as video games and further food products.

In an interview with fellow YouTuber Casey Neistat in 2019, Donaldson shared some of the secrets of his career success to date. He described his content as 'me being an idiot' and 'spending lots of money', revealing that he had dreamed of being a YouTube sensation from an early age, while never believing that it would actually happen. But he kept posting videos, despite having no money and no audience, and kept reinvesting the profits he did make. 'As I made more money, I was just like, now I want to spend it on videos somehow,' he said. 'That was just my mindset.'

Donaldson loves the process of making videos – and that is ultimately what drives him. As he said to Neistat: 'I'll be making videos until YouTube's literally not a thing.' In fact, he was so obsessed with the idea of becoming a successful YouTuber that he was prepared to sacrifice his teenage years to achieving that ambition. But while he is motivated by the number of clicks he receives on his videos, he also deeply values the fact his videos give him the opportunity to support his mother, employ his friends and help other people.

Donaldson also wants to challenge the idea that negativity is the secret to getting clicks on social media. He believes that when it comes to YouTube, 'positivity is just as much clickbait as negativity'. As far as he's concerned, being kind to people doesn't have to be boring; it can actually be great entertainment.

The audience is front of Donaldson's mind when he's planning a video as he likes to create content that people can't wait to see. 'I want to give people what they want,' he says. His advice to other would-be YouTubers is to put days into their videos when other people put in hours and to 'go above and beyond' so that they are not like anyone else.

Philanthropy is one of Donaldson's core values, as well as being the basis for his business model. 'I like helping people,' he told Neistat. 'Even when I didn't have much money, if I had money in my wallet I'd just give it away to homeless people.' He added that he enjoys seeing people's faces light up when they unexpectedly get large sums of money. Still, he admits that he's also motivated by the process of making money, saying: 'I want to make money so later on in life I can do big things.' One 'big thing' that Donaldson has already done is to found his own charity, Beast Philanthropy, which distributes food to underserved communities.[24]

Through his phenomenal success, Donaldson is directly challenging the perceptions of millions of parents around the world who advise their children that being a YouTuber or another type of social media influencer is not a viable career option. He has shown that you can build a career through being a fantastic entertainer and content creator, with YouTube being his platform of choice. 'A lot of people still see YouTubers as a subclass of influencers,' he told *Forbes*, adding that people underestimate the influence that a lot of creators have.[25] His own influence is such that he will undoubtedly be the inspiration for a whole new generation of content creators who succeed in monetizing entertainment via YouTube and other online platforms.

LEADERSHIP LESSONS FROM JIMMY DONALDSON

- **Develop original business models**. Capitalize on online platforms and emerging technologies to find new ways of generating revenue.

- **Continually nurture and explore great ideas**. Use creativity to stand out in a crowded marketplace.

- **Never stand still**. Only by pushing the boundaries of what is possible will you keep your brand fresh and relevant.

- **Ignore the doubters**. There will always be people who don't believe in what you are doing. Don't let them stand between you and the success you deserve.

- **Be philanthropic**. Develop a business model that allows you to profit while doing good for others.

Notes

1   Casey Neistat (2019) $2 MILLION in 12 months, the price of Mr. Beast's success (Online video) www.youtube.com/watch?v= UE6UkF9sABU (archived at perma.cc/28BR-7N6F)

2   Zilber, A (2018) YouTube star Jimmy Donaldson leaves $10,000 tip at a North Carolina diner after ordering just two glasses of water, *Daily Mail*, 22 October, www.dailymail.co.uk/news/article-6301253/ YouTube-star-leaves-10-000-tip-North-Carolina-diner-ordering-just-two-glasses-water.html (archived at perma.cc/56HT-RB3J)

3   MrBeast (2019) I opened a FREE BANK (Online video) www.youtube. com/watch?v=ORUX1lHbOa8 (archived at perma.cc/6YMV-SC4H)

4   MrBeast (2021) I sold my house for $1 (Online video) www.youtube. com/watch?v=vJH28ICkCdU (archived at perma.cc/X54R-FHAP)

5   Boyd, J (2022) The most-subscribed YouTuber and channels, *Brandwatch*, 15 December, www.brandwatch.com/blog/most-subscribed-youtubers-channels (archived at perma.cc/D44R-2JBQ)

6   Ariba (2022) MrBeast is now the most followed on YouTube. What's the secret to his success? *The Indian Express*, 17 November, https://indianexpress.com/article/explained/explained-culture/who-is-mrbeast-youtube-subscribers-pewdiepie-explained-8273863 (archived at perma.cc/9K6N-DZCQ)

7   Sorvino, C (2022) Could MrBeast be the first YouTuber billionaire?, *Forbes*, 30 November, www.forbes.com/sites/chloesorvino/2022/11/30/could-mrbeast-be-the-first-youtuber-billionaire/?sh=526a09f191a2 (archived at perma.cc/35LY-J8V9)

8   Ariba (2022) MrBeast is now the most followed on YouTube. What's the secret to his success?, *The Indian Express*, 17 November, https://indianexpress.com/article/explained/explained-culture/who-is-mrbeast-youtube-subscribers-pewdiepie-explained-8273863 (archived at perma.cc/9K6N-DZCQ)

9   Sorvino, C (2022) Could MrBeast be the first YouTuber billionaire?, *Forbes*, 30 November, www.forbes.com/sites/chloesorvino/2022/11/30/could-mrbeast-be-the-first-youtuber-billionaire/?sh=526a09f191a2 (archived at perma.cc/35LY-J8V9)

10 MrBeast (2021) I counted to 100,000 (Online video) www.youtube.com/watch?v=xWcldHxHFpo (archived at perma.cc/5EBZ-ECSS)

11 MrBeast (2017) Spinning a fidget spinner for 24 hours straight (Online video) www.youtube.com/watch?v=vtq3sSLImKs (archived at perma.cc/PQ3Z-GW2A)

12 MrBeast (2021) I spent 50 hours buried alive (Online video) www.youtube.com/watch?v=9bqk6ZUsKyA (archived at perma.cc/TW3B-K9EY)

13 MrBeast (2020) I spent 50 hours in solitary confinement (Online video) www.youtube.com/watch?v=r7zJ8srwwjk (archived at perma.cc/S9Q6-SBPT)

14 MrBeast (2021) I survived 50 hours in Antarctica (Online video) www.youtube.com/watch?v=7IKab3HcfFk (archived at perma.cc/ZG7P-T4GG)

15   Cacich, A (2021) YouTuber MrBeast reached 30 million subscribers with a little help from his friends, *Distractify*, 11 February, www.distractify.com/p/mrbeast-crew (archived at perma.cc/2TQQ-Z9EH)

16   MrBeast (2019) Planting 20,000,000 trees, my biggest project ever! (Online video) www.youtube.com/watch?v=HPJKxAhLw5I (archived at perma.cc/HW5Y-H2A7)

17   Sorvino, C (2022) Could MrBeast be the first YouTuber billionaire?, *Forbes*, 30 November, www.forbes.com/sites/chloesorvino/2022/11/30/could-mrbeast-be-the-first-youtuber-billionaire/?sh=526a09f191a2 (archived at perma.cc/35LY-J8V9)

18   Global Media Insight (2022) YouTube User Statistics 2022, www.globalmediainsight.com/blog/youtube-users-statistics/#stat (archived at perma.cc/V294-ALL3)

19   Sorvino, C (2022) Could MrBeast be the first YouTuber billionaire?, *Forbes*, 30 November, www.forbes.com/sites/chloesorvino/2022/11/30/could-mrbeast-be-the-first-youtuber-billionaire/?sh=526a09f191a2 (archived at perma.cc/35LY-J8V9)

20   Gray, G (2021) The untold truth of MrBeast, *SVG*, 17 December, www.svg.com/711096/the-untold-truth-of-mrbeast (archived at perma.cc/JG4C-NL8J)

21   Lorenz, T (2021) Mr. Beast, YouTube star, wants to take over the business world, *The New York Times*, 4 May, www.nytimes.com/2021/05/04/technology/mr-beast-youtube.html (archived at perma.cc/4R8R-ENPR)

22   Newman, J (2023) World's biggest YouTuber, MrBeast, 24, who paid to cure 1,000 blind people, finally responds to critics who blasted 'demonic' act for using the plight of the poor to boost content, *Daily Mail*, 1 February, www.dailymail.co.uk/news/article-11700877/YouTuber-MrBeast-responds-criticism-paying-cure-1-000-peoples-blindness.html (archived at perma.cc/WXV9-93BS)

23   Sorvino, C (2022) Could MrBeast be the first YouTuber billionaire?, *Forbes*, 30 November, www.forbes.com/sites/chloesorvino/2022/11/30/could-mrbeast-be-the-first-youtuber-billionaire/?sh=526a09f191a2 (archived at perma.cc/35LY-J8V9)

24   Casey Neistat (2019) $2 MILLION in 12 months, the price of Mr.
     Beast's success (Online video) www.youtube.com/watch?v=
     UE6UkF9sABU (archived at perma.cc/28BR-7N6F)

25   Sorvino, C (2022) Could MrBeast be the first YouTuber billionaire?,
     Forbes, 30 November, www.forbes.com/sites/chloesorvino/2022/11/30/
     could-mrbeast-be-the-first-youtuber-billionaire/?sh=526a09f191a2
     (archived at perma.cc/35LY-J8V9)

CHAPTER EIGHT

Sir James Dyson

Dyson

Leadership philosophy
'ENJOY FAILURE AND LEARN FROM IT. YOU NEVER LEARN
FROM SUCCESS.'[1]

Dyson is a multinational technology company founded in England but now based in Singapore. It is best known for manufacturing bagless vacuum cleaners – revolutionary when they were first introduced. Dyson's other products include hairdryers, lighting, hand dryers, air purifiers and robotic vacuums. The company, which prides itself on being 'unshackled from conventional thinking', employs over 14,000 people and is present in more than 80 countries. Around half the company's workforce are scientists and engineers and it conducts research in a wide range of areas including robotics, artificial intelligence, machine learning, battery development and high-speed electric motors.[2] A family-owned business, Dyson aims to remain a 'start-up in spirit with the freedom of experimentation and learning'.[3] In 2021, it reported revenues of £5.7 billion.[4]

Dyson's trailblazing founder, James Dyson, was born in May 1947. He is the son of a teacher who taught classics at an English public school – Gresham's in Holt, Norfolk – and the youngest of three siblings. Growing up in the wake of the Second World War, his childhood reflected the austere economic conditions of the time, with food rationing remaining in force until he was seven. In his autobiography *Invention*, he wrote that 'there was no television, never enough heating, no new toys and few, if any, consumer goods'. The family, he said, had just enough money to get by.[5]

At the age of eight, Dyson started to attend Gresham's. Soon afterwards, however, he was devastated by the death of his father, 'an ever-cheerful polymath' who passed away from throat and lung cancer in 1956, aged just 40. The loss of his father deeply affected the young Dyson, and has continued to affect him ever since.[6] More than 60 years after his father's passing, in an interview in 2021, he said that being told his father had died was the worst thing that anyone had ever said to him.[7]

Dyson was just nine when his father died and he boarded at his school, away from his family. But the bold inventor of today may not have existed had Dyson not lost his father so tragically. He has speculated that losing his dad may have encouraged him to take decisions for himself, be self-reliant and have a willingness to take risks.[8] He also lost his mother at a comparatively young age. She died of liver cancer in 1978, when Dyson was in his very early 30s.[9]

At school, Dyson did not excel academically and his school careers officer suggested that he become an estate agent. He enjoyed painting, however, and was encouraged in this pursuit by his mother, who was herself a keen amateur artist. In 1957, he won a painting competition in the boys' comic *Eagle*, with an oil painting of a Norfolk seascape. He also liked sport, music, drama and making model aeroplanes out of balsa wood.[10]

When Dyson left school he was unsure about what he wanted to do with his life. He decided to enrol for a foundation-year course at the Byam Shaw School of Drawing and Painting in London, which later became part of renowned art school Central Saint Martins. There he learned to draw well, met his future wife Deirdre, and discovered the possibility of a career in design. At the suggestion of his art school principal, he applied to study furniture design at the Royal College of Art.

It was during his time at the Royal College of Art that Dyson began to believe that 'anything was possible'. He realized that art and science could go together and began to dream of a career where he would simultaneously be an engineer, designer and manufacturer. Thinking big, he switched his course from furniture to interior design, a course similar to architecture, which gave him greater exposure to engineering.

While he was at the Royal College of Art, Dyson got to know the inventor and entrepreneur Jeremy Fry, who asked him to engineer the Sea Truck, a high-speed, flat-bottomed, fibreglass landing craft. The Sea Truck was

Dyson's third-year project. After leaving the college in 1969, he joined Fry's engineering business, Rotork, as head of the marine division, with responsibility for making and selling the Sea Truck. The Sea Truck ended up being sold to armies and navies around the world, as well as other buyers. Dyson saw the role as an opportunity to learn about manufacturing and sales, giving him knowledge that would allow him to make and market any products that he designed in future.[11]

By 1974, Dyson had decided to go into business on his own. He had an idea for a new type of garden wheelbarrow that he called the Ballbarrow. After mortgaging his house, he set up his first factory in a cart barn and a row of pigsties at his home, a farmhouse in the English county of Gloucestershire. Later the factory moved to an industrial estate in neighbouring Wiltshire. But while the Ballbarrow captured half of the garden wheelbarrow market in the UK, the business struggled to make money for several reasons, including not charging enough for its product.

In 1979, Dyson's fellow shareholders fired him from the company, known as Kirk-Dyson. He was left penniless since he had assigned the patent of the Ballbarrow to the company and the value of his shares had been heavily diluted as new investors were brought in. That experience of being fired, while painful, was a valuable lesson for Dyson. After that, he resolved that he would never again sign over his patents or work with shareholders. On a positive note, however, he had already struck upon the idea for a revolutionary vacuum cleaner – one that used the force of airflow to separate dust particles, removing the need for vacuum bags.[12]

Dyson spent four years developing his vacuum cleaner in a small coach house within the grounds of his house, funded by investment from his mentor Jeremy Fry, a bank loan, and the sale of his vegetable garden.[13] The vacuum cleaner made use of cyclonic action, pulling dust and particles at high force through a filter into a collection chamber. With dogged determination, Dyson built and tested 5,127 handmade prototypes until he finally produced one that worked. This was the pivotal moment that was to change the course of his fortunes, although that wasn't evident straightaway. He licensed his vacuum cleaner design to Rotork, as well as companies in Japan and Canada, but he also became embroiled in a lengthy lawsuit after suing two US companies for patent infringement. Once the lawsuit was settled – Dyson received $1 million, which didn't even cover his legal costs – he decided that instead of licensing out his technology, he would make it through his own company in future. To fund the venture, then known as Dyson Appliances Ltd, he borrowed more money against his house and remained heavily indebted for the next few years.[14]

In 1993, the first upright cyclonic vacuum cleaners with the Dyson name were produced in a factory in Wrexham, North Wales. Three months later, operations moved to a former Post Office depot in Chippenham, Wiltshire. Although the Dyson model, DC01, was more expensive than rival vacuum cleaners, it quickly became recognized as a quality product and was snapped up by house-proud consumers. In less than two years, the company had managed to secure 20 per cent of the UK vacuum cleaner market, profits were growing, and the business was expanding fast. In 1995, at the age of 48, Dyson finally managed to pay off all his debts,[15] including an overdraft that had mushroomed to £650,000.[16]

Since then, the business has expanded into a multi-billion-pound corporation that manufactures a wide range of domestic and commercial products. Inevitably not everything it has produced has been a success, however. For example, it ended up scrapping its Contrarotator washing machine after pricing it too low to cover its manufacturing costs.

More recently, the company invested £500 million in developing an electric car, a seven-seater electric SUV with a 600-mile range. But it pulled out of production at the last minute in 2019 after reaching the conclusion it wouldn't make any money on the vehicle. Other car-makers were willing to manufacture electric cars at a loss because they could subsidise their costs through the sale of traditional petrol and diesel cars. In an interview with *The Times*, Dyson spoke of his sadness and disappointment at the decision, but added: 'Ours is a life of risk and of failure – we try things and they fail.'[17]

Since 2019, Dyson Ltd has been headquartered in Singapore to enable the company to be closer to its supply chain, manufacturing capabilities and fast-growing markets in Asia. The company has manufactured its vacuum cleaners in Southeast Asia since 2002, having found it easier to source empty factories and highly skilled labour there than in the UK. Nevertheless, the company still employs around 4,000 people in the UK. Dyson has praised Singapore for its culture, which celebrates science and technology. This is in contrast to Britain, he says, where manufacturers are looked down on and seen as 'somehow rough and grubby'.[18]

Dyson has been criticized as a hypocrite for moving the headquarters of his company overseas while at the same time championing Brexit – the UK's decision to leave the EU, which took effect on 31 January 2020. His argument in favour of Brexit is that it enables Britain to compete more effectively around the world and to more easily recruit skills from a global talent pool.[19] But his thinking is also likely to be influenced by some major business battles he's fought over the years. In the 1990s he was dismayed to discover that a Belgian court was able to ban his company from talking about vacuum bags in its advertising.[20] Later, in 2014, he launched a legal case over an EU regulation on energy labels that he believed unfairly discriminated against Dyson – and ended up getting the regulation overturned.[21]

Brexit isn't the only controversy that Dyson has been caught up in. He became embroiled in a so-called 'sleaze' scandal after exchanging texts about tax with then prime minister Boris Johnson during the Covid-19 pandemic of 2020. Dyson had agreed to design and build 50,000 ventilators to treat Covid patients – in response to a direct request from the prime minister. But the government later dropped the request after it became clear to clinicians that it was better to avoid putting patients on ventilators if possible.

Dyson decided to swallow all £20 million of the costs that his company had incurred. Nevertheless, controversy arose after it emerged that he had written to the British Treasury asking for assurances that his staff overseas would not have to pay extra tax if they came to the UK to make ventilators. In a text exchange, Johnson told Dyson that as First Lord of the Treasury he would 'fix' the issue.

The controversy was further fuelled by the fact Dyson had temporarily moved his own tax residency to Singapore for a short period of time.[22] In his book, *Invention*, Dyson expressed disappointment that his exchange with Johnson was seen as 'lobbying' the prime minster and he said that the attempts by the media to mire both him and his company in political sleaze ended up failing because the allegations weren't true.[23]

In 2022, Dyson stirred up further controversy when he penned a column in *The Times* arguing against a UK government proposal that would give millions of employees the right to request working from home from day one of their employment. Working from home has 'superficial attractions for individuals in the short term', he wrote, but it is damaging to company competitiveness since it prevents in-person collaboration and in-person training. He also argued that to impose the policy amid a likely upcoming recession would be 'economically illiterate and staggeringly self-defeating'.[24] In response, a former Dyson employee blasted the company founder as being a 'complete dinosaur' who had a 'Victorian' approach to management.[25]

Dinosaur or not, Dyson is recognized as a great inventor and industrialist. He is also a passionate farmer who owns 36,000 acres of farmland across four different English counties. His farming business uses the latest science and technology with the aim of proving that agriculture can be profitable and sustainable while reducing the UK's reliance on imported foodstuffs. It grows large volumes of peas, potatoes and wheat, among other crops, and has a greenhouse for growing strawberries out of season. One of the farms has two anaerobic-digester power plants that produce biogas, which in turn provides energy to more than 10,000 homes.[26]

Alongside his activities in business and farming, Dyson is known for being a committed philanthropist and educationalist. In 2022, he set up the James Dyson Foundation to help combat the shortage in engineering skills. The Foundation organizes activities in 27 countries, such as school workshops and after-school clubs, and finances university facilities with the aim of encouraging young people from around the world to pursue an engineering career.[27] It also runs the annual James Dyson Award, which recognizes young inventors who have designed something to solve a problem. In September 2021, the Dyson Foundation announced that it was funding a five-year Fellowship into dementia research in partnership with Race Against Dementia, a charity founded by former Formula One racing driver Sir Jackie Stewart.[28]

In 2017, Dyson founded the Dyson Institute of Engineering and Technology, based in Wiltshire, England, in an attempt to help address the specific shortage of engineers in the UK. The Institute is a higher-education establishment where students combine studying for an engineering degree with working as an engineer for Dyson Ltd.[29] Between 2011 and 2017 Dyson was provost (head) of his alma mater, the Royal College of Art, the institution that played such a pivotal role in helping to shape his future career.

Today Dyson is one of the richest people in Britain, with the *Sunday Times* Rich List 2022 putting his net worth at £23 billion.[30] In December 2006, he was knighted for his services to business and has since been known as Sir James Dyson.

Secrets to success

Dyson is a great example of a 'free spirit' – someone who acts in an uninhibited, unconventional way and doesn't necessarily conform with normal social rules. He is the art school graduate who accidentally became an engineer. He is the industrialist who is helping to transform the British agriculture sector. He's been a relentless champion of manufacturing in an economy that is more geared towards the services industries. And he embraced the concept of failure being instrumental to success long before it was fashionable to do so.

Another way in which Dyson deviates from the norm is that he openly questions the value of experience, saying: 'Experience tells you what you ought to do and what you'd do best to avoid. It tells you how things should be done when we are much more interested in how things *shouldn't* be done.' He believes that inventors who develop new technologies must be prepared to step into the unknown and experience can be a hindrance to them doing that.[31]

Dyson is a very independent person and has described himself as someone who 'likes to learn on his own, by experiencing failure and discovering his own way to make things work'.[32] He admits to having a pronounced bloody-mindedness that drives him to keep on trying to crack a problem, regardless of how many times he fails.[33] When asked by the The Guardian to describe himself in three words, he said 'driven, impatient and thorough'.[34] Despite his own impatience, his advice to other would-be inventors is to show patience, determination and will power, however.[35]

Keeping his company private and family owned is important to Dyson since it means the business is cautious about how it uses its money while remaining free to take calculated risks should opportunities arise.[36] As an entrepreneur, Dyson is very hands-on. For example, he spends time working on production lines to see how they can be made more efficient.[37]

Dyson didn't set up his company with the intention of becoming fabulously rich. He did it because he derives huge satisfaction from the process of inventing, researching, testing, designing and manufacturing things. He admits that it can be hard to be a pioneer because 'you don't know whether you are going to succeed'. Hence, he believes that pioneers must be able to pick themselves back up when they stumble and to cope with feeling in a constant state of fear.[38]

In *Invention*, Dyson's wife, Deirdre, and his son, Jake, offer their own insights into what has made the inventor-entrepreneur so extremely successful. They describe a man with extraordinary confidence and powerful skills of persuasion, who is at ease with tackling difficult projects and who has 'an opinion about anything and everything'. He is competitive, determined, tidy and immensely practical. This is, after all, a man who plumbed and wired his entire house and hired a digger to build his own swimming pool. Dyson pays close attention to detail and likes to do things properly. He is also fearless, willing to take risks, and believes in learning and improving as he goes along. But perhaps his most important trait is optimism. As Deirdre says: 'He doesn't just hope for the best, he simply believes that everything will work out.'[39]

LEADERSHIP LESSONS FROM JAMES DYSON

- **Refuse to be defeated by your failures**. Instead, learn from them so that you come back better next time.

- **Focus on how things shouldn't be done**. The process of working out how to do things better will generate powerful insights.

- **Give responsibility to inexperienced members of your team**. They can help you come up with innovative solutions to the problems you face.

- **Pay attention to the details**. By doing things thoroughly, you are more likely to create an exceptional product or service.

- **Look on the bright side**. Having an innate sense of optimism will help you to overcome adversity.

Notes

1   Dyson, J (2022) *Invention: A Life*, https://www.dyson.co.uk/james-dyson (archived at perma.cc/PM67-36NL)

2   Dyson (2022) Sir James Dyson biography, www.dyson.co.uk/james-dyson (archived at perma.cc/5CES-652J)

3   Dyson (2022) Our story, https://careers.dyson.com/en-gb/who-we-are (archived at perma.cc/H8PG-3HR4)

4   Statista (2022) Revenue of Dyson Ltd worldwide 2010–2021, 12 December, www.statista.com/statistics/746505/worldwide-dyson-annual-revenue (archived at perma.cc/6V2X-CX7T)

5   Dyson, J (2021) *Invention: A life of learning through failure*, Simon & Schuster, United Kingdom, p 17

6   Dyson, J (2021) *Invention: A life of learning through failure*, Simon & Schuster, United Kingdom, pp 14–19

7   Greenstreet, R (2021) James Dyson: 'The worst thing anyone has said
    to me? That my father had died. I was nine', *The Guardian*, 4
    December, https://amp.theguardian.com/lifeandstyle/2021/dec/04/
    james-dyson-interview-father-died (archived at perma.cc/3CTJ-GZUX)

8   Dyson, J (2021) *Invention: A life of learning through failure*, Simon &
    Schuster, United Kingdom, p 20

9   Dyson, J (2021) *Invention: A life of learning through failure*, Simon &
    Schuster, United Kingdom, p 21

10 Dyson, J (2021) *Invention: A life of learning through failure*, Simon &
    Schuster, United Kingdom, pp 14–27

11 Dyson, J (2021) *Invention: A life of learning through failure*, Simon &
    Schuster, United Kingdom, pp 28–58

12 Dyson, J (2021) *Invention: A life of learning through failure*, Simon &
    Schuster, United Kingdom, pp 74–95

13 Dyson, J (2021) *Invention: A life of learning through failure*, Simon &
    Schuster, United Kingdom, pp 94–96

14 Dyson, J (2021) *Invention: A life of learning through failure*, Simon &
    Schuster, United Kingdom, pp 114–15

15 Dyson, J (2021) *Invention: A life of learning through failure*, Simon &
    Schuster, United Kingdom, pp 120–131

16 Dyson, J (2021) *Invention: A life of learning through failure*, Simon &
    Schuster, United Kingdom, p 31

17 Arlidge, J (2020) James Dyson interview: How I blew £500m on an
    electric car to rival Tesla, *The Times*, 16 May, www.thetimes.co.uk/
    article/james-dyson-interview-electric-car-tesla-tzls09t5m (archived at
    perma.cc/2FLG-U8CB)

18 Dyson, J (2021) *Invention: A life of learning through failure*, Simon &
    Schuster, United Kingdom, pp 202–04

19 Dyson, J (2021) *Invention: A life of learning through failure*, Simon &
    Schuster, United Kingdom, p 217

20 Dyson, J (2021) *Invention: A life of learning through failure*, Simon &
    Schuster, United Kingdom, p 138

21 Dyson, J (2021) *Invention: A life of learning through failure*, Simon &
    Schuster, United Kingdom, pp 219–20

22 Warrington, J and Boscia, S (2021) Sir James Dyson has moved back
    to the UK, docs show, as tax row continues, *City A.M.*, www.cityam.com/

boris-johnson-told-sir-james-dyson-he-would-fix-tax-issue (archived at perma.cc/5YEH-ZZ9Y)

23 Dyson, J (2021) *Invention: A life of learning through failure*, Simon & Schuster, United Kingdom, pp 252–53

24 Dyson, J (2022) UK's competitiveness is turning to dust under flexible working diktat, *The Times*, 8 December, www.thetimes.co.uk/article/uk-s-competitiveness-is-turning-to-dust-under-flexible-working-diktat-6x6pmq03k (archived at perma.cc/7E5N-6P5N)

25 Parsons, G (2022) Ex-Dyson employee says James Dyson has a 'Victorian' management approach, *LBC*, 8 December, www.lbc.co.uk/radio/presenters/tom-swarbrick/its-a-horrendous-place-to-work-says-ex-dyson-employee (archived at perma.cc/W47N-7TP2)

26 Dyson, J (2021) *Invention: A life of learning through failure*, Simon & Schuster, United Kingdom, pp 256–71

27 The James Dyson Foundation (2020) Our story: The accidental engineer, www.jamesdysonfoundation.com/who-we-are/our-story.html (archived at perma.cc/XQM3-W4EJ)

28 Dyson (2021) Dyson brings new perspective to Alzheimer's research, September, www.dyson.co.uk/newsroom/overview/news/september-2021/Dyson-Race-Against-Dementia-partnership (archived at perma.cc/FL87-KEXM)

29 The Dyson Institute of Engineering and Technology (2022) Education re-engineered, www.dysoninstitute.com (archived at perma.cc/HL8J-P3FQ)

30 Archambault, C (2022) Sir James Dyson net worth – Sunday Times Rich List 2022, 20 May, www.thetimes.co.uk/article/sunday-times-rich-list-sir-james-dyson-singapore-brexit-wealth-wfkqccw97 (archived at perma.cc/748N-CDUC)

31 Dyson, J (2021) *Invention: A life of learning through failure*, Simon & Schuster, United Kingdom, p 38

32 Dyson, J (2021) *Invention: A life of learning through failure*, Simon & Schuster, United Kingdom, p 24

33 Dyson, J (2021) *Invention: A life of learning through failure*, Simon & Schuster, United Kingdom, p 10

34 Greenstreet, R (2021) James Dyson: 'The worst thing anyone has said to me? That my father had died. I was nine', *The Guardian*, 4 December, https://amp.theguardian.com/lifeandstyle/2021/dec/04/james-dyson-interview-father-died (archived at perma.cc/3CTJ-GZUX)

35 Dyson, J (2021) *Invention: A life of learning through failure*, Simon & Schuster, United Kingdom, p 92

36 Dyson, J (2021) *Invention: A life of learning through failure*, Simon & Schuster, United Kingdom, p 343

37 Dyson, J (2021) *Invention: A life of learning through failure*, Simon & Schuster, United Kingdom, p 126

38 Dyson, J (2021) *Invention: A life of learning through failure*, Simon & Schuster, United Kingdom, pp 311–12

39 Dyson, J (2021) *Invention: A life of learning through failure*, Simon & Schuster, United Kingdom, pp 319–30

CHAPTER NINE

Kiran Mazumdar-Shaw

Biocon

Leadership philosophy
'INNOVATION IS BOTH ABOUT DOING DIFFERENT THINGS AS WELL
AS DOING THINGS DIFFERENTLY.'[1]

B iocon is one of India's largest biopharmaceutical companies with a market capitalization over $3.7 billion.[2]
The company is driven by the belief that everyone, everywhere, deserves access to affordable quality medicine.
Biocon has more than 13,500 employees who are constantly
trying to find new ways to treat diabetes, cancer and auto-
immune diseases. The company's medicines improve – and
save – the lives of millions of patients in over 120 countries.[3]

The driving force behind Biocon is Kiran Mazumdar-
Shaw, who founded the business from her garage in 1978,
at the age of 25. Notably, entrepreneurship was her second

choice of career. After graduating from Bangalore University with a bachelor's degree in zoology, she had wanted to pursue a career in brewing. Her inspiration was her father, the head brewmaster for one of India's largest beer companies. He told her that as a woman, she could achieve 'just as much, if not more, than any man'.[4] To fulfil her dream, she had headed to Australia to train in malting and brewing with the University of Melbourne. But, on her return to India, gender bias prevented her from securing a managerial role in the country's male-dominated brewing industry.[5]

Failing to break into the brewing industry was a major setback for Mazumdar-Shaw's career dreams. But through studying brewing, she had gained valuable knowledge of biotechnology and enzymes. Biotechnology – or biotech – is the process of using biological systems and living organisms to make useful products such as food ingredients, medicines, packaging and washing detergents. Enzymes are biological catalysts that are used to speed up biochemical reactions in living organisms as part of the biotech process.

After what she has described as 'an accidental encounter with an Irish entrepreneur', Mazumdar-Shaw decided to start her own business.[6] Initially, Biocon India was a joint venture with the entrepreneur's Ireland-based biotech business (called Biocon Biochemicals), and made enzymes for food processing, as well as industrial use. A year after its launch, Biocon India began exporting enzymes to Europe and the United States. Biocon Biochemicals in Ireland was later bought by giant British–Dutch consumer goods company Unilever.[7]

In the late 1970s, India's biotech industry was still in its infancy and Mazumdar-Shaw has said that until the mid-1980s, she was 'the lone entrepreneur in the Indian biotech landscape'. Among her challenges were persuading the market to accept biotechnology (which was then a new concept), unreliable power supplies in the city of Bangalore (now Bengaluru), and constraints imposed by red tape.[8]

Mazumdar-Shaw also had to overcome credibility barriers due to her gender, youth and lack of business experience. Writing in her blog, she recalled that 'entrepreneurship was a new phenomenon that was only for daring men and certainly not a "career" choice for women'. She continued: 'Banks were unwilling to lend to me because I was considered "high risk" in the business world. Professionals did not want to work for me as they felt I could not provide them with "job security".'[9] Eventually she did find financial backers who believed in her. But to secure funding from them she first had to make herself 'somebody worth investing in' by clearly articulating what she had set out to do.[10]

Motivated by her passion to make a difference, Mazumdar-Shaw persevered with growing her business, effectively helping to lay the groundwork for India's broader biotechnology revolution. Other biotech companies started up in Bangalore and across the country. Gradually the fledgling industry expanded and India began to emerge as a major destination for biotechnology and pharmaceuticals.[11]

The rise and rise of Biocon

Over more than four decades, Biocon has evolved from being a manufacturer of speciality enzymes to a global biopharmaceutical company that discovers, develops and produces life-saving medical treatments. In 1998, Biocon became an independent entity after buying out Unilever's shareholding. Three years later, it was the first Indian company to be approved by the formidable US Food and Drug Administration, for the manufacture of lovastatin, a cholesterol-lowering molecule. After successfully producing enzymes for many years, the company embarked on its biopharmaceutical journey when it started producing human insulin, for the treatment of diabetes, in 2003. Biocon listed on the Bombay Stock Exchange in March 2004, with a valuation of $1.1 billion.[12]

Since then, the company has continued to invest in its business, its people and the relentless pursuit of innovation. It has a publicly listed research subsidiary called Syngene, focused on problem solving and scientific innovation, and it even has its own learning institute, Biocon Academy, founded in 2013.[13] The academy provides advanced learning to biotechnology and engineering graduates. In a clear demonstration of her commitment to learning and development, Mazumdar-Shaw acts as the academy's chief mentor.[14] She is also highly committed to diversity and inclusion, describing them as business imperatives that are embedded in Biocon's core values since they promote both collaboration and innovation.[15]

When Covid-19 struck the world in 2020, Biocon and its subsidiaries helped to tackle the pandemic in several ways. As well as developing products to treat Covid-19 patients, it repurposed an existing drug to treat Covid-related complications. In addition, it provided support with testing and vaccinations and contributed to global research efforts to combat the disease.[16]

Biocon has a strong history of corporate social responsibility, dating back to its inception and heavily influenced by Mazumdar-Shaw's own ethical principles. In 2006, the company launched its own foundation, Biocon Foundation, which works with government agencies to address sustainable development issues. Its activities include making primary healthcare services available to underprivileged communities and investing in basic infrastructure and social services. It has also promoted responsible practices in the areas of environmental protection and conservation.[17]

Mazumdar-Shaw has been so successful as an entrepreneur that she became India's first self-made Indian female billionaire. She is also the recipient of numerous honours and awards. These include two of India's highest civilian honours, the Padma Shri and the Padma Bhushan. In 2014, the US-based Chemical Heritage Foundation awarded her the Othmer Gold Medal, which recognizes outstanding individuals who have contributed to progress in chemistry and science.[18] She featured in *Time*'s list of the 100 people who most affect our world in 2010 and was named the EY World Entrepreneur of the Year 2020.

Secrets to success

As a woman, Mazumdar-Shaw broke with convention by training as a brewmaster and then taking the huge risk of starting a business in biotech, at a time when the industry was little known or understood in India. It's hardly surprising, then, that she regards herself as an unconventional thinker.

She credits her unconventional approach to one of her teachers at Bishop Cotton Girls' School in Bangalore. That teacher's name was Anne Warrior and she was not just a teacher but a 'friend, philosopher, and mentor' to the young Mazumdar-Shaw. On one occasion, Warrior even got the class to transform a sad-looking garden patch into a designer cactus garden. Mazumdar-Shaw has said that England-born Warrior taught her 'to think for myself, to excel in everything I do and to do things differently and creatively in order to make a difference'.[19]

During her career, Mazumdar-Shaw has been coura-geous about taking calculated risks. One example of this was her decision to move into the field of biosimilar medi-cines (biological medicines that are very similar to medi-cines that are already in use). Biosimilar medicines help to widen access to life-saving treatments and lower health-care costs. Moving into biosimilars was a risk, says the entrepreneur, because it required huge investment and had 'not even been scripted' by the US and European regula-tory systems of the time.[20]

Nevertheless, this bold call turned out to be the right one. In 2017, Biocon became the first Indian company to receive approval from the US Food and Drug Administration for a biosimilar medicine called Trastuzumab, developed in partnership with US pharmaceutical company Mylan. Trastuzumab is used to treat some types of breast cancer, oesophageal cancer and stomach cancer.[21]

In a LinkedIn post, published that year, Mazumdar-Shaw described how the approval followed nine years of 'blood, sweat and tears'. She also highlighted the signifi-cance of the strategic collaboration between Biocon and

Mylan, which began in 2009. The partnership, she said, was structured as a 'sharing of risks and rewards' and drew on the complementary strengths of each partner. It was also 'a forerunner to many global partnerships that exist today in the biosimilar space'.[22]

Mazumdar-Shaw's business philosophy is based on the concept of 'compassionate capitalism'. She balances the pursuit of profitability with providing accessible and affordable treatments to patients. To achieve this balance, she recognizes that a sustainable business needs to deliver profits, but at the same time, it must deliver value to all its stakeholders, with the biggest stakeholder being the patient. Key to achieving this balance is keeping costs under control.[23]

As a female entrepreneur back in the 1970s, Mazumdar-Shaw was very much a pioneer in a man's world. As a result of her own experiences, she is a fierce advocate of gender equality and offers advice on how leaders can create an environment where women can thrive. She believes that it is essential to provide leadership opportunities to women based on their potential, even if they don't necessarily have the same level of experience as their male counterparts. She explains: 'I have taken those bets on people, and it's worked.'[24] Mazumdar-Shaw argues that women are 'change influencers and change makers' who are daring, willing to experiment and willing to explore.[25]

No leader can become hugely successful all on their own. They inevitably need the support of a committed and talented team. Mazumdar-Shaw recognizes this, which is why she believes greatly in the value of mentoring. As executive chair of Biocon, she has aimed to 'empower, enable and mentor' leaders at multiple levels within her organization. She has also mentored many female professionals.[26]

Arguably Mazumdar-Shaw's phenomenal success in business is down to her monumental sense of purpose. In particular, she is motivated to address the huge problem of health inequity – the unjust and avoidable differences between the ability of different communities to access healthcare. As she herself has said: 'Health equity, afford-able access is my business purpose.'[27]

LEADERSHIP LESSONS FROM KIRAN MAZUMDAR-SHAW

- **Be a compassionate capitalist**. Build a business that makes profits while delivering genuine value to its stakeholders.

- **Invest in building your credibility**. You cannot assume that people will automatically see or understand what you have to offer.

- **Be bold about taking calculated risks**. There's truth in the Latin proverb 'Fortune favours the bold'.

- **Take a chance on people, especially up-and-coming female leaders**. Given the opportunity, they will often exceed your expectations.

- **Let purpose be your guiding star**. Allow yourself to be guided by your sense of purpose in everything you do.

Notes

1 Mazumdar-Shaw, K (2022) Profile, LinkedIn, https://www.linkedin.com/in/kmazumdarshaw (archived at perma.cc/AK69-KGGU)

2 Companies MarketCap.com (2023) Market capitalization of Biocon, https://companiesmarketcap.com/biocon/marketcap (archived at perma.cc/6M76-D8K2)

3 Biocon (2022) Fact Sheet, www.biocon.com/about-us/factsheet-biocon (archived at perma.cc/N572-KHCQ)

4 Jewell, C (2018) From brewing to biologics: Biocon's Kiran Mazumdar-Shaw transforms global health, *WIPO Magazine*, April, www.wipo.int/wipo_magazine/en/2018/02/article_0005.html (archived at perma.cc/US3N-ZTQ7)

5 Kazmin, A (2020) The female Indian entrepreneurs who have overcome gender barriers, *Financial Times*, 24 August, www.ft.com/content/bab1e7a8-c395-4fe2-af20-9fd1ff6587ee (archived at perma.cc/JPV6-6F9V)

6 Spence, P (2020) And I think that's where my entrepreneurial journey began (Online video) *EY*, 19 October, www.ey.com/en_gl/life-sciences/how-an-accidental-entrepreneur-is-on-a-mission-to-change-capitalism (archived at perma.cc/KJG7-4LA2)

7 Biocon (2022) History, https://archive.biocon.com/biocon_aboutus_history.asp (archived at perma.cc/ZA84-RWGH)

8 Mazumdar-Shaw, K (2022) India's life sciences industry poised for the next level, 13 April, https://kiranshaw.blog/2022/04/13/indias-life-sciences-industry-poised-for-the-next-level (archived at perma.cc/367N-GXE7)

9 Mazumdar-Shaw, K (2021) Women can bring transformational change in India, 15 August, https://kiranshaw.blog/2021/08/15/women-can-bring-transformational-change-in-india (archived at perma.cc/4EKU-L5XK)

10 Mazumdar-Shaw, K (2022) Inspiring journeys with Ms Kiran Mazumdar-Shaw, 1 April, https://kiranshaw.blog/2022/04/01/inspiring-journeys-with-ms-kiran-mazumdar-shaw (archived at perma.cc/S5QC-2B7T)

11 Mazumdar-Shaw, K (2022) India's life sciences industry poised for the next level, 13 April, https://kiranshaw.blog/2022/04/13/indias-life-sciences-industry-poised-for-the-next-level (archived at perma.cc/367N-GXE7)

12 Biocon (2022) History, https://archive.biocon.com/biocon_aboutus_history.asp (archived at perma.cc/ZA84-RWGH)

13 Biocon (2022) History, https://archive.biocon.com/biocon_aboutus_history.asp (archived at perma.cc/ZA84-RWGH)

14 Biocon Academy (2022) Unlock your full potential for excellence in biosciences, https://www.bioconacademy.com (archived at perma.cc/5HXD-NM4Z)

15 Jewell, C (2018) From brewing to biologics: Biocon's Kiran Mazumdar-Shaw transforms global health, *WIPO Magazine*, April, www.wipo.int/wipo_magazine/en/2018/02/article_0005.html (archived at perma.cc/US3N-ZTQ7)

16 Biocon (2022) Addressing the COVID-19 pandemic, www.biocon.com/addressing-the-covid-19-pandemic (archived at perma.cc/XTG6-LPBP)

17 Biocon Foundation (2022) About Us, https://www.bioconfoundation.org/about/overview.html (archived at perma.cc/LCP6-2UHA)

18 Biocon (2022) Kiran Mazumdar-Shaw, www.biocon.com/about-us/our-leadership/kiran-mazumdar-shaw (archived at perma.cc/YPS2-KMRJ)

19 Mazumdar-Shaw, K (2015) The mentor who taught me to be unconventional, resourceful & fearless, 19 August, https://www.linkedin.com/pulse/mentor-who-shaped-me-taught-unconventional-fearless-mazumdar-shaw (archived at perma.cc/8KQY-FW3G)

20 Mazumdar-Shaw, K (2022) Inspiring journeys with Ms Kiran Mazumdar-Shaw, 1 April, https://kiranshaw.blog/2022/04/01/inspiring-journeys-with-ms-kiran-mazumdar-shaw (archived at perma.cc/S5QC-2B7T)

21 Mazumdar-Shaw, K (2022) Inspiring journeys with Ms Kiran Mazumdar-Shaw, 1 April, https://kiranshaw.blog/2022/04/01/inspiring-journeys-with-ms-kiran-mazumdar-shaw (archived at perma.cc/S5QC-2B7T)

22 Mazumdar-Shaw, K (2017) A journey of endurance, 29 December, www.linkedin.com/pulse/journey-endurance-kiran-mazumdar-shaw (archived at perma.cc/23JQ-65MC)

23 YouTube (2016) Kiran Mazumdar-Shaw 'Compassionate capitalism' (Online video) *Mint* www.youtube.com/watch?v=cQQsb7valrw (archived at perma.cc/38DV-QXWJ)

24 Spence, P (2020) And I think that's where my entrepreneurial journey began (Online video) *EY*, 19 October, www.ey.com/en_gl/life-sciences/ how-an-accidental-entrepreneur-is-on-a-mission-to-change-capitalism (archived at perma.cc/KJG7-4LA2)

25 Mazumdar-Shaw, K (2022) Inspiring journeys with Ms Kiran Mazumdar-Shaw, 1 April, https://kiranshaw.blog/2022/04/01/ inspiring-journeys-with-ms-kiran-mazumdar-shaw (archived at perma.cc/S5QC-2B7T)

26 Mazumdar-Shaw, K (2015) The mentor who taught me to be unconventional, resourceful & fearless, 19 August, https://www. linkedin.com/pulse/mentor-who-shaped-me-taught-unconventional- fearless-mazumdar-shaw (archived at perma.cc/8KQY-FW3G)

27 Mazumdar-Shaw, K (2022) Inspiring journeys with Ms Kiran Mazumdar-Shaw, 1 April, https://kiranshaw.blog/2022/04/01/ inspiring-journeys-with-ms-kiran-mazumdar-shaw (archived at perma.cc/S5QC-2B7T)

CHAPTER TEN

Elon Musk

SpaceX, Tesla and Twitter

Leadership philosophy
'WHEN SOMETHING IS IMPORTANT ENOUGH, YOU DO IT, EVEN IF
THE ODDS ARE NOT IN YOUR FAVOUR.'[1]

SpaceX, Tesla and Twitter are three of the most innovative – and influential – companies operating on our planet today. As a commercial aerospace company, SpaceX designs, manufactures and launches advanced rockets and spacecraft, with the aim of advancing a spacefaring civilization. Meanwhile, Tesla – which is better known to the general public – is helping to accelerate the world's transition to sustainable energy by manufacturing electric cars and other renewable energy products. As for Twitter, it's a microblogging and social media platform used by millions of people globally, including some of the world's most famous and powerful figures.

The man behind these pioneering businesses – and others – is Elon Musk, one of the world's most recognized and controversial entrepreneurs. Musk was born in the South African city of Pretoria in 1971. His father, Errol, was an engineer and his Canadian-born mother, Maye, was a model and dietician. A keen reader from an early age, it was not unusual for him to read for 10 hours a day and such was his thirst for learning that he ploughed his way through two sets of encyclopaedias as a child. He was nearly 10 years old when he got his first computer and subsequently taught himself how to code video games.[2]

Despite showing the signs of budding genius, Musk had a difficult childhood. Introverted and geeky, he struggled to relate to other children and spent much of his time absorbed in his own world. At school he was bullied and once ended up in hospital after being pushed down a flight of stairs.[3] Musk's parents divorced when he was nine. Initially he lived with his mother but later opted to move in with his father, believing him to be sad and lonely. He came to regret this decision as he found his father extremely difficult to live with, and the relationship between the pair has remained strained ever since.

When he was 17, Musk emigrated to Canada. He was able to acquire Canadian citizenship thanks to his mother and saw a move to Canada as a step towards his ultimate goal of living in the United States. He enrolled at Queen's University in Ontario, but later transferred to the University of Pennsylvania, where he graduated with dual degrees in economics and physics. While studying, he reached the conclusion that the internet, renewable energy and space were three areas that would undergo significant change in the coming years and where he would be able to have a positive impact.[4]

Musk started with the internet. In 1995, he and his younger brother Kimbal launched a searchable online business directory with map functionality. Musk did all the coding for the service, which became known as Zip2. Even at this early stage of his career, he was already displaying workaholic tendencies, sleeping in the office, on a beanbag next to his desk. His hard work paid off, however, since PC maker Compaq Computer Corporation bought Zip2 for $307 million in 1999. Musk came away from the deal with $22 million – the majority of which he ploughed into his next start-up, a would-be internet bank called X.com.[5]

X.com experimented with some concepts that were then considered radical for the banking industry, such as a payments system that enabled people to send money to each other via email. But the real game-changer proved to be the company's merger with Confinity – a fintech start-up that temporarily rented office space from X.com. Confinity developed a web and email payments service known as PayPal, which was used by the auction site eBay. After the two companies merged in March 2000, Musk became the largest shareholder in the combined company, known as X.com. He also became its CEO – although he was forced to stand aside in favour of Confinity co-founder Peter Thiel following a boardroom coup later that year. X.com was renamed PayPal and, in 2002, PayPal was bought by eBay for $1.5 billion. Musk, who had continued to invest in PayPal despite being deposed as CEO, netted around $250 million from the sale.[6]

A new dream

In 2001 Musk nearly died of malaria after contracting the disease on a vacation to South Africa. This experience appears to have prompted him to re-evaluate his life and focus on following his dreams. Having been interested in space travel since childhood, he decided to make space the focus of his next venture. So, in 2002, he founded Space Exploration Technologies (SpaceX) with the intention of building cost-effective rockets and making space travel economical and practical enough to enable the colonization of Mars.

Thanks to the eBay deal, Musk had sufficient money to fund the new venture, but aerospace is a challenging industry to break into and SpaceX endured some tough early years. After three failed launches, the company finally managed to launch its rocket, Falcon 1, on the fourth attempt, in September 2008, with the rocket becoming the first privately built machine to reach orbit.[7]

Incredibly, despite being a hugely demanding initiative in terms of both effort and money, SpaceX was not the only venture that Musk had on the go. Since 2006 he had been chairman of SolarCity, a solar panel business founded by his cousins Peter and Lyndon Rive, which he had also heavily invested in. Furthermore, he was the chairman of, and largest investor in, an electric carmaker called Tesla Motors. The company, which was named after electrical engineer Nikola Tesla, had been founded in 2003 by two Californian engineers, Martin Eberhard and Marc Tarpenning. Tesla had developed a stunning electronic sports car called the Roadster, but the company was draining cash while wrestling with production issues and bad publicity. By January 2008, Eberhard and Tarpenning had both left the company and Musk took over as CEO in October, amid the throes of the global financial crisis, which was expected to badly impact car sales.

The year 2008 was to prove hugely challenging for Musk. Tesla was running out of cash and so was Musk himself – between them, Tesla and SpaceX had consumed most of his fortune and were driving him to the brink of bankruptcy. In June, he also filed for divorce from his first wife. By the end of the year, he was relying on loans from friends, family and Tesla employees to keep the carmaker going.[8] He was under such pressure that he used to wake in the night, screaming with terror.[9]

But just when it looked like all was lost, Musk pulled off a remarkable turnaround. In December, he managed to secure a $40 million funding round that saved Tesla from bankruptcy. Then, just before Christmas, he landed a $1.6 billion contract for SpaceX to supply the International Space Station.[10] This marked the beginning of SpaceX as a viable commercial venture.

Reinventing the world

Since 2008 SpaceX has had some historic achievements, many driven by its determination to develop reusable rockets rather than traditional rockets that burn up on re-entry into the Earth's atmosphere. In 2012, its Dragon spacecraft became the first commercial spacecraft to deliver cargo to and from the International Space Station, and it even delivered humans to the station in 2020. In 2015, its Falcon 9 rocket delivered 11 communications satellites to orbit before achieving the first-ever orbital-class rocket landing back on Earth. Two years later, in 2017, SpaceX achieved the world's first re-flight of an orbital rocket.[11]

SpaceX also operates the world's largest commercial satellite constellation.[12] In fact, between 2008 and 2020, the company accounted for almost a quarter of all satellite launches worldwide[13] and provided internet services to Ukraine via its Starlink satellite internet service after Russia invaded the country in 2022.[14] In May 2022, SpaceX was valued at $127 billion and its ambitions keep growing.[15] It is reportedly aiming to send a crewed space-ship to Mars in 2029.[16]

Tesla (the company changed its name from Tesla Motors to Tesla Inc in 2017) has also notched up some impressive accomplishments over the past decade or so. These accomplishments have helped to totally transform consumer perceptions around electric cars and drive the growth of the electric car market. In 2009, Tesla unveiled its Model S sedan car – the next part of its plan to bring electric cars into the mainstream. A year later, the company went public and listed on the NASDAQ market with a valuation of $2.2 billion. Tesla displayed a prototype of its first SUV, the Model X, with its futuristic falcon-wing doors, in February 2012. But probably the most significant development of all came in 2017 with the launch of the Tesla Model 3, the first of its vehicles to be targeted at the mass market. Since then, Tesla has unveiled other vehicles, including the new-look Roadster sports car, the seven-seater Model Y, the Cybertruck and the Model S Plaid, its fastest vehicle ever.[17] As of January 2023, Tesla had a market capitalization of $402 billion.[18]

Musk sparked massive controversy when he bought Twitter for $44 billion in October 2022, taking the listed social media company private in the process.[19] Twitter, which had been founded by Jack Dorsey and three other entrepreneurs back in 2006, had taken off quickly, but it was unprofitable and recorded a net loss of $221 million in 2021.[20] While advertisers provided most of its revenues, the platform's advertising business was underperforming against competitors such as Facebook. Also, by the time the platform was sold, many of its most active users had defected to more fashionable rivals Instagram and TikTok.

A self-confessed 'free speech absolutist', Musk's motive for buying Twitter was to give people a trusted and transparent mechanism for exchanging ideas. The fact he planned dramatic changes for the business quickly became clear when he sacked the entire board and became Twitter's sole director, branding himself 'Chief Twit'. As part of a major cost-cutting drive, he cut nearly half of the company's 7,500-strong workforce [21] and told the remainder that they needed to commit to 'hardcore' working.[22] He also caused an outcry by announcing that Twitter would charge an $8 monthly fee to users who wanted a blue tick indicating a verified account. As they watched the unfolding chaos, many of the platform's advertisers dramatically scaled back their spending. Nevertheless, at the end of the year Musk proclaimed that Twitter was 'going in a good direction' and 'not on the fast lane to bankruptcy anymore'.[23]

It will be interesting to see what Musk does next with Twitter and whether he ultimately ends up reinventing the business model for social media platforms so that they no longer rely on advertising revenues and are either subscription-based or sell additional products and services. Prior to completing the purchase, Musk tweeted that buying Twitter was 'an accelerant to creating X, the everything app', a comment that suggests he is planning to revisit the original concept of his online bank, X.com. Significantly, he bought the domain name for X.com and relaunched the site in 2017.[24] In April 2023, newspaper reports revealed that Twitter Inc had changed its name to X Corp, although the social media platform itself continued to retain the Twitter branding. A month later, Musk hired seasoned media executive Linda Yaccarino to be Twitter's new CEO. He himself became the platform's executive chairman and chief technology officer.

Besides SpaceX, Tesla and Twitter, Musk has been involved in numerous other business and philanthropic endeavours. He co-founded Neuralink, a company that is developing brain–computer interfaces – otherwise known as chips in the human brain. These interfaces can potentially help people with paralysis gain independence by using their mind to control computers and mobile devices. Musk is also founder of The Boring Company, an infrastructure company that aims to combat traffic by building tunnels. In 2015, he helped to found OpenAI, a research laboratory that conducts research in the field of artificial intelligence with the aim of helping to develop AI that benefits all of humanity. OpenAI is best known for creating the revolutionary chatbot ChatGPT, which can confidently tackle a wide range of language-related tasks from answering questions to writing film scripts.[25] More recently, it emerged that Musk has plans to launch his own artificial intelligence start-up. Through the Musk Foundation, which he co-founded with his brother Kimbal, Musk makes grants in several areas including renewable energy research and human space exploration.

Courting controversy

In the past, Elon Musk has been described as a 'loose cannon'.[26] Certainly, he comes across as unconventional and far from the stereotype of the traditional, measured 'corporate' CEO. Some of his high-profile actions and decisions have also resulted in him receiving criticism and censure over the years.

In 2016, Musk incurred the ire of Tesla investors after the carmaker bought SolarCity for $2.6 billion. He claimed that the solar panel company – which was struggling at that point – was essential to Tesla's long-term goal of accelerating the transition to sustainable energy.[27] Musk ended up having to defend his actions in a lawsuit after some Tesla shareholders claimed the deal was a bailout and sought $13 billion in damages. He won the case in 2022.

Another controversy arose in 2018 when Musk claimed on Twitter that he was 'considering taking Tesla private' at $420 per share and had secured funding for the move. US market regulator the Securities and Exchange Commission charged him with making 'false and misleading statements', fined him and Tesla $20 million each, and forced him to step down as chairman of Tesla's board of directors.[28] Later, Musk was sued by Tesla investors who claimed that they had lost millions of dollars due to the stock volatility that accompanied the tweets. Again, he won the case.[29]

Also in 2018, Musk tweeted that a British caver who had helped to rescue 12 boys and their soccer coach from flooded caves in Thailand was a 'pedo guy'. The caver later sued for defamation, but lost the case after Musk's legal team managed to successfully argue in court that the tweet was heated rhetoric rather than intended as a statement of fact.[30]

Although he is primarily a businessman, Musk isn't afraid to wade into the world's biggest geopolitical problems. In 2022, he became embroiled in a row with the Ukrainian government when he put forward his own peace plan to end the war with Russia. The plan would have allowed Russia to keep the Crimean Peninsula, which it seized in 2014, among other concessions. This well-intentioned intervention only served to earn Musk a public dressing-down from Ukraine's ambassador to Germany, Andrij Melnyk, and its president, Volodymyr Zelenskyy.[31]

For most of 2022, Musk was ranked as the world's wealthiest person, but the poor performance of Tesla stock (which constitutes most of his wealth) resulted in him slipping to second place on the global rich list by the end of the year. In fact, he broke the world record for the largest loss of personal fortune in history after his net worth plummeted from a peak of $320 billion in 2021 to $138 billion in January 2023.[32] Regardless of exactly how rich he is, however, Musk is undoubtedly one of the most influential people on the planet.

Secrets to success

Musk is undoubtedly an extraordinary person who has achieved extraordinary things. His greatest achievements are probably that he not only broke into but totally transformed two established industries with extremely high barriers to entry – automotive manufacturing and aerospace. How did he manage to do this?

The simple answer to that question is that Musk is a great visionary. Arguably, one single vision has fundamentally underpinned all his business efforts, at least since 2002. This vision is to create a better future for humanity. He believes in using the power of technology to protect the planet where we currently live, hence his interest in electric vehicles and renewable energy. But he also believes that technology can help us to carve out a new future on Mars as a multi-planetary, space-faring species, which is why he is so committed to space exploration.

So compelling is Musk's vision that he succeeds in securing the services of the brightest and the best, and he motivates them to work backbreaking hours in pursuit of the end goal. He's known to be a difficult and demanding taskmaster, who doesn't suffer fools or negativity. Nevertheless, people still want to work for him because they find him truly inspiring. Dolly Singh, formerly head of talent at SpaceX, told a BBC documentary that Musk was 'arguably the best leader on the face of the planet'.[33]

Musk leads by example and is renowned for his immense work ethic. To keep production of the Tesla Model 3 on track, he worked 120-hour weeks and even missed his own birthday.[34] He also expects other people to work punishing hours and has been criticized in the past for driving his staff too hard. Once he reprimanded a Tesla employee for missing a work event to witness the birth of his child.[35]

Besides working incredibly hard, Musk is highly resilient and can handle extreme levels of stress and adversity. 'I don't ever give up,' he once said, when being questioned about the early failures of his space programme. 'I'd have to be dead or completely incapacitated.'[36]

As a great believer in the power of feedback, Musk argues that criticism is vital to evaluating what is going well with a project – and what is not going so well. 'Constantly seek criticism,' he has said. 'A well-thought-out critique of whatever you're doing is as valuable as gold. You should seek that from everyone you can, but particularly your friends.' Friends are not necessarily right in their criticism, he says, but very often they are. He also recommends that entrepreneurs should take the approach that they are wrong, saying: 'Your goal is to be less wrong.'[37]

Despite being one of the world's wealthiest people, Musk says he doesn't own his own house and stays in his friends' spare rooms for much of the time.[38] It might seem surprising that a billionaire should live such a minimalist lifestyle, but throughout his career, Musk has demonstrated that having money is not his primary motivator. In fact, he has been prepared to take huge risks with his personal wealth to realize his dreams. Some would describe him as reckless; to others, he is incredibly courageous.

He might be a man of formidable intelligence, but Musk is not neurologically wired in the same way as most other people. In 2021, while hosting the US comedy sketch show *Saturday Night Live*, he revealed that he had Asperger's syndrome.[39] Asperger's syndrome is a form of the developmental condition Autistic Spectrum Condition (ASC). People with Asperger's syndrome struggle to interact socially with other people and often have very restricted interests. Nevertheless, they can have some notable strengths, including remarkable focus and persistence and strong attention to detail. Musk certainly demonstrates these latter qualities, and they appear to be instrumental to his success.

Musk's ASC helps to explain why he struggled to form friendships as a child, why his speech lacks variety of intonation, and why he often avoids looking people directly in the eye. It also explains why he can come across to others as lacking in empathy.

In recent years, Musk has appeared to cut an increasingly eccentric figure, partly due to his flurry of erratic Twitter posts. During his *Saturday Night Live* appearance, he directly addressed criticism about his tweets, saying: 'Look, I know I sometimes say or post strange things, but that's just how my brain works.'[40]

LEADERSHIP LESSONS FROM ELON MUSK

- **Have a vision – and hold on to it through thick and thin**. Your vision is what will inspire your people to keep going through the most difficult times.

- **Don't be afraid to be different**. We might feel that we need to fit in, but success often comes to those who stand out. Capitalize on the attributes and skills that set you apart from others.

- **Nurture your resilience**. To achieve great things, you must be able to bounce back from adversity. Again and again and again.

- **Deliberately seek out criticism**. By gleaning the views of other people, you will be able to challenge your own thinking and plot a better way forward.

- **If you want to do something bold, then do it – even if the odds appear to be stacked against you**. If you only ever choose the 'safe option', you are effectively putting limits on your own potential.

Notes

1   YouTube (2021) When something is important enough, you do it, even if the odds are not in your favor… (Online video) 3 April, www.youtube.com/watch?v=ViOdlRzq3MY (archived at perma.cc/D4QH-2ZJF)

2   Vance, A (2015) *Elon Musk: How the billionaire CEO of SpaceX and Tesla is shaping our future*, Virgin Books, United Kingdom, pp 33 and 38

3   Vance, A (2015) *Elon Musk: How the billionaire CEO of SpaceX and Tesla is shaping our future*, Virgin Books, United Kingdom, p 40

4   Vance, A (2015) *Elon Musk: How the billionaire CEO of SpaceX and Tesla is shaping our future*, Virgin Books, United Kingdom, pp 43, 47, 51 and 54

5   Vance, A (2015) *Elon Musk: How the billionaire CEO of SpaceX and Tesla is shaping our future*, Virgin Books, United Kingdom, pp 60, 63, 72 and 80

6   Vance, A (2015) *Elon Musk: How the billionaire CEO of SpaceX and Tesla is shaping our future*, Virgin Books, United Kingdom, pp 88–89

7   Vance, A (2015) *Elon Musk: How the billionaire CEO of SpaceX and Tesla is shaping our future*, Virgin Books, United Kingdom, p 203

8   Vance, A (2015) *Elon Musk: How the billionaire CEO of SpaceX and Tesla is shaping our future*, Virgin Books, United Kingdom, p 207

9   Sherwin, A (2022) Elon Musk's ex-wife Talulah Riley says Tesla boss woke up screaming with terror over bankruptcy fears, inews.co.uk, 6 October, https://inews.co.uk/news/elon-musk-ex-wife-talulah-riley-tesla-boss-bankruptcy-1897540 (archived at perma.cc/GW4F-MYKC)

10 Vance, A (2015) *Elon Musk: How the billionaire CEO of SpaceX and Tesla is shaping our future*, Virgin Books, United Kingdom, p 210

11 SpaceX (2022) Making history, www.spacex.com/mission (archived at perma.cc/WC47-YMD8)

12 Henry, C (2020) SpaceX becomes operator of world's largest commercial satellite constellation with Starlink launch, *Spacenews*, 6 January, https://spacenews.com/spacex-becomes-operator-of-worlds-largest-commercial-satellite-constellation-with-starlink-launch (archived at perma.cc/52Y9-2EB8)

13 Statista (2022) Share of satellite launches worldwide by SpaceX from 2008 to 2020, www.statista.com/statistics/955928/spacex-satellite-launches-worldwide (archived at perma.cc/2AER-2KZL)

14 BBC (2022) Musk says SpaceX will keep funding Ukraine Starlink internet, 15 October, www.bbc.co.uk/news/world-us-canada-63266142 (archived at perma.cc/QX6K-PWMZ)

15 Forbes (2022) Elon Musk, CEO, Tesla, www.forbes.com/profile/elon-musk (archived at perma.cc/6FMH-XQ4V)

16 Torchinsky, R (2022) Elon Musk hints at a crewed mission to Mars in 2029, *NPR*, 17 March, www.npr.org/2022/03/17/1087167893/elon-musk-mars-2029 (archived at perma.cc/N3LV-7H6J)

17 Thompson, C, Lee, K and Levin, T (2022) Tesla just celebrated its 12th year as a public company. Here are the most important moments in its history, *Business Insider*, 11 July, www.businessinsider.com/most-important-moments-tesla-history-2017-2?r=US&IR=T (archived at perma.cc/3B4C-LVBU)

18 CompaniesMarketCap.com (2022) Market capitalization of Tesla (TSLA), https://companiesmarketcap.com/tesla/marketcap (archived at perma.cc/2SSZ-SZQ8)

19 Associated Press (2022) A timeline of billionaire Elon Musk's bid to control Twitter, 4 October, https://apnews.com/article/elon-musk-twitter-timeline-e0b41992f178a5221dd0410321068eb2 (archived at perma.cc/QS6H-VMVT)

20 Statista (2023) Net income/loss of Twitter from 2010 to 2021, www.statista.com/statistics/274563/annual-net-income-of-twitter (archived at perma.cc/4AH2-29J4)

21 Rushe, D, Oladipo, G, Bhuiyan, J, Milmo, D and Middleton, J (2022) Twitter slashes nearly half its workforce as Musk admits 'massive drop' in revenue, *The Guardian*, 5 November, https://www.theguardian.com/technology/2022/nov/04/twitter-layoffs-elon-musk-revenue-drop (archived at perma.cc/8QFC-EYJ9)

22 Sky News (2022) Musk says Twitter 'not on the fast lane to bankruptcy anymore', 25 December, https://news.sky.com/story/elon-musk-says-twitter-not-on-the-fast-lane-to-bankruptcy-anymore-12774290 (archived at perma.cc/2FLB-CJCG)

23 Kayali, L (2022) Musk tells Twitter staff: Work 'hardcore' or leave, *Politico*, 16 November, www.politico.eu/article/must-tells-twitter-staff-to-work-harder-or-leave (archived at perma.cc/LXA2-MW57)

24 Nolan, B (2022) Elon Musk says Twitter purchase will accelerate the creation of X, his long-discussed 'everything app', *Business Insider*, 5 October, www.businessinsider.com/elon-musk-twitter-accelerant-x-everything-app-2022-10?r=US&IR=T (archived at perma.cc/727F-Y7WJ)

25 Olinga, L (2022) Elon Musk sounds the alarm about ChatGPT, *The Street*, 26 December, www.thestreet.com/technology/elon-musk-sounds-the-alarm-about-chatgpt (archived at perma.cc/K7DB-B5YU)

26 Burnett, E (2022) Biden turns to Elon Musk to aid Iranian protestors. Defence official calls Musk 'a loose cannon', *CNN*, 22 October, https://edition.cnn.com/videos/business/2022/10/21/biden-elon-musk-starlink-internet-iran-protests-ukraine-white-house-dnt-marquardt-ebof-vpx.cnn (archived at perma.cc/9UT6-6HJS)

27 Hals, T and Jackson, S (2021) Musk defends timing of Tesla's $2.6bln deal for SolarCity, *Reuters*, 13 July, www.reuters.com/business/musk-set-take-stand-second-day-trial-over-solarcity-deal-2021-07-13 (archived at perma.cc/YF7Y-GR9Y)

28 U.S. Securities and Exchange Commission (2018) Elon Musk settles SEC fraud charges; Tesla charged with and resolves securities law change, 29 September, www.sec.gov/news/press-release/2018-226 (archived at perma.cc/5G9P-Y3BW)

29 Lee, D (2023) Elon Musk wins investor lawsuit over Tesla 'funding secured' tweet, *Financial Times*, 4 February, www.ft.com/content/f3a1e3d8-e6f2-45df-8856-aec6d069a01c (archived at perma.cc/PFJ9-7WZY)

30 Kolodny, L (2019) Elon Musk found not liable in 'pedo guy' defamation trial, 6 December, www.cnbc.com/2019/12/06/unsworth-vs-musk-pedo-guy-defamation-trial-verdict.html (archived at perma.cc/FZW8-QUTL)

31 Ingram, D (2022) Musk suggests Ukraine should cede Crimea, draws rebuke from Zelenskyy, *NBC News*, 3 October, www.nbcnews.com/tech/tech-news/musk-suggests-ukraine-cede-crimea-draws-rebuke-zelenskyy-rcna50528 (archived at perma.cc/CH73-ANMX)

32 Lock, S (2023) Elon Musk breaks world record for largest loss of personal fortune in history, *The Guardian*, 12 January, www.theguardian.com/technology/2023/jan/12/elon-musk-breaks-world-record-for-largest-loss-of-personal-fortune-in-history (archived at perma.cc/P4LH-L9HK)

33 BBC (2022) *The Elon Musk Show*, 19 October, www.bbc.co.uk/iplayer/episode/p0d3j60k/the-elon-musk-show-series-1-episode-2 (archived at perma.cc/G6E5-XV8Z)

34 Hern, A (2018) Will Elon Musk's 120-hour week stop us worshipping workaholism? *The Guardian*, 23 August, www.theguardian.com/technology/2018/aug/23/elon-musk-120-hour-working-week-tesla (archived at perma.cc/4QDY-TMER)

35 Vance, A (2015) *Elon Musk: How the billionaire CEO of SpaceX and Tesla is shaping our future*, Virgin Books, United Kingdom, p 177

36 YouTube (2019) Elon Musk: 'No, I don't ever give up. I'd have to be dead or completely incapacitated' (Online video) 14 December,

www.youtube.com/watch?v=wZZCTE1TCmw (archived at perma.cc/FV6L-VNHC)

37   YouTube (2015) Elon Musk on criticism, critique and not being right all the time (Online video) 23 January, www.youtube.com/watch?v=MQEMe0SFu-Q (archived at perma.cc/URJ8-6EFC)

38   O'Kane, C (2022) Elon Musk says he doesn't own a house and for the most part sleeps in friends' spare bedrooms, *CBS News*, 18 April, www.cbsnews.com/news/elon-musk-house-stays-friends-net-worth (archived at perma.cc/4MQ5-S8V2)

39   BBC (2021) Elon Musk reveals he has Asperger's on Saturday Night Live, 9 May, www.bbc.co.uk/news/world-us-canada-57045770 (archived at perma.cc/2UHC-BSBD)

40   YouTube (2021) Elon Musk monologue – SNL (Online video) 9 May, www.youtube.com/watch?v=fCF8I_X1qKI (archived at perma.cc/2GJF-BA6S)

CHAPTER ELEVEN

Satoshi Nakamoto

Bitcoin

Leadership philosophy

'IF YOU DON'T BELIEVE ME OR DON'T GET IT, I DON'T HAVE TIME
TO TRY TO CONVINCE YOU, SORRY.'[1]

B itcoin is the world's largest and best-known cryptocurrency – a type of peer-to-peer payment system that does not have any central issuing or regulating authority and only exists on computer networks. With cryptocurrencies, transactions are digital entries in an online database. These entries are secured using cryptography (the process of changing plain text into unreadable ciphertext using an encryption). Users store their cryptocurrencies in digital wallets, which they access using a key. In just over a decade, bitcoin has gone from being a paper concept to a financial asset that is prized by millions of people worldwide. As of

January 2023, the global value of bitcoin stood at a staggering $440 billion.[2]

The leader behind this multi-billion-dollar phenomenon is the mysterious Satoshi Nakamoto. On 31 October 2008, he effectively launched the world's most successful cryptocurrency when he published a white paper entitled *Bitcoin: A peer-to-peer electronic cash system*. Today, the white paper is considered seminal not just for bitcoin but for the wider cryptocurrency movement. Nakamoto is believed to be part of the 'cypherpunk' movement – people who see cryptography and software as means to achieve freedom and privacy. In fact, he had previously shared earlier versions of his white paper with Hal Finney and Wei Dai, two computer scientists who also belonged to the movement, which dates back to the 1990s.[3]

In his white paper, Nakamoto set out his vision for a decentralized digital currency system that would operate without central intermediaries such as banks and governments. The paper argued that a peer-to-peer version of electronic cash 'would allow online payments to be sent directly from one party to another without going through a financial institution'.[4] While the paper was not published until the end of October 2008, Nakamoto had begun coding the first implementation of bitcoin using the programming language C++ in May 2007.[5]

On the face of it, a currency stored on a digital ledger, without the backing of any recognized authority, might have seemed an eccentric idea that was very unlikely to take off. But the idea of cryptocurrencies had actually been circulating for more than two decades by that point. Nick Szabo, a US computer scientist, had previously floated the concept of bit gold, which used many of the same block-chain techniques that were later associated with bitcoin, such as a peer-to-peer network, a ledger, cryptography and mining.[6] Mining is central to bitcoin since it is the process by which new coins are created – miners are rewarded with coins when they solve complicated maths problems using specialist mining software.

Nevertheless, the timing of bitcoin's launch was apt, which undoubtedly contributed to it becoming the first cryptocurrency to go mainstream. In what was almost certainly no coincidence, Nakamoto's paper was published at the height of the global financial crisis – when public trust in banks and other financial institutions was badly fractured. Investment bank Lehman Brothers had filed for bankruptcy a month earlier as a result of being over-exposed to mortgage-backed securities amid a crash in the US housing market. Due to the interconnectedness of the global financial system, the collapse of the bank Lehman Brothers sparked contagion and the credit markets seized up.

In an effort to stave off the total meltdown of the global financial system, governments in a number of countries were forced to bail out their banks with the help of a monetary tool known as quantitative easing. With quanti-tative easing, central banks create new money for the purpose of buying government bonds (loans to govern-ments) or other financial assets. While it's a useful tool for keeping an economy going during a period of financial crisis, quantitative easing does bring risks such as inflation (rising prices) and stagflation (the combination of high inflation, high unemployment and low economic growth).

In January 2009, Nakamoto himself mined the first-ever bitcoin block (a set of transactions within a specific time period). To do this, he used blockchain, a new data ledger technology that he had invented. Known as the genesis block, the block he mined contained 50 bitcoins that were never used or could not be used, whether due to design or error. Embedded in the genesis block was a hidden message, referring to a headline from British daily newspaper *The Times*. The message read 'The Times 03/Jan/2009 Chancellor on brink of second bailout for banks'.[7]

Nakamoto carried on mining and reportedly mined up to 1.1 million bitcoins in the first seven months of 2009 – coins that would have been worth $22 billion as of August 2022 prices.[8] Intriguingly, despite the vast wealth they represent, those coins have never been touched since.[9] In theory, were the value of the coins to be directly converted into US dollars, they would make Nakamoto one of the 75 richest people alive in the world today.[10]

Nakamoto recognized that if his cryptocurrency vision was to succeed, he could not be the only person to mine and hold bitcoin. So, he made the code to mine bitcoin available to others.[11] On 11 February 2009, he posted a link to download the open-source software on the forum of the P2P Foundation, a non-profit organization dedicated to studying and researching peer-to-peer practices.[12] The opportunity soon piqued the interest of a small, but dedicated, group of fellow developers and the bitcoin project began to take off.[13]

Nakamoto remained in continuous contact with the growing, and increasingly vocal, bitcoin community for over two years. During that time, he actively collaborated with other developers to iron out issues and progress bitcoin. The spirit of that collaboration persists to this day, with hundreds of developers around the world continuing to work on the project.

To begin with, people who wanted to own bitcoin only had two options open to them. They either had to mine it themselves or arrange a peer-to-peer trade via a forum like Bitcointalk, which Nakamoto founded to host bitcoin-related discussions.[14] The market for bitcoin opened up in 2010, however, when it first became available to buy, sell and trade via online exchanges, including Mt. Gox. Founded in 2010, Mt. Gox was a Japanese exchange that famously went bankrupt four years later after thousands of bitcoins were stolen by hackers.

Awareness of bitcoin continued to increase, and in 2010, the fledgling cryptocurrency was first used to make a purchase. A developer called Laszlo Hanyecz bought two pizzas from another member of the bitcoin community with 10,000 bitcoins (worth around $223 million at early 2023 prices).[15] But while bitcoin's visibility was rising, so were tensions among bitcoin developers. The bitcoin network was hacked in August 2010, leading Nakamoto to focus heavily on security and become less collaborative with other developers. Towards the end of 2010, members of the bitcoin community became increasingly frustrated with Nakamoto's 'general lack of availability and inability to meet their many demands', according to Pete Rizzo, editor of *Bitcoin Magazine*.[16] On 12 December 2010, Nakamoto published what turned out to be his last-ever post on the Bitcointalk forum.

In February 2011, bitcoin achieved parity with the US dollar for the first time, a remarkable achievement for a currency that had only been in existence for just over two years. This could have been an opportunity for Nakamoto to bask in a little glory. Instead, two months later, he suddenly stepped aside as lead developer of the bitcoin project that he had initiated, passing on the responsibility to US software developer Gavin Andresen. After that, he disappeared.

Nakamoto sent a final email to fellow developers on 26 April, saying that he had 'moved on to other projects', and handed over the cryptographic key that he used to send network-wide alerts.[17] After he left, Nakamoto removed his name from the copyright claim in the bitcoin software, leaving the code to all 'Bitcoin developers'.[18]

The real Satoshi Nakamoto

Who is or was the real Satoshi Nakamoto? Which person or persons are behind the pseudonym? Surprisingly, the answer to that question is that no one really knows – or if they do know, they aren't telling. Frustratingly, the inventor himself avoided giving away any personal information in his forum posts and even in his private emails. As a result, the true identity of Satoshi Nakamoto remains one of the great mysteries of the 21st century.

Nakamoto's determined efforts to protect his own anonymity reflected his belief that individuals were less important than the collective good of the project. Nevertheless, discussions among early bitcoin developers, published on the site Building Bitcoin, show that speculation around the true nature of Nakamoto's identity began at an early stage. Developers questioned whether he was a single individual and whether he was really Japanese since he had never used a word of the language and didn't appear to work during usual Japanese hours. Nakamoto's professional competence as a coder was also questioned, with a developer called Kiba noting that 'some people say his code is crap'. More generously, Kiba continued: 'Whoever he is... he is brilliant to think of the idea.'[19]

In Japanese, Satoshi is a masculine given name that translates to 'clear thinking', 'wise' and 'intelligent history'. Of course, that doesn't necessarily mean that Satoshi is a man, but given that the majority of software developers are male, it is very likely that he is or was. Nakamoto, meanwhile, means 'one who lives in the middle'. It would appear that bitcoin's inventor had a legacy in mind – a decentralized currency system that would change the course of history – when coming up with the name Satoshi Nakamoto.

Yet while the name is intended to convey someone of Japanese origin, the evidence points to Nakamoto being British (or partly British if, as many believe, Nakamoto was, in fact, a group of people working together). The headline embedded in the genesis block came from the print version of the British newspaper, rather than the online version, suggesting that Nakamoto had access to a physical copy. The timings of his posts also suggest that he was based in either Europe or North America.[20] Nakamoto used British sayings, once remarking on the challenge of trying to come up with an accessible description for bitcoin: 'Sorry to be a wet blanket. Writing a description for this thing for general audiences is bloody hard. There's nothing to relate it to.'[21]

Analysis of Nakamoto's spelling choices reveals that he widely used British English as well as American English. This alternation between the two could suggest that while he used British English in his home life, he used American English in his work life. Or it could suggest that he was more than one person, living on more than one continent. Alternatively, it could simply be an indicator that spelling wasn't his strong suit. Notably, Nakamoto consistently used American English for his code.[22] In what may be another clue, Nakamoto listed his date of birth as 5 April 1975 for his profile on the P2P Foundation forum, with 5 April being the last day of the British tax year.

Over the years, a number of possible names have either been touted or put themselves forward as being bitcoin's enigmatic inventor. The more plausible suggestions include bit gold creator Nick Szabo and Hal Finney, who participated in the first-ever bitcoin transaction when he received 10 bitcoin from Nakamoto on 12 January 2009. Both denied being the bitcoin founder, however. Finney died in 2014.

Other possible candidates include Australian computer scientist Craig Wright, British cryptographer Adam Back and German entrepreneur Jörg Molt. In 2014, US magazine *Newsweek* claimed that the real Satoshi Nakamoto was Dorian Nakamoto, a Japanese-American man living in California. But he firmly refuted the suggestion that he was the bitcoin founder.

It has even been suggested that bitcoin's inventor is Elon Musk, one of the world's most famous entrepreneurs. How likely is this scenario? Certainly, Musk has knowledge of coding and economics. He also admits to holding the cryptocurrency personally while, in February 2021, his electric car company, Tesla, announced that it had bought $1.5 billion of bitcoin.[23] (The following year it sold approximately 75 per cent of its stake.[24]) Yet Musk himself denies having created bitcoin and at the time the white paper was published in 2008, he was frantically trying to save his companies Tesla and SpaceX. Whether he had the time or the headspace to launch a cryptocurrency at this juncture seems highly questionable.

Today, there is no real consensus around who Nakamoto is or was. Significantly, given that a lot of the evidence points towards Nakamoto being British, or at least based in Britain, few contenders for the crown have British origins. Many commentators think that the original Nakamoto is now dead – which would explain why we haven't heard from him in over a decade and why his original holding, mined in 2009, remains untouched. If he was terminally ill at the time the global financial crisis struck, he may well have seen bitcoin as his legacy to the world. Illness might also explain his increasing unavailability to developers before he disappeared and might provide poignant meaning to his final claim to have 'moved on to other projects'. It may be that bitcoin was a project he simply did in his spare time – something that his family and friends knew nothing about. And when he died, his involvement in the project died with him.

The timings of the posts and the use of a mixture of US and British English, as well as the sheer workload involved with getting bitcoin off the ground, are all arguments in favour of Nakamoto being a group of developers rather than one individual. Nevertheless, if Nakamoto is a group, it is a group that has succeeded in showing remarkable solidarity over the years – especially in the face of what must be considerable temptation to boast about being the bitcoin founder and to cash in on at least some of the original holding.

'My general sense is that the person who was using the Bitcointalk account was likely one person,' argues Pete Rizzo, of *Bitcoin Magazine*. 'There are some conceptual quirks – the speed with which he replies to messages, the speed with which he takes action, both in message and in what metastasizes in the technology itself.'

Rizzo notes that Nakamoto responded very promptly on certain occasions when the pressure was on. For example, when the bitcoin network was hacked in August 2010, he coded a fix within hours.[25] If Nakamoto had been more than one person, Rizzo believes, the response would likely have been slower as the group tried to work out what to do.

Dorian Banks, CEO of Looking Glass Labs, a Web3 platform based in Vancouver, Canada, takes the alternative view. 'I've always thought it's a group, or at least it became a group,' he says. 'I think maybe it started with one person who was from a position of hating the banking system, and the government controls over currency. Maybe they started the project on their own, but then I've always felt there was a transition to a group of people, with one or more of those people coming from a Commonwealth country.' His explanation for why all members of the group have managed to exercise self-restraint over time and not touch the original bitcoin holding is that whoever held the original key 'is no longer alive or they've lost the key'.

Of course, it is possible that Nakamoto is still alive and holds other bitcoin investments on an individual basis. In which case, he has probably become so rich that he has never needed to risk unsettling the market by selling the original holding. As for his refusal to blow his own anonymity, that is arguably the manifestation of his long-standing ideological commitment to put the group above the individual in order to preserve the integrity of the project. For Nakamoto, bitcoin was always about creating a better payment system. It was never about money and fame.

'One of the things that Satoshi Nakamoto had to confront early on was his control of the software,' says Rizzo. 'The aspiration for bitcoin was that it would be decentralized money that no one controls. Essentially, his admin rights were in conflict with the aspirations of the project. It was just a matter of time before he had to leave. He was just waiting until the community, the users, were ready to govern and control bitcoin.'

Rizzo believes that Nakamoto would also have taken steps to 'guard against his own self-interest' – in other words, to ensure that he did not give in to the temptation to profit greatly from the project at the expense of others. For that reason, he might have deliberately deleted the keys to the digital wallet that stored his initial holding.

While Nakamoto's true identity and appearance may remain unknown, that hasn't stopped Hungary's cryptocurrency community from managing to erect a statue in his honour. The statue, which stands in Budapest's Graphisoft Park, is a bronze bust with a plain face, wearing a hoodie that features the bitcoin logo. Viewers can see their own reflection in the statue's heavily polished face.[26]

Secrets to success

So, how did Nakamoto take a theoretical concept in a white paper and turn it into one of the defining financial and technological forces of our time? How did he become one of the greatest tech leaders of the early 21st century without anyone knowing who he really was? Certainly, he always seems to have understood that he was engaged in an all-or-nothing project. 'I'm sure that in 20 years there will either be a very large transaction volume or no volume,' he wrote on 14 February 2010, in a thread on Bitcointalk.[27]

In the early days, when it wasn't clear if his project would fly, he continued to persevere. He liaised with his fellow developers and answered their questions, with the aim of spreading awareness and understanding of bitcoin. He knew that if he was to succeed in his vision, ultimately the project would need to be taken forward by other people – what is not clear, however, is if he came to that realization through necessity (for example, because his health was failing) or through desire. Whatever his reasons for handing over the project in 2011, he evidently made the right decision since bitcoin took off in the years to follow.

Bitcoin is infamous for its price volatility – often giving its users the opportunity to get rich – or go broke – very quickly. Over its short life, it has been the focus of some spectacular market bull runs – and some equally spectacular crashes – with prices continuing to climb over time. A major driver of bitcoin boom-and-bust cycles is the bitcoin halving process – when the reward for mining new bitcoins is cut in half. Since halvings reduce the rate at which new coins are created, they reduce the available amount of supply even while demand increases. The historic bitcoin halving dates were 28 November 2012, 9 July 2016 and 11 May 2020, with the next halving expected in 2024.

Bitcoin's value over time shows a clear alignment with the halving process. The value of the cryptocurrency first passed the $1,000 mark towards the end of 2013, before subsequently crashing in 2014. In 2017, the price of bitcoin accelerated rapidly, peaking at nearly $20,000. Then it crashed in December. In November 2021, Bitcoin reached an all-time high of nearly $69,000, only to plunge 68 per cent by August the following year.[28] Its price was further rocked in autumn 2022 when leading crypto exchange FTX suddenly collapsed due to a lack of liquidity. Yet, at the market peak, on 9 November 2021, bitcoin – the currency that came from nothing – had a market capitalization of $1.28 trillion.[29] To put that figure into context, it is a higher capitalization than Facebook owner Meta had at the time.

But if investing in bitcoin is an emotional and financial rollercoaster ride, that hasn't deterred millions of people around the world from holding it. Despite its volatility, it is touted in some quarters as being comparable with gold in terms of a store of value. Certainly, its acolytes value its accessibility, liquidity and user anonymity, as well as its potential for capital growth. They also like the fact it is beyond government control, since governments cannot seize it or deflate it. Having said that, the currency is starting to be embraced by governments – somewhat contrary to bitcoin's anti-establishment image. It is now legal tender in the Central American country of El Salvador as well as in the Central African Republic.

Egalitarian principles have underpinned bitcoin's phenomenal success to date – it is organized in a way that ensures that no single individual or organization can take full control of the network. Anyone, anywhere, can potentially own bitcoin provided they can set up a digital wallet. What's more, they can easily take their money with them as they move across borders, without having to worry about capital controls or foreign exchange rates. Critics say bitcoin plays into the hands of money launderers and criminal gangs. Fans of the cryptocurrency claim it's a way to empower refugees and people who live in countries affected by hyperinflation. Bitcoin has also come under fire for being bad for the environment since the mining process consumes considerable amounts of energy. The counter-argument, however, is that bitcoin has a far less detrimental impact on the planet than the gold-mining industry and the traditional banking system.

A major reason for the confidence that exists in bitcoin, according to Dorian Banks, is the fact there's a limit on how many coins will ever be mined. That limit is 21 million. It is encoded in bitcoin's source code and cannot be changed thanks to bitcoin's decentralized nature. This restriction on supply is fundamentally what makes bitcoin successful as a store of value.[30] Gold has historically been regarded as a store of value for the same reason – there's only a finite amount of gold in the world.

Nakamoto himself certainly recognized the value of scarcity, which explains why he was philosophical about bitcoin users losing access to their digital wallets. 'Lost coins only make everyone else's coins worth slightly more,' he wrote on a Bitcointalk thread on 21 June 2010. 'Think of it as a donation to everyone.'[31]

LEADERSHIP LESSONS FROM SATOSHI NAKAMOTO

- **Trust is the foundation of long-term success**. If you can create a trusted product or service, people will use it.

- **Focus on the big picture**. The project, as a whole, is more important than any single individual.

- **Know when it's time to move on**. To achieve the desired results, it may be necessary to hand over management of a project to others.

- **Keep your ego in check**. You don't need everyone to know who you are to make a difference to the world.

- **Get your timing right**. If you come up with the right idea, at the right time, the magic will happen.

Notes

1   Bitcointalk (2010) https://bitcointalk.org/index.php?topic=532. msg6269#msg6269 (archived at perma.cc/VR9J-97E4)

2   Y Charts (2023) Bitcoin market cap, 23 January, https://ycharts.com/ indicators/bitcoin_market_cap (archived at perma.cc/6UK4-E3GM)

3   Qureshi, H (2019) Satoshi Nakamoto, *Nakamoto*, 29 December, https:// nakamoto.com/satoshi-nakamoto (archived at perma.cc/2GVU-QKJC)

4   Nakamoto, S (2008) *Bitcoin: A peer-to-peer electronic cash system*

5   Qureshi, H (2019) Satoshi Nakamoto, *Nakamoto*, 29 December, https://nakamoto.com/satoshi-nakamoto (archived at perma.cc/2GVU-QKJC)

6   Reiff, N (2022) What was the first cryptocurrency? *Investopedia*, 23 July, www.investopedia.com/tech/were-there-cryptocurrencies-bitcoin (archived at perma.cc/BC87-2S23)

7   CNBCTV18.com (2022) Everything you need to know about the bitcoin genesis block, 21 July, www.cnbctv18.com/technology/everything-you-need-to-know-about-the-bitcoin-genesis-block-14205612.htm (archived at perma.cc/P758-TQ5S)

8   Duggan, W (2022) The history of Bitcoin, the first cryptocurrency, *US News*, 31 August, https://money.usnews.com/investing/articles/the-history-of-bitcoin (archived at perma.cc/25KN-ST5R)

9   Philips, D (2021) How many Bitcoin does its inventor Satoshi Nakamoto still own?, *Decrypt*, 3 January, https://decrypt.co/34810/how-many-bitcoin-does-its-inventor-satoshi-nakamoto-still-own (archived at perma.cc/25KN-ST5R)

10 Forbes (2023) The world's real-time billionaires, www.forbes.com/real-time-billionaires/#2fe825a53d78 (archived at perma.cc/Z6FV-7W6K)

11 Held, D (2018) Bitcoin's distribution was fair, *Medium*, 4 October, https://danhedl.medium.com/bitcoins-distribution-was-fair-e2ef7bbbc892 (archived at perma.cc/QKS5-C5UU)

12 Nakamoto, S (2009) Bitcoin open source implementation of P2P currency, P2P Foundation forum, 11 February, https://p2pfoundation.ning.com/forum/topics/bitcoin-open-source (archived at perma.cc/G2HJ-ZNKQ)

13 Rizzo, P (2021) 10 years ago today, Bitcoin creator Satoshi Nakamoto sent his final message, *Forbes*, 26 April, www.forbes.com/sites/peterizzo/2021/04/26/10-years-ago-today-bitcoin-creator-satoshi-nakamoto-sent-his-final-message/?sh=14ad690c10dd (archived at perma.cc/HG6M-KCTD)

14 Cryptopedia (2022) The early days of crypto exchanges, 17 March, www.gemini.com/cryptopedia/crypto-exchanges-early-mt-gox-hack (archived at perma.cc/7KYV-FKJC)

15 Reiff, N (2022) What was the first cryptocurrency?, *Investopedia*, 23 July, www.investopedia.com/tech/were-there-cryptocurrencies-bitcoin (archived at perma.cc/BC87-2S23)

16 Rizzo, P (2021) 10 years ago today, Bitcoin creator Satoshi Nakamoto sent his final message, *Forbes*, 26 April, www.forbes.com/sites/peterizzo/2021/04/26/10-years-ago-today-bitcoin-creator-satoshi-nakamoto-sent-his-final-message/?sh=14ad690c10dd (archived at perma.cc/HG6M-KCTD)

17 Rizzo, P (2021) 10 years ago today, Bitcoin creator Satoshi Nakamoto sent his final message, *Forbes*, 26 April, www.forbes.com/sites/peterizzo/2021/04/26/10-years-ago-today-bitcoin-creator-satoshi-nakamoto-sent-his-final-message/?sh=14ad690c10dd (archived at perma.cc/HG6M-KCTD)

18 Rizzo, P (2021) 10 years ago today, Bitcoin creator Satoshi Nakamoto sent his final message, *Forbes*, 26 April, www.forbes.com/sites/peterizzo/2021/04/26/10-years-ago-today-bitcoin-creator-satoshi-nakamoto-sent-his-final-message/?sh=14ad690c10dd (archived at perma.cc/HG6M-KCTD)

19 Building Bitcoin (nd) https://buildingbitcoin.org/bitcoin-dev/log-2010-12-07.html#l-1600 (archived at perma.cc/6PJA-73SF)

20 Karaivanov, D (2020) Satoshi Nakamoto lived in London while working on Bitcoin. Here's how we know, *The Chain Bulletin*, 23 November, https://chainbulletin.com/satoshi-nakamoto-lived-in-london-while-working-on-bitcoin-heres-how-we-know (archived at perma.cc/J5QQ-DFHF)

21 Bitcointalk (2010) https://bitcointalk.org/index.php?topic=234.msg1976#msg1976 (archived at perma.cc/7FGX-FW2Z)

22 Ungeared (2020) The strange story of Satoshi Nakamoto's spelling choices, https://ungeared.com/the-strange-story-of-satoshi-nakamotos-spelling-choices-part-1 (archived at perma.cc/SC9X-EJHJ)

23 Kovach, S (2021) Tesla buys $1.5 billion in bitcoin, plans to accept it as payment, *CNBC*, 8 February, www.cnbc.com/2021/02/08/tesla-buys-1point5-billion-in-bitcoin.html (archived at perma.cc/8XVR-HB2S)

24 Novet, J (2022) Tesla has dumped 75% of its bitcoin holdings a year after touting 'long-term potential', *CNBC*, 20 July, www.cnbc.com/

2022/07/20/tesla-converted-75percent-of-bitcoin-purchases-to-fiat-currency-in-q2-2022.html (archived at perma.cc/2JKU-WHSX)

25 Shrem, C (2019) Bitcoin's biggest hack in history: 184.4 billion Bitcoin from thin air, Hackernoon, 11 January, https://hackernoon.com/bitcoins-biggest-hack-in-history-184-4-ded46310d4ef (archived at perma.cc/Q8LM-6HLL)

26 Davies, P with AP (2021) Hungary's Bitcoin fans unveil statue of mysterious crypto founder Satoshi Nakamoto, *Euronews*, 17 September, www.euronews.com/next/2021/09/17/hungary-s-bitcoin-fans-unveil-faceless-statue-of-mysterious-crypto-founder-satoshi-nakamot (archived at perma.cc/CD7W-6DWL)

27 Bitcointalk (2010) https://bitcointalk.org/index.php?topic=48.msg329#msg329 (archived at perma.cc/QF5Q-QZET)

28 Tham, N (2022) Bitcoin has crashed 68% from its peak – but one bull says the latest crypto winter is a 'warm winter', *CNBC*, 25 August, www.cnbc.com/2022/08/26/crypto-winter-is-coming-but-it-will-be-a-warm-winter-says-vc-firm.html (archived at perma.cc/KZH2-LU8Y)

29 Global Data (2022) Bitcoin's market capitalization history (2013–2022, $ billion), www.globaldata.com/data-insights/financial-services/bitcoins-market-capitalization-history (archived at perma.cc/G524-UFMF)

30 River Financial (2022) Can Bitcoin's hard cap of 21 million be changed?, https://river.com/learn/can-bitcoins-hard-cap-of-21-million-be-changed (archived at perma.cc/MAR8-BUVV)

31 Bitcointalk (2010) Dying bitcoins, 21 June, https://satoshi.nakamotoinstitute.org/posts/bitcointalk/threads/71/#7 (archived at perma.cc/Z2RA-JB7A)

CHAPTER TWELVE

Melanie Perkins

Canva

Leadership philosophy
'IT'S NEVER TOO LATE TO EXERCISE THE POWER OF
DETERMINATION.'[1]

Today, anyone, anywhere, can be a graphic designer
thanks to Canva. A powerful and easy-to-use graphic
design platform, Canva may be used to create a vast range
of visual content, from Instagram posts to business logos,
websites and Zoom backgrounds. To date, the platform
has produced over 10 billion designs and it boasts over 60
million monthly users living in 190 countries.[2]

The story of Canva is an inspiring tale of how one determined young woman overcame the doubters to bring her
vision to life.

Melanie Perkins is the daughter of an Australian-born
teacher and a Malaysian engineer of Filipino and Sri

Lankan heritage. Now in her late thirties, she demonstrated a flair for entrepreneurship at a very early age. She launched her first business at the age of 14, selling handmade scarves to shops and markets in her home town of Perth. That experience sparked her desire to build a business.[3]

Perkins was still a teenager – only 19 – when she came up with the idea of what became Canva in 2007.[4] While studying communications and commerce studies at the University of Western Australia, she taught other students to use basic computer design programs. The realization that these programs were complex and expensive ignited her mission to make affordable design accessible to all.[5]

Perkins dropped out of university and with her then-boyfriend (now husband), Cliff Obrecht, decided to test the idea of simplifying the process of design. The pair started out by targeting the niche market of school yearbooks, working from her mother's living room. Their graphic design start-up, Fusion Books, grew into the largest yearbook company in Australia and expanded into France and New Zealand.

While their business was going well, Perkins and Obrecht had even loftier dreams. They wanted to apply the design technology they had built on a much broader basis, beyond the yearbook market, so that it could potentially be used by anyone, anywhere to create professional designs. That's when Canva was born.[6]

Perkins realized that she would need venture funding to achieve her vision of building a graphic design platform at scale, one that would empower people everywhere to create their own professional designs. But although she believed passionately in the merits of her idea, the investors she initially spoke to weren't as convinced. In a LinkedIn post, Harvard board adviser Martin Roll described how, during her quest to raise venture capital, she was rejected by investors over 100 times.[7]

Realizing that she faced an uphill struggle, Perkins adopted some creative strategies to try to secure funding. She learned kiteboarding in an attempt to attract investment from a group of venture capitalists who were also kiteboard enthusiasts, including renowned angel investor Bill Tai.[8] She also made a point of learning from rejection. When an investor asked a hard question, or gave a reason for refusing to invest in her business, she would revise her pitch deck to answer the question or fix the reason for rejection.[9]

In the end her persistence – and willingness to take up kiteboarding – paid off. After three years, Perkins and Obrecht secured their first investment. They raised US$3 million in two tranches in 2012 and 2013, including a matching grant from the Australian government.[10] Among the investors was Tai, as well as Lars Rasmussen, a co-founder of Google Maps.[11] Canva was launched in August 2013, by which time the company's third co-founder, ex-Googler Cameron Adams, was on board. Adams later admitted that the youthful trio 'had no idea how to run a company'.[12]

From small fry to big fish

Fortuitously, Canva's launch coincided with the rise of social media and authors caring about their visual presence on platforms such as Instagram and Twitter. By 2014,

600,000 users had created 3.5 million designs using Canva and the platform was taking off in the huge market of China. Canva has been based in Sydney since 2012 and it also opened an office in Manila, the capital of the Philippines, in 2014.[13] In 2018, Canva acquired the status of a unicorn (a privately held start-up company with a valuation of over $1 billion) after raising $40 million in a funding round.[14]

Currently, the company's big challenge is cracking the corporate market since Canva is still predominantly used by individuals and small-to-medium-sized businesses.[15] With that in mind, it has launched its Visual Worksuite, a set of professional tools that can be used to create collaborative documents, websites and data visualization. In doing so, it is directly challenging the hegemony of established workplace tools such as Adobe, Google Docs and Microsoft Office.[16]

Canva's expansion hasn't come without growing pains, however. In May 2019, a hacker breached its systems and downloaded 139 million usernames and email addresses. This large-scale data breach resulted in the company significantly upping its investment in information security.[17]

As the company has expanded, it has resisted the lure of a move to Silicon Valley. Instead it has retained its base in Australia. In fact, Perkins has publicly stated that the company has 'no intention of moving elsewhere'. She would, however, like to see the country invest in growing its technology workforce and ensuring that people study tech subjects from a young age.[18]

Perkins remains CEO of Canva, which was valued at $40 billion in September 2021.[19] Meanwhile, *Forbes* estimated her own net worth to be $3.6 billion as of January 2023. Nevertheless, Perkins is patently clear that she does not view her business simply as a means to accumulate riches, saying: 'If the whole thing was about building wealth, that would be the most uninspiring thing I could possibly imagine.'[20]

Indeed, Perkins is known for her strong philanthropic principles. She and Obrecht each own an 18 per cent stake in Canva and they have pledged to transfer more than 80 per cent of their stake to the Canva Foundation for charitable causes.[21] In a statement, the couple said: 'We have this wildly optimistic belief that there is enough money, goodwill and good intentions in the world to solve most of the world's problems. We feel like it's not just a massive opportunity, but an important responsibility, and we want to spend our lifetime working towards that.'[22]

Ultimately, Canva's corporate values are an embodiment of the same values its founder had when she devised the idea for the business all those years ago. It aims to 'make complex things simple', 'set crazy big goals and make them happen', 'be a force for good' and 'empower others'.

Secrets to success

Perkins attributes her success to her self-confidence and to being 100 per cent committed to whatever she chooses to do. 'Everything I have done in my life I have poured my heart and soul into it, whether it was a school assignment or sport,' Perkins told the *Sydney Morning Herald* in 2015. 'I think that's such an important thing, especially when considering what you want to do in life. Confidence is key.'[23]

She also values communication highly. In a Q&A with *Entrepreneur* magazine in 2019, she said: 'Good communication is one of the most important aspects of being a good leader and helping the team make good decisions on achieving their goals.'

Perkins is known for her modesty and her down-to-earth leadership approach. She eats lunch with her employees and has described herself as 'not the boss of 600 people, but serving 600 people'.[24] She is very focused on helping her teams reach their potential, with Canva's success almost certainly linked to its nimble organizational structure. The company has a number of small, empowered teams, which have ownership over their own work, enabling them to maximize the results of their creative efforts.[25]

Henry Ford, founder of the Ford Motor Company, is often credited with the saying: 'If I had asked people what they wanted, they would have said faster horses.' This attitude towards innovation is shared by Perkins. 'I don't believe you can ask your users or customers what you should create,' she told *Entrepreneur* magazine, arguing that if she had asked the design students she was tutoring at university what they wanted, 'they would have asked for incremental improvements to the design software they were using'.[26]

Perkins is not your archetypal tech unicorn founder. She's not male, she's not white and she's not based in Silicon Valley. This probably explains why she's chosen to write about what it's like to be 'on the outside' in life, offering her advice to others in a similar position. Her top tip is 'don't worry about people who don't look like you'. In a blog for SmartCompany, she said: 'There are a number of people in this world who are archaic and small-minded – and there's almost nothing we can do about it. Just know it's their loss if they don't want anything to do with you.'

In the blog, Perkins offered a number of valuable suggestions for maintaining a positive mindset. These include concentrating on your goals, blaming things you can fix rather than things you can't control, believing in yourself and finding people like you. Unsurprisingly, she also underlined the importance of determination in the face of adversity – something she says has been 'like a magical superpower' throughout her life. As she puts it: 'If it were easy, it probably wouldn't be worth doing.' [27]

LEADERSHIP LESSONS FROM MELANIE PERKINS

- **Set yourself the biggest goal you possibly can**. The bigger your goal, the harder you'll try and the more you're likely to achieve.

- **Do what you're passionate about**. If you're doing what you love, you'll put more into it, which means you'll be more likely to succeed.

- **Keep going – no matter how many times you hear the word no**. If you believe in your dream, you can make it happen.

- **Learn from rejection**. Value all the feedback you receive – both positive and negative – so that you can improve your business or project and come back stronger next time.

- **Empower your people by giving them ownership over their work**. Ownership will give them the freedom to experiment, innovate and learn from their successes and failures.

Notes

1 Perkins, M (2018) A message for those who feel they're on the outside, from Canva co-founder Melanie Perkins, *Smart Company*, 24 September, www.smartcompany.com.au/startupsmart/advice/canva-co-founder-melanie-perkins-message (archived at perma.cc/7SB3-Z9NS)

2 Canva (2022) About Canva: Empowering the world to design, www.canva.com/about (archived at perma.cc/GNJ7-QVVW)

3 Zipkin, N (2019) She was told 'No' 100 times. Now this 31-year-old female founder runs a $1 billion business, *Entrepreneur*, 12 June, www.entrepreneur.com/leadership/she-was-told-no-100-times-now-this-31-year-old-female/310482 (archived at perma.cc/4GYS-5ZEN)

4 Konrad, A (2019) Canva uncovered: How a young Australian kitesurfer built a $3.2 billion (profitable!) startup phenom, *Forbes*, 11 December, www.forbes.com/sites/alexkonrad/2019/12/11/inside-canva-profitable-3-billion-startup-phenom/?sh=233109af4a51 (archived at perma.cc/DLJ2-TCBH)

5 The Economic Times (2022) It took Melanie Perkins 100+ rejections over 3 years (& some faith!) to give life to design platform Canva, 13 July, https://economictimes.indiatimes.com/magazines/panache/it-took-melanie-perkins-100-rejections-over-3-yrs-some-faith-to-give-life-to-design-platform-canva/articleshow/92845505.cms?from=mdr (archived at perma.cc/5LCD-6R4R)

6 Zipkin, N (2019) She was told 'No' 100 times. Now this 31-year-old female founder runs a $1 billion business, *Entrepreneur*, 12 June, www.entrepreneur.com/leadership/she-was-told-no-100-times-now-this-31-year-old-female/310482 (archived at perma.cc/4GYS-5ZEN)

7   Roll, M (2022) Did you know that Canva's founder was rejected more
    than a hundred times?, www.linkedin.com/posts/martinroll_
    womeninbusiness-womenentrepreneurs-techforgood-activity-
    6952522521644556288-cCXX/?trk=public_profile_like_
    view&originalSubdomain=lv (archived at perma.cc/L59R-3XF9)

8   Forbes (2022) Melanie Perkins, Cofounder & CEO, Canva, www.
    forbes.com/profile/melanie-perkins/?sh=7b7f396d1265 (archived at
    perma.cc/85FD-Z4B8)

9   Zipkin, N (2019) She was told 'No' 100 times. Now this 31-year-old
    female founder runs a $1 billion business, *Entrepreneur*, 12 June,
    www.entrepreneur.com/leadership/she-was-told-no-100-times-now-
    this-31-year-old-female/310482 (archived at perma.cc/4GYS-5ZEN)

10 Konrad, A (2019) Canva uncovered: How a young Australian
    kitesurfer built a $3.2 billion (profitable!) startup phenom, *Forbes*,
    11 December, www.forbes.com/sites/alexkonrad/2019/12/11/
    inside-canva-profitable-3-billion-startup-phenom/?sh=233109af4a51
    (archived at perma.cc/DLJ2-TCBH)

11 TechCrunch (2013) Canva raises $3 million to make design accessible
    to everyone, 19 March, https://techcrunch.com/2013/03/19/canva-
    raises-3-million-to-make-design-accessible-to-everyone (archived at
    perma.cc/UH5M-P54U)

12 Konrad, A (2019) Canva uncovered: How a young Australian
    kitesurfer built a $3.2 billion (profitable!) startup phenom, *Forbes*, 11
    December, www.forbes.com/sites/alexkonrad/2019/12/11/inside-canva-
    profitable-3-billion-startup-phenom/?sh=233109af4a51 (archived at
    perma.cc/DLJ2-TCBH)

13 Konrad, A (2019) Canva uncovered: How a young Australian
    kitesurfer built a $3.2 billion (profitable!) startup phenom, *Forbes*,
    11 December, www.forbes.com/sites/alexkonrad/2019/12/11/
    inside-canva-profitable-3-billion-startup-phenom/?sh=233109af4a51
    (archived at perma.cc/DLJ2-TCBH)

14 Canva (2018) Canva raises $40M to earn Unicorn title, 9 January,
    https://www.canva.com/newsroom/news/canva-raises-40m-round-earn-
    unicorn-title (archived at perma.cc/DLH8-NKUJ)

15 Enlyft (2022) Companies using Canva, https://enlyft.com/tech/
    products/canva (archived at perma.cc/6E5S-WMFY)

16 Recon Research (2022) Canva, the $26 billion design startup, launches a productivity suite to take on Google Docs and Microsoft Office, 15 September, https://reconres.com/canva-the-26-billion-design-startup-launches-a-productivity-suite-to-take-on-google-docs-and-microsoft-office (archived at perma.cc/3VDS-2Y75)

17 Crozier, R (2021) Canva's infosec resourcing 'still growing' two years after large data breach, *IT News*, 2 September, www.itnews.com.au/news/canvas-infosec-resourcing-still-growing-two-years-after-large-data-breach-569282 (archived at perma.cc/P27Q-DDK5)

18 Connelly, C (2015) From making scarves to building a $165 million tech start-up: Canva's Melanie Perkins, *The Sydney Morning Herald*, 6 October, https://www.smh.com.au/technology/from-making-scarves-to-building-a-165-million-startup-canvas-melanie-perkins-20151006-gk2nda.html (archived at perma.cc/EG4J-ZP4U)

19 Canva (2022) Canva announces USD 40 billion valuation fueled by the global demand for visual communication, www.canva.com/newsroom/news/canva-announces-usd-40-billion-valuation-fueled-global-demand-visual-communication (archived at perma.cc/48PC-J4YH)

20 Forbes (2022) Melanie Perkins, cofounder & CEO, Canva, www.forbes.com/profile/melanie-perkins/?sh=7b7f396d1265 (archived at perma.cc/85FD-Z4B8)

21 Forbes (2022) Melanie Perkins, cofounder & CEO, Canva, www.forbes.com/profile/melanie-perkins/?sh=7b7f396d1265 (archived at perma.cc/85FD-Z4B8)

22 The Giving Pledge (2022) Melanie Perkins and Cliff Obrecht, https://givingpledge.org/pledger?pledgerId=427 (archived at perma.cc/5CZR-HL68)

23 Connelly, C (2015) From making scarves to building a $165 million tech start-up: Canva's Melanie Perkins, *The Sydney Morning Herald*, 6 October, https://www.smh.com.au/technology/from-making-scarves-to-building-a-165-million-startup-canvas-melanie-perkins-20151006-gk2nda.html (archived at perma.cc/EG4J-ZP4U)

24 Nine News Australia (2019) Australia's Melanie Perkins is the co-founder of Canva (Online video) 3 July, www.youtube.com/watch?v=CzJFy-TfP_s (archived at perma.cc/WH4B-XNUD)

25 Zipkin, N (2019) She was told 'No' 100 times. Now this 31-year-old female founder runs a $1 billion business, *Entrepreneur*, 12 June, www.entrepreneur.com/leadership/she-was-told-no-100-times-now-this-31-year-old-female/310482 (archived at perma.cc/4GYS-5ZEN)

26 Zipkin, N (2019) She was told 'No' 100 times. Now this 31-year-old female founder runs a $1 billion business, *Entrepreneur*, 12 June, www.entrepreneur.com/leadership/she-was-told-no-100-times-now-this-31-year-old-female/310482 (archived at perma.cc/4GYS-5ZEN)

27 Perkins, M (2018) A message for those who feel they're on the outside, from Canva co-founder Melanie Perkins, *Smart Company*, 24 September, www.smartcompany.com.au/startupsmart/advice/canva-co-founder-melanie-perkins-message (archived at perma.cc/7SB3-Z9NS)

CHAPTER THIRTEEN

Zhang Ruimin

Haier Group

Leadership philosophy
'THE KEY TO LEADERSHIP IS TO TRANSFORM YOUR EMPLOYEES
OR WORKERS INTO ENTREPRENEURS.'[1]

Haier is the world's biggest home appliances manufacturer,[2] employing more than 100,000 people globally and selling its products to over 160 countries and regions worldwide. Along with the Haier brand itself, the company's recognized brands include Candy, Hoover, Fisher & Paykel and GE Appliances. In 2021, the company achieved global revenues of $33.5 billion.[3] Not only is it a market leader in the white goods space, Haier is widely considered to be one of the most innovative companies in the world.

Haier was founded by Zhang Ruimin, who remains the company's honorary chairman after retiring as CEO and chairman in 2021. He was born in January 1949, in Laizhou City, in the eastern Chinese province of Shandong, to parents who worked in a clothing factory. Zhang's journey to becoming a world-renowned business leader and thinker effectively began in December 1984 when, aged 35, he became director of the Quingdao Refrigerator Factory. The factory was the predecessor business of Haier, which Ruimin subsequently established in 1991.[4]

At the time Zhang took charge, the Quingdao Refrigerator Factory was struggling with a lack of money and skills, while those workers it did have had gone several months without pay. Zhang managed to secure enough money to pay his dispirited employees and keep the business going.[5] He also focused on growing and training the factory staff to address the skills shortage.[6] Over the course of 30 years, Zhang turned the small, collectively owned, debt-ridden, loss-making factory into a multinational home appliances and electronic goods company that has been closely studied due to its ground-breaking approaches to business, leadership and management.

Over the years, Zhang has determinedly followed several principal business strategies including brand building, diversification and internationalization. These have enabled the company to enhance its reputation, expand its product portfolio well beyond refrigerators, and move into new markets. Besides pursuing organic growth, Haier has made several significant acquisitions – with the most prominent being the $5.4 billion purchase of GE Appliances in 2016. Haier's business philosophy is to have 'zero distance' with its customers so that it can respond to their rapidly changing daily needs.[7]

The Rendanheyi model

Zhang believes that today's fast-moving and technologically driven world demands employees with an entrepreneurial spirit. For that reason, he implemented a decentralized organizational approach at Haier, which is known as the Rendanheyi model. Rendanheyi effectively means that every employee should get to create value for customers.[8]

Under the Rendanheyi model, teams and individuals are empowered to create microenterprises within the context of the wider organization. These microenterprises can make their own business and hiring decisions, set compensation and decide how they want to allocate their resources. Some of these self-managing enterprises are known as 'users' and are market-facing. The others – known as 'nodes' – supply the users with component products, such as design and manufacturing, and support services such as HR, finance and IT. Regardless of whether the microenterprises are users or nodes, they are ultimately accountable to the company's customers.[9]

One of the most revolutionary aspects of the model is that microenterprises can choose whether they want to buy services from other microenterprises. If they prefer, they can go outside the organization and source external service providers. User microenterprises can request proposals from nodes and then negotiate with them over terms. Nodes that fail to deliver the quality of service demanded by their users risk losing their internal customers. To ensure collaboration in key areas, such as investment in technology, microenterprises are organized into platforms that are based on either the products they produce (such as washing machines) or their business activity (such as marketing).[10]

The Rendanheyi model was first proposed in 2005, but it wasn't an overnight success. It took time for employees' mindsets to adjust to the new approach and for them to get used to the idea of not working in silos. As part of the transition to the Rendanheyi model, the company let go more than 10,000 middle-level managers. It also started out with small pilot projects at first, then replicated them once they became successful. Not until 2016 did the model's impact on performance really start to show – the accumulated effect of many years' persistence with the microenterprise way of working.[11]

Haier has now organized itself into more than 4,000 microenterprises, with most having between 10 and 15 employees. The market-facing user microenterprises are divided into those that are helping to reinvent Haier's legacy appliance business and those that are entirely new businesses, serving new markets or developing new business models. They are set ambitious growth and profit targets and are expected to build their own ecosystems by collaborating with other businesses. Meanwhile, the node microenterprises also have their own targets, which may relate to areas such as reducing costs, improving quality, and driving greater use of automation. When targets are exceeded, workers in the microenterprise benefit from bonuses and profit sharing. On the other hand, a change of leadership is automatically triggered should a microenterprise fail to hit its baseline targets for three months in a row.[12]

In Zhang's view, innovation is not about new products and technologies but about developing new ways to create value for customers. Every individual in a microenterprise should be able to create value for customers. Zhang says that successful microenterprises within Haier are motivated, well-organized and good at seizing market opportunities. Those that do not embody all three of these characteristics do not tend to last. Some microenterprises manage to secure external venture capital and achieve IPOs. One of Haier's microenterprises, gaming computer brand ThundeRobot, successfully achieved an IPO in 2017 and was earning revenues of $394 million by 2021.[13]

To date, Haier's Rendanheyi model appears to have brought the company much success – along with praise from management experts. This is because it encourages employees to collaborate, innovate and compete with one another while taking direct ownership of a business activity. It also enables employees to enjoy the fruits of their efforts. Critics might argue, however, that it is a slightly unforgiving approach to business that punishes failure and could discourage truly radical experimentation and innovation. Time will ultimately be the judge as to whether such criticism is valid.

Over the years, Zhang has been awarded numerous accolades for his pioneering approach to business and leadership. In August 2004, for example, he was ranked sixth among Asia's most influential business figures by *Fortune*. A year later, the *Financial Times* included him on its list of the world's 50 most respected leaders.[14] In 2016, he was awarded the Legend in Leadership Award by the Yale School of Management. The following year, he was named in the *Fortune* list of the World's 50 Greatest Leaders.[15] Zhang, who is a member of the Chinese Communist Party, has also regularly featured on the prestigious Thinkers50 ranking of the world's leading management thinkers.

Many of China's top entrepreneurs are largely unknown to Western business audiences. That is not the case with Zhang, who has shared his business philosophy with the world through writing articles and speaking at events. Furthermore, he has himself been the subject of numerous media stories over the years. Notably, in 1998, Zhang became the first Chinese entrepreneur to lecture at Harvard.

Secrets to success

In an article for the *Harvard Business Review*, published in 2007, Zhang outlined how his approach to leadership had evolved over the previous two decades. In his early days at the Quingdao Refrigerator Factory, he focused on restoring goodwill with staff members who had not been paid. Once that was achieved, he cracked down on discipline, introducing new rules that prohibited urinating and defecating in the workshops and stealing company property. This helped to improve the atmosphere in the workplace, boosting employee morale. He also made a point of setting a good example and bearing hardships – which might involve sitting on a camp stool in the aisle if he could find no available seat on a train. Later, he prioritized acting with conviction so that his people knew he'd do whatever it took to make sure that things happened.[16]

The same article revealed that Zhang had a deep inner resilience that he had developed from living through China's Cultural Revolution. In 1966, Mao Zedong, then Chairman of the Communist Party, unleashed a brutal campaign against his perceived enemies within the party. Between 500,000 and two million people are thought to have died during the purge, which caused social and economic turmoil and effectively plunged the country into a state of virtual civil war. The revolution finally ended with Mao's death in 1976.[17] What Zhang took away from this tragic episode in his country's history was that 'all kinds of challenges can be overcome'.[18]

To develop his unconventional business strategy, Zhang has combined traditional Chinese culture with techniques from Western management gurus. For example, his thinking on individual empowerment is influenced by the ancient Chinese philosopher Lao Tzu, who said: 'In the highest antiquity, the people did not know they had rulers.'[19] Zhang has also read numerous management books by the late management thinker Peter Drucker, whose views he admires. In particular, he learned from Drucker that what counts in business is not how many people you manage, but the results you get out of them. Indeed, Drucker's thinking influenced Haier's entrepreneurial Rendanheyi model.[20]

Zhang is known for setting high standards and has always been committed to producing high-quality products. In fact, soon after his appointment to the Quingdao Refrigerator Factory, he famously directed employees to smash up 76 defective refrigerators.[21] He also believes that timing is crucial in business and advocates doing the right thing, at the right time. For example, he puts his company's early successes in the 1980s down to it producing quality goods during a period when they were sought after, but hard to find.[22] In addition, he argues that it's essential to keep up with the times.[23]

In terms of his attributes as a business leader, Zhang has described himself as having 'an indomitable will'. Once he has set his mind to achieving a goal, he won't stop until he achieves it.[24]

LEADERSHIP LESSONS FROM ZHANG RUIMIN

- **Bring out the entrepreneurial nature of your team**. Empower them to make their own business and hiring decisions and allocate their resources as they see fit.

- **Stay close to your customer**. The closer you stay to your customer, the more easily you will be able to adapt to their needs and wants over time.

- **Make quality the cornerstone of your business model**. There will always be customers for quality goods and services.

- **Don't expect overnight success when you roll out a new project, initiative or organizational model**. It takes time to change people's mindsets and get them used to new ways of working.

- **Be positive in the face of challenges**. Even the most difficult obstacles can be overcome.

Notes

1 Wharton School of the University of Pennsylvania (2018) For Haier's Zhang Ruimin, success means creating the future, *Knowledge at Wharton*, 20 April, https://knowledge.wharton.upenn.edu/article/haiers-zhang-ruimin-success-means-creating-the-future (archived at perma.cc/HQ3R-M4CW)

2 Statista (2022) Selected leading home appliances manufacturers worldwide ranked by revenue in 2021, www.statista.com/statistics/266689/net-sales-of-leading-home-appliance-manufacturers-worlwide (archived at perma.cc/RA8T-9RLU)

3 Haier (2022) Haier in a nutshell, www.haier-europe.com/en_GB/about-haier (archived at perma.cc/T5BZ-9AWJ)

4 Haier (2022) Zhang Ruimin, www.haier.com/global/about-haier/ceo (archived at perma.cc/85PA-JZNU)

5 Ruimin, Z (2007) Raising Haier, *Harvard Business Review*, February, https://hbr.org/2007/02/raising-haier (archived at perma.cc/889V-8DGF)

6 Wharton School of the University of Pennsylvania (2018) For Haier's Zhang Ruimin, success means creating the future, *Knowledge at Wharton*, 20 April, https://knowledge.wharton.upenn.edu/article/haiers-zhang-ruimin-success-means-creating-the-future (archived at perma.cc/HQ3R-M4CW)

7 Haier (2022) Haier in a nutshell, www.haier-europe.com/en_GB/about-haier (archived at perma.cc/T5BZ-9AWJ)

8 McKinsey Quarterly (2021) Shattering the status quo: A conversation with Haier's Zhang Ruimin, 27 July, www.mckinsey.com/capabilities/people-and-organizational-performance/our-insights/shattering-the-status-quo-a-conversation-with-haiers-zhang-ruimin (archived at perma.cc/UX3Z-E4VQ)

9 Gordon, J (2022) Rendanheyi model – explained, *The Business Professor*, 5 October, https://thebusinessprofessor.com/en_US/mgmt-operations/rendanheyi-model-explained (archived at perma.cc/CHL3-NARP)

10   Hamel, G and Zanini, M (2018) The end of bureaucracy, *Harvard Business Review*, December, https://hbr.org/2018/11/the-end-of-bureaucracy (archived at perma.cc/5QNP-3MYD)

11   Wharton School of the University of Pennsylvania (2018) For Haier's Zhang Ruimin, success means creating the future, *Knowledge at Wharton*, 20 April, https://knowledge.wharton.upenn.edu/article/haiers-zhang-ruimin-success-means-creating-the-future (archived at perma.cc/HQ3R-M4CW)

12   Hamel, G and Zanini, M (2018) The end of bureaucracy, *Harvard Business Review*, December, https://hbr.org/2018/11/the-end-of-bureaucracy (archived at perma.cc/5QNP-3MYD)

13   Wharton School of the University of Pennsylvania (2018) For Haier's Zhang Ruimin, success means creating the future, *Knowledge at Wharton*, 20 April, https://knowledge.wharton.upenn.edu/article/haiers-zhang-ruimin-success-means-creating-the-future (archived at perma.cc/HQ3R-M4CW)

14   Warton University of Pennsylvania (2009) Zhang Ruimin, http://www.whartonbeijing09.com/bio-zhang-r.html (archived at perma.cc/4T3N-QYZL)

15   Haier (2022) Zhang Ruimin, www.haier.com/global/about-haier/ceo (archived at perma.cc/85PA-JZNU)

16   Ruimin, Z (2007) Raising Haier, *Harvard Business Review*, February, https://hbr.org/2007/02/raising-haier (archived at perma.cc/889V-8DGF)

17   Phillips, T (2016) The Cultural Revolution: All you need to know about China's political convulsion, *The Guardian*, 11 May, www.theguardian.com/world/2016/may/11/the-cultural-revolution-50-years-on-all-you-need-to-know-about-chinas-political-convulsion (archived at perma.cc/S5RQ-JVHW)

18   Ruimin, Z (2007) Raising Haier, *Harvard Business Review*, February, https://hbr.org/2007/02/raising-haier (archived at perma.cc/889V-8DGF)

19   Ruimin, Z (2007) Raising Haier, *Harvard Business Review*, February, https://hbr.org/2007/02/raising-haier (archived at perma.cc/889V-8DGF)

20 Wharton School of the University of Pennsylvania (2018) For Haier's Zhang Ruimin, success means creating the future, *Knowledge at Wharton*, 20 April, https://knowledge.wharton.upenn.edu/article/haiers-zhang-ruimin-success-means-creating-the-future (archived at perma.cc/HQ3R-M4CW)

21 McKinsey Quarterly (2021) Shattering the status quo: A conversation with Haier's Zhang Ruimin, 27 July, www.mckinsey.com/capabilities/people-and-organizational-performance/our-insights/shattering-the-status-quo-a-conversation-with-haiers-zhang-ruimin (archived at perma.cc/UX3Z-E4VQ)

22 Wharton School of the University of Pennsylvania (2018) For Haier's Zhang Ruimin, success means creating the future, *Knowledge at Wharton*, 20 April, https://knowledge.wharton.upenn.edu/article/haiers-zhang-ruimin-success-means-creating-the-future (archived at perma.cc/HQ3R-M4CW)

23 McKinsey Quarterly (2021) Shattering the status quo: A conversation with Haier's Zhang Ruimin, 27 July, www.mckinsey.com/capabilities/people-and-organizational-performance/our-insights/shattering-the-status-quo-a-conversation-with-haiers-zhang-ruimin (archived at perma.cc/UX3Z-E4VQ)

24 Ruimin, Z (2007) Raising Haier, *Harvard Business Review*, February, https://hbr.org/2007/02/raising-haier (archived at perma.cc/889V-8DGF)

CHAPTER FOURTEEN

Uğur Şahin and Özlem Türeci

BioNTech

Leadership philosophy
'WE ARE NOT IMPORTANT, IT'S THE TASK WE ARE DOING.'[1]

On 9 November 2020, the Covid-19 pandemic was raging around the world, spreading fear and uncertainty, triggering onerous social restrictions, and having already claimed more than 1.2 million lives.[2] It was on this day that US drug-manufacturing giant Pfizer unveiled a pioneering vaccine against the Covid-19 virus. The vaccine had been developed in partnership with a then little-known German biotechnology company called BioNTech. 'Today,' said Pfizer in a press release, 'is a great day for science and humanity.'[3]

The Pfizer-BioNTech vaccine – which boasted an efficacy rate above 90 per cent – made use of a 'messenger

RNA' (mRNA) molecule created in a laboratory. The mRNA molecule in the vaccine was a synthetic version of the mRNA that naturally exists in human cells and carries protein information from the DNA in a cell's nucleus to its cytoplasm, the watery interior of a cell beyond the nucleus.

The role of the synthetic mRNA module was to teach real bodily cells how to make a protein that would trigger an immune response against the virus. Essentially, it was a set of do-it-yourself instructions to help the human body make the antibodies that would enable it to fight Covid-19. Since the mRNA vaccine did not contain an actual virus, it marked a departure from traditional vaccines that trigger an immune response by inserting a weakened or dead germ directly into the body.

Scientists had been studying, and experimenting with, mRNA since the 1960s. In fact, mRNA vaccines were seen as potential methods to elicit immunity against cancer and infectious diseases such as influenza, rabies and Zika virus. Nevertheless, mRNA technology had not been approved for widespread use prior to the pandemic.

The pandemic showed that not only were mRNA vaccines safe, they could be manufactured quickly at scale and modified easily in response to virus mutations. In fact, so successful were both the Pfizer-BioNTech vaccine and another mRNA vaccine developed by US drug manufacturer Moderna that mRNA technology is now seen as a promising option for fighting other life-threatening diseases, including cancer, HIV, malaria and tuberculosis.

History of innovation

Husband-and-wife team Uğur Şahin and Özlem Türeci, together with their co-founders, started BioNTech in the western German city of Mainz back in 2008. At that time, they could not have foreseen that one day their business would play a pivotal role in turning the tide against a pandemic of respiratory illness, helping to save millions of lives in the process. The pair – who are both oncologists specializing in immunotherapy – had a history of innovating in the field of fighting life-threatening diseases. They had previously co-founded Ganymed Pharmaceuticals, a developer of antibody drugs for the treatment of solid cancers. BioNTech, likewise, was mostly focused on developing cancer treatments – using a wider range of technologies, including mRNA – but it had never brought a product to market by the time the pandemic struck.[4]

While Şahin and Türeci are German citizens, they both have Turkish roots. Şahin was born in Iskenderun, Turkey, in September 1965, but moved with his family to the north-west German city of Cologne when he was four years old. His parents worked at a Ford factory, but he wanted to become a doctor and ended up becoming a physician at the University of Cologne. Türeci was born in Siegen, West Germany, in March 1967, to Turkish immigrants. Her father was a surgeon, which sparked her interest in medicine at an early age, and she studied to become a doctor.

After meeting on a hospital ward, the pair discovered a shared passion for treating cancer and decided to work in medical research. Specifically, they sought to explore whether the body's own immune system could be trained to destroy tumours. Initially they focused on research and teaching, with Şahin working in the lab of Rolf Zinkernagel, winner of the 1996 Nobel Prize in medicine, at the University of Zurich. Then they cofounded Ganymed Pharmaceuticals in 2001 and later BioNTech. The scientists married in 2002, but such was their dedication to their work that on the day they tied the knot, they returned to the lab after the ceremony. In 2016, Ganymed Pharmaceuticals was sold to Japanese pharmaceutical company Astellas Pharma for €422 million.

Despite suddenly finding themselves very wealthy, Şahin and Türeci continued to persevere with their immunotherapy research. By 2019, BioNTech had gone public, listing on the NASDAQ stock exchange, and was collaborating with the Bill & Melinda Gates Foundation – a not-for-profit fighting poverty and disease – on programmes to prevent HIV and tuberculosis infections.[5] That same year, Şahin received the German Cancer Award, a prestigious award that recognizes outstanding achievements in the field of clinical oncology research, translational research and experimental research in Germany, Austria and Switzerland. He was also awarded the Mustafa Prize, a biennial prize granted to top Muslim researchers and scientists in the fields of science and technology.

After reading an article in medical journal *The Lancet* in January 2020, Şahin became convinced that a virulent new coronavirus, then spreading quickly in parts of China, would metamorphose into a full-blown pandemic. He also believed that his own business, BioNTech, could use the mRNA technology it had already developed as part of global efforts to develop a vaccine. Recognizing that it was in a race against time, BioNTech set to work on what it called Project Lightspeed, assigning hundreds of staff to the initiative. 'It felt not like an opportunity but a duty to do it,' Şahin said in an interview.[6]

Şahin realized that BioNTech would need a partner to bring a vaccine to market and Pfizer was a logical choice since the two companies had been working together on a flu vaccine since 2018. In March 2020, with the deadly new virus beginning to sweep the planet, the pair agreed to collaborate on a vaccine against what became known as Covid-19.

After the vaccine was unveiled in November, it received swift approval by countries around the world. Soon it started being injected into people's arms. By October 2022, more than 3.8 billion Pfizer-BioNTech Covid-19 vaccines had been shipped to 180 countries around the world.[7] In August 2021, it was announced that the vaccine had been rebranded and would henceforth be known as Comirnaty.

Spurred on by their success with the Covid vaccine, Şahin and Türeci are now exploring how mRNA technology can be used to treat cancer by targeting affected cells for destruction. They have several trials under way, including one where patients are given a personalized vaccine to spur their immune system to attack the disease. The pair are hopeful that mRNA technology could lead to new treatments for cancers such as melanoma and bowel cancer, and believe that cancer vaccines could be widely available before 2030. For now, however, they are careful to manage public expectations. 'As scientists, we are always hesitant to say we have a cure for cancer,' Türeci told the

BBC in October 2022. 'We have a number of break-throughs and we will continue to work on them.'[8]

They were never in it for the money, but today Şahin and Türeci are billionaires. Their company, BioNTech, was valued at $35 billion as of January 2023[9] and by the end of 2021 it employed nearly 3,100 full-time staff members.[10] Şahin remains CEO of the company; Türeci is its chief medical officer. Türeci is also president of the Germany-based Association for Cancer Immunotherapy. In 2021, the pair of scientists received Germany's Order of Merit for their achievements in developing a Covid-19 vaccine, one of the country's highest honours.

Secrets to success

They might be two of the world's most successful scientists, but Şahin and Türeci are renowned for their immense modesty. An article in *The New York Times* in November 2020 gave some insight into their living circumstances at the time, highlighting that they lived in a modest apartment near their office, rode bicycles to work and did not own a car. The same article also quoted Albert Bourla, Pfizer's chief executive, saying that Şahin is a 'scientist and a man of principles'.[11]

As scientists, Şahin and Türeci took a matter-of-fact approach to the challenge of finding a vaccine and refused to contemplate defeat. 'We have been in the innovation field for many years, we are habitualized not to think about the scenario that it might not work but rather to ensure that we address all potential flaws,' Türeci told *The Times*.[12]

In the same interview, Türeci described science as her 'high passion', explaining: 'I think the most noble thing you can use science and technology for is to serve the people.' Meanwhile, Şahin admitted to being driven by curiosity and wanting to understand how things work. He was also motivated to try to change the world for the better after having to tell cancer patients in hospital that nothing more could be done to help them. 'As a scientist, I knew that we are not doing everything that is possible so we need to do more,' he said. 'That's what drives me on.'[13]

When founding BioNTech, Şahin wanted to ensure that everyone who worked at the company not only had scientific skills but also had the ability to become a leader who managed others. He also wanted to promote an open culture where all employees felt able to contribute and has said: 'It's about people feeling encouraged to express their opinions, concerns, and lessons learned from mistakes.'[14]

Şahin and Türeci were willing to take risks. Nevertheless, they also understood their own limitations as businesspeople. That is why they were careful to bring into BioNTech people who understood finances, dealmaking and business development.[15]

Şahin's advice to other would-be entrepreneurs is to 'identify what you love'. Talking about the mission in business that he and his wife share, he has said: 'If we can do something useful for humanity, and if we can do something useful for patients, then it could be also a business. At the end of the day, the pharmaceutical business is about helping people. We are really driven by the fact we want to help, and to reduce the disease burden, and to reduce suffering.'[16]

LEADERSHIP LESSONS FROM UĞUR ŞAHIN AND ÖZLEM TÜRECI

- **Good partners are key**. Identify like-minded people and organizations that share your vision.

- **Understand your own limitations**. By hiring other people with specific expertise, you will be able to compensate for your own weaknesses and build a strong team to accomplish the common goal.

- **Don't expect overnight results**. You need to be patient and persistent to succeed in the long run.

- **Do what you love**. If you focus on what you really care about, you are setting yourself up to excel.

- **Understand how you can serve humanity**. Helping others is what drives success.

Notes

1 Thomson, A and Sylvester, R (2020) The Covid-19 vaccine is our duty and passion. We're not important, *The Times*, 14 November, www.thetimes.co.uk/article/the-vaccine-is-our-duty-and-passion-were-not-important-qxj0bnkw6 (archived at perma.cc/K488-VKZ2)

2 World Health Organization (2020) Weekly epidemiological update, 10 November, www.who.int/publications/m/item/weekly-epidemiological-update---10-november-2020 (archived at perma.cc/6XKG-AKU9)

3 Pfizer (2020) Pfizer and BioNTech announce vaccine candidate against COVID-19 achieved success in first interim analysis from phase 3 study, 9 November, https://www.pfizer.com/news/press-release/press-release-detail/pfizer-and-biontech-announce-vaccine-candidate-against (archived at perma.cc/Y9AF-4NF4)

4   Gelles, D (2020) The husband-and-wife team behind the leading vaccine to solve Covid-19, *The New York Times*, 10 November, www.nytimes.com/2020/11/10/business/biontech-covid-vaccine.html (archived at perma.cc/NKU9-BRB2)

5   Gelles, D (2020) The husband-and-wife team behind the leading vaccine to solve Covid-19, *The New York Times*, 10 November, www.nytimes.com/2020/11/10/business/biontech-covid-vaccine.html (archived at perma.cc/NKU9-BRB2)

6   Gelles, D (2020) The husband-and-wife team behind the leading vaccine to solve Covid-19, *The New York Times*, 10 November, www.nytimes.com/2020/11/10/business/biontech-covid-vaccine.html (archived at perma.cc/NKU9-BRB2)

7   Pfizer (2022) Our commitment to equitable access, www.pfizer.com/science/coronavirus/vaccine/working-to-reach-everyone-everywhere (archived at perma.cc/CJB6-969C)

8   Walsh, F (2022) BioNTech: Could Covid vaccine technology crack cancer?, *BBC*, 15 October, www.bbc.co.uk/news/health-63247997 (archived at perma.cc/LAL6-LSLG)

9   CompaniesMarketCap.com (2023) Market capitalization of BioNTech, 23 January, https://companiesmarketcap.com/biontech/marketcap (archived at perma.cc/5LFV-82KD)

10 Mikulic, M (2022) Number of employees at BioNTech SE from 2019 to 2021, *Statista*, 4 April, https://www.statista.com/statistics/1300627/biontech-employees-number (archived at perma.cc/BWL5-P8TA)

11 Gelles, D (2020) The husband-and-wife team behind the leading vaccine to solve Covid-19, *The New York Times*, 10 November, www.nytimes.com/2020/11/10/business/biontech-covid-vaccine.html (archived at perma.cc/NKU9-BRB2)

12 Thomson, A and Sylvester R (2020) The Covid-19 vaccine is our duty and passion. We're not important, *The Times*, 14 November, www.thetimes.co.uk/article/the-vaccine-is-our-duty-and-passion-were-not-important-qxj0bnkw6 (archived at perma.cc/K488-VKZ2)

13 Thomson, A and Sylvester R (2020) The Covid-19 vaccine is our duty and passion. We're not important, *The Times*, 14 November, www.thetimes.co.uk/article/the-vaccine-is-our-duty-and-passion-were-not-important-qxj0bnkw6 (archived at perma.cc/K488-VKZ2)

14 Wright, W (2020) How one professor built two billion-dollar biotechs, *Life Science Leader*, 1 June, www.lifescienceleader.com/doc/how-one-professor-built-two-billion-dollar-biotechs-0001 (archived at perma.cc/2Z26-NY2W)

15 Frankly Speaking, S1 E9 (2021) Dr. Ugur Sahin Founder and CEO of BioNTech (Online video) *Arab News*, 8 March, www.youtube.com/watch?v=2q8qR3i2u0I (archived at perma.cc/W5SA-8QK7)

16 Frankly Speaking, S1 E9 (2021) Dr. Ugur Sahin Founder and CEO of BioNTech (Online video) *Arab News*, 8 March, www.youtube.com/watch?v=2q8qR3i2u0I (archived at perma.cc/W5SA-8QK7)

CHAPTER FIFTEEN

Whitney Wolfe Herd

Bumble

Leadership philosophy
'GO AFTER THE LIFE YOU WANT.'[1]

Bumble is an online networking platform that connects people with others with the aim of building romantic relationships, friendships and business connections. It has three modes: Date, BFF and Bizz. In the case of heterosexual dating, women make the first move on Bumble Date, which puts them in the driving seat when it comes to initiating new romantic relationships. Bumble BFF is a way for people to expand their social circle or make new friends when they move to a new city. Bumble Buzz enables people to expand their professional network, allowing them to find mentors, team members and potentially exciting career opportunities.

In an internet world that can be cruel, unforgiving and even downright dangerous, Bumble prioritizes kindness and respect, 'providing a safe online community for users to build new relationships'.[2] Today Bumble boasts a community of over 100 million people, living across six different continents.[3] Its revenues for 2021 stood at $765 million.[4]

Bumble was founded in 2014 by Whitney Wolfe Herd who had a mission to 'challenge the antiquated rules of dating'.[5] The entrepreneur was born Whitney Wolfe in Salt Lake City, Utah, in July 1989, only changing her surname to Wolfe Herd after she married Texan oil heir and restauranteur Michael Herd in 2017.

Prior to starting Bumble, Wolfe Herd was aware of many 'smart, wonderful women' who were 'waiting around for men to ask them out, to take their numbers, or to start up a conversation on a dating app'. She believed that in an age when women were making huge advances in their professional careers, the gender dynamics of dating and romance remained very outdated. 'I thought, what if I could flip that on its head?' she has said. 'What if women made the first move, and sent the first message?'[6] The name of the platform is inspired by queen bees and the idea of women being in charge.[7]

Bumble follows the same fundamental principle as another well-known dating app, Tinder, which was founded in 2012. In other words, you swipe right if, yes, you like the look of someone's profile and swipe left if no, you don't. If two people swipe yes for each other, it's a match and they can connect with each other. They then have 24 hours to connect.

Where Bumble differs from Tinder is that in the case of heterosexual matches, it is always down to the woman to make the first move or the connection will expire. With Tinder, which is owned by online dating giant Match Group, women have to enable a specific setting if they want the power to make the first move with a male match. As a basic service, Bumble is free – like Tinder – but it also offers premium subscription features, such as Bumble Boost, which gives users additional features including the option to extend their time on their current matches. Additionally, users can make in-app purchases.

The similarity between the designs of Bumble and Tinder is no coincidence. Wolfe Herd was vice-president of marketing and co-founder of Tinder before she left the company in 2014 and subsequently sued it for sexual harassment and discrimination. She alleged that Justin Mateen, her former boss and boyfriend, had called her a 'slut' and a 'whore' in front of Tinder's then-CEO, Sean Rad.[8] The case was later resolved, with no admission of wrongdoing.[9] While she was waiting for the case to settle, Wolfe Herd was subjected to a barrage of online abuse that extended as far as rape and murder threats. In response, she deleted her Twitter account and started to work on the idea of a women-only social network that focused on positivity.[10]

Wolfe Herd ended up embarking on a new course, however, after meeting with Andrey Andreev, a Russian-born, London-based entrepreneur who had founded online dating network Badoo back in 2006. Andreev had previously met her when she was working at Tinder, and had been impressed with her energy and passion. He offered to back her if she started an online dating app that focused on the needs of women. Significantly, Wolfe Herd's legal settlement with Tinder had not included a non-compete clause so she was free to take the other entrepreneur up on his offer.

Andreev made an initial investment of about $10 million and took 79 per cent of the Texas-based company. Wolfe Herd was to be the founder and CEO with a 20 per cent ownership stake, leaving 1 per cent of the equity to share with other investors. The Bumble app went live in December 2014, and proved to be an instant hit despite the online dating market already being a crowded space. It turned out that women were keen to empower themselves. The app was downloaded 100,000 times in the first month alone.[11] By 2020, it had become Tinder's primary competitor among people aged under 35.[12] In fact, Bumble's success ultimately led to Tinder's owner, Match Group, offering to buy it – only to be turned down.[13]

Today Bumble is used by people in more than 150 markets around the world. In 2018, it attracted headlines when it launched in India with the support of Indian actress Priyanka Chopra, herself a Bumble investor. The move was considered risky at the time due to India's high levels of sexual violence as well as casual dating being a new and mostly urban phenomenon in the country. Indian women only need to provide the first initial of their name on the app, not their first names or surnames, and they can use the app to report bad behaviour.[14] Wolfe Herd believes that the markets with the most misogynist mindsets present the greatest opportunities for Bumble.[15]

In November 2019, Wolfe Herd stepped up to become CEO of MagicLab, Bumble's parent company, after Andreev sold his majority stake in MagicLab to private equity firm Blackstone for approximately $3 billion. The sale followed an investigation by *Forbes* earlier that year, which alleged a toxic culture at Badoo's London headquarters. Allegations of racism and sexism were also made against Andreev himself – allegations that he denied.[16] The controversy put Wolfe Herd in a very difficult position since Andreev was her friend, her business partner and her mentor, and yet misogyny and other forms of prejudice went against everything that she and her brand stood for. In a statement she admitted to feeling 'mortified' by the allegations while stating that she had 'never seen or heard' any of the behaviour described in the *Forbes* report.[17]

In July 2020, MagicLab was renamed Bumble, making Bumble the parent company of Badoo, which has a big following in Europe and Latin America. Wolfe Herd said the move would give the business 'one constructive, cohesive, and unified mission and value set'.[18] MagicLab's other dating apps, the gay dating app Chappy, and the over-50s dating app Lumen, were both merged with Bumble by the end of that year.

In February 2021, Bumble became a public company when it listed on the NASDAQ stock exchange, closing the first day of trading with a market capitalization of around $7.7 billion.[19] At that point, Wolfe Herd became the world's youngest self-made female billionaire[20] and the youngest woman to have taken a company public. She was just 31 at the time.

Secrets to success

Certainly, Wolfe Herd 'walks the talk' when it comes to being a successful and empowered woman. Not only is she the CEO of a publicly listed company with customers right across the planet, she is also a tireless advocate of gender equality, who is determined to fight the ongoing misogyny that continues to exist in the world. In 2019, for example, she successfully lobbied the Texas state legislature to pass a law that banned the sending of unsolicited nude images.

Wolfe Herd's belief in equality also extends to other aspects of diversity and inclusion. She is committed to fighting racism, with Bumble being a public supporter of the Black Lives Matter movement. She also has a diversity team that is working to solve the challenges around prejudice faced by users of the Bumble app who come from minority or marginalized groups, including those with disabilities and sight impairment.[21]

From Wolfe Herd's perspective, the point of being in business is to make a positive difference to the lives of others. 'I am a firm believer that you cannot start a business just to start a business,' she has said. 'You have to start a business to solve a personal pain point. You have to wait till your life hands you that struggle and innovate from there.'[22] Her personal pain point is online toxicity and abuse – something she has dedicated her life to addressing.[23] What keeps her going through difficult days is remembering the people she's brought together – and the marriages, babies and general happiness that have ensued.[24]

Wolfe Herd showed a natural entrepreneurial bent from a very young age, which helps to explain her rapid rise to success in business. While she was still in college, she started the Help Us Project, which sold organic bamboo tote bags for the benefit of the Ocean Futures Society. Subsequently she founded the Tender Heart clothing line, based in Nepal, to raise awareness around human trafficking and fair trade. After graduating from the Southern Methodist University in Dallas, Texas, she worked for New York incubator Hatch Labs, which is where she first got to know several of the Tinder co-founders.[25]

A famously hard worker, Wolfe Herd once used to check her emails every two hours through the night and get up at 4.30 am to start work. She has since recognized this as toxic behaviour that does not set a good example to other would-be entrepreneurs.[26] Nevertheless, she openly admits to being 'obsessed' with Bumble. That includes being obsessed with the company's customers, its team, and its commitment to future innovation.[27] She said: 'I don't think you can create change unless you have a certain level of addiction to what you're doing because you have everybody waiting for you to fall.'[28]

A marketing genius, Wolfe Herd has ensured that Bumble stands out in a crowded marketplace through the delivery of a compelling user experience. The branding of the dating app is clear and bright, but feminine and very much in keeping with the 'queen bee' theme. The company's headquarters in Austin, Texas, are painted a bright yellow colour and inside the décor pays homage to beehives. Bumble's values – including kindness, respect, safety and accountability – inform the experience that the brand delivers to its customers.[29] Since its launch, the company has deployed a wide range of marketing methods including social media ads, content marketing, influencer marketing and 'offline marketing' on subways and buses. Over time, Bumble has consistently innovated – during the Covid-19 pandemic, for example, it released 'Virtual Dating' badges for users who were exclusively available to date online.[30]

On a personal level, Wolfe Herd is authentic and honest about the challenges she has faced, both as a leader and as a person. She has admitted to suffering from serious post-natal depression and anxiety after her son was born.[31] She also says that, as a very shy person, she didn't particularly set out to become the public face of her company. That came about as a result of the effort she put in to making it a success and the fact the business was built out of her personal story. She says what's beautiful about Bumble now is that 'it's so much bigger than me… It will outlive me and that's the goal'.[32]

LEADERSHIP LESSONS FROM WHITNEY WOLFE HERD

- **Don't get mad, get even**. If you find yourself treated poorly in business, don't waste your time and energy on feeling resentful. Instead, focus on being even better than you already are and proving your capability to others.

- **Start a business to solve your personal pain point**. The chances are other people will have similar pain points and want to use your product or service.

- **Embed strong values right at the heart of your organization**. People will want to buy from you if they know what you stand for and believe that your values align with theirs.

- **Don't be afraid of entering a crowded market**. Even if you have competitors offering the same product or service, you can still set your business apart through clever execution and marketing.
- **Be a little bit 'obsessed'**. By focusing relentlessly on your business, you will outperform your competitors and prove your doubters wrong.

Notes

1   CNN Business (2018) Men swipe right but women make the first move (Online video) https://edition.cnn.com/2018/10/03/tech/bumble-india-priyanka-chopra/index.html (archived at perma.cc/3BMH-2FUR)

2   Bumble (2022) We're not just for dating anymore, https://bumble.com/en (archived at perma.cc/YG8Y-SBDT)

3   Wolfe Herd, W (2022) A letter from Whitney Wolfe Herd, Bumble founder and CEO, https://bumble.com/the-buzz/a-letter-from-whitney-wolfe-herd-founder-and-ceo (archived at perma.cc/6YCE-ECYX)

4   Curry, D (2022) Bumble revenue and usage statistics, *Business of Apps*, 6 September, www.businessofapps.com/data/bumble-statistics (archived at perma.cc/KR9M-U463)

5   Bumble (2022) We're not just for dating anymore, https://bumble.com/en (archived at perma.cc/YG8Y-SBDT)

6   Wolfe Herd, W (2022) A letter from Whitney Wolfe Herd, Bumble founder and CEO, https://bumble.com/the-buzz/a-letter-from-whitney-wolfe-herd-founder-and-ceo (archived at perma.cc/6YCE-ECYX)

7   Planet Bee Foundation (2022) The bee in popular culture: Bumble, www.planetbee.org/planet-bee-blog/the-bee-in-popular-culture-bumble (archived at perma.cc/JV4V-TXKQ)

8   Gayles, C (2014) Tinder dating app hit with sexual harassment lawsuit, *CNN*, 1 July, https://money.cnn.com/2014/07/01/technology/social/tinder-sexist-lawsuit/index.html (archived at perma.cc/438A-7WUF)

9 O'Brien, SA (2019) She sued Tinder, founded Bumble and now, at 30, is the CEO of a $3 billion dating empire, *CNN*, 13 December, https://edition.cnn.com/2019/12/13/tech/whitney-wolfe-herd-bumble-risk-takers/index.html (archived at perma.cc/D8E2-GBMR)

10 O'Connor, C (2017) Billion-dollar Bumble: How Whitney Wolfe Herd built America's fastest-growing dating app, *Forbes*, 14 November, https://www.forbes.com/sites/clareoconnor/2017/11/14/billion-dollar-bumble-how-whitney-wolfe-herd-built-americas-fastest-growing-dating-app/?sh=2e1b1c97248b (archived at perma.cc/7WF9-4WGK)

11 O'Connor, C (2017) Billion-dollar Bumble: How Whitney Wolfe Herd built America's fastest-growing dating app, *Forbes*, 14 November, https://www.forbes.com/sites/clareoconnor/2017/11/14/billion-dollar-bumble-how-whitney-wolfe-herd-built-americas-fastest-growing-dating-app/?sh=2e1b1c97248b (archived at perma.cc/7WF9-4WGK)

12 Curry, D (2022) Bumble revenue and usage statistics, *Business of Apps*, 6 September, www.businessofapps.com/data/bumble-statistics (archived at perma.cc/KR9M-U463)

13 Tepper, F (2017) Match Group tried to acquire Bumble for $450 million, *TechCrunch*, 23 August, https://techcrunch.com/2017/08/23/match-group-tried-to-acquire-bumble-for-450-million (archived at perma.cc/7RVV-ZRQC)

14 O'Brien, SA (2018) Bumble to expand to India with the help of actress Priyanka Chopra, *CNN Business*, 4 October, https://edition.cnn.com/2018/10/03/tech/bumble-india-priyanka-chopra/index.html (archived at perma.cc/3BMH-2FUR)

15 O'Brien, SA (2019) She sued Tinder, founded Bumble and now, at 30, is the CEO of a $3 billion dating empire, *CNN*, 13 December, https://edition.cnn.com/2019/12/13/tech/whitney-wolfe-herd-bumble-risk-takers/index.html (archived at perma.cc/D8E2-GBMR)

16 Au-Yeung, A (2019) Sex, drugs, misogyny and sleaze at the HQ of Bumble's owner, *Forbes*, 8 July, www.forbes.com/sites/angelauyeung/2019/07/08/exclusive-investigation-sex-drugs-misogyny-and-sleaze-at-the-hq-of-bumbles-owner/?sh=62f154606308 (archived at perma.cc/F4KK-9TFZ)

17 Matney, L (2019) Bumble chief responds to reports of misconduct at parent company, *TechCrunch*, 9 July, https://techcrunch.com/2019/07/09/

bumble-chief-responds-to-reports-of-misconduct-at-parent-company-badoo (archived at perma.cc/9TU9-HCRC)

18   Laporte, N (2020) Bumble hits 100 million users – and has new plans to take over the dating world, *Fast Company*, 15 July, www.fastcompany.com/90527896/bumble-hits-100-million-users-and-has-new-plans-to-take-over-the-dating-world (archived at perma.cc/CT8U-MQCL)

19   Bursztynsky, J (2021) Bumble stock closes up 63% after soaring in market debut, *CNBC*, 11 February, www.cnbc.com/2021/02/11/bumble-ipo-bmbl-starts-trading-on-nasdaq.html (archived at perma.cc/3KUF-4H3V)

20   Forbes (2022) Whitney Wolfe Herd, www.forbes.com/profile/whitney-wolfe-herd/?sh=5577283e3147 (archived at perma.cc/97XJ-3LHS)

21   Mulkerrins, J (2021) Whitney Wolfe Herd: How Bumble made her the world's youngest female self-made billionaire, *The Times*, 24 April, www.thetimes.co.uk/article/whitney-wolfe-herd-how-bumble-made-her-the-worlds-youngest-female-self-made-billionaire-5vvrzfkx9 (archived at perma.cc/PQE8-KUCN)

22   CNN Business (2018) Men swipe right but women make the first move (Online video) https://edition.cnn.com/2018/10/03/tech/bumble-india-priyanka-chopra/index.html (archived at perma.cc/3BMH-2FUR)

23   Mulkerrins, J (2021) Whitney Wolfe Herd: How Bumble made her the world's youngest female self-made billionaire, *The Times*, 24 April, www.thetimes.co.uk/article/whitney-wolfe-herd-how-bumble-made-her-the-worlds-youngest-female-self-made-billionaire-5vvrzfkx9 (archived at perma.cc/PQE8-KUCN)

24   Forbes (2022) Bumble CEO Whitney Wolfe Herd describes how life has changed since company went public, 14 December, www.forbes.com/sites/premium-video/2022/12/14/bumble-ceo-whitney-wolfe-herd-describes-how-life-has-changed-since-company-went-public/?sh=469f8b0e2848 (archived at perma.cc/LW49-SLTM)

25   Miller, H (2022) Whitney Wolfe Herd: Standing out in a saturated market, Leaders.com, 10 March, https://leaders.com/articles/leadership/whitney-wolfe-herd (archived at perma.cc/FL5X-P7NS)

26   Mulkerrins, J (2021) Whitney Wolfe Herd: How Bumble made her the world's youngest female self-made billionaire, *The Times*, 24 April, www.thetimes.co.uk/article/whitney-wolfe-herd-how-bumble-made-her-the-worlds-youngest-female-self-made-billionaire-5vvrzfkx9 (archived at perma.cc/PQE8-KUCN)

27   Forbes (2022) Bumble CEO Whitney Wolfe Herd describes how life has changed since company went public (Online video) 14 December, www.forbes.com/sites/premium-video/2022/12/14/bumble-ceo-whitney-wolfe-herd-describes-how-life-has-changed-since-company-went-public/?sh=469f8b0e2848 (archived at perma.cc/LW49-SLTM)

28   CNN Business (2018) Men swipe right but women make the first move (Online video) https://edition.cnn.com/2018/10/03/tech/bumble-india-priyanka-chopra/index.html (archived at perma.cc/3BMH-2FUR)

29   Miller, H (2022) Whitney Wolfe Herd: Standing out in a saturated market, Leaders.com, 10 March, https://leaders.com/articles/leadership/whitney-wolfe-herd (archived at perma.cc/FL5X-P7NS)

30   Ian (2022) Bumble founder: Guide to PR and marketing, *Pressfarm*, 31 October, https://press.farm/bumble-founder-whitney-wolfe-herd-guide-to-pr-and-marketing (archived at perma.cc/7SJ2-VT4E)

31   Mulkerrins, J (2021) Whitney Wolfe Herd: How Bumble made her the world's youngest female self-made billionaire, *The Times*, 24 April, www.thetimes.co.uk/article/whitney-wolfe-herd-how-bumble-made-her-the-worlds-youngest-female-self-made-billionaire-5vvrzfkx9 (archived at perma.cc/PQE8-KUCN)

32   Forbes (2022) Bumble CEO Whitney Wolfe Herd describes how life has changed since company went public (Online video) 14 December, www.forbes.com/sites/premium-video/2022/12/14/bumble-ceo-whitney-wolfe-herd-describes-how-life-has-changed-since-company-went-public/?sh=469f8b0e2848 (archived at perma.cc/LW49-SLTM)

CHAPTER SIXTEEN

Mark Zuckerberg

Meta Platforms

Leadership philosophy
'THE BIGGEST RISK IS NOT TAKING ANY RISK.'[1]

Every day Meta connects billions of people with each other through its popular websites and apps including Facebook, Instagram and WhatsApp. Today, Facebook alone has nearly three billion users worldwide – more than a third of the planet's entire population.[2] As one of the world's largest companies, Meta has successfully tapped into the fundamental desire of humans to talk to, share with and learn about each other.

Mark Zuckerberg co-founded Facebook back in February 2004. At the time he was a 19-year-old sopho-more (second-year student) majoring in psychology and computer science at the prestigious Ivy League school of

Harvard. His co-founders were fellow students Eduardo Saverin, Dustin Moskovitz and Chris Hughes. The online directory they created was then known as TheFacebook. com and intended to connect college students. But so popular was the web service that its fame quickly grew beyond college circles. Within a comparatively short space of time, it was being used by millions of people over the age of 13.

The origins of Facebook were mired in controversy for several reasons. Firstly, Zuckerberg had been the primary developer on an earlier service called Facemash, which allowed students to rate the attractiveness of their peers. Despite being an instant hit with visitors, the site incurred strong criticism and Zuckerberg quickly took it down. Nevertheless, in November 2003, he was called before the Harvard Administrative Board (the body responsible for enforcing undergraduate academic regulations and stand-ards of social conduct) to address accusations that he had breached security and violated copyrights and individual privacy.[3]

Undeterred by his setback with Facemash, Zuckerberg launched TheFacebook.com a few months later. In April 2004, The Facebook was first formed as a limited liability company under Florida law. With the site taking off quickly, Zuckerberg and Moskovitz decided to spend the summer working in the Californian city of Palo Alto, known colloquially as the 'Birthplace of Silicon Valley'. Saverin, meanwhile, headed to New York to do an intern-ship with investment bank Lehman Brothers. In California, Zuckerberg met Sean Parker, founder of peer-to-peer file-sharing application Napster, who joined the company. He also met with Peter Thiel, co-founder of online payments service PayPal, who was to become Facebook's outside investor. Realizing that he was on to a winner, Zuckerberg decided to drop out of Harvard to focus on growing the business.[4]

By this time, the relationship between Saverin and Zuckerberg had soured. Tensions had arisen after Saverin ran ads on The Facebook for his own, separate jobs board site called Joboozle. Also, Zuckerberg felt that his co-founder was being uncooperative when it came to business decision making and had not managed to secure any funding for the company, which urgently needed finance to keep going.

At that point, Saverin owned 30 per cent of The Facebook. To cut him out of the business and bring in Thiel as an investor, Zuckerberg came up with a plan. He formed a new company under Delaware law that would buy the old company, formed under Florida law. In October 2004, Saverin signed a shareholder agreement that allotted him three million shares and he handed over his voting rights to Zuckerberg, who became The Facebook's sole director. In January 2005, the new company issued nine million shares, diluting Saverin's stake in the business to less than 10 per cent without diluting those of the other shareholders.[5] Saverin later sued the company for breach of fiduciary duty and was reportedly awarded $5 billion in shares. In 2005, both the company and the site rebranded as Facebook instead of TheFacebook.com after the company bought the domain name Facebook.com for $200,000.

Saverin's lawsuit was not the only legal battle that Zuckerberg was involved in during the early days of Facebook. In 2008, Facebook reportedly paid $65 million to brothers Cameron and Tyler Winklevoss and Divya Narendra, the founders of ConnectU, a social networking site for Harvard students and alumni.[6] The trio claimed that in 2003 they had hired Zuckerberg to write code for their site, then called Harvard Connection, but he had stolen their idea and technology to launch Facebook instead.[7]

The tumultuous story of Facebook's beginnings was documented in the hit 2010 biopic *The Social Network*. Zuckerberg has noted, however, that many elements of the plot were fictionalized because the reality of building Facebook was not glamorous enough to base a movie on. Apart from anything else, the movie depicted him as a self-centred single man who had recently been ditched by his girlfriend. In fact, he was already dating his now-wife, Priscilla Chan, whom he met at Harvard and is mother to his three daughters.[8]

The next chapter

Facebook may have had a turbulent beginning, but that didn't stand in the way of its meteoric rise. By December 2006, Facebook had 12 million users worldwide. Three years later that number had grown to 350 million.[9]

In 2008 Facebook overtook Myspace as the world's most-visited social media site. As advertising began to take off, revenues and profits grew. The company undertook an initial public offering in May 2012, listing on the NASDAQ stock exchange. In total, it raised $16 billion, giving it a market value of $102.4 billion. At that point, it was the largest-ever IPO of an internet company, even exceeding the IPO of search engine Google, which had raised $1.9 billion when it went public in 2004.[10] Zuckerberg himself was worth $19 billion, aged just 26.[11] By October 2012, Facebook had one billion monthly users, an achievement that its founder described as 'humbling'.[12]

Shortly before the IPO, Facebook bought photo-sharing app Instagram for $1 billion. Instagram had over 30 million users who were uploading more than five million new pictures a day.[13] The move, while questioned by market commentators, turned out to be a stroke of genius. Instead of acting as a potential rival to Facebook, Instagram became a strategic asset to the company, enabling it to connect with younger social media users, including teenagers. Over time, Facebook has invested in Instagram, adding new features that have helped the app to grow to more than a billion users.[14]

Another major development was the acquisition of messaging app WhatsApp for $19 billion in 2014. Again, the purchase was an opportunity to take control of a rising competitor to Facebook, which has its own Messenger app.[15] Facebook's two high-profile acquisitions, and its success in integrating them, led to the company facing accusations of anti-competitive behaviour, however. In 2020, Facebook was sued by the US Federal Trade Commission, which claimed that it had acted illegally to maintain its social media monopoly. If the company loses the lawsuit, it could be forced to sell both Instagram and WhatsApp.[16]

In October 2021, Facebook the company was renamed Meta Platforms, or simply Meta, although the social media platform kept its own name. This reflects the company's

desire to shift the focus of its brand from social networking to a visionary business that will help to realize the
metaverse – a virtual world in which humans can immerse
themselves by using virtual reality and augmented reality
headsets. Writing in his *Founder's Letter*, Zuckerberg said
the world was 'at the beginning of the next chapter of the
internet', a chapter that he described as 'an embodied
internet where you're in the experience, not just looking at
it'.[17] In the letter he envisaged a future where people could
teleport themselves as holograms to the office, to concerts
and to relatives' houses.

Zuckerberg is a man who has made his fortune out
of taking risks. Nevertheless, his focus on the metaverse
is perhaps his biggest risk to date since it has already
consumed billions of dollars in investment and the business model is still unproven. During 2022, investors questioned the wisdom of investing heavily in the virtual world.
They also had other concerns, not least declining revenues
linked to falling advertising sales. By the end of October,
Meta's share price had fallen by a whopping 71 per cent,
effectively knocking $676 billion off the company's valua-
tion. Zuckerberg maintained his belief that the bet would
pay off, however, and appealed for patience, saying that he
believed 'those who are patient and invest with us will end
up being rewarded'.[18] To reassure investors that Meta was
serious about maintaining its profitability, Zuckerberg
subsequently laid off 13 per cent of Meta's workforce,
more than 11,000 employees.[19] In a statement, he admitted that the decision was 'a sad moment'.[20]

It's a case of watch this space to see if Zuckerberg
ultimately ends up being proved right on the metaverse.

In the meantime, he remains one of the world's richest people, with a net worth of $52 billion as of January 2023.[21]

String of scandals

Zuckerberg's commitment to creating a more open, transparent and connected world has led to his company becoming embroiled in numerous scandals. These scandals have involved data privacy, disinformation and information security, as well as accusations that its Facebook platform has inadvertently played a role in inciting violence against individuals and communities.

Over the years, the company has been repeatedly criticized for making changes to its privacy settings, often on the grounds that it has been making too much information about its users publicly available. It has also attracted controversy over various other incidents. For example, in 2012, Facebook conducted psychological tests on 70,000 users without their consent to see how they reacted to posts when certain words were removed from newsfeeds. Subsequently the company apologized for its actions. Four years later, in 2016, it was accused of influencing the outcome of the US presidential election by allowing the dissemination of 'fake news'.[22]

In 2018, negative headlines abounded following the high-profile Cambridge Analytica scandal. It emerged that the data of up to 87 million Facebook users globally had been harvested by Cambridge Analytica, a political consultancy that worked for the Trump presidential campaign and had used the data to influence several elections worldwide. In response, Facebook made changes to its platform to restrict the amount of information that app developers are able to access.[23]

The same year that the Cambridge Analytica scandal broke, Facebook was used to incite violence as part of a genocidal campaign against the Rohingya Muslim minority in Myanmar. Facebook commissioned an independent human rights assessment of the role of its services in the southeast Asian country, with the report concluding that the company wasn't doing enough to prevent its platform from being used to incite offline violence. This led Facebook to admit that it 'can and should do more'.[24]

Three years, later, however, supporters of Donald Trump, who had just lost the 2020 presidential election, besieged the Capitol Building in Washington DC, the seat of the US Congress. Trump's supporters believed that the election had been 'stolen' from him by the Democrats. Five people died due to the siege, which took place on 6 January 2021, and over 100 were injured. While the siege was not primarily organized on Facebook, the company was nevertheless blamed for allowing hate and misinformation to spread. The day after the insurrection, Facebook suspended Trump's own account on its platform.[25] The former president was not allowed to return to the site until more than two years later.

For many people, Meta, more than any other tech company, exemplifies arguably the most famous dictum of the internet age: if you're not paying for the product, then you *are* the product. Facebook doesn't sell user data to advertisers, however. Instead, it sells targeted advertising based on the information that it has on its users.

It is also worth noting that when Facebook was founded – nearly two decades ago at the time of writing – it was not intended to be a company. It was, as Zuckerberg high-lighted in his 2012 *Founder's Letter*, built to accomplish the social mission of making the world more open and connected. He also saw the platform as a tool to help ordinary people get their voices heard by governments. Zuckerberg was clear that the aim of Facebook was to strengthen interpersonal relationships between people. These, he pointed out, are what bring long-term happiness.[26]

Secrets to success

In his 2012 *Founder's Letter*, Zuckerberg wrote: 'We don't build services to make money; we make money to build better services.' That observation reflects his view of what being in business should be about. It shouldn't be about the pursuit of profits, but rather the pursuit of a passion to deliver high-quality goods or services to customers.

Notably, Zuckerberg – who is both CEO and chair of Meta – controls more than 54 per cent of the company's voting-class shares despite owning only 13 per cent of its stock. This is the result of a dual-class share structure that is typically used to enable entrepreneurs to retain control over their businesses after they have gone public. While the investment community has reservations around this kind of share structure, it has enabled Zuckerberg to run his business with a long-term perspective in mind.

Along with taking a long-term view, Zuckerberg is known for being a risk-taker who believes that businesses should take calculated risks to avoid becoming stagnant and falling behind competitors. While speaking at Stanford University in 2011, he said that in a fast-changing world 'the only strategy that is guaranteed to fail is not taking risks'.[27]

Something else that Zuckerberg believes in is moving at speed. For a while, Facebook was known for its motto 'Move fast and break things'. Later the motto changed to the less catchy 'Move fast with stable infrastructure'. Now 'move fast' is one of Meta's corporate values, along with five others including 'focus on long-term impact', 'build awesome things' and 'live in the future'.[28]

Zuckerberg is a divisive figure in the court of public opinion, mostly due to fears that Meta is overly powerful. Nevertheless, Zuckerberg is undoubtedly a great visionary who draws highly talented people to work for him. Among them are Sheryl Sandberg – a respected executive who acted as chief operating officer of Facebook and then Meta between 2008 and 2022 – and Sir Nick Clegg, the former deputy prime minister of the United Kingdom, who is Meta's president for global affairs. Sandberg grew the advertising side of Facebook, helping to make the business more profitable. Clegg leads the company on policy matters, a role that requires him to interact with regulators while making a case for the company's products.

Zuckerberg has never just been a computer nerd – despite the unflattering depiction of him in the movie *The Social Network*. As someone who majored in psychology at Harvard it is no surprise that he is deeply interested in – and sensitive to – human behaviour. In fact, this helps to explain his immense achievements in the world of social media. Facebook might be a powerful technological tool, but its fundamental success lies in understanding people – and what drives them. People want the opportunity to show their approval – hence the popularity of Facebook's 'Like' button. They also want to be able to interact with others and express their views, hence the comment functionality. And they are fundamentally curious, hence they want to see where their friends have gone on holiday and what their children look like.

Zuckerberg is known for being a fast talker who can come across as socially awkward to others. Nevertheless, he's also been described as warm, inquisitive and a good listener.[29] Unsurprisingly for someone who became incredibly successful at a very young age, he has a strong work ethic – and expects other people to demonstrate that same quality.

Giving back is important to Zuckerberg. Together with his wife, he operates the Chan Zuckerberg Initiative, which is on a mission to help build a more inclusive, just and healthy future by eradicating disease, improving education and meeting the needs of local communities. The initiative makes grants to support individuals and organizations working in science, education and the community. It also makes venture investments in impact-focused companies. In 2015, Zuckerberg announced that over the course of their lifetimes he and Priscilla would give 99 per cent of their Facebook shares (then worth about $45 billion) to advance this mission.[30]

Famously, Zuckerberg has a penchant for wearing grey t-shirts. Yet this is more of a statement about his decision-making approach than his fashion sense. He has said that he'd prefer to use his energy on things that make a difference to the world rather than on deciding what to wear.[31]

LEADERSHIP LESSONS FROM MARK ZUCKERBERG

- **Stay true to your vision**. Doing that will sustain you when you encounter criticism and find yourself confronting difficult times.

- **Move at speed**. By acting quickly, and taking calculated risks, you will gain first-mover advantage in the marketplace and stay ahead of your competitors.

- **Remember that great people build great businesses**. Find talented leaders to work with you and empower them to make decisions.

- **Learn about human psychology**. If you understand what motivates people, you have the foundation for business success.

- **Continually think about the future**. That's the only way to ensure you don't get left behind.

Notes

1 Pozin, I (2018) One piece of advice from Mark Zuckerberg that will determine your success (or failure) in 2018, *Inc.*, 19 February, www.inc.com/ilya-pozin/one-piece-of-advice-from-mark-zuckerberg-that-will-determine-your-success-or-failure-in-2018.html (archived at perma.cc/9QPK-7VUR)

2 Statista (2022) Number of monthly active Facebook users worldwide as of 3rd quarter 2022, www.statista.com/statistics/264810/number-of-monthly-active-facebook-users-worldwide (archived at perma.cc/V25J-TB5K)

3 Kaplan, C (2003) Facemash creator survives ad board, *The Harvard Crimson*, 19 November, www.thecrimson.com/article/2003/11/19/facemash-creator-survives-ad-board-the (archived at perma.cc/BAD7-UQ8V)

4   Carlson, N (2012) How Mark Zuckerberg booted his co-founder out of the company, *Business Insider*, 15 May, https://www.businessinsider.com/how-mark-zuckerberg-booted-his-co-founder-out-of-the-company-2012-5?r=US&IR=T (archived at perma.cc/5WFP-3NP9)

5   Carlson, N (2012) How Mark Zuckerberg booted his co-founder out of the company, *Business Insider*, 15 May, https://www.businessinsider.com/how-mark-zuckerberg-booted-his-co-founder-out-of-the-company-2012-5?r=US&IR=T (archived at perma.cc/5WFP-3NP9)

6   Gaudin, S (2009) Facebook, ConnectU reportedly reach $65 million settlement, *Computerworld*, 11 February, www.computerworld.com/article/2530833/facebook--connectu-reportedly-reach--65-million-settlement.html (archived at perma.cc/ZFB4-RJBP)

7   Lawson, S (2007) ConnectU suit against Facebook continues, *Computerworld*, 26 July, www.computerworld.com/article/2542696/connectu-suit-against-facebook-continues.html (archived at perma.cc/UP8R-GL6G)

8   Batty, D and Johnston, C (2014) Social Network 'made up stuff that was hurtful' says Mark Zuckerberg, *The Guardian*, 8 November, https://www.theguardian.com/technology/2014/nov/08/mark-zuckerberg-social-network-made-stuff-up-hurtful (archived at perma.cc/45NC-TNBK)

9   Grossman, L (2010) Person of the Year 2010 Mark Zuckerberg, *Time*, 15 December, https://content.time.com/time/specials/packages/article/0,28804,2036683_2037183_2037185-1,00.html (archived at perma.cc/5EK6-N6PR)

10 Hall, M (2002) Facebook, *Britannica*, 18 October, www.britannica.com/topic/Facebook (archived at perma.cc/A6ZU-SRGQ)

11 History.com (2023) Facebook raises $16 billion in largest tech IPO in U.S. history, www.history.com/this-day-in-history/facebook-raises-16-billion-in-largest-tech-ipo-in-u-s-history (archived at perma.cc/QMT5-DBEF)

12 Smith, A, Segall, L and Cowley, S (2012) Facebook reaches one billion users, https://money.cnn.com/2012/10/04/technology/facebook-billion-users (archived at perma.cc/35DM-LEJ4)

13 BBC (2012) Facebook buys Instagram photo sharing network for $1bn, 10 April, www.bbc.co.uk/news/technology-17658264 (archived at perma.cc/VEB2-ZDGW)

14   Ghaffary, S (2022) The Facebookification of Instagram, *Vox*, 27 July, https://www.vox.com/recode/23274761/facebook-instagram-land-the-giants-mark-zuckerberg-kevin-systrom-ashley-yuki (archived at perma.cc/XS8H-5YSD)

15   Warzel, C and Mac, R (2018) These confidential charts show why Facebook bought WhatsApp, www.buzzfeednews.com/article/charliewarzel/why-facebook-bought-whatsapp (archived at perma.cc/9BGA-ADFL)

16   Reuters (2022) U.S. sets high bar to settle Facebook antitrust suit – FTC chair, 9 June, https://www.reuters.com/technology/us-sets-high-bar-settle-facebook-antitrust-suit-ftc-chair-2022-06-09 (archived at perma.cc/F6MZ-LJQT)

17   Zuckerberg, M (2021) Founder's Letter 2021, Meta, 28 October, https://about.fb.com/news/2021/10/founders-letter (archived at perma.cc/5BRQ-X3S4)

18   Barinka, A (2022) Meta plummets 25%; Zuckerberg plea for 'patience' falls flat, *Yahoo!Finance*, 27 October, https://uk.finance.yahoo.com/news/zuckerberg-asks-patience-meta-costs-011642485.html (archived at perma.cc/T7ZY-SSGA)

19   Reuters (2022) Meta to cut more than 11,000 jobs in one of the biggest layoffs this year, 9 November, www.reuters.com/technology/meta-cut-more-than-11000-jobs-one-biggest-us-layoffs-this-year-2022-11-09 (archived at perma.cc/2QAU-WLLM)

20   Meta (2022) Mark Zuckerberg's message to Meta employees, 9 November, https://about.fb.com/news/2022/11/mark-zuckerberg-layoff-message-to-employees (archived at perma.cc/Z3HH-TW5D)

21   Bloomberg Billionaires Index (2022) Mark Zuckerberg, 6 November, https://www.bloomberg.com/billionaires/profiles/mark-e-zuckerberg/?leadSource=uverify%20wall (archived at perma.cc/3XHN-X29J)

22   Meisenzahl, M and Canales, K (2021) The 16 biggest scandals Mark Zuckerberg faced over the last decade as he became one of the world's most powerful people, *Business Insider*, 3 November, www.businessinsider.com/mark-zuckerberg-scandals-last-decade-while-running-facebook-2019-12?r=US&IR=T (archived at perma.cc/DAP3-2VRC)

23 Zialcita, P (2019) Facebook pays $643,000 fine for role in Cambridge Analytica scandal, *NPR*, 30 October, https://www.npr.org/2019/10/30/774749376/facebook-pays-643-000-fine-for-role-in-cambridge-analytica-scandal (archived at perma.cc/B3ZX-G9RD)

24 Warofka, A (2018) An independent assessment of the human rights impact of Facebook in Myanmar, *Meta*, 5 November, https://about.fb.com/news/2018/11/myanmar-hria (archived at perma.cc/L9DV-9T54)

25 Akhtar, A (2021) Sheryl Sandberg says the US Capitol siege was not primarily organized on Facebook, but acknowledges Facebook moderation not perfect, *Business Insider*, 12 January, https://www.npr.org/2021/10/22/1048543513/facebook-groups-jan-6-insurrection (archived at perma.cc/SX73-5LFB)

26 Zuckerberg, M (2012) Founder's Letter, 2012, Facebook, www.facebook.com/notes/261129471966151/?paipv=0&eav=Afb2qo_aLaz6kOgPIZHORhSs7i5HyxM2MmYjyecC1GwpLA3qW7v61VGWPiPjPfWql08 (archived at perma.cc/3K3R-RSJX)

27 Pozin, I (2018) One piece of advice from Mark Zuckerberg that will determine your success (or failure) in 2018, *Inc.*, 19 February, www.inc.com/ilya-pozin/one-piece-of-advice-from-mark-zuckerberg-that-will-determine-your-success-or-failure-in-2018.html (archived at perma.cc/9QPK-7VUR)

28 Southern, M (2022) Mark Zuckerberg announces Meta's new company values, *Search Engine Journal*, 15 February, www.searchenginejournal.com/mark-zuckerberg-announces-metas-new-company-values/438298/#close (archived at perma.cc/V52R-DRFN)

29 Grossman, L (2014) Inside Facebook's plan to wire the world, *Time*, 15 December, https://time.com/facebook-world-plan (archived at perma.cc/54SQ-2Q7Q)

30 BBC (2015) Facebook's Mark Zuckerberg to give away 99% of shares, 2 December, www.bbc.co.uk/news/world-us-canada-34978249 (archived at perma.cc/A6DL-8UV3)

31 Wilson, R (2021) Know why Mark Zuckerberg wears same grey t-shirt every day, *Marketing Mind*, 31 March, www.marketingmind.in/know-why-mark-zuckerberg-wears-same-grey-t-shirt-every-day (archived at perma.cc/FZU8-CKGS)

PART TWO

The next generation

In leadership, just as in any other field, it's always exciting to wonder about who's around the corner. Which people will shape the future of our world? While the first section of this book focuses on leaders who are already well established, this section explores five leaders who you might not yet have heard of, but who could have a transformative impact on their own markets, and internationally, over the years to come. These leaders also act as a bellwether for the changing nature of leadership – what is expected of leaders today, compared with, say, a decade ago? What stands out, in particular, is that these leaders tend to have a strong social and environmental focus, they prioritize the wellbeing of their people, and they have a powerful vision for how the world can be a better place. From their stories, we can learn just as much – if not more – about the transformative power of great leadership as we can learn from the leaders profiled in Part One. Read on to find out more …

CHAPTER SEVENTEEN

Lucrezia Bisignani

Kukua

Leadership philosophy
'IF YOU'RE NOT READY TO FAIL BIG, YOU'RE NOT READY
TO WIN BIG.'

Italian entrepreneur Lucrezia Bisignani is based in the
Kenyan capital of Nairobi, where she is transforming the
world of children's entertainment with her educational
cartoon company Kukua. Having lived in Europe, North
America and now Africa she has a global mindset, which
she credits to her parents, who liked to travel to remote
places, taking her and her three siblings with them. Born
and brought up in Rome, Bisignani later attended boarding
school and drama school in the English town of Oxford.

When she founded Kukua in 2014, Bisignani was just
23 years old. The business, she says, combined all the

different passions that she'd developed during her life until that point. Not only did she have a love of acting and storytelling, she had been entrepreneurial from an early age, making and selling things. As a teenager she had also launched her own non-profit organization, Staanoi, to raise money for projects that she cared deeply about. She sold photos from her travels, using the profits to build water wells in Africa. She also created a fashion calendar, inspired by the environment, which funded the development of Gamechangers, a programme that aimed to equip school children with 21st-century leadership skills such as empathy, entrepreneurship, negotiation and resilience.

After completing a one-year foundation course at the Oxford School of Drama, Bisignani worked briefly in a fundraising consultancy firm and then in a tech start-up accelerator in San Francisco. A major turning point for her came in 2014 when she was accepted onto the prestigious Graduate Studies Program of Singularity University, a US education provider that brought together individuals who wanted to use technology to tackle global challenges. Never technically a university, the organization is now known as Singularity Group. At the time, Singularity University was based at NASA's Ames Research Center in Silicon Valley, California.

Bisignani attended Singularity University's 10-week programme, along with 79 other individuals who had either already achieved something impressive in techno-logy or the sciences or who had a deep passion to solve a big problem. Singularity's mission was to help and empower these 80 individuals to use exponential techno-logies – such as artificial intelligence, gaming, nanotech and biotech – to address issues in areas such as cyber-security, education, the environment, housing, poverty and water usage.

During her time on the Singularity programme, Bisignani learned from a string of successful entrepreneurs, along with other experts and speakers. She was the youngest person in her cohort, which put her regularly out of her comfort zone – something she relished. 'I was always learning something new from really extraordinary people,' she says. 'My mindset switched completely.' In particular, Singularity taught her to think big and she started Kukua just months after finishing the programme.

The Kukua story

Passionate about education, Bisignani researched education-related problems while she was at Singularity University. She discovered that illiteracy is a major problem in many developing countries, especially in Africa. At the time, the non-profit organization XPRIZE had created a challenge to solve the problem of child illiteracy in Africa, offering $15 million of investment to a team that could develop software enabling children to teach themselves basic reading, writing and arithmetic.

Inspired to solve the illiteracy challenge, and win the prize, Bisignani spent two months after Singularity travelling across Gambia, Kenya and South Africa to study illiteracy. She sat at the back of hundreds of classrooms, in both rural and urban areas, to understand how kids were being taught. After that, she began raising money and put together a team to build some apps for teaching primary school children how to read, write and do maths. The apps all had an African setting and featured African characters.

Bisignani was convinced that she and her team were in a really good place to win the competition, so she wasn't mentally prepared for what came next. They didn't win – which came as a devastating blow after all the hard work she'd put in and the people she had rallied to believe in her project. 'It was a moment of failure that knocked me to the ground,' she recalls. 'But I believe it was all so I could ask myself the next most important question: where do I go from here?'

Remembering that what kids had most liked about her apps was that they featured characters who looked like them, and aware of the huge gap in the market for cartoons based in Africa, she decided to move into the entertainment industry. 'I realized our entire business model was around creating a massive story world for kids to love these characters, through animated content, films and TV series,' she says. 'Then we would monetize that with licensing, merchandising and consumer products, and eventually experiences, whether those were online or theme parks.'

As luck would have it, the American movie *Black Panther* came out in 2018, featuring an African superhero. The movie was a box office hit, attracting audiences from across the globe. At the same time, the world was starting to wake up to the importance of diverse characters. 'Suddenly, these characters made sense to the investors I was pitching to,' Bisignani recalls. 'And they completely saw the importance, the need.'

Fast forward a few years and Kukua has produced an animated series based on Super Sema, an African girl with superhero powers relating to science, technology, engineering, maths and the arts. She uses these powers to solve major problems in her community, whether that's replanting trees to reforest the environment or creating a 3D printer that prints pizza. As Bisignani explains: 'The goal is to get kids excited about these skills, and to be inspired, so that when they're in their next science lesson in school, they're like, "Oh that's what Sema did in that episode! I want to do that, too."' Super Sema's futuristic world is inspired by many different parts of Africa in terms of the words, music and colours used, and such is her appeal that she has fans not only in Africa but also in the US and Europe. 'The cartoon series is relatable to anyone who watches,' says Bisignani, 'not just kids who have the same colour skin.'

The *Super Sema* franchise, now in its fourth season, began as a series of YouTube Originals. In future it will also be distributed on other platforms. Additionally, Kukua is partnering with other companies to produce consumer products based on the characters in the series – products such as toys, books, activity books, STEM kits and clothing. The Super Sema talking doll is already available on Amazon, promoted by Oscar-winning actress Lupita Nyong'o. Nyong'o acts as an ambassador and executive producer for Kukua and is also a shareholder in the company. The next step, according to Bisignani, is interactive experiences – for example, giving children the opportunity to join Super Sema in the lab while she performs a science experiment.

As CEO of Kukua, Bisignani is 'super involved' in every aspect of the company's creative activities, as well as with

THE NEXT GENERATION

the overall business strategy and fundraising. 'Creativity is the most important part of our business,' she says. 'If we don't have an extraordinary story world and characters, there is nothing else.' The company hired a global team of award-winning writers, producers, franchise builders and designers to create and develop its show. The in-house company staff numbers just 15, which helps to keep the business agile and lean. Some of the team previously worked for Disney. Most of the in-house staff – including the show producers – are African women but there are other employees dotted around the world. The actors who do the voiceovers are all Kenyan. Bisignani's twin brother, Giovanni, acts as chief financial officer and is based in Rome.

In terms of scaling the business, Bisignani says the greatest challenges have firstly been to create a compelling story world and loveable characters and secondly to make sure that everyone knows about the *Super Sema* cartoons. 'The growth of the fan base is our next most important challenge, along with maintaining the quality of the creative and the brand,' explains Bisignani. To date, the business has raised $8.5 million in funding from venture capital firms, as well as a major Chinese conglomerate. In 2019, Bisignani was listed on the *Forbes* 30 Under 30 Europe list of social entrepreneurs.

Secrets to success

Bisignani believes that a good leader is someone who empowers others to be better and do better. They put the best resources at the disposal of their team so that they can grow 'and eventually grow the business alongside you'.

Nevertheless, she thinks that to make the right strategic decisions, it's essential to know what's going on within the business. 'It's important for me, as a leader, to know everything about every single department in the company,' she says.

As someone who takes a keen interest in education, it's no surprise that Bisignani herself is fuelled by learning. 'I'm obsessed by learning and I love learning new things,' she says. 'I really deep-dive into subjects, like how do we set up a world-class animation process or grow our social media presence? These were things I had never done before. I have to learn, and I have to learn really quickly.' The way that she learns is by reading as much as possible, whether it's books or online resources, and by finding mentors – people she can turn to for advice and support. Some of her most important mentors are her investors, including 'future of entertainment' expert Matthew Ball, Brent Hoberman and Spencer Crawley of Firstminute Capital, Paolo Barletta of Alchimia Investments and Eghosa Omoigui of EchoVC Partners. Another important mentor is Claudia Lloyd, a four-times BAFTA winner who works with Bisignani to write, produce and co-create *Super Sema*, and who is a shareholder in the company. Bisignani also looks out for 'best in class' examples of how others in her field have succeeded, such as US animation studio Pixar's journey to become one of the leading storytelling companies in the world, or leadership lessons from Disney's CEO, Bob Iger.

Bisignani sees her ability to learn as one of her greatest strengths. She is also, she says, 'incredibly efficient' and can switch through the different tasks she needs to address every day in an organized and methodical manner, 'from giving notes on a new script, to reviewing a legal contract or analysing our growth performance'. In terms of her weaknesses, she believes that she could be 'a lot less apologetic and own things a lot more'. 'I just love leaders who are humble,' she explains. 'But sometimes I wish I could just state myself with a little bit more confidence and be unapologetic about my strengths, and who I am as an entrepreneur, and as a person, as opposed to maybe playing it smaller.'

Female leaders have a valuable advantage in the workplace in that they don't just see employees, they see people 'with everything they come with', says Bisignani. 'The most interesting part of any human being is their story, their baggage, and when you are able to let that shine in a workplace, people really give their best because they feel understood.' She argues that women are inclined to allow more personal conversation and openness in meetings. She herself is relaxed if the first 10 minutes of a meeting cover personal topics or are completely off the agenda. 'I don't think that's time wasted,' she says. 'I think that makes the meeting a lot stronger, and the overall outcome a lot stronger, than if the meeting is just very transactional.'

Over the coming years, Bisignani believes that leadership will evolve so that soft skills, such as empathy and creativity, become more important. Future generations should focus on these skills, she says, since they cannot be automated by robots.

The most important leadership lesson that Bisignani has ever learned is to be comfortable with failing. 'The motto of my drama school was "fail, fail again, fail better"', she says. 'If you're not ready to fail big time, you're not ready to win big time.'

LEADERSHIP LESSONS FROM LUCREZIA BISIGNANI

- **Nurture a global mindset**. Our planet is a very big place. The ideal location or target audience for your business might not be where you are living right now.

- **Embrace your inner creativity**. You can change the world by using your imagination to create concepts and ideas that other people engage with.

- **Have a Plan B**. If your first business plan doesn't work out, think about how you can apply the knowledge and learning you've acquired in different ways.

- **Be comfortable with failing**. If you're too afraid of getting hurt, you won't grow anything big. Confront your fear of failure and focus on taking away valuable lessons when things go wrong.

- **Aim to connect closely with the people in your business**. Recognize them as individual humans with their own stories and aspirations rather than simply as employees.

CHAPTER EIGHTEEN

Mette Lykke

Too Good To Go

Leadership philosophy
'HIRE GREAT PEOPLE AND EMPOWER THEM
TO HAVE REAL IMPACT.'

M ette Lykke is CEO of Too Good To Go, a Denmark-based foodtech business that is on a mission to reduce global food waste. She was born and brought up in Ringkøbing, a small town on Denmark's west coast and home to the country's largest onshore wind farm. After studying political science at the University of Aarhus, she joined prestigious global consultancy McKinsey as a management consultant when she was 25.

McKinsey, says Lykke, was an important learning experience. 'What you get there is really a toolbox for how to solve problems,' she says. 'I also found the culture to have this very strong can-do attitude, which I've also tried to take with me. I'm quite optimistic and believe that we can do a lot if we just set a high bar.'

As it happened, Lykke ended up staying with McKinsey for only around 20 months. In November 2007 she left the company to found a start-up with a couple of colleagues who had joined on the same day that she did – Christian Birk and Jakob Jønck. 'We started talking about starting our own company, and how much fun it would be to work for a more noble purpose and to actually follow through,' she says. 'Because as a consultant, you come in, you diagnose, you problem-solve a bit, and then you leave before you know if it even worked. We wanted to follow through from beginning to the end. We also wanted to work for ourselves and decide for ourselves how to do things.'

Lykke's background offers some insight into why she was attracted to the idea of running a business with a noble purpose. Entrepreneurial blood has run in her family since her grandfather founded a chain of lumberyards and construction material stores. She also has a strong commitment to social causes, having volunteered at the local riding school as a teenager. But what did her parents think about her walking away from a career with McKinsey? 'My father thought it was a great idea,' she explains. 'His take was that you can always take the corporate job. But if you have two partners that you like, and you have an idea, you can't be sure that that chance will ever pop up again.' Her mother, concerned for her future security, needed a little more convincing, however.

As the three would-be entrepreneurs all had a background in sports, they decided to focus their efforts on helping to address the global obesity problem through making fitness fun. They wanted to bring a social dimension into individual sports such as running and cycling. So, they developed a social fitness app called Endomondo. Its name combined the word 'endorphins' with 'mondo', the Esperanto word for 'world', to effectively mean 'a world of endorphins'. The app offered free real-time GPS tracking of running, cycling and other distance-based sports and enabled people to share their progress and targets, as well as challenge their friends. Endomondo used what Lykke describes as the 'classic "freemium" model' – users could download a free version supported by ads, or an ad-free premium version, with additional functionality.

Launching the app was a major challenge at first due to the general lack of smartphones at that time, particularly those that could support GPS tracking. The first iPhone was launched in January 2007, but Apple only introduced a built-in GPS for the product in 2008. Meanwhile, the App Store did not open until July 2008. 'It was quite complicated to launch an app when nobody knew what an app was,' says Lykke. 'And funding was hard to get because people thought we were way ahead of our time.' The founding team didn't take any pay for the first two years, but they managed to survive as they were young and their costs were low. 'It's a relatively small price to pay for pursuing your dream,' is how Lykke puts it.

To build momentum behind the app, the three founders travelled to weekend running races around Denmark. 'We would set up shop, with a desk, a computer and a TV, and we would try and show runners how it worked,' Lykke recalls. 'The problem was that only about 7 per cent of people had GPS on their phone. So, we had to seed the idea and then ask them to get a new phone. It's a bit of a tough one, but that's how it started. Then we built a great product. And once they did try it out on their new phone, they did get hooked, and they did invite their friends. It helped that people wanted to brag about their sports so back then they put a lot on Facebook and Twitter.' The trio also worked hard on PR to drum up free publicity for their app. Endomondo's fame and popularity spread and, by 2015, it had 20 million users globally.

Lykke learned some notable lessons from scaling Endomondo, with the biggest one being not to give up, even when times are really tough. Another was 'the importance of doing something that you really love and that you're very passionate about'. She also says it's key to work with great people – people you enjoy spending time with.

In 2015, US athleticwear brand Under Armour offered to buy Endomondo. By this point, Lykke was running the company on her own as both her co-founders had left and she was ready for a new adventure. She also believed that Endomondo would fit well with Under Armour. 'I liked the brand and the vision they had for how we could make the combination a good one,' she explains. So, Endomondo was sold to Under Armour for $85 million, proving that Lykke's decision to walk away from her career with McKinsey was, as she says, 'a good call'.

Lykke stayed on with Endomondo, now part of Under Armour, for a couple of years to help bed in the acquisition. But being back in the corporate world had ignited a yearning to return to the world of start-ups. 'I started having this itch for the early days and building something from scratch,' she explains. 'The energy, the speed, the freedom and, of course, the pressure.' And soon a chance meeting was to change the course of her life once again.

Too Good To Go

In 2016, Lykke was sitting on a bus, on her way to attend an event outside Copenhagen. She happened to strike up a conversation with the woman sitting next to her, who showed her an app on her phone. 'The app had been out for eight months,' Lykke recalls. 'And I just thought it was the coolest, coolest idea.' The app that the woman showed her was Too Good To Go, a mobile service that ensures good food doesn't go to waste by connecting consumers with restaurants and stores that have surplus food. Consumers can go to the store or restaurant, buy the food at a discount, and then take it home to enjoy. Blown away by the concept, Lykke got in touch with the app's founders – Brian Christensen, Thomas Bjørn Momsen, Stian Olesen, Klaus Bagge Pedersen and Adam Sigbrand – to congratulate them on their brilliant idea. They asked her to start advising them and, within a couple of months, she had not only invested in the business, she had also been asked to take over as CEO.

Lykke was charged with scaling Too Good To Go, growing the team and making the social impact business as big and impactful as it could possibly be. 'I was a little bit hesitant about five young guys asking me, a woman, to take over,' she admits. 'Because if you put me in the front seat, I'm gonna drive. But the agreement was that they would take a backseat.'

Since then, Lykke has more than delivered on her remit. The workforce of Too Good To Go has grown from eight people when she started in 2017 to more than 1,000 today, based in five different countries. The app covers a total of

17 countries – all of Western Europe, Poland, Canada and the US – with plans to expand further. The business is now backed by three different venture capital funds and has raised €150 million in funding to date.

Lykke believes that Too Good To Go has a huge opportunity to expand further since far too much food is still wasted. Its greatest challenge, she says, is motivating people to see the urgency of the need for change. In 2022, it acquired CodaBene, a French company that has developed artificial intelligence-based software that helps stores to better manage the expiry dates of food products and make effective use of food that is about to expire, perhaps by donating it to charity. 'We want to have a whole toolbox of different things you can do to reduce food waste,' Lykke explains. 'Because with the app alone, we can't get all our partners to zero waste. And that is the ambition. So, we need to expand our offering.'

Lykke believes it is critical to tackle the issue of food waste for three major reasons. Firstly, food waste is a huge environmental problem. Over a third (37 per cent) of greenhouse gas emissions are created by food production[1] and food production is a major contributor to habitat and biodiversity loss. Yet almost 40 per cent of food produced goes to waste annually.[2] Secondly, there is the social prerogative. 'We talk about how we can produce enough food for everyone on the planet, when, in fact, we do,' she explains. 'But still, hundreds of millions of people go to bed hungry.[3] I think there's a moral obligation to reduce food waste in the countries where we have enough food.' Finally, food waste doesn't make financial sense – over $1.2 trillion of food is wasted on an annual basis.[4]

Already Too Good To Go is saving around 300,000 meals a day from going into the waste bin. But Lykke believes it can have a much greater impact going forward, not only by saving more meals but also through the 'halo effect' of making people think differently about food, whether that's through giving them recipes to use up their leftovers or tips for better organizing their fridge. Furthermore, she's also seeing that business schools are beginning to use Too Good To Go as a textbook example of a social impact business. She says: 'If we can help inspire people to start better companies, that's a third level of impact.'

Asked about the long-term vision for her business, Lykke's answer is this: 'I think we will be a true force in the fight against food waste. Too Good To Go should be a household name and be integrated into the way we think about food. So, you would open your fridge and ask your spouse: "Is this milk too good to go?" We should have changed the way people think about food and built out solutions for our partners to get them to zero waste. We want to help prevent them from building up a surplus to begin with, then if they do have a surplus, they can put it into Too Good To Go or donate it. Then we'll be saving millions of meals from going to waste on a daily basis.'

In 2020, Lykke was named as one of the World Economic Forum's Young Global Leaders. She sees the honour as belonging to Too Good To Go as a business rather than to her as an individual, however. 'I think we are on a really important mission,' she says, 'and we want to do something good. So, when I got that recognition, it was less about me as a person and more about our company and our mission. We want to inspire creative people to build better companies and just set the bar higher. So, I'm happy with the recognition because I think it will help towards that.'

With the money she made from the sale of Endomondo, Lykke could have chosen never to work again and to lead a comfortable life of leisure. So why didn't she take that route? 'I'm really motivated by building something that matters, something that has a strong purpose,' she explains. 'I like seeing the impact of that scaling and growing day by day. That's what I find fun. That's where I find my energy. It's nice to go to the beach every now and then. But it's not something that would make me thrive every day. I really need a mission.'

Secrets to success

As a leader, Lykke believes in being authentic and in growing and empowering others. 'The most important thing, in my experience, is to be yourself,' she says. 'I find that people are inspired by people, not machines. So be yourself. Have a clear purpose, set a clear direction, but then give people a lane to run in. Make sure to remove any barriers and really set people free. Then, naturally, they will want to have as much impact as they can.'

She also tries hard to take feedback well so that she gets better over time. 'I make a point of asking for input and being open to feedback,' she explains, 'whether it's from my direct reports or from people in the company in general. I try to welcome that, otherwise it won't happen. And I make sure I show some gratitude whenever people are willing to share their thoughts.'

To develop herself, Lykke makes a point of talking to external people to try to get new perspectives. These include her coach as well as other business leaders in her network. She also reads widely. 'I don't think you can read your way to being a leader,' she says. 'But I do think it adds some additional perspectives.'

When it comes to developing her team, Lykke focuses on building trust. She's a big fan of US management expert Patrick Lencioni's book, *The Five Dysfunctions of a Team*, which lists an absence of trust as the first dysfunction. 'I really believe that because once you have trust, you can give feedback openly and you can have professional arguments, and you can still work together,' she says. 'You can disagree and commit, or agree and commit, and deliver results. So, creating that trust, I think, is worth a real investment.'

Lykke believes that transparency is key to building trust. 'If I want people to trust me, I also have to give them enough context that they understand the decisions I take, especially the tough ones,' she says. 'So, I do try to be as transparent as I can.'

In terms of her strengths, Lykke says she's 'good at attracting people who are better than me'. She also describes being 'patiently impatient' as one of her virtues. 'Every day I'm hungry,' she says. 'And I definitely have a big urgency to get things done. I get restless if a meeting lasts too long, or if a project is just dragging on and on. I want to see some action and results. But I'm also patient in the sense that I do get that Rome wasn't built in a day. So, we have to be impatient for many days in a row, in order to see the real results. I think that balance between patience and impatience is key in a good leader.' Other people, she says, would cite personal courage as being among her strengths – although what they see as courage she sees as her taking calculated risks.

As for her weaknesses, Lykke admits that she can be a little too slow to delegate, which is stupid, she says, when she's so good at attracting brilliant people. She also believes that she could be faster at taking tough decisions.

Expectations of leaders are changing and are going to change further over the next few years, Lykke believes. 'It's not enough anymore to show up in your suit and deliver good results,' she says. 'With trends like the Great Resignation and quiet quitting, a lot of people are starting to ask themselves more existential questions like, 'Do I really want to be doing this work every day?' Also, with time, fewer people will commit themselves fully to a job. As a leader, that's really challenging because you have to overcome finding people a little bit entitled because that opinion is not going to help you. Both sides need to find each other a little bit in the middle here. And I think keeping people engaged is a real challenge. It's a big plus to be able to offer something meaningful. If you have a strong mission in your company, then it should be more attractive than traditional companies where it's hard to see how you're making the world better. So, I try to put a lot of focus on our mission.'

The most important leadership lesson that Lykke has ever learned is 'to be a leader in a sustainable way'. By that she means she's had to find a leadership style where 'I'm basically just myself – and that has to be good enough'. She's also aware that she needs to maintain her energy to remain a leader in the long term. This was a lesson that she learned way back at McKinsey when a colleague told her that she could have a long career, or a fast career, but she would have to decide between the two. 'It's about setting a pace that's appropriate for the marathon and not the sprint,' she says. 'This is something I've had to learn.'

LEADERSHIP LESSONS FROM METTE LYKKE

- **Never give up**. If you can keep your dream alive through the most difficult of times, you will emerge the other side stronger in the end.

- **Set a high bar**. Even if you don't achieve the lofty results that you are aiming for, you will achieve a lot more than if you had set a lower bar.

- **Be patiently impatient**. Have a sense of urgency about getting things done, but accept that progress is incremental – it takes time to bring about change.

- **Build trust and foster transparency**. Your team will be stronger if they trust each other and trust in you.

- **Aim to be a sustainable leader**. If you want a long-term career, you must preserve your energy for the things that matter most.

Notes

1   Charles, K (2021) Food production emissions make up more than a third of global total, *New Scientist*, 13 September, www.newscientist.com/article/2290068-food-production-emissions-make-up-more-than-a-third-of-global-total (archived at perma.cc/D8L3-5JV8)

2   World Wildlife Fund (2021) Over 1 billion tonnes more food being wasted than previously estimated, contributing 10% of all greenhouse gas emissions, 21 July, https://wwf.panda.org/wwf_news/?3211466/Over-1-billion-tonnes-more-food-being-wasted-than-previously-estimated-contributing-10-of-all-greenhouse-gas-emissions (archived at perma.cc/YK8B-9A6Q)

3   World Food Programme (2011) A 7 billionth child – 1 in 7 chance of being hungry, 31 October, www.wfp.org/videos/7-billionth-child-1-7-chance-being-hungry (archived at perma.cc/UH9K-LGYE)

4   Food Nation (2023) Food loss and waste is also a $1.2 trillion USD business opportunity, https://foodnationdenmark.com/news/food-loss-and-waste-is-also-a-1-2-trillion-usd-business-opportunity (archived at perma.cc/PRM9-MRDS)

CHAPTER NINETEEN

Nthabiseng Mosia

Easy Solar

Leadership philosophy
'BUILD YOUR PEOPLE TO TAKE OWNERSHIP OF WHAT THEY NEED
TO DO TO ACHIEVE THE ORGANIZATION'S GOALS.'

N thabiseng Mosia is the co-founder and chief commercial officer of Easy Solar, a fast-growing, off-grid solar energy company based in the West African countries of Sierra Leone and Liberia. Born in Ghana, her mother is Ghanaian and her father is South African. At the time of her birth, her father was in exile from South Africa as he was a member of the African National Congress (ANC), a liberation movement that opposed the country's apartheid regime. The family moved to Johannesburg following the release from prison of Nelson Mandela, the ANC leader who later became president of South Africa. Mosia grew up in Johannesburg and subsequently attended the University of Cape Town, graduating with a degree in business, science, finance and accounting with first-class honours.

While she was at university, Mosia had thought herself on track for a career in finance – either as a chartered financial analyst or as a chartered accountant. But after doing an internship with an investment management firm she wasn't convinced that she wanted to enter the world of finance. Instead, she became interested in a career in management consulting, seeing it as a 'cool way to solve problems and learn about different industries'. After leaving university, Mosia spent some time in the UK and India. Then she joined professional services firm Deloitte as a consultant, specializing in strategy and innovation. While she was based in Johannesburg, she worked in several African countries. Mosia had always been interested in African development but, during her time with Deloitte, she came to appreciate the close connection between development and energy. She was also increasingly aware that clean, renewable energy is the way of the future.

Inspired by her interest in energy, Mosia headed to the United States where she spent two years studying for a master's degree in energy, finance and policy at Columbia University's School of International and Public Affairs. At Columbia she took a class where she met the other two co-founders of what was to become Easy Solar – Alexandre Tourre and Eric Silverman. The trio's class project – a plan to distribute solar energy to underserved communities in Africa – evolved into a fully fledged business after it secured funding from D-Prize, an initiative to support aspiring entrepreneurs who are helping to end extreme poverty. The young entrepreneurs raised additional funding from entering other competitions. Prior to studying at Columbia, Silverman had spent several years in Sierra Leone, where he had served in US volunteer development organization the Peace Corps. It was his suggestion that the business should initially focus on Sierra Leone.

Easy Solar's vision is to make energy accessible and affordable for all in the countries where it operates, by bringing energy to 'the last mile' (the final step of the distribution process). The energy is accessible because it is provided through a network of shops and agents. It is affordable thanks to flexible financing options that allow people to pre-pay for their energy and stagger their payments using smartphone technology. The company also supplies consumers and businesses with a range of solar-related products such as solar panels, lanterns that can charge smartphones, and solar-powered fans. Through its environmentally friendly business model, it is transforming lives.

'If people ask me what's the problem we're trying to solve, I say it's the fact that more than half of the African continent is in the dark,' Mosia explains. 'In the 21st century, people are walking two to three kilometres to charge their phone at a little kiosk in rural communities. They leave their phone there for two hours and it's charged by the one person who can afford a generator. Electrification is a problem that has, by and large, been solved in most parts of the world. It just so happens that the fastest, least-cost, most modular way to electrify people in Africa is to do solar.'

Building grid infrastructure and large power plants across Africa will take many years and require a lot of investment. At the same time, Africa is home to some of the poorest markets in the world, with flailing health and education systems, and which lack money to spare. 'Unfortunately, grid expansion could take up to 10–20 years,' says Mosia. 'In the meantime, solar can be deployed rapidly at a price point that is way more competitive than alternative solutions. It's the fastest, and most supportable and environmentally friendly way to electrify homes.' With Africa being the world's sunniest continent, it also makes sense to draw on a resource that is so widely available.

To date, Easy Solar has largely operated in Sierra Leone and neighbouring Liberia, where it has provided power to around 800,000 people. But it is also expanding into Guinea and possibly Nigeria. Additionally, it has plans to expand into the Democratic Republic of Congo, which has a population of over 92 million people – of whom less than 10 per cent have access to electricity.[1] Easy Solar deliberately chooses markets where a large proportion of the population is off-grid so that it can 'fill the gap' as Mosia puts it. This solar capacity can then be fed into the grid as and when it should arrive.

Easy Solar's business model has captured the attention of venture capitalists and development finance institutions from around the world. So far it has raised a total of $20 million and it fundraises on a near-constant basis. Nevertheless, the business has needed to navigate some significant obstacles to make progress. 'Access to capital has been a challenge,' Mosia admits. 'We have a good team that is pretty skilled at tapping into the capital markets, but people have a super-risky appetite when it comes to Africa, and even more so if it's not South Africa or North Africa.' The volatile global context – including the Covid-19 pandemic and the war in Ukraine – has also presented issues, not least an inflationary environment that has reduced the disposable incomes of Easy Solar's rural customers.

Alongside the challenges, there are also opportunities, however. In particular, Easy Solar has an opportunity to issue carbon credits against its solar range. These credits would enable companies in the developed world to compensate for their greenhouse gas emissions by subsidizing the provision of solar energy to low-income households in rural Africa.

Already Easy Solar's annual revenue exceeds $8 million and it employs more than 800 people across its business. These include sales representatives who work in its shops, commission-based agents who win customers in rural communities, after-sales representatives who ensure that the solar systems are serviced and maintained, and brand ambassadors who help to market the company, along with call centre and head office staff.

As a tech-enabled company, Easy Solar is evolving its business model beyond solar products and services. For example, because of the credit data it holds, it can provide finance to customers who have previously been unbanked to allow them to buy products such as smartphones and clean cooking stoves. 'In a country where there isn't really a strong banking sector, we're providing asset finance,' Mosia explains. 'In terms of growth, we're looking at what we're calling "productive use appliances", mainly anchored through solar. So, solar freezers, solar water pumps and solar generators to displace diesel generators. We're looking at solar-powered appliances that can generate income for people.' As well as serving consumers, the company sees opportunities to provide solar energy to the business community, including factories.

Mosia has some powerful stories to tell about the difference that Easy Solar has made to people's lives. Girls can walk around safely at night thanks to solar lighting in their communities. Children can do their homework after school because they can see what they are working on. Families whose only source of lighting was once a smoky kerosene lamp can now watch television comfortably while breathing in clean air. Mosia is bringing solar energy to African communities that are currently off-grid, driving up standards of living, improving health and safety, and creating new opportunities for people to build wealth.

Secrets to success

As a leader, Mosia is driven by her huge sense of purpose. 'Most countries' electrification stories have involved dirty, harmful fuel,' she says. 'In Africa, we have an opportunity to look forwards and backwards at the same time and learn from everybody's mistakes. It would be such a great story for humanity to say, "We learned from the past and we did electrification in a clean, affordable way that had human dignity. And that didn't leave the world worse off than how we found it."'

In 2019, Mosia was listed on the prestigious *Forbes* Africa 30 Under 30 ranking, in the technology category. That same year, she was recognized as one of the social entrepreneurs of the year by the World Economic Forum, alongside her co-founders. In 2020, she was also named Young Female Entrepreneur of the Year by *Forbes* Africa. This recognition gives her a powerful voice – a voice that she is using to be an advocate in the battle against climate change. 'We're seeing the impact of the climate crisis everywhere in the world, but here we are already on the borderline of survival,' she says. 'I'm trying to amplify that. And I want to use my platform to add to the amazing voices that are already out there.'

Going forwards, Mosia believes that leaders will be expected to have a strong moral compass, and to take society and the environment into account when making decisions. 'Principles and ethics matter,' she says. 'People are starting to get called out for arrogant behaviour. But I still don't think we're celebrating enough of those quiet leaders who build solid, stable, healthy and happy workforces.'

Mosia sees leadership as being able to navigate people on a course through turbulent and uncertain events. 'I don't think leadership is just getting stuff right,' she says. 'If that were the case, anybody who did something achievable would be a leader. I see business as constant firefighting. Which problem am I going to confront today? And how am I going to respond to it? And how am I going to enable and build my teams to respond better and better every single time?'

Getting people to achieve goals is good management, Mosia believes, but given the constraints of the markets where Easy Solar operates, she sees leadership as 'building people to move through any context to achieve their goals and to respond accordingly when things go out of turn'. She herself has had to fight to overcome the disadvantage of being a woman and an African woman at that. 'I've been undermined a lot in my life,' she says. 'And I have to endure life's challenges in a way that perhaps my male co-founders don't have to.' Nevertheless, these experiences have resulted in her having empathy, strong collaboration and listening skills, the ability to read a room, and the capacity to 'lead from the back' by empowering others.

Mosia sees her strengths as being able to set a vision, act as an inspiration to others and have a willingness to accept failure – at least to some extent. 'Our team is always very clear about where we are supposed to be going,' she says. 'And I believe in giving people ownership and allowing them to fail. I think failure is great, once or twice. Then we need to have a conversation!' Her main weakness, she says, is that despite everything she's achieved, she still suffers from imposter syndrome. 'I still have to train myself to believe that I am worthy,' she explains, 'and that I am supposed to be where I am, that I've worked very hard for it, and that I deserve every success that has come my way.'

The most important leadership lesson that Mosia has ever learned is to 'endure'. By this she means putting up with difficult things in the short term to achieve her bigger, longer-term objectives.

LEADERSHIP LESSONS FROM NTHABISENG MOSIA

- **Follow your passions**. When you do something you care about, you are more likely to achieve great things.

- **Understand the part you play in the 'bigger picture'.** How can you make a difference to the world through what you do?

- **Lead from behind**. Empower others to respond to the challenges they face. You will help them to build their resilience in the process.

- **Don't expect the journey to be easy**. At times you will probably have to struggle in the short term to achieve your long-term goals.

- **Retain your moral compass at all times**. The most successful leaders will be measured by the values they hold and the business cultures they create.

Note

1   Spencer Jones, J (2021) Democratic Republic of Congo – an off-grid solar opportunity, *Smart Energy International*, 6 May, www.smart-energy.com/renewable-energy/democratic-republic-of-congo-an-off-grid-solar-opportunity (archived at perma.cc/RZE9-LCLK)

CHAPTER TWENTY

Akindele Phillips

Farmcrowdy

Leadership philosophy
'LISTEN MORE THAN YOU SPEAK.'

Serial entrepreneur Akindele Phillips is co-founder and CEO of Farmcrowdy, an agtech company that is focused on improving the efficiency of food production in Nigeria and other African countries. He also runs his own outsourced accounting services firm called Porter's World Consult and has co-founded a logistics platform called Haul247, which connects manufacturers with truck owners who can deliver their goods.

Unsurprisingly for a man who runs three businesses, Phillips hails from an entrepreneurial family. His doctor father founded a hospital while his mother runs schools. After leaving school himself, he studied accounting at Obafemi Awolowo University, in the ancient Nigerian city of Ile-Ife. He then joined professional services firm KPMG, where he trained as an auditor before moving to a logistics firm called PhilandMove as strategy director. Since then, he has continued in his role with the logistics firm while pursuing his entrepreneurial interests.

It was through his accounting services firm, Porter's World Consult, that Phillips came into contact with Farmcrowdy's first two co-founders, Onyeka Akumah and Ifeanyi Anazodo. The pair asked him to join the business as chief financial officer in 2016, a role he did for four years before moving on to become chief risk officer and then CEO. He has balanced his work with Farmcrowdy with his accounting services firm, the logistics firm, and later with running Haul247, which was launched in 2020. It's a lot to juggle but Phillips manages to do it all by staying focused on what matters and delegating to his team. Does this system work perfectly? 'No,' he admits. 'Sometimes I miss a few things, but I don't miss much.'

Farmcrowdy's business model is aligned with the United Nations Sustainable Development Goal 2, which aims to end hunger, achieve food security and improved nutrition, and promote sustainable agriculture. Nigeria has around 38 million smallholder farmers – around 20 per cent of the country's population[1] – who grow crops such as palm oil, cocoa beans, maize, nuts, rice and soybeans. Unfortunately, these smallholder farmers struggle to access the inputs they need to produce higher-yield commodities – inputs such as seeds and fertilizers. They are also not necessarily aware of the latest agricultural practices that can help ensure they use inputs in the right way.

Farmcrowdy supports smallholder farmers by working closely with the small retail businesses that sell them seeds and fertilizers. It provides financing to these retail businesses to enable them to buy and store higher volumes of seeds and fertilizers, meaning they can then sell the inputs to farmers at affordable prices. Farmcrowdy has also created an app called 'Agraina', which enables these small businesses to better manage their inventory volumes and collect payments from customers. The app will even allow them to open a bank account.

Farmcrowdy has developed several other apps that the retail businesses can use to explain good agronomic practices to farmers. It also works with the retailers to buy produce from individual farmers for a good price and then sell it in aggregate to buyers inside and outside of Nigeria. In the same way, it helps producers of meat to sell their products to food manufacturers.

To fund its business model, Farmcrowdy has raised money from development finance institutions (DFIs) and other institutional investors. When the small retail businesses earn a profit from selling their seeds and fertilizers, they repay their loans from the sales proceeds. Farmcrowdy earns commission from the retailers' profits when they sell their inputs.

The critical issue of food security

Russia's invasion of Ukraine in 2022 highlighted the issue of food security at both a global and a continental level. Africa, for example, suffered from significantly reduced wheat supplies as a result of the crisis, which drove up the price of bread. The result has been that DFIs and companies in the food industry have recognized the need to invest in different parts of the world to ensure stable production of different commodities. 'I don't think any country or continent can be self-sufficient,' says Phillips. 'We have to continue to interact and exchange commodities.'

Over the longer term, Farmcrowdy's priority is to provide greater visibility around the agricultural output of the countries where it operates. 'A lot of the time you cannot predict the volume of the commodities that will be harvested in certain regions,' says Phillips. 'But once retailers of farm inputs – seeds, fertilizers and chemicals – are onboarded and they're selling to farmers, we have an idea of the total volume of these inputs that has gone to certain regions. And we can predict how much harvest, all things being equal, is expected from that region.' Equipped with this knowledge, Farmcrowdy will be able to work with leading food manufacturers to help them plan which regions they should source commodities from and which regions they should sell products to. It will also be able to better support the small retail businesses that serve the smallholder farmers by ensuring that they have sufficient working capital to buy essential inputs.

Farmcrowdy currently operates in Nigeria and Rwanda, but has plans to expand to the Ivory Coast, as well as run a pilot in Jamaica. In 10 years' time, it hopes to exist in all the African countries that have advantageous conditions for agricultural production. At the time of writing, the business had raised around $1.8 million in funding and was looking to raise a further $25 million to provide working capital to the retailers that serve the smallholder farmers as well as improve its own technology, invest in skills, develop its marketing and expand into new markets.

Phillips believes that in today's world, businesses must consider their social and environmental impact and bear in mind the needs and expectations of all their stakeholders when making decisions. 'If we want to continue to exist as a planet for the next 50 to 100 years, we need to pay attention to society and the environment,' he says.

Secrets to success

Phillips puts his success in life down to having good mentors, which include businesspeople such as the renowned Nigerian lawyer Asue Ighodalo, as well as religious figures. 'I get guidance from them on specific questions,' he says. He is also an avid reader of business books and a great believer in getting 360-degree feedback from his colleagues. When seeking 360-degree feedback, he asks what he should do more of, what he should change and what he should stop doing. Over the years, he's learned a lot from asking those three questions. For example, he's realized that there were occasions when he wasn't empathetic enough, or when he failed to check back in with someone over a particular issue.

In Phillips' view, a good leader is someone who grooms other people for success. 'You need to immediately identify a mentee,' he says. 'When I'm in a new organization or community group and I'm taking up a leadership position, I'm thinking, "Who can I groom?" Because you can't do it alone. You need to create a system where if you're not there, things are working, at least to an extent.'

As a leader, it's vital to be able to identify the strengths and weaknesses of other people, says Phillips, and to help them work on their areas of strength by giving them tasks that will enable them to further improve. He invests in regular training sessions for his team and promotes the sharing of information – for example, sharing articles via a WhatsApp group.

Phillips sees his own strength as being able to assimilate and balance information and present solutions to problems in a clear and articulate way. He also believes that he's a good listener – in fact, he believes that being able to listen is the most important leadership skill that he's ever learned. As for his weaknesses, he admits to being a perfectionist. 'I always want everything to work perfectly, but life is not that way,' he says. 'I try to balance that out with more patience.'

What motivates him is a desire to help other people. In fact, he points out that his entire entrepreneurial career stems from his consulting service, which has involved him supporting many start-ups to solve their problems. He's also proud of his role in helping to address the global issue of food security, emphasizing the existential nature of food. As he points out: 'You need to have eaten before you can think of any other thing you want to do on Earth.'

To stay motivated and inspired, Phillips has a vision board that he looks at every morning. The vision board contains pictures that capture where he wants to be in different areas of his life in future. These include the lives he wants to impact, how he sees his business developing and the different nations he wants to connect with, as well as his personal and family goals.

He has already seen the impact of the vision board in practice. For example, when he started his outsourced accounting services firm, it only operated in Nigeria. Since then, it has developed partners in a number of other African countries – and he believes this has happened because he's kept adding more countries onto the board. Meanwhile, in 2021, Farmcrowdy was selected for inclusion in Evolve, an initiative by news channel CNN and Afreximbank, which showcased some of Africa's strongest B2B technology companies. Prior to that, Phillips had simply put up 'CNN' on his vision board. 'The vision board has really helped to give me ideas,' he says. 'Sometimes it's not clear why I'm writing certain things. But I don't limit my mind when I'm writing it.'

Looking ahead, Phillips believes that the leaders of the future will have to pay more attention than ever to multiple stakeholders. 'Leaders will need to embrace the fact they're not in business for themselves,' he says, 'but for their shareholders, their employees, their customers, their regulators and their governments, as well as non-governmental organizations. We have to consider our impact on multiple stakeholders – we cannot ignore them any longer.'

LEADERSHIP LESSONS FROM AKINDELE PHILLIPS

- **Invest in developing the next generation of leaders**. This allows you to delegate some of your responsibilities and have a more effective impact within your organization.

- **Seek 360-degree feedback**. Other people will be able to give you useful insights into where you can improve and you may learn things about yourself that you never realized before.

- **Be a good listener**. You will engage more effectively with other people if you pay close attention to what they're saying and resist the temptation to talk too much yourself.

- **Understand your stakeholders**. Identify the different stakeholders who are connected to your organization and get to know their expectations and needs. That will help you to ensure the long-term sustainability of your organization.

- **Create your own vision board**. If you visualize the future you want, you are more likely to make that future happen.

Note

1   Adeite, A (2022) Uncommon facts about smallholder farmers in Nigeria, *Babban Gona*, https://babbangona.com/uncommon-facts-about-smallholder-farmers-in-nigeria (archived at perma.cc/8NRU-9ESY)

CHAPTER TWENTY-ONE

Andrea Thomaz

Diligent Robotics

Leadership philosophy
'A GOOD LEADER SEES THE VISION OF WHERE THE BUSINESS NEEDS TO GO.'

Andrea Thomaz is CEO and co-founder of Diligent Robotics, which builds robots that work alongside clinical staff in hospitals, helping them to work more lefficiently and effectively. She first became interested in artificial intelligence (AI) when she was studying electrical and computer engineering at the University of Texas in the late 1990s. 'I was fascinated by machines that you could teach new things,' she says. 'And I started getting really interested in the new era of AI, driven by machine learning.'[1]

After leaving the University of Texas, Thomaz briefly worked as a junior engineer for tech giant IBM. But she began to hear about interesting artificial intelligence and human–computer research taking place at the Massachusetts Institute of Technology (MIT). 'I felt like I needed to go to grad school,' she explains. 'So, I went to get a master's degree. I didn't have a plan to go into academia. I just wanted to gain expertise in machine learning and artificial intelligence and see how I could change my career path.'

What started out as a two-year master's degree turned into a multi-year fascination with developing artificial intelligence as a skillset. At MIT, Thomaz came across the institute's robotics lab and realized it was 'really, really fun to see your software actually work in the world'. With that, her passion for robotics was born. She went on to study for a PhD and wrote a thesis on the topic of 'socially guided machine learning'. Her thesis explored how robots could learn how to do new things from people and which machine learning algorithms would support that process.

Thomaz completed her PhD in 2006. At that time, she was not aware of any companies where she could continue to work on the kind of robotics she was already pursuing. So, she decided to remain in academia and moved to the Georgia Institute of Technology where she was assistant and then associate professor, leading the Socially Intelligent Machines Lab at the institute's School of Interactive Computing. While at the Georgia Institute of Technology, she broadened her research focus to investigate topics such as how a robot could interpret what people are saying, how it should interact in a dialogue, and what it should pay attention to in a demonstration. At that time – around 2007–8 – very few scientists were exploring this area of robotics. So, Thomaz and her students were effectively pioneers in their field, building their robots from scratch.

After nine years at the Georgia Institute of Technology, Thomaz switched to the University of Texas, becoming leader of the university's robotics lab.

One of Thomaz's PhD students at the Georgia Institute of Technology was a young woman named Vivian Chu, who had a strong interest in finding a commercial application for the research they were doing. By that time, more companies had become involved with robotics. As they discussed possible career paths for Chu, the pair began to explore the idea of founding their own start-up. 'We couldn't find any start-up that had our perspective, where you could build robots that work side by side with people,' says Thomaz. 'What the world needs is not just autonomous robots doing jobs by themselves, although there is a place for that in warehouses and manufacturing. There is also a whole host of jobs and service tasks that are about robots doing things together with people as part of a team. That's what we really got excited about.'

The pair founded their business, Diligent Robotics, in December 2017, initially with funding from the National Science Foundation. From the start, their idea was to develop robots that would learn from demonstration. They decided to focus on serving the health sector because they had become aware of workforce shortages in hospitals. After building several prototypes, the co-founders eventually ended up with Moxi, a service robot that works alongside teams of people in hospitals. For fun, they initially used the pronoun 'she' to refer to Moxi, says Thomaz, but once they had reflected on their brand, the pair decided that they did not want to 'gender the lowest level of work these robots are doing'. So, now they make a conscious effort not to refer to Moxi by gender although they don't try to correct other people who refer to the robot using 'he' or 'she'. 'It's hard when you have robots going round in your environment not to use pronouns,' Thomaz admits.

Moxi was first deployed in a Dallas hospital in 2020, in the midst of the Covid-19 pandemic. It was used to transfer personal protective equipment and other supplies around the hospital building. Now the robot is in service in dozens of hospitals across the US. 'Moxi supports nurses, pharmacy departments and lab technicians, taking on delivery tasks and carrying things that people would normally have to hand carry around the hospital,' Thomaz explains. 'Instead of running across the hospital to deliver a lab sample or fetch medication, they can send a Moxi robot to go and do that for them.' The hospitals that use Moxi do not actually own the robots outright. Instead, they hire them on a 'robot-as-a-service' basis, paying a monthly fee based on the work that the robot does. The robots are assembled and tested in Austin, Texas, although they contain components from all over the world.

Diligent Robotics' business model evidently appeals to investors given the company has raised $50 million from investors to date, including from some leading venture capital firms. According to Thomaz, Diligent's appeal lies in the fact that 'we are the first company that is developing mobile robots that are able to manipulate the world – reach out and push a button to open a door, and work next to people in a human environment. And, yes, we're in hospitals today, and we have a lot more expansion we can do in healthcare. But I think this has the potential to impact service in general.' Thomaz believes that in the long term there are use cases for robots like Moxi in numerous commercial settings, including shops, restaurants and office buildings, but not necessarily in people's homes. While Moxi is currently only deployed in the United States, it is likely that the robot will be adopted internationally over the coming years.

Today, Diligent Robotics is at an interesting inflection point in terms of its growth, according to Thomaz. 'The main opportunity we face right now is extreme demand from the customer,' she explains. 'Demand is definitely outpacing our ability to service the market at the moment. So, our challenge is to really grow as a business, and to build up our operations and ability to build fleets of robots and get them up and running as fast as possible.' The company has already expanded from being a small, technically focused team to having a core staff of around 85 – including client success, manufacturing and production teams – as well as additional staff who service the robots.

Making the jump into the world of business after spending the best part of two decades in academia was a major move for Thomaz, who took on the role of CEO while Chu became chief technology officer. For the first couple of years, the company was focused on product research and discovery, so its work closely matched the work Thomaz had done as a professor. Once the product was fully developed, however, and some initial customers had signed up, she started to feel much more like a businesswoman and much less like an academic. Her time was increasingly taken up with sales, hiring staff, thinking about the financials, considering key performance indicators, and reflecting on what would drive the business to succeed.

'Coming from academia, you feel like you have so much catching up to do on the business side of things,' she says. 'You feel like you're always asking a dumb question. But, later on, I got to a point where I was really comfortable saying, "Hey, I don't know how to structure this part of the business. Help!" And, you know, it's not usually a dumb question…'

Thomaz had to overcome some initial bias within the investment community due to her academic background. Initially, investors were afraid that she would either move too slowly or lack the business experience to really drive the company forward. Nevertheless, she now believes that coming from academia has been an advantage in many ways. 'To build the kind of technology that we were building, you had to have a research mindset and you had to have this "iterate quickly, iterate quickly" mindset that we have in academia,' she says. 'Then, over time, as you show that you are able to run the company, it becomes so much easier to convince investors that you're not just an academic. Instead, it's almost like a superpower. Investors say: "Oh, my gosh, you've got this academic background and you've got the ability to run a company. That's amazing."'

As CEO, Thomaz focuses on setting the high-level objectives for Diligent and on making sure that all the teams are aligned and understand those objectives. Despite her strong technical background, she's enjoying taking a step back from doing the detailed work as she concentrates on the business side of things. 'I'm really motivated by the number of people we're able to impact,' she says. 'One of my favourite things is to visit our clients, watch Moxi robots go round, and see the frontline staff get work done with these robots. It's fun when they're excited and taking selfies with Moxi, but it's almost more exciting when it's just a normal part of their work.'

The enthusiastic reception that Moxi gets from hospital staff contradicts many of the negative social perceptions of robots that exist today. 'There is a lot of sci-fi baggage with robots, both good and bad,' Thomaz acknowledges. 'We have this notion that robots should be here, and they should be doing a lot of stuff for us. But, at the same time, there are a lot of movies about robots going rogue and taking over the world, and I think that is also in the back of people's minds.'

Still, she says that when Moxi arrives at a new hospital, people quickly overcome their sci-fi baggage, especially once they've learned how Moxi can help them in practice. 'They realize it's not, you know, super-advanced artificial intelligence,' says Thomaz. 'It's a delivery robot. And it's doing things for me that I really need done in a reliable way – and it's taking real work off my plate.' People tend to rapidly conclude that they do, in fact, like robots. 'I think that's how we're always going to have robots in society,' Thomaz explains. 'There is a place for augmentation tools.'

Secrets to success

Thomaz believes that it is the role of a leader not only to set the vision for the business but also to break that vision down into a series of executable steps that everyone in the business can align on. 'Maintaining that alignment so that everyone understands they're part of the mission, that's one of the most important things that a good leader does,' she says. She also thinks the leader plays a vital role in helping to shape the culture of the business, saying of

Diligent: 'We don't want this to be a start-up that burns people into the ground. This is a marathon, not a sprint, and we're building a culture, not a *thing*.'

Robots feature in both Diligent's mission and in Thomaz's personal mission since she believes they can play a major role in society, provided they are used in the right way. 'The success or failure of robots in society will stem from their ability to work successfully together with people,' she predicts. 'We're showing the right way to bring robots into a team of people. At Diligent, we say that we want to build beautiful robots. We build beautiful robots that do useful things for people.'

This mission is vital to attracting the talented people that Diligent needs to thrive and grow. 'Everyone I interview – without me bringing it up – usually says within the first five or 10 minutes that why they want to work for Diligent is the social mission,' says Thomaz. 'They want to be working on technology that they can feel good about. They want to be building state-of-the-art machine learning, AI and robotic systems that are for the benefit of society.'

Thomaz sees her main leadership weakness as 'some of the baggage that I probably bring from academia'. Not having a huge amount of corporate experience, she is aware that she has some blind spots when it comes to business. 'On the other hand, when it comes to my strengths, I would say I'm quick to take action and it's pretty easy to get me to make a decision,' she explains. 'As a start-up, we have to make a lot of decisions with a lack of information. People need the CEO to be comfortable making those decisions because taking too long results in a lot of ambiguity.'

As an academic by background, it's not surprising that Thomaz has turned to books to develop herself as a leader. 'I was fascinated to read about different leaders, and different start-up stories,' she says. 'I think you learn from reading. *The Hard Thing About Hard Things*, by Ben Horowitz, was really impactful early on.'

Throughout her career Thomaz has also sought support from mentors – a strategy she describes as 'seeking out the right mentors at the right time'. These mentors include fellow start-up founders, as well as Diligent Robotics independent board member Lance VandenBrook (who is CEO of IAM Robotics, a provider of fulfilment robots) and Cynthia Breazeal, the leading US robotics scientist who was Thomaz's PhD adviser at MIT.

Thomaz believes that, in future, technology leaders will need to evolve to become more empathetic and to 'think about the whole person' when it comes to managing their staff. Employees, she argues, want to be recognized as individuals and they want their leaders to be committed to helping them along their development pathways. The most important leadership lesson that Thomaz has ever learned is 'you can never assume that you've said something too many times'.

LEADERSHIP LESSONS FROM ANDREA THOMAZ

- **Don't be afraid to start your own business – even if you have no business experience**. You can learn and develop business skills and source advice from experts.

- **Push the boundaries with your use of technology**. You can develop a valuable niche in the marketplace if you have a product or service that people want and no one else has.

- **Align your people with the vision**. They will achieve the best results if they understand exactly what they are working towards.

- **Frequently repeat your key messages**. People need to hear information many times over to remember it.

- **Turn your disadvantages into your superpowers**. Having different experiences and skillsets from other leaders might seem a negative at first, but it can set you apart in the long run.

Note

1   AI is the simulation of processes that normally require human intelligence, such as speaking and making decisions, while machine learning is the development of computer systems that can learn and adapt without following explicit instructions.

Conclusion

The major question that naturally arises at the end of this book is surely the following: What do the 21st-century business icons profiled here have in common with each other? Is there such a thing as a single blueprint for success?

Perhaps the most common theme – if a rather unexciting one – is the overwhelmingly strong work ethic that these leaders seem to have. None of the leaders profiled in this book has as their secret to success a propensity to overindulge on Netflix series or spend half their Sundays scrolling through their smartphones (or not that they admit to, at least). The carmaker Henry Ford might have been a 20th-century business icon, but he was effectively speaking for 21st-century business icons as well when he said: 'It has been my observation that most people get ahead during the time that others waste.'

Alongside hard work and self-discipline, several other important themes prevail. One of these is purpose. The business icons have a strong sense of purpose – they know what they want to do with their business, and why they want to do it. And they care deeply about what they do. As a result, they take a very long-term perspective when it comes to business strategy. They are prepared to make short-term sacrifices if it means achieving their overall objectives.

Purpose helps to inform vision and the leaders featured in this book are great visionaries. By painting a vivid picture of what they want to achieve, they inspire talented people to work with them. What's more, they make a point of empowering their people, by giving them agency and ownership of tasks. That helps to build determination, loyalty and an entrepreneurial spirit within their workforce.

Business icons know that they can't do everything all on their own. Hence, they build strong teams and prioritize collaboration, both within their organization and between their organization and its external partners. They are not afraid to hire people who are better than they are at certain aspects of the business. They actively seek out advice, support and, in many cases, funding from others. They listen to mentors and act as mentors themselves.

A willingness to take risks – extreme risks, in many cases – is also key. But, at the same time, those risks are calculated. We are not talking about random punts here. The risks that the business icons take are based on their understanding of evolving economic, social and techno-logical trends. Similarly, the icons are also prepared to fail – even many times over – since they see failure as a fundamental part of the journey to success. They are persistent and resilient and will repeatedly bounce back from setbacks that would cause other people to simply give up.

Another common theme of business icons is perfectionism. They tend to demand a lot of others, sometimes more than those people feel able to give. While this perfectionist streak can lead to them losing talented staff, it is also what drives them to push the boundaries of what is possible so that they end up delivering the goods and services that genuinely transform the world.

Yet while there are common themes, there is no single blueprint for a business icon. Icons can be male or female. They can be young or old. They can be extraverted or introverted. They can send people into space or sell slimming pants. They can be based anywhere on the planet. But if there is any one thing that does unite all the business leaders in this book, it is probably their belief in the power of business to do good. Through the actions they're taking to solve specific problems, and address particular pain points, they are helping to make the world a better place.

About the author

Sally Percy has nearly 20 years' experience as a business journalist and editor. She is editor of *Edge*, the official journal of the UK's Institute of Leadership, and a leadership contributor to Forbes.com. During her career, Sally has written for numerous publications and also works as an editorial consultant, creating thought leadership articles for well-known businesses. In 2017, she published her first book, *Reach the Top in Finance: The ambitious accountant's guide to career success*. Earlier in her career, she worked as a management consultant for Accenture. Sally has a degree in modern history from the University of Oxford.

Ovidia Yu is one of Singapore's best-known and most acclaimed writers. She has had over thirty plays produced and is the author of a number of comic mysteries published in Singapore, India, Japan and America.

She received a Fulbright Scholarship to the University of Iowa's International Writers Program and was awarded the S.E.A. Write Award for Singapore.

Also by Ovidia Yu

The Frangipani Tree Mystery
The Betel Nut Tree Mystery
The Paper Bark Tree Mystery
The Mimosa Tree Mystery
The Cannonball Tree Mystery

The Mushroom Tree Mystery

Ovidia Yu

CONSTABLE

CONSTABLE

First published in Great Britain in 2022 by Constable

1 3 5 7 9 10 8 6 4 2

Copyright © Ovidia Yu, 2022

The moral right of the author has been asserted.

A CIP catalogue record for this book
is available from the British Library.

ISBN: 978-1-47213-205-5

Typeset in Contenu by SX Composing DTP, Rayleigh, Essex
Printed and bound in Great Britain by Clays Ltd, Elcograf S.p.A.

Papers used by Constable are from well-managed forests
and other responsible sources.

Constable
An imprint of
Little, Brown Book Group
Carmelite House
50 Victoria Embankment
London EC4Y 0DZ

An Hachette UK Company
www.hachette.co.uk

www.littlebrown.co.uk

Dedicated to the memory of the real Fukutarō Suzuki
(pen name Keikichi Ōsaka), prolific pioneer writer of
mystery stories. Drafted into the Japanese Army
during the Second World War, he died in the
Philippines in 1945.

Historical Note

———◆———

The 'true' story of the Japanese bomb plans was even more dramatic than I've dared put down here. One of their ideas was to send bombs via gas balloons to America, following wind patterns. In 1945 one killed six people, including five children, in Oregon. There are also records that plague-infected rats were bred in laboratories in Singapore as hosts for the plague-infested lice that Japanese planes scattered over China.

I based Mrs Maki very loosely on the wife of a moderate Singapore-based Japanese official who spoke out against the growing militarisation in Japan before the war. He was assassinated after returning to Japan, likely by the right-wing group she later joined.

I based Professor Kutsuki (very, very, very) loosely on Professor Ryokichi Sagane, a physicist at the University of Tokyo. Copies of a letter to Professor Sagane were dropped over Nagasaki before the bombing, from 'three of your former scientific colleagues during your stay in the United States', urging him to tell the public about the danger involved in weapons of

mass destruction. But, though aware of the dangers of the bomb contamination, Professor Sagane was neither blind nor based in Singapore during the war.

After news of the Hiroshima bomb reached Singapore, the Japanese military ordered *all* of the PoWs in Changi prison to be killed in revenge. Also, the risk of the Japanese wiping out Singapore's population rather than surrendering was very real. Fortunately, those orders weren't carried out.

In addition to anchoring historical facts to published sources, I've incorporated variations on stories I was told by my late relatives ('Just think of seventeen people sharing one WC!' my late mother said, every time we complained about something at home), as well as stories passed on from the families of friends. I hope this story reflects the spirit of all those who survived as well as their memories of those who didn't.

The Mushroom Trees

———◆———

I remember it was some hours before dawn, that Monday morning, when I heard the planes approaching. I was out by the mushroom trees and had already been there for at least an hour.

I found it hard to sleep because of the August heat, and because we were close to the Swan Lake, the humidity was so thick that you couldn't tell if the damp soaking your sheets was coming out of you or the air.

It was hot outside too, but I've always preferred to be outdoors than inside a building, especially now I was living in Moss House, on the grounds of the Singapore Botanic Gardens, since renamed the Shōnan Botanic Gardens by the Japanese. Moss House was where the Kew Gardens–trained British administrator and his family had lived. Now they, with all the other botanists and researchers, were either locked up as PoWs or doing hard labour on the Siam–Burma Railway.

Because of the blackout and curfew, I was safer out there at night than I was during the day. Also, the mushrooms seemed

to grow better by night, and it was less traumatic to lift the tarpaulin to look at them when it was dark.

I extinguished my coconut-oil lamp. I'd improvised it from an old cough-tincture bottle, coconut oil, and lamp wicks made from strips of old dishcloth twisted, sewn together and pulled through the hole I'd made in the lid. I'd ducked under the tarp covering the mushroom trees and pulled it over me when I heard the planes coming, straining to pick up the whistle before the impact. They say it's good to hear the bombs explode, because if you're alive to hear it, it hasn't got you. They passed over without incident. I waited a while more, then crawled out. Born in 1920, the year of the metal monkey, I was twenty-four years old. I didn't know if I would live to turn twenty-five.

Here in Syonan-To – Japanese Occupied Singapore – there were daily air raids from British and American bombers. Radios were still banned, with harsh penalties, so it was impossible to know what was happening in the rest of the world. The official Japanese version was that the war was over for Singapore: we were now part of the great Japanese Empire. But the bombers told a different story.

These days, the sky black with smoke in the middle of the day and thick with the smell of wood and attap houses burning, it must have sunk in with even the most victory-focused Japanese that their success in the East wasn't absolute.

Of course, the Allied bombs destroyed local homes as well as Japanese fortifications but that didn't turn the locals against them. In fact, most welcomed the raids. The incendiary bombs were part of the healing process, like the pain of cutting infection from a rusty nail out of your foot. And the daily bombings were

a sign that, whatever the Japanese said, we hadn't been forgotten. It was a small price to pay.

The laboratory building was on the other side of Swan Lake, at the small opening that stood at the foot of the steep slope from the primary forest area. You either walked the ten-minute scenic loop around the lake or, as I had done, crossed a precarious plank bridge laid over the marsh garden – the narrowest part of the lake, which was thick with water hyacinth, lotus pads and horsetail reeds. Swan Lake was now officially called 'Main Lake'. We called it 'Snakehead Lake' because the snakeheads, eels and catfish in it were our main source of protein. There was fencing around the perimeter of the garden but, like everything else, it was in a state of disrepair.

While foraging for edibles behind the laboratory building, I'd found three huge half-rotted tree trunks covered with tarpaulin and thick with mushrooms. They bore a plastic-encased order to 'keep the substrate covered to prevent cross-contamination by wild mushroom spores'. It was clearly an experiment and I'd decided to continue it. I didn't have any scientific education, but I was good at experimenting, analysing results and not giving up.

The teachers at the Mission Centre school I'd attended had drummed it into us that we could succeed at anything we really wanted to, as long as we converted our 'want' into 'work'. Of course, they'd been talking about getting a teacher-training certificate or secretarial post: when I'd admitted my dream of becoming a journalist I was told it was neither realistic nor respectable. But, to be fair, they'd encouraged my equally unrealistic goal of going to university.

3

All of that had evaporated when the Japanese came. Now my only goal was to stay alive.

I'd found soil and fertiliser, and helped myself to the bins of mulch and wood chips and added them to what was already there. As with everywhere else on our island, the hill slope was granite beneath the surface layer of loam – clay, sand and organic matter – which was precious and had to be carefully preserved. The supplies were probably intended to keep fancy exotic plants alive but I'd put them to good use growing vegetables to keep us common people alive. We were the endangered species now.

Foraging for wild mushrooms is dangerous, because you can't tell the good from the bad until it's too late. Trusting labels written by scientists was risky too, but though I never took risks if I could help it, you have to trust some people or you'll spend all your time reinventing the wheel.

Mushroom-growing felt like part craft and part magic. I had to do the work but there was no way of telling whether they would spawn until they did – or didn't. I'd already managed to grow shiitakes, and my experimental mushrooms hadn't killed anyone. I considered that a success.

I'd kept the tarp tied over the trunks to prevent wild spores coming in. I'd also warned – almost threatened – the houseboys to stay away, despite their curiosity. They meant well but they were young and clumsy. I'd heard them joking, 'Miss Chen has a tree spirit boyfriend!' but they knew better than to disobey me.

I was hoping to get some wine-cap mushrooms to spawn from the last of the *saketsubatake* sent from Japan, and there were signs of life, but I didn't know if they would survive to grow large enough to eat.

Whenever I could, I brought food scraps from the house to the mushroom trees, like people brought food offerings to the shrines. Maybe that was how it all started. The birds and bugs, worms and animals that ate them would leave droppings to enrich the soil. Mushrooms were virtuously vegetarian and had a deliciously umami 'meatiness'.

I'd learned from the scientists' notes that once the spawn was placed it must not be disturbed or the mushrooms would not grow. So I moved down the trunks of the mushroom trees according to the markings, tying down the tarp at different points.

I'd also tried to grow the *maitake* or 'dancing mushroom', Mrs Maki's favourite variety. So far I hadn't succeeded. They're normally found in Japanese hardwood forests and perhaps didn't like the soft wood or Singapore's hot, humid climate.

From what I was seeing, the Japanese didn't like our climate either. Mrs Maki complained almost as much about how hot she was as she did about how stupid I was.

I was using mushrooms to distract myself. I've always found the best way to avoid thinking about something you can't change is to focus on something else. I didn't want to think about what I was doing there. Mrs Maki had come to find me at my grandmother's house when she came back to Singapore. Years ago, she had been my first Japanese teacher. Now she wanted me to set up and run a household for her since she knew I could speak Japanese as well as English, Malay, Hokkien and Cantonese. She also said it had been Hideki Tagawa's suggestion. I think we both knew he wanted to keep an eye on me.

Hideki Tagawa had no official military post, but he was close to Prince Chichibu and had been instrumental in establishing the military dictatorship in Japan. Since the death last year of Colonel Fujiwara, Hideki Tagawa had been 'chief adviser' to the military administration in Syonan. His first and most complicated task had been to cover up what had driven the top administrator to his death while making sure his reputation and pension remained pristine for the sake of his wife and children in Japan.

When I'd first met him, Hideki Tagawa had been so sure Japan was doing what was best for Asia: freeing us from Western colonial rule. And, like my former boss Chief Inspector Le Froy of the Singapore Police, Hideki Tagawa had tried to create a system that was fair to locals, as well as their Japanese lords and masters, in which justice applied to all.

Was it so wrong for me to help the Japanese run our island if I'd been willing to work with the British?

Hideki Tagawa's mother, Mrs Maki's mother and my mother's mother had been three sisters who were the last true generation of the Sakanoue clan. That meant we were cousins. I'd learned this only after the Occupation had taken place.

They weren't my only family with 'pride'. My grandfather's family in China had cut him off after he'd dishonoured the Chen family by marrying a Straits-born woman without bound feet. But my grandfather had thrived, building up a lending (loan shark), gambling and property empire, which my grandmother had continued to run after his death. Ah Ma wasn't cowed by convention. She'd taken me in after the death of my parents, even though fortune-tellers had advised her that I would expose her and the family to the bad luck I was carrying. 'Those

know-it-alls also told me to sell your grandfather's business after he died. Instead I kept it and you.'

Anyway, the bad luck of being born a girl, then having polio, no longer held true. Most of the healthy men my age were dead or in prison.

Though Hideki Tagawa was the official resident of Moss House, the main reason the household had been arranged was for Professor Nobutsuna Kutsuki, the genius scientist. He had been evacuated to Singapore after all his work records were destroyed in the laboratory explosion and fire that had blinded him. His official reason for being here was to re-document the work that had been destroyed. The explosion had also damaged Professor Kutsuki's hands so it was difficult for him to manage his chopsticks and toothbrush. There were always ink and food stains on his clothes, and although I made sure they were washed, there was always a sour, rank smell about him. That must have been painful for a man as particular as he must once have been – everything within his reach, like his water glass, was always very precisely placed. As well as the books he could no longer read.

Professor Kutsuki's assistant, Morio Goda, and Yoshio Yoshimoto, the officer responsible for recovering lost material, were there too. My work wasn't difficult, but the atmosphere in the house was.

The security around Professor Kutsuki was so high I couldn't leave the Botanic Gardens even to visit the market. I had to make do with the food that was sent in. We were given the best there was, but it still wouldn't have been enough if I hadn't been able to supplement it from the Botanic Gardens and the jungle beyond.

Professor Kutsuki was the brilliant scientist whose secret research project had been supposed to win the war for Japan, but I hadn't seen him doing any work since he'd arrived. I'd been told to stay away from his room, so I had nothing to do with him, other than preparing his meals and washing his clothes, but I'd heard them alternately cajoling and yelling at him to no avail. I felt sorry for the old man.

I wondered how long they would keep this up. And whether I would continue to work there after they gave up on him. Even now I suspected the only reason we were still there was because Mrs Maki passionately admired Yoshio Yoshimoto and didn't want to admit failure to him. I don't know whether she thought she was in love for the first time or believed this was her last hope. Maybe she wasn't even aware of it.

When Hideki Tagawa said she was behaving like a foolish girl, she said she was a patriot and told him he was thinking like a traitor.

Next to Yoshio Yoshimoto, Hideki Tagawa looked even more like a rat. Especially now he was increasingly secretive and preoccupied.

Yoshio Yoshimoto resembled a Japanese Humphrey Bogart. He hated the West, especially Americans, so you wouldn't think he'd take that as a compliment when Mrs Maki told him so. But I think he did. At least, I heard him repeat it more than once to tease Mrs Maki.

Mrs Maki was no Ingrid Bergman.

Yoshio Yoshimoto also looked a bit like the hero, Oishi, of *The 47 Ronin*. I suspect that was why Mrs Maki had insisted on screening *The 47 Ronin: Part 2* at Moss House when it was announced there would be no public screenings.

I reminded myself this was none of my business and, trying not to breathe on them, continued laying the minute spores on squares of damp cloth in rows close, but not too close, to each other. I didn't want to overcrowd them, but at the same time I wanted to fit in as many as I could.

Unfortunately this reminded me of Hideki Tagawa saying last night at the dinner table, 'We're trying to keep as many as possible of them alive, but they keep dying.'

He'd been talking about PoWs locked up in Changi Prison. More than five thousand were crammed into a facility intended to house just over five hundred. But the alternative was worse. Earlier in the war, the Japanese had got rid of PoWs and locals by tying them together, marching them into the sea and shooting them.

'Shot or beaten to death?' Mrs Maki had asked. 'Prisoners of war are always dying. Please try the steamed egg, Professor. It will give you energy for your work.'

'Malaria and dysentery mostly.' I didn't miss Hideki Tagawa's quick glance at me, standing by to clear the dishes or in case anyone needed more tea or water. He knew I had friends in Changi Prison – Dr and Mrs Shankar, the parents of my best friend Parshanti, who was now somewhere in the up-country jungles with her fiancé, my old teachers from the Mission School and, of course, Chief Inspector Le Froy, who'd given me my first job and who'd taught me so much ...

'We don't have enough food or medicine for our own soldiers. It's hard for everyone.' Hideki Tagawa shoved his bowl at me, 'I have no appetite. Clear this away.'

I suspected he knew how eagerly table scraps were devoured in the kitchen.

'Any man who surrenders instead of fighting to the death is guilty of dishonouring his country and family,' Yoshio Yoshimoto said. 'Why are we feeding cowards who surrendered when our own soldiers need food? I don't understand you.'

Yoshio Yoshimoto was big on honour and duty, and had been involved in the distribution of *The 47 Ronin* propaganda film that no one seemed interested in now. Most found it too slow-moving and depressing.

I kind of liked it, though. Of course I'd looked as miserable as everyone else when Mrs Maki had forced the entire household to sit through it after dinner last night to justify the expense of the electricity. In brief, this is what happens in the film: the master of the forty-seven samurai is killed. The samurai kill the murderer in revenge, then themselves. It seemed more about the pointlessness of war than a celebration of Japanese imperialism.

Hideki Tagawa had said as much: 'The military told Kenji Mizoguchi to make a ferocious morale-booster based on the forty-seven Ronin, all about us battling the Western demons. Mizoguchi had no choice but to go ahead, but he made us look like idealistic fools instead of heroes, and all those military men don't know the difference!'

'Don't talk nonsense,' Mrs Maki had scolded him. 'Don't talk at all!'

I had to admit the film was kind of romantic and touching. In *Part 2* (I hadn't seen *Part 1*) the forty-seven Ronin, led by the handsome Oishi, give up everything, including their own lives, to avenge their master. Oishi is the last to commit *seppuku* and courteously excuses himself with 'I have to go now.' It's a poignant

moment. It made me think of Le Froy ceremonially writing notes to dismiss us formally from our jobs at the Detective Unit. He'd known enough of the Japanese military mentality to see the need to protect us, even before they started targeting all those who'd worked with the British.

I don't think Mrs Maki realised the film was about deceiving the powerful and playing the fool to appear harmless. But maybe she was distracted by Professor Kutsuki constantly asking Morio Goda, 'What's happening now?'

'They're eating. And drinking.'

'Eating what? Drinking what?'

'How would I know? It's a film!'

'It's a stupid film, then!'

I didn't have to act helpless or stupid to be seen as a harmless fool, thanks to the childhood polio that had left me crippled. But without a mission like Oishi's, I couldn't see what good that did me.

A shout from the other side of the lake cut into my thoughts.

'Missy! Missy Chen! Come back to the house! You are wanted!' It was Tanis, one of the houseboys.

Thanks to the Japanese killing off anyone who was good at anything, it was impossible to get adult staff. But I'd worked with Tanis and the other houseboy before so when Mrs Maki had asked me to find servants for Moss House I'd thought of them. Between the three of us we managed to keep her and her project team happy.

'Mrs Maki says come quick!' He spoke in Japanese in case he was overheard. Using any other language was an offence, but by now both boys had adequate Japanese. Most locals picked

up languages easily, which wasn't surprising since we grew up on a mash-up of Chinese dialects, Malay and Tamil.

'Now? What happened? Why is Mrs Maki awake?'

My thoughts jumped to Professor Kutsuki. Mrs Maki and Yoshio Yoshimoto had said the rebels and traitors were after him, but there had been no attempts to kill or kidnap him so far.

'The *kempeitai* are here! Mrs Maki says come quick!'

The *kempeitai*?

'Coming!' I stood up at once, dusting damp earth off my shins. Despite the recent calm I hadn't forgotten the killings of the early days. With luck it was just another routine questioning. Despite Hideki Tagawa's protection, I'd worked with the British-run police so my presence at Moss House was regularly questioned. 'Coming,' I repeated, trying for a steadier voice. But I was tense enough to yelp and scramble away when someone burst out of the bushes above, skidding and sliding down the steep slope towards me.

'Wait! I'll walk back with you!'

It was Morio Goda, Professor Kutsuki's assistant. I almost didn't recognise him. Normally so particular about his appearance, he was sweaty and dishevelled from ploughing through the tangle of vines and branches.

'Where did you come from?' Looking up, I couldn't see anything but the dangerous darkness of thorny undergrowth and thick foliage. 'What were you doing up there?'

'Come on,' he said. 'Don't keep the *kempeitai* waiting.'

A Lighter and a Poison Pin

———◆———

'So, what did you think of *The 47 Ronin*?' Morio Goda said conversationally.

I was so taken aback I almost forgot to worry about the *kempeitai*. Professor Kutsuki's assistant looked to be in his early twenties. He and I were the youngest in the household, apart from the houseboys. At first I'd hoped we might be friends – it was so long since I'd been around anyone under forty – but Morio Goda had been very cold and distant.

All right, not 'cold and distant': he'd been rude and superior, making clear he saw me as a servant. That was why I was more than surprised to find him out there, talking to me as though I was a human being.

'What?'

'The film. Last night.'

'I don't know. Where did you come from? What were you doing up there?'

'What was I doing? What were *you* doing? You looked like you were hiding a body – or an escaped prisoner or something!'

Tanis, who'd just reached us, rolled his eyes and staggered, as though he was drunk, while making kissing sounds. In other words, he behaved like a brat – or the small boy he was.

I pointed at the fish traps on the other side of the makeshift plank bridge we were coming to. 'Go and check them,' I ordered him. Tanis ran ahead, giggling.

'What are you hiding under there?' Morio Goda asked, as we crossed the bridge after him. 'Why are you messing around with those dead trees, anyway?'

'Told you. I'm growing mushrooms,'

'You can't grow mushrooms here.'

'You had some of them for dinner last week.'

'She grows mushrooms there,' Tanis shouted. 'She cooked them for the house. She lets us help cook them but she won't let us help grow them. She's scared that we'll steal her precious mushrooms!'

'I told you to stay away from the mushroom trees because I'm still figuring out how to keep them alive,' I said. 'Mushrooms prefer to grow in the dark. I don't want to let too much light in, but I have to keep them moist. I don't want you messing them up.'

'You grew all those mushrooms you served us? Do you have to fertilise them or are they feeding on the dead tree?'

'Both. Mushrooms digest whatever they grow in, so the rotting tree trunk is a good start. But I also scatter dead leaves and kitchen scraps over them.' Much as I loved talking about my mushroom trees, I returned to the topic that, right then, interested me most. 'What were you doing up there? Were you spying on me?'

'What?' Morio Goda managed to look affronted. He was still patting down his hair and smoothing his shirt as he hurried to keep up with me.

I always walk as fast as I can when I'm around people like him, so they have no chance to call me slow. I knew I had to be careful around Morio Goda, and I remembered that now, even though he looked so uncharacteristically grubby and untidy. He was always very particular about his clothes and once accused the houseboys of stealing one of his vests. He'd demanded they be beaten till they admitted it and only stopped when Professor Kutsuki admitted he'd taken it to dry his feet after stepping in mud. 'Why would I want to spy on you? You're nothing!'

'That's true,' I said agreeably, 'so what *were* you doing?'

'I didn't know why you were sneaking out so I followed you to see. Just in case you were doing something like contacting the rebels. I went the long way round so you wouldn't see me following you and I could find out what you were up to.' He sounded uncomfortable, as if he was trying to be nice but struggling to squeeze out his words through painfully constricted vocal cords.

I'd learned more about the differences between individual Japanese since moving into Moss House. Some, like Hideki Tagawa and Mrs Maki, believed in the war because they were tired of being treated as animals by Westerners. But they seemed not to realise they were just as bad, perhaps worse (though probably unaware of it), in the way they treated 'lower class' Japanese. Like Morio Goda. And Morio Goda was very aware of it.

I could tell Yoshio Yoshimoto and Morio Goda spoke with accents that made Mrs Maki wince. It was like the British Oxbridge-educated officers mocking men with regional dialects and calling them Brummies or Scousers. I think Mrs Maki forgave Yoshio Yoshimoto because he was so good-looking. But Morio Goda wasn't much taller than I was and almost as skinny.

Morio Goda wasn't looking for equality with Westerners. He'd not had anything to do with foreigners until the war. But he came from a class so put down by other Japanese that they were banking on Japanese superiority to all other races. It was their only chance to despise others as they were despised at home.

So how come Morio Goda was being nice to me now?

Chen Tai, my grandmother, had always warned me, 'Never trust any man who is nice to you.'

'I told you what I was up to,' I said. 'I was growing mushrooms.'

'Mushrooms are a waste of time. Some people like Yoshio Yoshimoto can't eat mushrooms. Can't even be near them,' Morio Goda said. He dropped his attempt to be nice, 'That's what's wrong with your people. You don't understand true heroism. You need to pay more attention. The film is about bringing back the old days when Japan was great and everyone knew it. Did you see *Part I*?'

I knew *The 47 Ronin: Part I* had been released the week of the attack on Pearl Harbor and received with the military and nationalistic fervour that had been at its peak in Japan. That had been before I'd been recruited to work at Moss House.

'No.'

'See? That's your problem. No culture. The films are about what is at the heart of Japan. It will never surrender. That's why it will always be victorious!'

I'd thought (from *Part 2* at least) that the film was about fighting on for revenge even if you could no longer fight for victory – even if all you could hope for was the honour of committing ritual suicide.

I didn't get it, frankly. I don't know whether it was because I wasn't honourable enough or wasn't Japanese enough. I'd rather start building a new life. But I knew Morio Goda wasn't interested in what I thought so I just nodded and looked properly ashamed.

But I remembered being startled by the intensity with which Hideki Tagawa's eyes fixed on the screen when Oishi said, 'Excuse me, I must go now.' It was as though he was watching a personal prophecy of doom.

That fitted with rumours I'd heard that the tide of war had turned against the Japanese. Other rumours said Germany had surrendered to the Allied forces in Europe, but here in Syonan, and especially in Moss House, we were cut off from all news. In any case, regardless of what happened in the West, we knew Japan would never surrender the East.

The Japanese told us the Americans were bombing Singapore and Laos because we were outposts of the Greater Japanese Empire. It was their revenge for how the Japanese had attacked Hawaii, and because it was too far and too dangerous for them to bomb mainland Japan.

I think they wanted us to believe we were in more danger from the American bombers than from our Japanese occupiers. 'This is the most dangerous time for you. That's why it's vital for you to report any sighting of Americans so that Japan can protect you.'

But I knew that locals still prayed for the safe flight home of the very bombers that had just destroyed their homes. If it was true that the Allies had given up on us, why were they still sending the planes? Every attack on our Japanese-held island was a reminder that we had not been forgotten.

'Of course, I also speak American,' Morio Goda said.

'I thought Americans spoke English.'

'It's just a dialect of English. Like Chinese is an inferior dialect of Japanese.'

I ignored the challenge.

'Listen. Da doo da da doo da da da/Da doo da da doo da da da/Da doo da da doo da da da /Da doo da da doo da da.' I couldn't make out what he was singing. There weren't any words until: "'He's the boogie-woogie bugle boy of Company B.'"

Oh. He was singing an American song. Then he said, 'A lighter and a poison pin. Just like Yoshio Yoshimoto, I always carry a lighter and a poison pin.'

'Sorry, what?'

Ostentatiously he pulled a small box out of his pocket and shook it at me, then replaced it without letting me see its contents. 'It's what all the top operatives carry on missions.'

'What missions?'

'That's secret. I can't tell you. A lighter and a poison pin. The pin is a regular pin that you have to dip in poison once a week to keep primed. That's all a modern warrior needs to carry,' Morio Goda said. 'I do important top-secret work.'

'Yes, I know Professor Kutsuki's work is very important,' I said, meaning to flatter him.

Instead, he looked offended. 'I'm not just some pen-pushing secretary. I'm a warrior, a patriot. Like the super-patriots!'

The 'super-patriots' had been famous for organising the assassinations of politically moderate statesmen, industrialists, military generals and admirals before the war. When they were caught, their sympathisers in the government gave them light sentences and regarded them as patriot heroes. I didn't see

Morio Goda as one of them. But even if he hadn't assassinated anyone, I'd no wish to provoke him into starting with me.

Besides I was getting the strangest feeling that he was trying to ingratiate himself, though he wasn't very good at it. With me? This was even more startling than his bursting out of a tangle of shrubbery above me.

'Like Yoshio Yoshimoto,' I suggested.

'Yes! Exactly!'

Now I'd finally found the right flattery track Morio Goda took over: 'Yoshio Yoshimoto is a great warrior. What's happening isn't going to keep him down.'

'What isn't?' I tried not to sound too interested.

'Prime Minister Koiso resigning, of course. Because the damned Americans sank the Imperial *Yamato*.'

The *Yamato* had been the flagship of the Imperial Japanese Navy. I was careful not to look happy or interested. 'Why would that affect Yoshio Yoshimoto?'

'Prime Minister Koiso was Yoshio Yoshimoto's patron. You really don't know anything, do you?'

I knew that Prime Minister (now former Prime Minister) Koiso, an ardent supporter of state Shintoism and Japanese supremacy, had been instrumental in starting the war against China and then against the Allies. It sounded like things were really changing, then. I managed to look appropriately chastised, and Morio Goda was pleased enough to help carry the young coconuts that the houseboys had harvested earlier and left in a heap under the trees. I was surprised. And a little intrigued.

Morio Goda had made clear he had no time for me and Mrs Maki because we were only women. That didn't bother me, but

Mrs Maki seemed to throw the two of us together on purpose, like asking Morio Goda to teach me things that would help me get on in life.

It's really hard to pretend to be dumb when the person instructing you knows so little. But the smartest thing a woman can do is let men think they're smarter. It's not hard but, as with killing chickens, you need to stay in practice, so I'd have gone along with it if I'd had to. Still, I'd been glad when he turned Mrs Maki down rudely.

But what if something she'd said had set him against me?

What if her interfering had annoyed him, and his previous rudeness to me was a reaction to it? He certainly seemed to want to be friendly now. 'How's it going with Professor Kutsuki?' I'd nothing against making a new friend.

'I think the gas affected his brain as well as his eyes,' he said. 'Now he's like a baby. He likes folding origami, always wants me to read him *honkaku* mystery stories instead of working on the gas bomb.'

'What gas bomb?'

'Nothing.'

'I thought no one was supposed to use gas. There was an official statement.'

'But the use of gas here isn't against the US forces so it doesn't count. The Americans won't retaliate if it's used against Asians.'

The way Morio Goda said that made me realise how dangerous Professor Kutsuki could be if he got his mind back to his work.

We were passing through the plant nursery section I'd set up so I grabbed some red chillies and fat kaffir limes as I passed.

'You're growing all this stuff?'

'Most of it. The wild mango and rambutan trees were already here. I planted the ginger, lemongrass, limes, kaffir limes and chillies, as well as vegetables like *kang kong* and *pak choy*.'

'Who gave you the seeds or whatever you used?'

'I just used seeds from the vegetables brought to the house.' I'd grown up doing it at Chen Mansion, and found it odd that everyone didn't grow their own vegetables. 'In this climate, everything grows all year round.'

'Your climate is horrible. Too hot all the time!'

'It feeds us.'

'No fish today, Missy.' Tanis, panting, had caught up with us. 'All the fish traps are empty.'

'Not even small fish? We need to make more fish sauce soon.'

There was no soy sauce, so we fermented tiny fish in barrels of seawater to flavour our food.

'No, Missy. Just one water snake. Too small to eat. I let it go.'

'Stay away from us. You're all wet,' Morio Goda said. 'I didn't know you could catch fish here. What kind of fish do you normally get?'

'Eels and snakehead, mostly. Sometimes catfish.'

'That's disgusting,' Morio Goda said. 'Only outcasts eat such crap.'

'Hey, you ate snakehead two nights ago. Everyone said it was good!'

'I won't eat it again, now that I know. It's poisonous!'

'Snakehead meat is firm, white and flaky. The poisons are in the fat under the skin, so I removed it before grilling it over charcoal and letting the rest of the fat drip off.'

Morio Goda licked his lips and I knew he was remembering the taste. 'I thought it was sea bream.'

'If you like, next time I'll tell you it's sea bream. Will that help?'

He had the grace to smile and say nothing.

Anyone who's ever had to cater with limited supplies knows how good it feels to produce a meal out of practically nothing. Well-fed people are easier to manage than hungry ones.

We turned towards the house with just the vegetable produce we'd collected along the way.

Moss House was a colonial style 'black and white' house built for the elite British, black because of the dark timber beams and white for its whitewashed walls. There were servants' rooms behind the house next to the external kitchen, as well as an external servants' staircase leading up to the first floor so chamber pots could be dealt with and cleaning equipment stored invisibly.

It was a mish-mash of a traditional house, with many long windows for ventilation. As it was on sloping ground the first floor was well off the ground, with large verandas and high ceilings. It had Western-style innovations, like an electricity generator, and indoor lavatories with running water downstairs.

Moss House wasn't as big as Chen Mansion, where I'd grown up. But at Chen Mansion I'd slept on a mat in the corner of my grandmother's bedroom while at Moss House, as cousin to Hideki Tagawa and Mrs Maki, I had my own room. I had nothing to complain about but I didn't like the house.

There were worse places to live, like my grandmother's house in a now-quarantined cholera zone. Seventeen people were packed into a house with one outdoor WC but part of me still wished I was there.

Here, Moss House and the Botanic Gardens offices and

laboratory might have been created by the British and commandeered by the Japanese, but the vegetation was all local and reclaiming its territory. Already the indigenous weeds were knee-high, overwhelming the imported carpet grass.

In front of the house, the military cars bore flags with the Hinomaru, now our state flag: a red circle on a white background.

I'd been so taken aback by Morio Goda's sudden appearance that I'd forgotten until now why Tanis had come for me. I saw Ah Peng anxiously looking around the house. He should have been in the kitchen in case someone wanted something, but he came running to us.

'You two, take the coconuts, get back to the kitchen and start boiling the water for the professor's tea,' I told them. I was fond of Tanis and Ah Peng, and had tried to teach them how to please the Japanese so they were less likely to be destroyed on a whim.

'Yah, Missy.'

'On the way, Missy!'

All we had to do was survive until the British came back to save us. It might not be long now. I'd drummed into them, 'Don't stick your head out, don't get noticed. Don't try to be a hero. The best thing you can do is stay alive.'

I meant to follow my own advice. But what did the *kempeitai* want with me?

With the bombers overhead daily, and deadly submarines preventing food and fuel from getting through, it was hard to pretend we believed Japan had already won the war. But it's the cornered rats that are the most dangerous. The important thing now was to stay alive until they were forced to accept they had lost.

Hiroshima Bombed

◆

One good thing about the Occupation: there were so many real threats that we stopped imagining what could go wrong. There just wasn't enough energy to go on worrying about everything. Instead, unless there was actually a gun pointed at you, you got on with your life.

And if there was a gun pointed at you?

Then either you got shot and died – or you got on with your life.

A tremendous kerfuffle was in full swing. News had come in of the bombing of Hiroshima. But all the reports were garbled.

'A female high-school student sent a message to Fukuyama headquarters saying Hiroshima was attacked early on the sixth of August by a massive new type of bomb and the city was totally destroyed.'

'A high-school student?' Yoshio Yoshimoto sounded derisive. 'Probably some nonsense prank. Besides Fukuyama is a hundred kilometres from Hiroshima. Can't you get news from anywhere

closer? We know there's been no major enemy raid. And there's nothing stored there that could blow up.'

Even though Hideki Tagawa held no official post in the government, most of the Japanese in Syonan respected or feared him. It was really the same thing. Hideki Tagawa had had the final say on the island since the unexpected death of the previous military administrator. In the chaos since, no replacement had yet been sent out from Japan. It was said that the powers-that-be in Japan had problems enough with the war dragging on without worrying about conquered territories like ours.

We were pretty much left to run our island on our own. Much like the British had left us earlier in the war.

In person, Hideki Tagawa was a small, dark man, who had a way of hunching and dipping his head as though he was trying not to be noticed. In fact he had helped Prince Chichibu establish the military dictatorship in Japan and steered the country into the alliance with Nazi Germany.

But Hideki Tagawa liked to say that the more power people believed you had, the more vulnerable you were. He'd always run things from the shadows until he was forced into view after Colonel Fujiwara's death.

'What's happening?' I whispered.

'They're saying the Americans dropped a huge bomb over Hiroshima. Yoshio Yoshimoto says it's just a bluff and the Americans are trying to trick them into surrendering but they never will.'

'A really big bomb?' I whispered again, since no one seemed to be paying attention to us.

'Really big,' Tanis said. 'Tagawa-san went crazy at first.'

'Tagawa-san?' I couldn't imagine that. Hideki Tagawa was always the most controlled of men.

'He was crying and shouting and banging his head on the wall. Yoshimoto-san had to calm him down. He said Army Control in Hiroshima wasn't responding, that all the telegraph lines north of Hiroshima had stopped working just like that, so it was just an American bluff. But then he said they had sent a plane to fly over and had seen from a hundred and sixty kilometres away that the city was destroyed. They couldn't get any closer because of the great cloud of smoke. It was like the Americans opened a gate to Hell and the fire came out and swallowed Hiroshima.'

'Bigger than big,' Ah Peng agreed. 'Bigger than the biggest. Tagawa-san was crying. I cried a bit too. I didn't know what was happening, but he scared me.'

'We must wait for orders from Japan,' Hideki Tagawa said. Whatever state he'd been in earlier, he was calm now. 'We can't do anything until we know what's really happening there. The main-line telegraph has stopped working just north of Hiroshima. All we're getting is reports of a great explosion in the city. The Imperial Japanese Army General Staff say the only verified reports are from some small railway stops sixteen kilometres outside Hiroshima.'

'Exaggerations,' Yoshio Yoshimoto said. 'If there was an enemy raid of any size they would have been warned. And with no large storage of explosives in Hiroshima, there's no way there can be an explosion of such a size. The communications are down. That's all it is. The Americans found some way to block

26

communications and are trying to scare us. Only fools – fools and railway workers – would believe this.'

'Complete silence from the Army Control station in Hiroshima,' Hideki Tagawa said. 'No alarms issued. The Tokyo control operator noticed Hiroshima Broadcasting Corporation had gone off air and tried to call on another telephone line, but all the lines, all telegraph communications, are down. How can that be?'

'We've known for a while that something's been planned,' Yoshio Yoshimoto said. 'You think we *don't* know you've been suppressing those orders? You won't even tell the men what they're supposed to do.'

'I'm waiting for further instructions. I sent a query back to Japan that hasn't been responded to yet. I'm going to Headquarters,' Hideki Tagawa replied. 'I can't get any information here.'

There was one radio in the house but a whole system set up at Headquarters.

'Can it really be as bad as they say?' Mrs Maki's voice trembled.

'Not likely, I think,' Hideki Tagawa said. 'Hiroshima's reinforced concrete buildings should withstand almost any bomb damage. But communications are down and Hiroshima is the communications centre for the mobilisation of all of southern Japan. That's most likely why they targeted it.'

'If the Americans agree Emperor Hirohito will not be put on trial–'

'You trust the Americans?' Yoshio Yoshimoto snorted.

I didn't understand the sudden change of subject. But–

'Captains X and Y want to see you,' Mrs Maki said abruptly to me. 'They're in the house. In the dining room. Hurry up,'

A Cripple in a Blue Coat

———◆———

I hurried to the dining room, which was still set up for last night's screening of *The 47 Ronin*.

Captains X and Y had been assigned to keep an eye on Professor Kutsuki when he arrived in Singapore. The first couple of weeks they'd been in Moss House day and night and there had been some discussion – fierce and tedious – as to where their meals would be taken. I'd assumed we'd feed them – just add more water to the porridge as any local household would do – but Mrs Maki objected unless the military supplied their rations, which it did not.

Now Captains X and Y were ensconced in a security box all the way down the driveway at the Cluny Road Gate where they doubled as security guards and from which they could be summoned if needed. I sent the boys down with snacks when I could, and they sent up semi-illegal hawkers, with vegetables and pickles, who passed by.

They had names, of course, something like Captain Ichikawa and Captain Yamasaki, but after Professor Kutsuki insisted on

calling them Captain X and Captain Y that was how we all addressed them.

Captain X was broader and Captain Y taller, so I tended to think of them as the X-axis and Y-axis, something that usually made me smile, but not today. I got the feeling they'd been standing in silence for some time.

'We have come for Chen Su Lin,' Captain X said, when he saw me.

They were standing by the long dining table and the chairs still pointed to the screen at the end of the table which Mrs Maki had set up for *The 47 Ronin* screening.

I was too taken aback to be scared. 'What's it about?'

'Who sent you? And what do you want with her?' Mrs Maki demanded.

'We are to take her to Headquarters immediately for questioning.'

My throat seized up. I couldn't breathe. I could feel every heartbeat painfully in my throat.

'Why?' I swore that if she sorted this out I'd never again mind Mrs Maki's questions and interference.

If this wasn't sorted out, though, I mightn't be in a position to mind anything ever again.

'We got a call saying that sometime in the night, a crippled woman in a fancy blue coat went to Kempeitai East District Branch,' Captain Y said. 'She said she was there to see Hideki Tagawa and was allowed into his office. Tagawa-san was not there at the time. She was alone in his office and could have seen top-secret papers,'

The Kempeitai East District Branch was the headquarters of

the Japanese military police. It was located at the old YMCA building on Stamford Road.

'Tagawa-san wasn't there,' Mrs Maki said. 'He was here all night. You must have seen him before he left.'

'And I was here all night,' I said. All right, I hadn't been in the house but I'd been on the premises. 'It wasn't me.'

'Who says she was there?' Mrs Maki ignored me.

'She matches the description we were given.'

'What were you told?'

'A crippled woman. She spoke bad Japanese and was walking with a limp and wearing a dark blue *michiyuki*,' Captain X said. 'Several people testify to the blue *michiyuki*. It was a hand-drawn indigo design.'

Childhood polio had left me with a limp. But I hadn't been anywhere near the Headquarters building in months.

'She gave her name and said she was a relation of Tagawa-san and that he had told her to wait for him in his office. The guards on duty had heard all about her. They recognised the name and let her in,' Captain Y said.

So it wasn't just the local community that gossiped about my relationship to Hideki Tagawa and Mrs Maki. Only since the Occupation had I learned my dead mother had been their cousin Ryoko. She'd run away from her family and Japan, and ended up marrying my father in Singapore. They'd died within a day of each other when typhoid and cholera hit the slums they were living in after my grandmother had disowned her son for marrying a Japanese.

'They should have known Hideki Tagawa wasn't in his office in the middle of the night,' Mrs Maki said. 'What's the big deal?

Some woman sneaks in to try to see him. That's hardly a military crisis. In case you haven't noticed there are far more serious things going on. We still don't know what's happening in Hiroshima—'

'There are security concerns. She was gone when the security guard went in to check. And the safe in Tagawa-san's office was broken into and emptied. And the briefcase set by his door to receive incoming top-secret photo-tele-autograph printouts was also gone.'

'Hideki Tagawa would not leave secret papers lying around in his office,' I said. He was fanatical about security and wrote down as little as he could, preferring to depend on his memory.

Mrs Maki pinched my arm, telling me to shut up. 'Did you go to Headquarters?' she hiss-whispered.

'No!'

It was notorious as a site of interrogation and torture. Locals like me stayed well away from it.

'Then shut up!'

'We are to search for the briefcase and the contents of the safe and bring them in too.'

'Without looking at them.'

'Do you mean anyone could give you any name and get in without showing papers? What kind of security do you have here?'

'The person entered via the side gate, so the guards didn't pay attention.'

The side gate was the one the informers used.

'That was why they only noticed the name she signed, the blue *michiyuki* she was wearing and the limp. And the big coolie

hat. And she spoke very poor Japanese, so they knew she was a local.'

'My cousin speaks very good Japanese. I taught her myself,' Mrs Maki said. 'You've talked to her, you should know that. As for her limp – get up and walk to the door and back.'

I obeyed her. My left leg was shorter than the right, thanks to the polio. But with a hefty cork sole nailed to the bottom of my left clog I could walk pretty evenly. Unless you were trying to race me up or down the stairs, I could probably keep up without anyone noticing anything was wrong.

'Anyone can walk with a limp and speak bad Japanese.'

'She gave her name as Chen Su Lin. That's how we knew to come here.' Captain X sounded strained.

'Do you think anyone trying to get secret papers out of Headquarters would give their real name?'

'She had a permit marked with Tagawa-san's personal seal.'

Meaning it had to be someone with access to his office at Headquarters or Moss House. Or someone he was working with.

'What's going on here?' It was Professor Kutsuki, tapping his way in with his cane. 'Are you eating without telling me?'

Captains X and Y looked uncomfortable.

Professor Kutsuki was supposed to be a genius, but didn't look like one. He was a tall, thin man wearing a Western-style shirt and trousers. His spectacles had pieces of paper stuck over both lenses, a pair of frowning eyes with huge eyeballs drawn on them. They looked like they belonged to a demon and would give children nightmares.

Professor Kutsuki said he kept his eyes covered because, since the firebomb attack on his lab in Philippines, their

condition was too awful for people to witness. I'd never seen him without his shielding spectacles, but if his eyes were worse than those drawn on the paper they must have been truly terrible.

'Come closer!' Professor Kutsuki had a very strong sense of smell and was sniffing in the direction of the two captains. 'I can't smell you apart. Did you get that? That's a joke. Of course I can tell you apart. What makes you so sure it was a girl? Just because whoever it was signed in as a girl doesn't mean it was a girl. You always swear that no one looks at your secret informers, so why shouldn't it have been a man dressed in woman's clothing? Like Morio Goda, for instance. He's so skinny and walks around on tiptoe. Sometimes I think he's a woman sneaking into my room and going through my drawers!'

'He's a real joker,' Morio Goda said. He'd been so quiet until now that I hadn't realised he'd followed us into the house.

'You think this is a joke?' Professor Kutsuki turned the terrible cartoon eyes on him.

Morio Goda ignored him.

'This is boring,' Professor Kutsuki said. 'I want some tea.'

'Later,' Mrs Maki snapped. 'When Tagawa-san gets back. And Yoshimoto-san. They'll sort out all this—'

'Hideki Tagawa hasn't left yet,' the blind professor said. 'He's standing over there and Yoshio Yoshimoto is hiding behind the wall, listening. Who's the blind one here, I ask you?'

The two men entered, nodding to acknowledge the salutes Captains X and Y gave them.

Hideki Tagawa took his time unclipping and wiping his spectacles. He seemed totally engrossed in polishing his lenses

33

but I knew he was studying the situation in the room. He was good at assessing situations. He'd been in Malaya as a spy long before war was declared. Undercover as a travelling photographer, he'd documented the British camps and island defences and helped plan the attack. My former boss, Chief Inspector Le Froy, who'd been mocked by the British Home Office for seeing Japanese spies everywhere, had once described Hideki Tagawa as one of the most dangerous men in Japan's military secret service.

Behind him, Yoshio Yoshimoto said, 'What's going on here? Is it a coup?'

'No, sir.' Captains X and Y stood to attention but smiled at the joke.

People tended to smile and relax when Yoshio Yoshimoto was around. He wasn't just good-looking, he was also charming and much better at winning over people in difficult situations than Hideki Tagawa.

Even I had to smile when he put a hand on my shoulder and said, 'You can't take Miss Chen away. Who will cook my favourite spicy green papaya soup?'

I swore to myself I would make him the best papaya soup if he got me out of this. With no hope of chicken or pork or pomfret it wouldn't be much compared to the soups I'd prepared before the war, but I knew I could turn out a good dish with my homemade fish sauce. Thinking about cooking had calmed the pulse that was throbbing painfully in my throat. That seemed worth remembering, though I doubted it would come to mind when I needed it most.

Yoshio Yoshimoto saluted Hideki Tagawa, who ignored him and looked even more nondescript next to him. Then he turned back to me.

'I hear you were trained in criminal detection by the *gaijin* detective Le Froy,' Yoshio Yoshimoto said. 'Were you trying to detect something at Headquarters? Something you could pass on to the British?' His tone was light and teasing, as though he thought it a huge joke, but was it? And if he was teasing, was he teasing the captains or me?

'No, sir.'

'That's what Tagawa-san used to justify his interest in you, wasn't it? Thanks to him, we also know your grandfather was a very powerful man. He ran the local triads, didn't he? The British knew very well what he was up to, but even they didn't dare tackle him.'

'My grandfather has been dead for over forty years, sir. I never knew him.' I stared indignantly at Hideki Tagawa, but now he was ignoring me as well as Yoshio Yoshimoto.

'She was described . . .' Captain X tried to steer the interrogation back to the present.

'. . . as a girl speaking bad Japanese, walking with a limp and wearing a dark blue *michiyuki*,' Captain Y said.

'Do you see Miss Chen limping?'

'There's something wrong with her left leg,' Captain Y said, with some triumph.

'Did you see her limping?' Mrs Maki repeated her question. 'I'd say the adjustment to her shoe is very well done. I checked it myself.'

'The intruder said she was Tagawa-san's close relation. They knew Tagawa-san has a cousin here, and that was why they let her in, even though it was against rules. They will be reprimanded. But she said that he had told her to meet him there, so they could not turn her away.'

'Chen Su Lin is cousin to Hideki Tagawa and myself.' Mrs Maki went to stand by Yoshio Yoshimoto. 'You know that very well. I don't know what game you're trying to play. Who set you up to this?'

'We have orders from Headquarters to bring her in,' Captain X said, with a look at Hideki Tagawa, who remained expressionless. 'Papers are missing. And a briefcase that was empty but must have been used to carry away the contents of the safe.'

'We have orders to bring her to Headquarters to answer questions,' Captain Y agreed.

I was getting more scared as the situation sank in. Was I being set up by Hideki Tagawa?

Or, worse (kind of, but in a way that made no difference to me): was I being used to take him down? It would have been poetic justice, since Hideki Tagawa had tried to use me to get to Le Froy. My mind started to spin towards panic, but—

'Nothing is missing,' Hideki Tagawa said. 'I know what is in my office better than anyone else. The night security made a mistake.'

'But, still, the security breach, these are orders from Headquarters—'

'We are under orders to bring the limping girl with a blue coat back immediately—'

'Morio, you were off somewhere with Su Lin, weren't you?' Professor Kutsuki said. 'You just came back with her. You two were out together all night?'

Morio Goda's eyes dilated in shock. I saw him dart a look at the old professor, then at the captains, at me and back to the

captains. Then: 'Yes, I was,' Morio Goda said. 'We were together all night. It couldn't have been Miss Chen. She hasn't left the grounds of the Shōnan Gardens.'

'What are you talking about?' Captain X demanded.

'It can't have been Miss Chen,' Morio Goda said firmly. 'I was with Miss Chen all night. She didn't leave the grounds.'

'What?' Mrs Maki turned on me. 'How dare you sneak off with him? You're going to end up worse than your mother!' She glared at Morio Goda, seeming to forget the accusation against me. Her disapproval of him was clear. At least, her disapproval of his behaviour. I was disconcerted to see she was assessing his person.

'All night?' Captain X said to Morio Goda, ignoring her.

'Yes.'

'What were you two doing together?' Captain Y asked, with a leer.

'Trying to grow mushrooms for the household,' Morio Goda said. 'Mushrooms can't take too much sunlight so they have to be cultivated at night.'

That was smart of him. Growing food was then the only acceptable activity. Thanks to the Australians and Americans disrupting sea transports and blocking land supply routes, the Japanese soldiers were starving along with us locals. Most had lost the mad nationalistic brutality of the early days and even come to depend on help from locals to survive.

'So is everything sorted out here?' Yoshio Yoshimoto said. 'The two young ones are innocent, then. Good night, men. Let me see your reports tomorrow.'

'But, sir, we have orders—'

'We must find what is missing – Tagawa-san, you yourself told the security officer—'

'What I said is my concern,' Hideki Tagawa said. 'Now go and do something useful. Like informing those fools in charge of security they need to improve if they hope to pass the next surprise assessment.'

It was almost funny seeing Captains X and Y simultaneously relax and re-tense as they processed (a) that it had been a security assessment and (b) they had been part of an assessment with no idea how they'd done. They made their farewell salutes rapidly and left.

As soon as Captains X and Y had gone, even as we heard their car starting outside, Mrs Maki hissed at me, 'You've been spending time with Morio Goda? We don't know anything about his family or where they come from!'

Yoshio Yoshimoto laughed at her. 'Leave the young people alone. Things are different now. A man you would not consider in peacetime might prove himself worthy in war.' He raised his eyebrows at Morio Goda. 'More than worthy, in fact.'

Morio Goda looked sullen and embarrassed. I tried to catch his eye but he refused to look at me. I didn't care.

Morio Goda had saved me.

'Thank you for what you did just now.' I ran to catch him at the door as he waited to follow Yoshio Yoshimoto out of the dining room.

'Shut your stupid mouth,' Morio Goda said. 'I don't know what you're talking about. Anyway, I hate mushrooms.'

He was so stiff and awkward that he reminded me of Hideki Tagawa when we'd first met. Later Hideki Tagawa explained his

rudeness had been exaggerated to hide how moved and disturbed he'd been by my resemblance to his cousin Ryoko, my late mother. He'd been very fond of her.

A snort of derision or amusement made me look at Professor Kutsuki, forgotten in his chair. He wasn't looking in our direction. But I somehow knew he'd been listening. He might have been brilliant, but I found him creepy.

I wondered if Morio Goda liked me. He was right. It was best not to say anything. I would cook for him, though. Even if I could never thank him, I would find out what his favourite foods were and prepare them for him.

'Mushrooms are good, sustainable food,' Hideki Tagawa said quietly. He'd been listening too, then.

'Some are poisonous,' Professor Kutsuki said. 'Mushrooms, people, it's impossible to tell by looking whether they're going to nourish you or kill you.'

Do the Right Thing:
The 47 Ronin

'Oh, Missy! So happy they didn't take you away, Missy!'
'So good to see you, Missy! Have the *kempeitai* gone?'

Tanis and Ah Peng had clearly expected me to be arrested. When I went to the kitchen I found them crouching by the back door whispering over their precious cache of unripe fruit, as though planning to run away.

'We found some *chiku*. Do you want some? We didn't eat because we waited for you.'

'We thought those wicked soldiers were going to take you away!'

'You know Captain X and Captain Y.' I was really trying to comfort myself rather than them. 'Remember you always take leftover food to them at the guard post?'

Instead of answering, they threw their arms around me and hugged me. Ah Peng was crying, Tanis barely managing not to as he muttered, 'I will never bring them food again. Never! I will eat it all myself!'

They were so young. And, in their limited experience, people taken away by the *kempeitai* were never seen again. I understood that all too well.

'Come on.' I untangled them gently. 'We must work. Better roll up your *chikus* in a towel to get ripe.'

I set them chores and got out the wooden chopping board for myself. Whatever happened, there was a houseful of people who would need to be fed. I reminded myself that preparing food made me feel better. I think it's an animal instinct, like feeling sleepy when it rains because we want to curl up in a cave. Peeling and chopping was the best cure I knew for stress and anxiety. Maybe because it promised my body nourishment to come.

Anyway, I knew it was the right thing to do and I always tried to do what was right.

But what exactly did 'Do the right thing' mean?

I was only alive because my grandmother had refused to do the right thing. Ah Ma, Chen Tai, the brain behind the Chen family's pre-Occupation black-market empire had kept me in the family despite the fortune-tellers' warnings. That had clearly been the wrong thing to do. Even worse, she'd sent me to the Mission Centre school to learn English and arithmetic so I could handle the British and the family accounts. Then, instead of shunning the Japanese when the war against China started, she'd apprenticed me to a Japanese hairdresser to learn Japanese. All my life, my grandmother had encouraged me to be smart and watch out for myself, instead of warning me that I'd never find a husband if I didn't learn to act stupid.

But as far as I was concerned, her biggest error had been in not telling me why I'd been condemned as bad luck: my late

mother had been Japanese. But how would life have been different if I'd known?

The boys had collected a mass of wood sorrel for dinner and I grabbed a bunch of it from the bucket where it was soaking to clean and chop it. There still wasn't any news about what had happened in Hiroshima. The bomb damage couldn't be as bad as the early reports made out, but how bad was it?

And how bad would the Japanese reprisals be?

Whatever was happening, people had to be fed, and I always felt better with a knife in hand. I shook out a bunch of wood sorrel with its clover-shaped leaves and picked off the fruits that looked like tiny okra, but had hard seeds inside. Then I started to chopping. I think any woman always feels safer when she's holding a good, sharp kni— It was dashed out of my hand.

I cried out, startled. It was Mrs Maki. She slapped me. 'What do you think you're playing at now?'

'What's happening here?' Yoshio Yoshimoto said, from the back door. He looked between me and Mrs Maki. 'Clearly she's preparing a meal.'

Mrs Maki looked startled. She'd smacked me so often that she was hardly aware she was doing it. I don't think she meant anything by it. If you were around her you got nudged, pinched and hit. It was the way she communicated. I guessed it was how she'd been brought up so, naturally, she assumed that was the only way to train girls and other servants.

'I came in and caught her stealing food,' Mrs Maki said. Then, seeing his eyes move from the soggy weeds in my hand to the cloth on which I'd been draining fish bones salvaged from the stew pot, 'All servants steal food. It's in their nature. You

have to watch them non-stop or they'll eat you out of house and home.'

'Maybe you should feed them more.' Yoshio Yoshimoto smiled. He came to me and squeezed my shoulder. 'This one could do with more meat on her bones.'

I saw the jealousy flash in Mrs Maki's eyes. He might have thought he was helping me, but he was actually getting me into worse trouble with her.

I pulled away from him, which made him laugh. 'What's wrong? Is there someone you're more interested in? A young man named Goda, perhaps?'

'It's my time of the month,' I said, looking down at my feet. 'I'm sorry, I mustn't contaminate you, sir.'

It was almost funny how fast his face and manner changed.

He muttered a curse and stepped back quickly.

I'd been around Yoshio Yoshimoto enough to know women's menstrual blood was taboo to him. Like many other right-wing Shintoists, he was fiercely conservative about things like the weakening and contaminating effect of women and foreigners.

'You should have said something. You shouldn't be around our food. Get away from the kitchen and stay away until your cycle is over.' He turned on Mrs Maki. 'Things are bad enough. No point adding to the problems.'

'I was not expecting it yet, sir,' I said, still staring at my feet. I didn't have to act to appear embarrassed and awkward.

'Sir?' Morio Goda stood in the back door. He must have gone outside and around the house after Yoshio Yoshimoto. 'I have to speak to you, sir.'

43

Yoshio Yoshimoto recovered his good humour as he dipped the hand that had touched me into the water barrel and dried it on his uniform. 'I'm not the one you have to ask permission to speak to, young man. I know who you really came looking for.' He jerked his thumb in my direction.

Morio Goda ignored me and glared at him. 'Sir. I must speak to you. In private.'

'Not now. I have to go to Headquarters to get the latest news. It's going to be a long day. I'm leaving now. They're probably shouting for me already. Wait till tonight. Anyway, you clearly don't need my permission to spend time with whoever you want!'

'Sir! It's not what you think. This is very important and urgent. Nothing to do with this stupid girl!'

'Who are you calling stupid? You're not thinking you're too good for her, are you? Our family is as good as yours any day!' Mrs Maki said at once.

'Let the young people be.' Yoshio Yoshimoto laughed. 'Don't forget, it's them sneaking off together that gave your niece her alibi. Sneaking out in the middle of the night to do gardening together, producing mushrooms to feed the population. So patriotic!'

'Not together,' Mrs Maki said. 'They shouldn't have been alone together. It's not proper. Su Lin, you should know better. You should not have been meeting with a strange man in secret.'

It was funny how she'd instantly switched to protective female relation worrying about my reputation and marital prospects. But even I could see she was worried about the bomb the Americans had dropped on Hiroshima. She didn't want to believe it could be as bad as people said. And she was applying

so much pressure to disbelieving it that, as soon as a crack appeared, it all burst out of her.

'She's feeding the houseboys more than she should and supplementing the household diet with her dirty mushrooms,' Morio Goda said. 'That's why I was watching her. I wanted to find out why she was stealing food bought for the household.'

There was something strange about Morio Goda's manner to Yoshio Yoshimoto, I thought. Or maybe his manner was just odd that day. I saw clearly he was lying and he was nervous. The others must have seen it too. But what was he so nervous about?

Morio Goda had saved me from a tricky situation, I owed him for that, but it didn't mean I was going to do anything that Mrs Maki would worry about.

And it certainly didn't give Morio Goda the right to criticise my housekeeping or my mushrooms.

'I don't know what we should do now,' Mrs Maki said. 'Shall we just sit and wait for the Americans to bomb us again? You know what? I'm going to play *The 47 Ronin* again. The machine and screen are already set up in the dining room and we can watch it over breakfast.'

Yoshio Yoshimoto had no objection. But he didn't offer to help her set up the film as he had last night. Nor did he sit down to watch it over his breakfast, which, I suspect, was what Mrs Maki had been hoping for. He left, via the back door, with a handful of dried mango strips.

Morio Goda stormed out after him (kicking over the slop pail on the way), ignoring Mrs Maki calling to him to take the professor's breakfast tray up to his room.

In fact, no one wanted breakfast, but maybe they just didn't want to sit through the film again. I don't think it mattered to Mrs Maki, who perhaps wanted something to distract her while we waited for updates and orders from Japan.

I didn't think *The 47 Ronin* was the best choice of distraction. The film's message was bleak: it's better to die than to adapt. But then again maybe that was exactly the message Mrs Maki was subconsciously trying to accept.

'Should I soak the dried mushrooms for tomorrow before I leave?' This served two purposes. In addition to plumping up the dried mushrooms, the soaking water served as the base for the morning porridge and soup.

'Mushrooms. That's all you're interested in. You and your stupid mushrooms. Where do you think you're going?'

'Yoshimoto-san told me to go to my room and stay there till—'

'Never mind what he said. He's not living in a Shinto temple here. He'll just have to eat whatever we put in front of him.'

But I saw that just thinking of him made her smile a little.

I'd seen Yoshio Yoshimoto criticise and point out her errors and then, just when she was about to yell at him, he would praise something she'd done or reach out to tuck a strand of hair behind her ear and tell her she was so womanly and graceful. Then it didn't matter what he'd said before.

'You mustn't let that boy frighten you. But whatever he says to you, I don't want you going anywhere alone with him. If he tries to persuade you to do anything that makes you uncomfortable, I want you to come and tell me straight away.'

'It's Professor Kutsuki who makes me uncomfortable,' I said.

'Don't be ridiculous. He's a brilliant scientist. He just needs

to get over the shock of what happened. He can't be bothered with a nobody like you,' She seemed to think a man who was brilliant was automatically a saint.

'I don't mean that. But he's always watching—'

She snorted.

'Listening, I mean. And when nobody's around, he moves about quite easily.'

'What he does is none of your business. You just get on with your job and stay away from him.'

I was quite happy to stay away from Professor Kutsuki. And from Morio Goda?

I wanted to get to know him better. He went out of his way to be offensive, but when I was in trouble he'd come to my rescue.

I wouldn't be stupid enough to fall in love with a Japanese (unlike my father), but he'd lied for me. I wouldn't talk to him if it made him uncomfortable, but I didn't want to think about what might have happened to me if I'd been arrested for breaking into Headquarters.

I made the houseboys start preparing something for lunch. Even if no one else wanted to eat, there was no point in giving them an excuse to take it out on us.

Mrs Maki came to watch as I finished picking over the fish heads. She wasn't as furious as she'd sounded earlier. 'So you've hooked that young man. How long has this been going on?'

I could tell she was really trying to find out what had been happening between me and Morio Goda. It was easy to be honest. 'There's nothing going on between us,' I said. 'He came to look at the mushroom trees. That's all.'

'I know what men are like, and they're all the same. There's never anything going on until it's too late. I don't want you going near that place with him again. I mean it.'

'I was just working on the mushrooms. I didn't even know he was there.' I sounded sullen because I knew that was what she wanted.

'You expect me to believe that?'

But at the same time I sensed she was trying to matchmake us.

I didn't think Mrs Maki had anything against Morio Goda. In fact, all along I'd suspected she had a soft spot for him. It was in the way she pressed him to eat, took his side whenever anyone else (well, Professor Kutsuki) spoke harshly to him, and worried about his comfort. 'Are you sleeping all right? This horrible country, so hot with so many mosquitoes. I don't know how anyone stands it. You must miss your family and home so much.' Or 'Have you thought about what you're going to do with yourself after the war? There will be many opportunities for clever young men like you in the colonies.' In other words, she used all of her usual conversational gambits, though they were clearly wasted on him. Morio Goda was awkward and gauche, which was part of what I liked about him. But maybe she thought there was still a chance he'd be useful after the war.

This morning, though, after hearing him say he'd spent part of the night with me, she was assessing him, like a butcher eyeing a pig. Or, worse, a matchmaker eyeing a landowner's son.

But it must have caused her a certain pang.

I'm not saying Mrs Maki was one of those older women who pick younger men to toy with, but she was the kind who didn't

get along with other women – younger or the same age as herself. She'd always said she got along much better with men. And while she became irritated with Professor Kutsuki for being facetious, and with Hideki Tagawa and Yoshio Yoshimoto for not confiding in her or asking her opinion, when it came to Morio Goda she'd almost adopted him as a surrogate son. Her own children were so far away in Japan.

Morio Goda didn't appear at lunchtime and wasn't in his room. I carried a tray up to Professor Kutsuki, but he refused to open his door and shouted at me to go away. I could understand them all being on edge.

That evening, Hideki Tagawa told the professor and Mrs Maki that Tokyo Military Command had sent another plane to Hiroshima. The official report was that after flying for three hours, while still more than a hundred and sixty kilometres from Hiroshima, the officer and his pilot had seen a great mushroom cloud of smoke over what was left of the city. The initial reports of a 'huge' bomb hadn't been exaggerated. In fact, they didn't begin to describe what had happened.

Hideki Tagawa couldn't answer Professor Kutsuki's many questions about the bomb. 'We just don't know yet. The important thing now is to take care of the victims. Most of the medical staff in Hiroshima are dead or injured themselves.'

Mrs Maki alternated between crying and raging, 'All those students! What did they ever do to deserve this?'

She was talking about the thousands of recent recruits, most of them students, who had been killed while training in the grounds of Hiroshima Castle. Well, at least I knew her own

children weren't in Hiroshima but almost two hundred miles away in Nagasaki where Hideki Tagawa also had relatives.

'Those damned Americans! How dare they attack us in our own homes?'

If I'd been feeling suicidal, I might have pointed out the Japanese had done the same to the Americans – when there hadn't yet been war between them. But, not being suicidal, I kept my mouth shut.

I tried to crush the hope that stirred in me. It would be suicidal to look happy now. And in my experience, things always got worse just when they looked like they were getting better. But there was some hope at last.

That night I fell asleep thinking about what I might cook for Morio Goda to thank him without embarrassing him.

Missing Morio Goda

◆

The next thing I knew I was waking up out of a strange dream of slicing green papaya for soup while trying to find enough dried shrimps to flavour the stock, but there were none. Then I was walking on the high-tide line behind my grandmother's house looking for clams and, to my amazement, lobsters were crawling around. I tried to grab as many of them as I could. I would make Yoshio Yoshimoto the best green papaya soup he'd ever tasted! But the lobsters started dragging me into the sea ... I was glad to wake up.

Everything had sorted itself out in the night and I knew what I was going to do: nothing.

I'd almost been dragged into a huge mess yesterday, but Morio Goda had saved me.

I owed him. But that didn't mean I was going to marry him or even that I liked him, so Mrs Maki had nothing to worry about.

I wouldn't even show I remembered it, when I saw him again. Pleased by this idea, I wiped my face and dressed quickly. I couldn't wait to find him and show him I had nothing to say

to him. Plus I had some pickled ivy gourds that should be just ready to fry with some dried shrimps for the morning congee.

I hardly thought about the destruction that had been wrought upon Hiroshima the day before.

Reports and rumours had continued to come in all day and all night. Hiroshima was a big city and military base. It was at least double the size of our little island and at least five to ten times (depending on who was speaking) more significant in terms of cultural, social and historical importance. It seemed that everyone in the house (except the houseboys and me) had friends, relatives and former colleagues in that unfortunate city.

Mrs Maki persisted in calling reports of the destruction 'greatly exaggerated'. According to her, they were designed to frighten us, though it wasn't clear who she thought was coming up with these lies.

Yoshio Yoshimoto and Hideki Tagawa, who knew much more about such things, said much less. I was more inclined to believe them. According to Hideki Tagawa, the Japanese had been so unprepared that, though reconnaissance planes had been spotted before the blast, the all-clear was sounded over Hiroshima at a little after seven in the morning. The bomb had landed on the city at just after eight fifteen.

'They say everything turned white,' Hideki Tagawa said, 'like a hundred thousand camera flashes all going off at the same time. People say it was like the light slammed them violently into the ground. It peeled the skin off their bodies so that it was hanging from their faces and arms like ribbons dragging on the ground. There are bodies everywhere, people and cattle lying

swollen on the road and in the river. And the sky turned purple and grey for the rest of the day, maybe for ever.' He looked grim and tired. 'It was like an earthquake, a shockwave and a firestorm all at the same time.'

'The Americans don't have the ability to develop, let alone transport such a bomb,' Yoshio Yoshimoto insisted. 'It is just lies and manipulation. Japan will never be defeated. We must be prepared to fight on.'

I could see why Morio Goda looked to Yoshio Yoshimoto as a role-model warrior. I was looking forward to hearing what Goda himself had to say about the American bomb. Like the rest of the Japanese here, I doubt it had occurred to him until a few months back that they hadn't already won the war. Well, now he would have to admit the Americans had reached mainland Japan with a powerful bomb of their own.

'The American President Truman announced, sixteen hours after the bomb was dropped, that Hiroshima had been destroyed by a new American atomic-energy bomb with more power than twenty thousand tons of TNT,' Hideki Tagawa said.

'And because they dropped one bomb, the Americans expect Japan to surrender?' Yoshio Yoshimoto said.

'Japan will not discuss disarmament unless four conditions are met,' Hideki Tagawa said. 'Japan's imperial institution must be preserved and respected. Japan will be responsible for disarmament with no outside interference. No foreign troops will be allowed on any Japanese territory, and any war-crimes trials of Japan's military officers will be conducted by Japan alone.'

'In other words, you're ready to surrender,' Yoshio Yoshimoto said. 'You just want it put in nice words.'

'You think the Americans will agree to that?' Mrs Maki asked. I couldn't tell if she was hopeful or not.

'Only cowards even consider surrender,' Yoshio Yoshimoto said. 'Even if the great victory once hoped for is now unlikely, continuing the war is still our best option. We can outlast the Americans. We can out-wait them. They lack the character and devoted service of our one hundred million people willing to die for Japan's advantage. What good is their having one new and most cruel bomb? They've shown their hand. If we prove we're not intimidated, they're left with nothing.'

I served my dried shrimp fried with strips of pickled ivy gourds but Morio Goda didn't come down for breakfast.

'He went off in a huff because of something Professor Kutsuki said,' Mrs Maki told me, when I asked if I should prepare a tray for him. 'Or something he did. He'll get over it and come back. If he can't be bothered to turn up for meals, why save food for him?'

Professor Kutsuki didn't come down to breakfast either, so my clever innovation went unremarked – they ate blindly, as though I'd served stir-fried cardboard – except by Ah Peng and Tanis who wolfed down the leftovers with even more gusto than usual. But those two children ate like goats, anything and everything, so the best I could say was that the food wasn't wasted.

Then Professor Kutsuki decided to have one of his massive temper tantrums. I heard Mrs Maki even before I reached his room. She was shouting at one of the houseboys but I knew her words were directed against the old man. 'Why is there such a mess? Don't you fools know how to clean? You should all be shot!'

I hurried to rescue whichever of the boys she was scape-goating.

'I don't want anyone in my room. Why are you in here? Get out!'

I heard a crash.

I stopped at the doorway. The room was indeed in a mess. There were things all over the floor, strange substances spilled, as well as stacks of books and clothing bundled in heaps.

Mrs Maki saw me. 'Go and find that useless Goda fellow. He's supposed to be taking care of the professor. Get him in here at once!' She turned back to Professor Kutsuki. 'Where is he? Did you send him to town to get something for you?'

'Why ask me? You're the ones who lured him away. What did you do with him?' Professor Kutsuki groped around and grabbed a notebook, hesitated and put it down, then seized the burned-out mosquito coil and threw it at us. It landed harmlessly on the floor, leaving a trail of ash.

'Morio Goda is missing?' I asked Mrs Maki quietly. I hoped the captains hadn't taken him away for questioning to try to break the alibi he had given me.

'All his things are still here. He probably just went off and got drunk. Looking after this old man is enough to drive anyone to drink. He'll be back.'

'He's gone off like this before?'

'He used to take time off when the professor was dictating into his machine. But since the machine disappeared he's had to record everything by hand. Pah! I didn't make that useless lout work any harder than I did myself. What are things coming to that young people can't do a day's work without falling apart? This younger

generation is feeble, soft, rotten at the core! See if you can do anything with him. At least get him dressed and make sure he uses the chamber pot, if he refuses to go down to the WC. I'll start lunch.' Mrs Maki left the room, grabbing a terrified Ah Peng along the way. She almost walked into Yoshio Yoshimoto.

'What's all the commotion?' Yoshio Yoshimoto asked.

'Nothing for you to worry about. Oh, you don't look well, Yoshimoto-san. It's the horrible climate here. You're coming down with something. You've been working too hard,' Mrs Maki said. 'I can give you something for it. Su Lin, go and get—'

'Oh, no. No, it's just an allergy. Please don't trouble yourself.'

'He won't dare eat anything you give him. He's afraid you'll poison him!' Professor Kutsuki shouted. 'It's always the murderers who are most afraid of being murdered, you know! What does that tell you about him, eh?'

Yoshio Yoshimoto laughed as he went down the stairs with Mrs Maki.

But I realised I'd never seen Yoshio Yoshimoto eating anything prepared especially for him. He would eat off common plates, but only after others had started. Was that just courtesy or did he believe someone here might try to poison him?

I remained quietly by the door, watching Professor Kutsuki. He was growling to himself. Presently he stopped and listened. I stayed still. 'You can't fool me. I know you're there.'

'I'm not trying to fool you.'

'You're trying to sneak up on me and spy on me.'

'No, sir. I'm standing still, not sneaking anywhere. And I'm not spying. I know you know that I'm here.'

'Why are you here?'

'I think Mrs Maki wants me to clean your chamber pot.'

'So, you want to clean my pot? That's the kind of thing you enjoy doing most? Pah!'

'No, sir. But I would rather clean the pot than the floor.'

It was a risk, but it worked. Professor Kutsuki froze. I could tell he was processing that – and me. He sniffed in my direction.

Suddenly he giggled, like a schoolgirl, with jerky little gasps. 'If you have to clean up shit, at least clean it from the pot!'

And I was laughing too. 'If you had to, which would you prefer?'

'All right. You can stay. But I still don't trust you,' Professor Kutsuki said. 'Nothing personal, but I distrust all women, all Chinese, all stupid people, all military officers. Do you find my appearance frightening?'

'No, sir.'

'Not even the eyes on my spectacles?'

Fine. If he wanted to frighten me, okay, I'd be frightened. 'A little, sir.'

'The eyes on my spectacles were copied from *A Demon Woman Beating a Samurai*. Do you know what that is?'

'No, sir.'

'Of course you don't. You're a fool. I'm a fool for expecting anyone here to know anything.'

'Please tell me what it is, sir.'

'Why should I?'

'So that the next time I look at your spectacles I'll know what they are, sir.'

'Pah! Are you so insolent to all of your Japanese masters? I'm surprised you're still alive. It's a Takamizawa print. Not that you'll know what that means.'

'A woodblock print?'

'How would you know that?'

'Before the war, when Mrs Maki was posted to Singapore with her husband, there were *ukiyo-e* prints of Japanese scenery at their house. She told me they were Takamizawa prints. But I never saw anything like a demon woman.'

'Your Mrs Maki drew them for me. Demon eyes drawn by the demon woman!'

After that Professor Kutsuki let me clean his room. He didn't really need my help to get dressed. Most of the mess he'd made came from the breakfast tray he'd overturned, so there was tea and rice and miso everywhere. But I noticed that, after I'd wiped it all up, if I replaced something a little to the left or right of where it had been, he was quick to correct me.

I understood. Without his eyesight, he could still find his things as long as nothing was moved.

And he apologised several times for my having to empty his chamber pot, which he fortunately hadn't knocked over. 'I can make my way down the stairs to the lavatory, but that fool Goda locks me in when he wants to sneak out at night. So at my age it's safer to have an option in here.'

Maybe he wasn't as crazy as he was trying to appear.

'And you two are not the only ones in the house sneaking around. Mrs Maki walks about at night too. Thinks she can do it without me hearing her. Pah! Come here,' he said. 'Stand in front of me so that I can smell you.'

Then again, he might just have been crazy in a different way.

I did as he asked. It was a bizarre request, but I'd survived

under the Japanese by not questioning what I didn't understand. And his manner didn't feel threatening.

Professor Kutsuki leaned forward. Without touching me, he sniffed at the cotton material of my *samfoo* top, then asked me to hold out my arms and sniffed at my hands.

'Your fingers – your fingernails – that's the smell. That's it. It's good that you wear *monpe* instead of frivolous Western skirts.'

I was wearing my usual cotton trousers but I suppose they counted as *monpe* or work trousers.

'I'm sorry, sir. I'll go and wash my hands.'

'Don't be a fool, girl. If I thought your hands would poison me, I wouldn't have let you into my room. This is the smell I was looking for. Decaying organic matter. And mould. You've been sneaking around outside my laboratory spying on me, haven't you? Don't try to lie to me. I know. I can smell it on you.'

He had to be smelling the mushroom spores and decaying tree matter from my mushroom trees. This stuff was deadly for papers and records but good for growing things. I'd scrubbed my hands, as best I could, but we'd long since run out of carbolic soap and no doubt some traces remained under my nails.

'And there's something else too. I wasn't sure but, yes, it's there. It's an echo of something from long ago. When I could still see. In those days I paid less attention to what I was smelling, fool that I was. All the years I wasted. No, don't move away. I haven't finished.'

He took one of my hands and, like a dog, sniffed up to the bend of my elbow then back to my wrist.

'After I lost my eyesight, I deliberately developed my sense of smell. I used myself as a test subject. I still have all the smells from my past, but I haven't catalogued them for retrieval as

59

efficiently. You are a cousin of that woman who won't stop talking?'

'My late mother was her cousin.'

'That's it, then.'

He let go of my arm and seemed to forget me, sunk in reverie. It was hard to tell whether or not he was asleep because of those ridiculous painted spectacles. But I guessed from his breathing that he was thinking hard.

'The only frustrating thing is how to put things down to be seen by the right people. How do I know, when I'm dictating, that you got it right? The fools they send me don't know anything about science. And anyone who does is incapable of recording and typing. This generation is totally useless.'

'I can take down your dictation if you like, sir. Then when I read it back to you, you can correct what I got wrong.'

'Women only know how to talk. Always full of excuses. Always trying their tricks and games. But I don't fall for all that. Do you understand?'

'Yes, sir.'

'What's so funny?'

I had smiled, but how had he sensed it?

'Well?'

'You remind me of my friend's father. The way you sniffed at my arm. During our school holidays, Dr Shankar would pay us two cents for every new plant we could find and identify. He always sniffed the plants like that. Carefully first, to make sure it wasn't poisonous. Then more deeply, to try to figure out what it might be related to.'

'Dr Shankar who wrote about common plant poisons in the

Malayan Straits?' Professor Kutsuki straightened and directed his left ear towards me.

'Yes, sir. I was at school with his daughter.'

'I've read translations of his papers. The range of medical uses. How on the edge of toxicity you can get the greatest benefits because you want to kill off the weakest, diseased cells to preserve the organism. He sounds like a truly remarkable man.'

I hoped Dr Shankar was still a remarkable man ... but I didn't say so as I didn't want to draw attention to him. As far as I knew, he was still interned with the PoWs and enemy aliens. The Japanese had not been as harsh towards Indian locals as the Chinese, but Dr Shankar had compounded his crime of gaining a medical degree from the University of Edinburgh by marrying a Scottish wife.

'He was trying to teach you girls to identify poisonous plants? Did he teach you to extract poisons? Is that what you've been sneaking out to do?'

'No, sir! I was trying to spawn mushrooms from dried spores. Dr Shankar was happiest when we brought back something we could eat or he could show his wife how to cook. Like noni fruit and ivy gourds that looked like baby watermelons,'

I'd cooked them too, serving them in curry with wild pepper leaves.

'The noni fruit is the Indian mulberry he was investigating as a cancer treatment?'

'I don't know. I just know he was so happy when his wife said something tasted good. He used to say the best thing his wife did for him was learning to make better vegetable curry than any Indian woman he knew.'

'She wasn't Indian?'

'She was from Scotland.'

'We all had happy families once,' Professor Kutsuki said. 'I saw only Shankar's one book on plant poisons. That's gone now, along with all the other books in my home. Are there others? Did he stop writing?'

'No, but he made notes in his books all the time. To record what he learned.'

'Where are his papers? His research? Why didn't he publish further?'

Without the backing of a university, Dr Shankar had found it difficult to get his work published. Even though he had access to a wealth of raw material unavailable to other researchers. 'He didn't know if anyone would ever read them. But he recorded notes to get them out of his own head he always said.'

'Where are all his notes? Why would he show them to you?'

'During the school holidays, Dr Shankar taught his daughter and me to cut out the unused pages from the backs of our school exercise books and turn them into notebooks with a hole-punch and split pins. He challenged us to record every day something we'd learned. If we hadn't learned anything, we could go through his notebooks and pick out one fact to copy into our own.'

'So, in a way, you have come to me as a student of Dr Shankar. That is a sign, you know. Where are his notebooks?'

'Destroyed by soldiers. They wanted to save them to use as lavatory paper but they were ordered to destroy them. Their officers thought they might be codes.'

'Soldiers are fools!' Dr K said loudly. 'The more important the soldier, the bigger the fool! What a waste! Not even good enough for lavatory paper? Pah!'

He sank into a reverie. I began to wonder whether I should go downstairs to see to the lunch preparations. Professor Kutsuki was dressed and the room was as clean as I could make it. He'd broken surprisingly few things. Indeed, I'd say his tantrum had been carefully orchestrated to make the greatest mess with the least damage.

'If you're all right here, I'll take this tray downstairs and bring you something fresh to eat. And some tea. Or maybe try some coconut water. The houseboys are going to harvest young coconuts this morning.'

He ignored this.

Quietly, I picked up the tray and was moving to the door when he said, 'You can read English, can't you? I know you can talk English. I've heard you talking English to Hideki Tagawa. He shouldn't be surprised people don't trust him. Who wants to trust a man who says things they can't understand? Pah! I've got nothing against people who speak other languages. When Yoshio Yoshimoto wanted me to take Morio Goda as my assistant, he said the boy could read and translate English, German and Chinese to Japanese for me. But he would not. I think he cannot. Just one more of Yoshio Yoshimoto's false promises. That man thinks just because he can talk himself into believing anything he can make it come true. If the useless Goda was a horse or dog I would have returned him to Yoshimoto as being of inferior quality. Or I could have had him shot! But because he is supposedly a man, I must put up with him. Pah!'

I was surprised by his vehemence. 'Why not just tell him – or tell Yoshio Yoshimoto – that it's not working out? I'm sure he'll find you someone else.'

63

'That boy lies about me. Says I'm being difficult. That I'm losing my mind. Now that's what everyone wants to believe. He'll just tell Yoshimoto some lies and get me locked up in a lunatic asylum. Well, why not? I'm just a stupid, blind old man to him. You're wondering why I'm so angry?'

'Well – yes.'

'I'm starving, that's why. All the English scientific books in the research library here, all that information so close to me, and I'm starving because I can't read them.'

I understood his pain. 'I didn't know there were English scientific books here.'

'In the Botanic Gardens laboratory. Not that many and none that I could have read as they're all in English.'

'I can read and translate any of the English books for you,' I said. 'I'll have to look up the scientific terms, but there should be reference books too.'

Professor Kutsuki froze, nose up, like a dog scenting the air. 'You'll read me anything I want? Are you sure Yoshio Yoshimoto will approve?'

'It has nothing to do with him,' I said firmly. 'You can give Morio Goda some other work to do, and while he's busy I can read to you. If the books were left behind by the British scientists, there won't be anything top secret that they have to shoot me for seeing, right?'

The truth was, I suspected Professor Kutsuki was right about Morio Goda exaggerating his English proficiency. In that case, if I read and translated books for him, it would take some pressure off Goda. I would be repaying some of the debt I owed him. And if it put Professor Kutsuki in a better mood, it would benefit everyone in the house.

'Pah!' Professor Kutsuki gave another disbelieving snort, then heaved himself to his feet and shuffled to the shelf nearest the mat he slept on. He bent and ran his fingers over the books and papers stacked there, then pulled out a magazine, in Japanese, not English. 'Read this to me.'

It was a mystery story.

'Morio Goda thought it was beneath him to read me stories so he kept hiding the magazine. But I'm better at finding things than he is at hiding them.'

He was testing me? Well, I was perfectly happy to read stories. I put down the tray and took the magazine.

The story was called 'The Demon in the Mine'. It wasn't very long but it was creepy. Workers in an underground mine were being killed off one by one, supposedly by the demon haunting the place. There was a creepy atmosphere, thanks to the claustrophobic underground setting, but the man-made conditions the men were working under were worse. In the end that was the greatest horror, nothing supernatural. The 'demon' turned out to be the foreman who'd been promised money by his bosses on condition that he kept quiet about dangerous fissures in the mine until they'd sold their shares. Not only did the foreman not warn his men about the danger, he spread rumours then pretended to be the demon's first victim, subsequently dressing up as the demon and killing anyone else who came close to discovering the threatening fissures.

'Do you like it?' Professor Kutsuki asked.

By the end of the story he was sitting cross-legged on his sleeping mat, rocking back and forth gently. Whenever I paused, for breath or effect, he cried, 'Don't stop! Go on!' like my niece Little Ling did when I read to her.

'So, do you like it? What do you think?'

'It's a good story,' I said, 'I'd never heard of Keikichi Ōsaka before. But it paints a very dark picture of people.'

'An all too believable picture. The writer's real name was Fukutarō Suzuki.'

'Was?'

'He was my assistant before this fool Goda. But he died in the explosion that did this.' He gestured to his eyes. 'Do you know what I was working on?'

'Something top secret.'

'That's all they told you? You're lying. I can't stand people lying to me.'

'I heard Mrs Maki telling someone that Yoshio Yoshimoto is in charge of developing a great poison-gas bomb that's going to turn the tide of the war. I guess that's what you're working on.'

'That woman talks too much. But what do they expect? Especially from the kind of older woman who would be flattered when a heroic young soldier invites her to help execute Japan's Divine Mission.'

'Japan's Divine Mission?'

Professor Kutsuki was a respected scientist. I could be punished for hearing what he wouldn't be penalised for telling me, but I wanted more. Especially now, after the huge bomb the Americans had dropped on Hiroshima.

But just then footsteps pounded up the stairs and the door was pushed open, revealing two terrified houseboys.

'Big Sister Chen! You must come right away! It's urgent!' Tanis said.

'Big Sister Chen! It's him! We found him and he's dead!' Ah Peng said, and burst into tears.

Dead Morio Goda

Morio Goda was indeed dead. He was lying in the mud on the other side of the Swan Lake, close to the boardwalk bridge. The boys had pulled him out of the water before running back to the house.

I tried to pump his chest through his wet shirt though I knew there was no hope. No water came out of his lungs. My attempts dislodged a small box in his pocket. A cheap lighter and a tiny screw fell out. I remembered the poison pin he'd talked about.

Had Morio Goda have killed himself? But the bottom of the screw didn't look sharp enough. Besides, it wouldn't still have been in his pocket if he'd used it.

'Did he kill himself?' Professor Kutsuki had followed me and the boys out. It was damned odd and inconvenient that this old blind man, who couldn't make his way to the toilet, had trailed us down the stairs, out of the house and across the rickety wooden bridge. 'What happened?'

Suicide wasn't impossible or even unlikely. After three and a half years of the Japanese Occupation, it wasn't unusual for

people to go mad and provoke the Japanese soldiers into killing them. Sometimes the soldiers went mad and killed without needing an excuse. The human mind is resilient only for so long under constant stress and fear before it cracks.

'I don't know.' I looked up at the steep slope above us. 'He could have tripped and fallen down the slope.'

'Then he should be wet and dirty, not dead.'

'I don't know,' I repeated. There was something very wrong here. The worst of it was, I didn't know what it was.

If only Professor Kutsuki hadn't been there, I would have told Tanis and Ah Peng to run back to the kitchen and forget what they'd seen.

But we were all in for it now.

'Go back to the house and tell Mrs Maki that Mr Goda fell into the lake. Don't say anything to anybody else. Then go straight to the kitchen and stay there. If anybody asks you anything, just say you don't know.'

The boys ran off.

'You could go back to the house with them, you know,' Professor Kutsuki said.

'Oh, I'm sorry – I should have asked one of the boys to guide you back. I will stay with – him until someone comes.'

'I can find my way back on my own if I want to. I know where we are. I am familiar with the laboratory building over there, with your mushroom-tree experiments outside it. But I will stay here with you. They may want to hear me say I was with you all day so you couldn't have killed the boy. I'll be your alibi, just like the boy was. Maybe I'll be the next one to die.'

Professor Kutsuki spoke lightly but I felt he was telling me he knew Morio Goda had lied for me. Yet he seemed not to

expect me to say anything. I saw Captains X and Y appear around the corner of the house. They walked with the air of men who knew this was yet another wasted journey – an attitude that changed when they caught sight of Professor Kutsuki standing next to a body on the ground. They were *kempeitai*, but their assignment was to keep Professor Kutsuki and his project safe.

'It's that secretary,' Captain X asked. 'Did you kill him?'

'Shut up,' Captain Y told him, before either the professor or I said anything. Apparently they were also there to protect him from the consequences of his actions. 'You, both get back to the house. We'll handle things from here.'

'Where did you find him? Was he attacked by locals? It must have been the resistance fighters,' Mrs Maki said.

'It looks like he fell behind the research-lab building. There's some stuff there. Some tarpaulin tied down with ropes over some old tree trunks. He must have tripped over them and tumbled down the slope to the lake,' Captain X said.

'Why would he fall? There's a perfectly good path by the lake.'

'It probably happened last night when it was dark,' Captain Y said. 'We've reported the death to Headquarters. Now we must wait until they send someone round. It's possible it was an accident, but we can't be too careful. And what was he doing out there in the middle of the night?'

The blackout due to the Allied bombers was enforced strictly in the area.

If he had been there to meet someone ...

Mrs Maki turned on me. 'Did you sneak out to meet Morio Goda again last night?'

'No!'

'I'm sick of you sneaking around and lying to me!'

She raised a hand to smack me but Hideki Tagawa stopped her. 'Su Lin. Were you out last night?'

I'd come to accept that Hideki Tagawa felt protective towards me. Or, as Mrs Maki put it, he was unnaturally jealous and protective of me.

'Not last night,' I said. 'Or the night before.' I wanted to tell Hideki Tagawa I'd never spent any time planting mushrooms with Morio Goda. That he'd lied and I'd gone along with it. But this wasn't the right time.

'It was probably those soldiers,' Mrs Maki said, looking at Captains X and Y. 'They're looking for someone to blame for their incompetence so they killed him themselves and are blaming it on him.'

Nobody answered her.

Hideki Tagawa said, without turning around, 'We're all doing what we can because we have to. Most of us are here only because we landed on a certain track and have no choice but to keep going.'

'How can you say that?' Mrs Maki said. Normally so calm, she was blinking and twisting her fingers together. 'Of course we must believe in what we're doing. Otherwise, what's the point? What's the point of anything?' Her voice shrilled to a crack.

'It's no use being scared,' I said. 'Whatever happens, being scared won't help. What would help is if you go and boil water to make tea.'

'I'll do that.' Mrs Maki was so eager to go she was out of the door before she had finished speaking.

'You want tea? Now?' Hideki Tagawa said.

'I wanted her to change tack,' I said. 'Making tea will give her time to calm down.'

It was something I had learned from the Mission ladies. The first thing they did in any emergency, whether childbirth, drunken soldiers or a wild boar attack, was to start the water boiling. It was the act of making tea rather than drinking it that made you feel you were doing something useful and therefore could do more.

'When she comes back she'll have stopped feeling scared and instead be angry with me for ordering her around. She'll feel better.'

Hideki Tagawa smiled wryly. 'Sometimes I forget how well you read us. Go out and sweep or something so that you're not around when she gets back.'

I didn't need to be told twice.

I was glad to get away by myself for a bit. Since Mrs Maki was in the kitchen, I went to the side of the house to check the laundry drying there. I had barely had time to reach for a towel when—

'Su Lin?' a dear, familiar voice said.

I jerked round, startled. Then I ran over and flung my arms around the square, smiling officer in local police uniform. 'De Souza! What are you doing here?'

'Representing Major Dewa. The death of a Japanese aide has to be investigated by the police, but a secretary isn't important enough for the big guns, so Major Dewa's local driver, interpreter and dogsbody, one Captain de Souza, is here at your service.'

I was so glad to see him. We'd worked together in the Detective Shack before the war. Then, when things settled down

under the new regime, de Souza had accepted an invitation to rejoin the now Japanese-run local police force. As we'd seen, the Japanese were less aggressive towards Eurasian and Indian locals than they were to Chinese and Malays. It was part of their trying to sow dissent between the different races in Singapore.

The Japanese didn't understand that most or all of us were descended from people who'd left their old ancestral lands to make new lives for themselves. Being a Singaporean wasn't about having a certain skin colour or religion. It was about whether you were willing to work to survive, and for your family and the island to survive. Apart from a few informers, most of those working with the Japanese were doing it for the good of us all.

'So you're here to investigate Morio Goda's death?'

'Major Dewa's already decided it was suicide, but wants it registered as an accident.'

'What? Why?'

'Too many soldiers are committing suicide. The major doesn't want any more of them to get the idea.'

'But you can't—'

'You want me to go against my orders?' De Souza grinned at me. 'Where is the poor fellow? No, just point me in the right direction. Better if you don't come with me. Are you doing okay? Apart from all this, I mean.'

'Like that, *lor*. You?'

'Same-same. See you later, sister.'

De Souza was all wet when I next saw him. Although the boys had dragged Morio Goda's body out of the lake, de Souza had waded in to examine where he'd gone in. It was the kind of

thoroughness Le Froy had tried to instil in all of us when we'd been part of his Special Investigations Unit at the Detective Shack.

For all their teasing, the others – especially de Souza and Prakesh Pillay – had always treated me like a sister. And Le Froy like . . . I wanted to believe he'd treated us all equally but the others claimed I got special treatment. 'Not because she's a girl. Because she's the smartest,' Le Froy always said.

I'd been proud of that then.

'You tried to resuscitate him?'

'I knew it was hopeless, but, yes, I tried.'

'His neck was broken. Could that have happened when you were trying to . . .' De Souza mimed tilting back a head and lifting the chin.

'No. I'm sure not. And I didn't break any ribs doing chest compressions either.'

'Nothing wrong with his ribs. But his neck is broken.'

'Morio Goda's lungs weren't full of water when I tried to revive him. Nothing came out when I pulsed his lungs. Meaning–'

'Meaning he was dead before he went into the lake? He could have broken his neck in the fall. I spoke to that old blind man, his boss, Professor Kutsuki. He seemed pretty certain Goda drowned, says he was so stupid he could have drowned in a footbath. But even so, Morio Goda wouldn't have drowned if he hadn't lost consciousness. He wouldn't have lost consciousness if he hadn't struck his head on a stone. That much is obvious, right? The problem is that there aren't any stones in the water around here. The bottom of the pool is soft and muddy, and the bank is clay with cow grass growing. None of that could have

produced the bruise on the side of his head. And there's no way he could have fallen hard enough to break his neck.'

I reflected on the implications of what he'd told me. 'You're not saying that—' I stopped. Suggesting anything other than suicide would be going against what de Souza's boss had already decided had happened.

'Yah.' De Souza nodded.

We jumped when someone else said, 'You two trying to make trouble for all of us as usual?'

'Prakesh!'

He was an unfamiliar figure in his Indian National Army uniform, but it was indeed Prakesh Pillay and his grin.

'This big oaf sent a message,' Prakesh said, jerking his head at de Souza, 'saying a situation had come up here and to look into it. So I did. Goda was being paid out of military funds so I'm here officially to confirm he's dead. What's the verdict?'

'Accidental death by drowning,' de Souza said.

'You said he didn't drown,' I objected. 'And you don't think it was an accident.'

'That's how it's being written up. Major Dewa signed off on it even before I left the office. He didn't see any point in me coming out here, but I told him we had to make sure your Hideki Tagawa sees us treating the investigation with due respect.'

'There won't be any investigation,' Prakesh said. 'So many soldiers killing themselves, these days, it's practically an epidemic.'

'You all think he killed himself? Why did you bother to come, then?'

'Any excuse to see you, Su Lin. And pay attention. It's the one

thing they're being very careful *not* to say. Can't have people thinking the troops are demoralised, can they? Much better to say they were killed in battle. Then their families get to do all their war shrine stuff.'

'But you think he killed himself.'

'Don't you?'

Before the moment of connection I'd shared with Morio Goda, I wouldn't have thought twice. But while walking back from the mushroom tree I'd have sworn he had something other on his mind than suicide, something he'd been a little upset – but more excited – about.

'No.'

I saw them exchange looks.

The war had been going on for so long that depression and despair were everywhere. Sometimes it seemed that the only control left to us was deciding how we would die instead of waiting to be killed.

'Why not?' de Souza said.

'How well did you know the man?' Prakesh asked, at the same time. He sounded suspicious now. 'Well enough to know he wouldn't kill himself?'

'Not at all! I just meant someone thinking about suicide wouldn't dress as carefully as he did. Hair and nails trimmed, hands smooth. You don't worry about things like that when you're driven to the point of destroying yourself.'

De Souza was nodding and Prakesh looked relieved.

'Either it all starts falling apart gradually and there are signs, or there's some big reason that should be obvious, but there wasn't. And it wasn't true that Morio Goda had nothing to live for. He was

all gung-ho about serving the empire – and he had his lighter to set off dynamite and his poison pin to kill himself. If he'd wanted to die he would have used that, not drowned himself, right?'

'It sounds like you knew him quite well,' de Souza said, as Prakesh remained silent.

'I want to know what happened to him, that's all.'

'Does it matter? Come on. One dead Nip after they killed so many of us? We have to show up and record it but, really, does it matter?'

'Of course it does.' De Souza gave Prakesh a warning look. Prakesh started to protest but stopped when de Souza jerked his head in my direction. 'Is this the poison pin you were talking about?' He held out the little case I'd seen earlier.

Prakesh opened it. 'What's this poison pin all about? It's just an ordinary screw. Maybe dipped in something but it looks like it's dried out. I doubt it's deadly. It would've oxidised and lost its strength in the air anyway. If he bought it off someone, he was cheated.'

'Are you sure? I thought he got it because he was an agent of some kind.'

Prakesh shook his head and tossed away the screw. I noticed he kept the lighter, though. So did de Souza, who held out his hand for it – he was investigating the case, after all. These imported lighters were a precious commodity, now that matches were so scarce.

'So Goda was telling you about his exploits as an agent?'

'Not really. We hardly talked before yesterday, but then he lied for me. Someone accused me of stealing something and he said, no, I couldn't have because I was with him, even though I wasn't. I mean, I feel like I owe him something for that.'

Given all that had just happened I didn't feel up to explaining the whole business about a girl breaking into Hideki Tagawa's office. Anyway, all that had been overtaken by news of the Americans' big bomb.

'I'm sorry about your friend, Su Lin. But, hey, it still doesn't make any difference. I mean, dead's dead, however it happened, right? Nothing we find out can bring him back,' Prakesh said.

'Right.' De Souza rolled his eyes heavenwards. 'Remind me again why you joined the police back when there was a choice.'

'Free uniforms, and I had a thing for baggy khaki shorts. Still do.' He put his hands into the pockets of his INA uniform shorts and shook them. 'They want it to be an accident. So that's what it is. We just used it as an excuse to come and see you. You know all of this ...' he gestured around us '... is a high-security zone? We can't just drop in on you and demand food like we used to.'

We were silent for a moment.

'I don't see any checkpoints,' I said.

'It's the difference between on paper and in practice. Manpower shortages and all that. That's also why no one bothers about one more death.'

'It matters how they died because they mattered. Like we all do,' de Souza said. 'Even under the British, remember? Unless local lives matter, nothing matters.' Chief Inspector Le Froy had drummed it into us when we were working under him. 'You have to believe you're worth something or you don't bring anything to the job.'

I missed those days almost as much as I missed Le Froy ... or maybe it was all part of the same loss. 'A lot of people died

in Japan yesterday,' I said to change the subject. 'Did you hear about the American bomb?'

Of course they had.

'It's hard to know how much to believe,' de Souza said. 'Reports say eleven square kilometres of the city were on fire for hours. Even if it was just a tenth of that – just one square kilometre from one bomb – it's hard to imagine. What must it be like on the ground over there, even now?'

We'd all seen the aftermath of firebombs. No matter who dropped them, their effect was horrifying.

'Hey, anyway,' Prakesh said, 'you know Parshanti and Dr Leask said they wouldn't talk about getting married until all this is over? I thought they were crazy. I mean, who knows if it's ever going to be over, or if any of us will still be alive? But now maybe it's really going to happen.'

For years Prakesh Pillay had had a huge crush on my best friend Parshanti Shankar. Of course he'd been far from the only one. Parshanti had been popular. But I knew what he was saying. Coming through the war alive was all that really mattered.

'Sounds like the resistance fighters in the jungle up-country are pretty sure the end is in sight,' de Souza said. 'Let's hope they're right. Parshanti and Dr Leask want their parents and everyone else around for the wedding. I just hope Leask survives Mrs Shankar after surviving the Japanese.'

'That's one good thing about the war,' I said. 'Even the most protective parents will be so glad their children came out of it alive that they won't make a fuss about who they marry.'

'It won't last,' Prakesh said. 'Human nature. We forget things fast, both good and bad. Hey, speaking of marriage, you'd better

decide which of us you prefer and make it a double wedding. Cheaper. And you know you'll have to marry one of us. After seeing us in action at the Detective Shack, no other man is ever going to measure up.'

'You're going to scare her off men altogether,' de Souza said. 'But, Su Lin, you know I'm a better bet than this guy, right?'

So it was settled. Morio Goda's broken neck would be recorded as an accident, though clearly they believed he'd killed himself, like so many other Japanese soldiers. The Japanese seemed to revere suicide as much as the British despised it.

The rest of us, like animals, did what we could to stay alive. One good thing that had come out of this was seeing my old colleagues again. But that made me remember what Hideki Tagawa had said about the shortages in the PoW prison.

'Have you heard anything from Le Froy? I heard the PoWs now have to pay for their food and medicine, but how?'

'They can work outside the camp for cash if they sign an agreement not to try to escape,' Prakesh said. 'Though not one man did till a commanding officer ordered them to do so, incidentally pointing out that such a document was non-binding if signed under duress.'

'Le Froy?' I asked.

'Yes, that was Le Froy's idea. At least now there's some food going in. And once they're out of the prison compound, people try to help by passing them stuff.'

'On the other hand, the prison has stopped giving them any rations at all, and they're made to do really heavy work. Digging trenches, clearing sewers and bomb damage, loading munitions

at the docks and for only thirty cents a day. Not much when one coconut costs twenty-five to thirty dollars in banana money,' Prakesh said.

'What? For coconuts? How can anyone charge for them?' They grew in profusion everywhere on the island so we'd always taken them for granted – and for free. Not only did the young coconuts provide food and drink, but the milk made anything you cooked taste better, and coconut pulp could be used to thicken gravy.

Now, with no imports coming in, we even made our own *gula melaka*, coconut-palm sugar, for sweetening. I'd watched it being made while I was growing up and managed to replicate it after some experimenting. In the old days it hadn't been high class enough for the British (white people used white sugar) but it was all that was available now. You had to cut into the bud of the coconut flower to collect the sap, like tapping rubber trees for latex. The sap was then heated slowly till most of the water had evaporated and you were left with a soft paste or crystals, depending on how long you heated it.

So, coconuts helped us survive – and we saw them as gifts from the gods.

'Why would anyone pay thirty dollars for a single coconut?'

'They have no choice. The guards decide what goes into the prison.'

I thought of Le Froy, who'd lost a foot to gangrene last year. 'What if they can't work?'

'Those who can are sharing what they have. I know I've complained about the British in the past, but they're the ones you want on your side when the chips are down. I don't know how long they can last, though. It's getting really bad. The

Japanese have been shipping men out to Borneo as free labour, and now to Thailand where they're building this crazy overland railway into Burma. And the men sent to Japan to work the mines don't live more than two weeks. Anyone who gets injured or can't keep up is left behind to die. If this isn't over soon . . .' Prakesh shook his head.

Maybe a single death wasn't so terrible in comparison to what would happen if the war dragged on. But Le Froy had always said that figuring out answers to seemingly trivial questions was the way to prevent them becoming giant problems.

De Souza and Prakesh were only concerned that I didn't get into trouble over Morio Goda's death. But I would keep my eyes and ears open. I owed him that, at least.

No One Is Irreplaceable

———◆———

Was Mrs Maki crying over Morio Goda? I wondered, after the visitors had left, taking the sodden bundle of dead body with them.

But it was not Mrs Maki who was sniffing. It was Yoshio Yoshimoto, up in Professor Kutsuki's room. In fact, they were all there, though they'd all had dinner alone on trays in their rooms. I'd dared to hope they might stay closeted away all night: it would reduce the cleaning that had to be done after Yoshio Yoshimoto had scattered cigarette ash or Mrs Maki had inspected supplies that she always tasted and never put back in the right place.

When Yoshio Yoshimoto saw me he came out of the room, and drew me a little down the corridor. 'War is hard on everyone,' he said. 'Once things settle down it will be different. The Allies are on their last legs. That bomb of theirs is clearly a desperate attempt to impress us. Now they've played their last card, there's nothing they can do if we don't respond. But what was Morio Goda really doing with you by the laboratory building yesterday?'

Did Yoshio Yoshimoto suspect me of having lured Morio Goda there? And of doing it a second time and killing him? There was no point in lying now. My alibi was dead. 'I told you, I was working on my mushroom trees, watering and harvesting them before the sun came up. I didn't even know he was there until the houseboy called me. Then he appeared from the slope above.' I waved vaguely in the direction of the primary-forest conservation area between us and Tyersall Avenue.

Yoshio Yoshimoto nodded. It was an acknowledgement that he'd heard me, not that he believed me.

'What's happening in Professor Kutsuki's room?' I asked. 'Should I bring up a mop and bucket?'

'Hideki Tagawa's making the professor go through all his things and see whether anything is missing. Any samples, any notes, any medicines ...'

Professor Kutsuki's voice rose, shrill and petulant: 'You are the one with the eyes and you want me to check whether anything is missing? How am I supposed to know?'

Hideki Tagawa appeared in the doorway, clearly looking for Yoshio Yoshimoto, who said, 'Tagawa-san's thinking Morio Goda was bribed to spy on the professor and his project. Isn't that right? You're thinking that Morio Goda was a spy?'

Hideki Tagawa didn't deny it. 'You suggested him as assistant to Professor Kutsuki. Why?'

'Because he's a distant relation who needed a job. You know what families are like. He was a smart boy and he wanted to serve the nation. Why not give him something to do?'

'So you recommended him to Professor Kutsuki even though he had no other recommendations?'

'Pah! Now we get the real story!' the professor interrupted loudly, from inside the room. 'You told me, "This is the perfect assistant for you. He will help you do all your translations. He is an expert in five hundred languages." I knew Morio Goda was spying on me and copying my notes. I could hear him and smell his deceit. But I kept quiet about it because it stopped you pushing other people at me. I never let him see anything important. You thought I was taken in. You also thought that you were so clever. Ha! Who's the clever one now?'

'Look, if Morio Goda was a spy, I'm the one he was sent to spy on.' Yoshio Yoshimoto looked tense.

He must have been fonder of Morio Goda than he'd let on, I thought, or than he'd realised. Or maybe he just felt responsible for getting him the post with Professor Kutsuki. Especially if they were distantly related.

'No one could know that Professor Kutsuki would lose his assistant and need a new one. I'm the one who should be upset.'

'That poor boy. That poor, poor boy!' Mrs Maki said yet again – she'd been saying it pretty much continuously since the body was taken away. 'They said he had a broken neck. He must just have fallen in the dark. There are trails but everything is overgrown in this horrible country. And the slope down to the lake is very steep. He must have tripped over those stupid mushroom trees. Those trunks just lying there are a menace. A death trap! Why don't you tell those two useless guards to clear that area instead of just standing at the gate doing nothing? I told them to do something useful for once, but they won't listen to me.'

'Hideki Tagawa thinks Morio Goda may have been killed by people trying to get to Professor Kutsuki,' Yoshio Yoshimoto said.

Mrs Maki's mouth fell open. I could almost see the new ideas rearranging themselves in her head. 'You mean Goda was protecting the professor?' She looked back into the room as though to remind herself of who he was. 'From whom? Or what?'

The others went back into Professor Kutsuki's room and I moved to where I could see him rocking on his sleeping mat. I remembered how easily he'd made his way across the stretch of lawn and over the bridge, and how calm he'd been in the presence of death. I could no longer think of him as helpless.

What if Morio Goda had been asked to sabotage the professor's work? What if he'd refused and been killed? But if so, as Mrs Maki was asking, who could have murdered him?

'Did Goda ask you to meet anyone?' Hideki Tagawa asked Professor Kutsuki. 'Did he mention anything or anyone? Do you know if he communicated with anyone outside this house?'

'I don't see why you're questioning me so fiercely. I'm the one who's been taken advantage of.' I saw the old professor was enjoying himself hugely. 'Interrogate the man who sent that boy to spy on me.'

'He was sent to me and I only asked him to work for you because I couldn't use him,' Yoshio Yoshimoto said.

'They're not questioning you because they suspect you. They're worried about you,' Mrs Maki told Professor Kutsuki.

'Pah! If you're all so worried about me, let me tell you this is not a safe room to sleep in,' Professor Kutsuki said. 'All night, I can hear people sneaking up and down that staircase outside.'

The external spiral staircase had been originally designed so that night-soil carriers wouldn't pass through the house with their loads.

'That's the fire escape. Nobody uses it now. In any case the door's locked.'

'What happens if there is a fire? How will I get out?'

'There isn't going to be a fire. Don't be so stupid!'

Mrs Maki had just called 'stupid' the man who had been described as one of the greatest Japanese scientific minds of his generation. No one commented.

I saw Professor Kutsuki run his tongue over his lips. I suspected he had registered the insult, enjoyed it and meant to bring it up when he felt things were getting dull. Despite everything else, I was learning new things about him.

'Su Lin!' Distracted by the professor, I jumped when Mrs Maki gripped my arm painfully, 'Do something to make him go to sleep,' she whispered to me. 'You're supposed to be looking after him so give him something that will make him settle down.'

She had evidently forgotten that Professor Kutsuki's hearing was preternaturally acute. He hissed in our direction, 'I think Madam wants you to read me a bedtime story. Either that or put sleeping powders in my tea.'

'I'm sure that's not what she meant,' I said, 'but if you like, I'll read you something.'

'Not now,' Hideki Tagawa said. 'Can you walk Professor Kutsuki downstairs to the WC? He doesn't want to use his pot.'

'Of course. Sir?'

'They want to search my room without me here to keep an eye on my things,' he said, but he was quite amenable to going downstairs. He probably wanted to get away from them for a bit too.

Professor Kutsuki didn't need me to guide him down the stairs and to the back where the WC was. If the lights hadn't been on, I'd probably have needed his guidance.

'Do you want to know how I recognise your smell?'

'The mushrooms,' I said. We'd already talked about that.

'I recognise the smell of your mother on you. I knew her a long time ago, before I went blind. I didn't know her that well, but I knew who she was, and I heard Morio Goda telling someone about you. My hearing was good before I lost my eyes and is superior to anyone else's now. All information gatherers should be blinded as part of their training.'

'You knew my mother? What did Morio Goda say about me? Who was he telling?'

He ignored my questions. 'Your eyesight isn't so good. Not much better than mine was. It would do you much good to lose it completely and focus on your other skills and senses. All you are doing now is straining your eyes and weakening them further. It is stupid to try to strengthen what will always be your weakest point. Anyway, Morio Goda was spying all the time, and not just on me. He was spying on Mrs Maki too. I could smell that woman's perfumed powders on him when he came back after searching through her drawers. Women are fools. They layer on alien scents to cover their body's odours. It is like covering faeces with flower petals. The original smell is still there, and you need to expel its cause from your body because you can only stay healthy if you keep all the systems going.'

I'd emptied his chamber pot in the early days when he'd stayed only in his room. I hoped I wasn't going to have to discuss the contents. But I found his pride in his spatial awareness and

sense of smell very touching. I clung on to my poor eyesight because it was my most precious sense. If I couldn't read, I would lose access to any minds beyond those immediately around me.

I suspect it had been the same for him. He was making the best of things.

'If you ask me, that woman upstairs is driving everyone else mad.' Once we were out of earshot of those in his room above, he had dropped his high-pitched playful voice.

I could still hear them upstairs. Mrs Maki had rejoined them and sounded on the verge of hysteria. The men's voices were lower and I couldn't make out their words. They were clearly searching for something in the professor's room. Mrs Maki seemed convinced it had to be there, hidden somewhere devious.

'Why is she so angry with you?' Professor Kutsuki asked, then answered himself: 'It's not you. She's angry – she's scared – because of that new bomb the Americans used on the Second Army Headquarters in Hiroshima. Everybody is scared of the big bomb that fell there, so they make a fuss about small things here.'

That was true. But: 'I don't think it's me Mrs Maki's angry with. I think it's my mother, for running away and abandoning them. But Hideki Tagawa insists on her having me here, so she has to settle for hating me while I work. Like you have to settle for not trusting me while I work for you.'

'Oh, no, she doesn't hate you. It would be easier for her if she did. And she would probably be a lot nicer to you. She would dress you up a lot more so she could send you out to entertain men in high positions. No. In her way she's trying to hide and protect you. She believes your mother tried to protect her. That is what she cannot forgive her for.'

In a weird way this made sense. Mrs Maki couldn't bear owing anyone anything.

We didn't go straight back upstairs when he had finished. At the foot of the stairs, Professor Kutsuki picked up a piece of propaganda paper from the hall table. He folded it into a triangle, pressed down and tore off a strip to leave a perfect square. Then he pinched, folded and refolded the flimsy paper until at last he handed me an origami lotus flower. It was beautiful. 'This is art that I can see with my fingers,'

It was intricate and detailed. The print on the petals, already smearing, added somehow to its delicate beauty. 'It's lovely.'

'You're a good girl,' Professor Kutsuki said. 'If you weren't, that woman would probably like you a lot better.'

'What are you two doing, standing there in the dark?' Mrs Maki's voice preceded her down the stairs.

'Everything is dark to the blind. Blindness is part of evolution.' The professor's high-pitched singsong tone was back. 'Every man's eyesight grows weaker with age. It means the stage of taking in external information is coming to an end, just as the caterpillar stops eating to focus on creating a protective carapace. I was young enough to need to develop my other senses. Most men don't try. They go for spectacles and other artificial means.'

'Oh, be quiet!' Mrs Maki said.

I remembered her late husband had worn glasses. I also remembered the rumour that Mrs Maki had passed his schedule to his assassins. Was it true – and was she wondering whether that had been for nothing? Was that part of what was upsetting her?

When we got back Hideki Tagawa and Yoshio Yoshimoto were still in Professor Kutsuki's room.

'I'm going to ask Captains X and Y to take turns to supervise your needs,' Yoshio Yoshimoto said. 'Since they're already assigned to you we won't have to apply for extra staff. And we won't have to feed an extra man. Good for the housekeeping budget, eh?'

'Pah! I hate soldiers!' Professor Kutsuki said. 'I hate them as much as I hate the spies you try to plant on me.'

'Somebody has to clean you up, not to mention write down your notes. Remember, you're supposed to be working.'

'You are a bully! I hate men like you!'

'I could do it.' I heard the words come out of my mouth before realising I'd decided to speak.

'You?' Yoshio Yoshimoto was apparently trying to figure out if I was still unclean. 'A female assistant?'

That seemed to be the case.

'Professor Kutsuki said Morio Goda couldn't take dictation because he was too slow. I can take dictation and I'm very fast,' I said.

'I'll do it,' Mrs Maki said. 'I taught the girl to write Japanese. I'm much better at translating Japanese and English than she is. You should have let me handle his note-taking from the start. I'll soon get him organised and working.'

'Not you!' Professor Kutsuki barked. 'You talk too much and I don't like your smell!'

'How dare you?'

Of course Professor Kutsuki couldn't see that Mrs Maki's mouth had fallen open in shock, but he grinned, rocking

backwards and forwards gleefully, as though he'd been waiting to say that for a long time.

'You think I don't know you sneak into my room and go through my things. Remember the time I found you going through my cupboards and you tried to pretend you weren't there? Pah! As though I couldn't hear your breath and smell your sweat. That's why I can say I don't like your smell. Then when I poked you with my stick you had the gall to pretend you'd just come in.'

Hideki Tagawa didn't manage to hide a smile, which made Mrs Maki glare at him. 'I'm in charge of this house. How do you expect me to run things if I can't walk around?'

'You'll be paid double what you're getting now,' Yoshio Yoshimoto said to me.

Like all Singaporeans, I had a healthy respect for money. For us, love of money is the only thing that comes close to our love of food. But given I wasn't being paid anything (apart from free board and lodging) double of nothing was still nothing.

'The professor should be guarded by trained men,' Hideki Tagawa said. 'Your suggestion about those two captains assigned to watch the house, why not go with that?'

'Jurisdiction,' Yoshio Yoshimoto said. 'The military won't pay them to take dictation. Besides, I doubt they can read. And they won't wipe his butt.'

'Are you scared that I'll do something terrible,' the professor asked, 'or that somebody will do something terrible to me?'

'I might do something terrible to you myself. Anyway, Su Lin has too much work to do in the house already. She can't take you on as well,' Hideki Tagawa said.

Mrs Maki recovered herself. 'Don't get the girl involved. Can't you ask Headquarters to send somebody here for him? All this has nothing to do with Su Lin. I should never have given her a job and I'm not going to keep her here any longer. She eats more than she's worth. I'm sending her back to her family tonight. Never mind the cholera or whatever you say is going on in that district. It's probably just an excuse so they don't have to feed her.' She turned on me. 'Why are you standing around doing nothing? Pack your things! What are you waiting for? Go now!'

I took a step towards the door, resentment welling inside. I'd not wanted to come to Moss House: Mrs Maki had corralled me. And I certainly hadn't been useless. I'd set up the food and fuel suppliers, plus the cooking and cleaning systems that had the household working so well.

Still, there was no point in arguing. Meanly I hoped things would fall apart once I was gone and that Mrs Maki would be blamed. Sadly, though, it was more likely Tanis and Ah Peng would get into trouble. I hoped they would be all right. They could understand basic Japanese, but their grasp was shaky and they had trouble understanding Mrs Maki when she got angry and talked too fast.

'If you don't need Su Lin to work in the house, why can't she help Professor Kutsuki?' Yoshio Yoshimoto said. 'Just for now, until we make further plans.'

'No,' Hideki Tagawa said, at the same time. 'Why Su Lin? What's so special about her? Nothing. Let her go on running the house and kitchen. Let Mrs Maki take notes for Professor Kutsuki. She understands the project. Su Lin doesn't. Anyway, Su Lin doesn't have clearance.'

'You don't trust her?' Yoshio Yoshimoto said.

'I don't trust him,' Hideki Tagawa said. 'Mrs Maki can look after herself better.'

'He doesn't trust me!' The professor giggled. 'Tagawa-san is scared of me!'

I suddenly saw Hideki Tagawa suspected the blind genius of sending Morio Goda out to his death. At first sight it was a ridiculous idea ... but I'd seen for myself how easily Professor Kutsuki moved around in the dark of his room, seeming to sense the people around him. Could he have asked Morio Goda to take him out that night, then pushed him down the slope? In the blackout a blind man might find his way around as easily as anyone without a torch. Better even, if he knew the terrain and was used to getting around without seeing.

'Miss Chen?' Yoshio Yoshimoto addressed me formally, as an equal. 'What do you think?'

I hesitated. So many thoughts were spinning in my head. But most of all I felt a growing anger that no one seemed to care that Morio Goda was dead. All they were concerned with was how to replace him.

'I would like to help Professor Kutsuki,' I said.

'You feel responsible for him,' Yoshio Yoshimoto said, 'like your cousins feel responsible for you. But they have a much more pleasant duty. Do you think you can guide the professor around and transcribe his notes for him? That's not so difficult, is it? Do you think you're capable of it?'

'Yes, sir. I believe I am. I will do my best.'

He turned to the professor. 'What do you think of this arrangement?'

We waited for him to complain about my smell.

'She moves quietly and is careful. She's like a mouse. I'll call her Zu Mi, short for Ne Zu Mi instead of Zu Lin.'

'She's Su Lin, not Zu Lin,' Mrs Maki said. 'It's only a Chinese name. It doesn't have any real meaning.'

'And you don't have any thoughts in your brain but you never stop talking! I like the girl because she is quiet. Not sneaking around but also not talking nonsense non-stop.'

'I know you're up to something. I'm going to be watching you.' I think Mrs Maki didn't realise she'd spoken aloud till she noticed everyone looking at her.

Except for Professor Kutsuki, of course. He held a piece of paper curved behind his left ear, like a loudspeaker cone, and pointed in her direction with it. Somehow that was even more unnerving than if he'd been staring at her.

'If you want to jump off a cliff why should I stop you?' Mrs Maki said, in her normal voice. 'Just make sure he has his food and medicine for his stomach. And don't believe any nonsense he tells you about having to go outside. Make sure he stays in the house.'

So she was also suspicious of the professor.

'That's settled, then. Make sure he doesn't poison himself or you.' Yoshio Yoshimoto might have been joking, but I wasn't sure.

'Yes, sir.'

'Someone may be out to get him. Whoever approached Morio Goda might approach you too. If any stranger talks to you, come to me at once. And if he sends you out to meet anyone, especially at night, don't go alone. Tell us first.' So Yoshio Yoshimoto wasn't joking.

'Professor Kutsuki has said previously he doesn't want a female assistant,' Hideki Tagawa said. 'I'll get HQ to send over a young man tomorrow. He'll be quiet. Didn't you say you didn't want females around, sir?'

'Some people seem to think I say too much.' The blind genius pursed his lips sulkily.

'Professor Kutsuki should be properly guarded. Especially now his assistant is dead.' Mrs Maki's silence had ended. 'Can't you get the *kempeitai* to send more soldiers to guard him? We brought him over here because everyone says Singapore is supposed to be safe and now Morio Goda is dead—'

'The stupid boy had an accident!' Yoshio Yoshimoto snapped.

'No soldiers. I hate soldiers. I hate soldiers even more than I hate women!' Professor Kutsuki said.

'Su Lin,' Yoshio Yoshimoto said to me, 'we need your help. Professor Kutsuki needs your help. You will be his temporary assistant until we can work out something better. The matter is settled for now.'

Later, carrying clean laundry to the rooms, I found Yoshio Yoshimoto standing just inside the open doorway of Morio Goda's room. He was staring as though he was trying to understand what had happened.

I was touched by how moved he was by Morio Goda's death. More so than Professor Kutsuki, for whom Morio had been working. 'It's all right to be upset,' I said, 'but he wouldn't want you to feel guilty.'

'What?' He jumped and glared at me. 'Guilty of what? What are you saying?'

I was way out of line, but since I'd started I would push through. 'Of course you feel responsible for him. I know how much he respected you as a *sensei* and as a role model. But he wouldn't want you to feel bad,' I offered him a (clean) handkerchief. 'Would you like some hot tea or soup?'

He gave a laugh, then took the cloth and wiped his face. 'Little mother,' he said. 'I thank you.'

I felt I owed him something for his confidence in me. He'd shown he trusted me more than Hideki Tagawa or Mrs Maki did. 'If someone approaches me about the professor's work I will tell you.' I wanted him to know I was aware that whoever had approached Morio Goda might approach me too.

'Good girl. But recovering the old man's final assembly notes, that's what's important now.'

'What?'

'He doesn't need to do any new work. Get him to tell you what he was working on just before his laboratory was blown up. Then write down everything he says.'

Trying Out

———◆———

'Where do you think you're off to? I told you to stay in the house. No sneaking out!' Mrs Maki snapped that afternoon, when I lifted the rattan vegetable basket off its hook on the wall.

'I'm only going to get the vegetables.'

'Send one of the boys. I don't want you leaving the house at all. You think I don't know what you get up to outside?'

What did she think I got up to? The Botanic Gardens were fenced in from the road on all sides.

'I go out and over the lake bridge—'

Mrs Maki shuddered at the mention of the lake. Did she suspect me of drowning Morio Goda? I wished she'd make up her mind. Was I supposed to be his lover or his killer? All right, maybe the two weren't mutually exclusive. 'You don't leave this house at all, do you hear me?'

'Yes, ma'am.'

She meant it too. At least for now.

I handed Ah Peng the basket, since Tanis was occupied in

splitting a jackfruit. We would be having jackfruit curry over sweet potatoes for dinner.

Well, the houseboys were perfectly capable of taking care of the vegetable gardens.

'Get the red stem *saan choy*. Don't take too much and kill the plant, ah!'

What really hurt was being forced to desert my mushroom trees just when I was starting to get somewhere with them. I still didn't trust Tanis and Ah Peng to harvest the fungi. They tended to get carried away with enthusiasm. I was most afraid of contamination from spores of other, possibly poisonous, mushrooms.

'You don't realise how serious this is,' Mrs Maki said, when Ah Peng had left – at a run: he was happy to be outdoors. 'You think everything's a game you can solve by cooking one of your soups! Well, there are bigger issues at stake here than you're capable of imagining. I'm not going to risk you messing everything up. You're not to have any communication with anyone outside this house. No sneaking off to meet your policeman boyfriend, no leaving the house at all. Just get Professor Kutsuki to put down his notes. That's all you have to do and you'd better do it!'

I started to say that de Souza wasn't my boyfriend, but Mrs Maki was already gone. It didn't make any difference: she wouldn't have listened to me anyway. Besides, she was wrong about one thing: a good soup could make all the difference in the world.

Tanis grinned at me and twirled a finger around his temple. '*Siao*,' he said. That was Singlish for 'crazy'. I had to agree.

I should have headed up to see what Professor Kutsuki was

doing but first I started a stock with dried fish and dried mushrooms. The wonderful thing about stock is that once you get it going it cooks itself. 'Watch it,' I told Tanis. 'Add water if it gets low.'

Whatever happened upstairs, there would be good soup cooking in the kitchen. It's little things that remind you it's possible to go on living.

'I never said I don't like the girl but I also never said I wanted to work with her. Why can't I work on my own? You told me not to trust anybody.'

Professor Kutsuki wasn't alone, so I paused outside his door.

'You don't like anybody.' Yoshio Yoshimoto's charm sounded strained. 'You need somebody to help you. It doesn't have to be somebody smart, just someone who can see. You don't even have to trust her. It doesn't matter what she learns – who is she going to tell?'

It was wrong to listen, wrong to interrupt and also wrong not to obey Mrs Maki's instructions. What was the safest thing to do in such a situation?

I froze in position with a hand raised so it looked like I was about to knock on the door. If accused of listening, I would say I'd just arrived. If accused of being late, I'd say I heard voices and didn't dare enter. And, of course, I listened hard.

'Unless you agree to have one of the soldiers with you, the girl is your best choice. And she probably reads and writes better than any of the men. It won't be easy to find anyone else with even a basic education. What do you say?'

'I don't want a soldier.'

'That's settled, then.'

I scurried backwards enough steps that I was coming down the corridor when Yoshio Yoshimoto left the room. He went past without looking at me, his face hard.

'How much did you hear?' Professor Kutsuki asked. I noticed he didn't speak immediately, but waited till we heard the officer's footsteps going down the stairs. I would remember to do the same.

'I wasn't listening,' I lied politely.

'Pah! Of course not.' You are a smart girl. You know I have to object to you working with me or they will never let me keep you. You must listen to everything you can, provided you tell me what you hear! What do you say to that?'

'I'll try not to disappoint you.'

'At least you're not stupid, like that boy was. You don't know what it's like being blind and surrounded by fools who've got eyes and don't know how to use them.'

'I'm sorry.'

'Why sorry? It's not your fault that I'm blind. Unless you know something I don't, and I seriously doubt that.'

'I'm sorry that you're blind and you can't read. I'm sorry that I'm here and don't know enough about physics and chemistry to help you. But at least I can read. Do you want me to read to you?'

'What for? The only books here are English books. You can't read English.'

I picked up a book on the floor by the door (which had clearly been thrown at someone) and started reading. It was about soil types with a focus on residuals. I translated the best I could so he would see I wasn't just making up gibberish.

'Properties of residual soils depend on the weathering of the rocks in the area.' At least I knew the lyrics to the Andrews Sisters' 'Boogie Woogie Bugle Boy' better than Morio Goda had. Though I wasn't sure I could translate them in any way that would make sense to Professor Kutsuki.

'All right, all right. So you understand English. Why are you doing this? I know you are here to spy on me. I may be blind, but I can see your plans, clear as daylight.'

'I'm supposed to look after you and I'll do my best. That's all.'

'I hear things. I know you slip out of the house at night. If you didn't have something going on with Morio Goda, why would he lie for you?'

Did everyone know Morio Goda had lied for me?

Sometimes I walked around outside at night. It was safer now than at any time since the start of the Occupation because the threat of Allied bombers kept *kempeitai* on duty, staring skywards close to shelter. Besides, most of the soldiers were as starving, sick of war and depressed as the locals. I hadn't realised Professor Kutsuki had heard me, but somehow I sensed he wasn't serious.

'I think you could have killed Morio Goda yourself,' I countered. 'I know you can get around just fine when you want to. You could have asked him to take you out for some secret business without telling anybody. There's only your word that you didn't know he went out last night. Outside in the dark, being able to see would be no advantage. You could have pushed him down the slope into the lake and come back into the house yourself!'

'Me? You think I killed Morio Goda? Me? An old blind man?'

'Why not? You probably had more reason to do so than I did.'

Professor Kutsuki pursed his lips, tried to frown, then giggled, 'Good point. Very good point, girl. I'm honoured. But that doesn't mean I trust you. Come closer, so that I can smell you better. So you liked that useless boy, admit it. Even though he was so rude to you?'

'I didn't dislike him.'

'The firebomb attack on my lab in Luzon in the Philippines was like the Pearl Harbor attack,' Professor Kutsuki said. 'Like the staged Manchurian attack, engineered by Japanese military personnel to give them an excuse for invading and taking over. Now the people who came up with those schemes remove Morio Goda and plant you in his place. They've already attacked my research lab once. What do they want you to do to me?'

'They want me to go on cleaning your room and washing your clothes. And now write down your notes for you.'

'Pah! Why should I trust you?'

'Because even if they have a plan, I don't know about it. And plans don't always work. The attack on Pearl Harbor, meant to disable the American navy and warn them to stay out of the war, actually brought them into it.'

'That was so stupid of them. The Americans would have been happy to mind their own business if they hadn't gone to poke the tiger in its cave.' He nodded. 'We can make a truce,' he said. 'You're not stupid and I know you have a good sense of smell and taste because it shows in the food you prepare. You don't know how many cooks are taste-blind. My sharp hearing and sense of smell are a curse, I tell you. Your Mrs Maki uses perfume because she thinks she smells bad. She's smell-blind. But her perfumes don't mask what I can smell. I can tell when she's been

arguing with Hideki Tagawa because she sweats when she's angry with him. And when she spends time with Yoshio Yoshimoto? Oooh!' Professor Kutsuki giggled. 'I can't explain that to you. I would get into trouble for corrupting Hideki Tagawa's pure young virgin!'

I laughed too, 'I'm not that innocent. And I know Mrs Maki's angry with Hideki Tagawa for not giving Yoshio Yoshimoto a more influential position.'

'She likes to run things, doesn't she?'

Because Hideki Tagawa was unmarried and had no sister, Mrs Maki, as his cousin, served as his housekeeper and hostess. She seemed to think this gave her the right to advise him as a wife would. Except she wasn't able to fulfil the most important function of a military wife. Now all the officers' wives had been sent to safety in Japan, she could no longer get useful information (such as whose husband was drinking too much, gambling or meeting up with strangers) from them.

'And she likes that man. Yoshio Yoshimoto is an upstart and a social climber,' Professor Kutsuki said. 'Morio Goda was always his man, not mine. He might have been working for me, but everything he did was designed to please Yoshio Yoshimoto.'

'Why a social climber? He says he's from an old family.' I had an idea, but poked gently for more information.

'His father was the youngest son of a samurai family, who joined the army but failed to rise in the ranks, and his mother was the daughter of a Buddhist monk who left the temple to become a shoemaker. His family is hanging on to respectability by their fingernails, trying not to drown in poverty. Of all people for her to pick!'

It was funny to see Mrs Maki looking at Yoshio Yoshimoto with admiration, offering him the few delicacies we could scrounge (though he ate nothing that wasn't served to all) and hanging on his every word as if she worshipped him. Especially when he was only in the position he occupied thanks to her.

'I don't think she picked him. I think she likes him.'

'Who trained you?'

'What?'

'I said who trained you? You'd better not try to cheat me. We're on a truce, remember? Anyway, I just answered your question so it's your turn to answer mine. Who trained you?'

'I learned to cook and clean from my grandmother mostly, with the black and white amahs. The teachers at the Mission School taught me to read, write and keep household accounts. Then Mrs Maki provided instruction in Japanese.'

'You expect me to believe that? You needn't pretend. Girls dream of growing up to marry handsome men who promise them two or even three rice crops a year. Now if they're still alive they're bitter and disappointed because the men they would have married are dead. So, why aren't you bitter? Why aren't you saying you'd be better off dead?'

'Do you think you'd be better off dead, sir?'

'Pah. Do you imagine I want to be here? Do you know why I finally agreed to come? They told me I'd be working with the former director of the Scientific Studies Bureau. But by the time I got here, he had been sent on to Laos. And I was allowed to bring just one assistant with me – the useless assistant they chose for me. He was supposed to help me but he was offended to be asked to carry my bags. Now do you think I'm sorry he's dead?'

What was he trying to get at? I couldn't tell if the old professor was asking for sympathy or threatening me. I suspect he wasn't sure either. Like a fisherman throwing pebbles into a pond, he was trying to see what he could stir up.

'I need someone I trust. I have no eyes. I need someone who has eyes but no tongue. But that wouldn't work. How would you read to me without a tongue? What I need is someone with eyes and no brain. I could trust someone like that.'

The old man got up, took the two steps to the side table and picked up the bottle there, pouring two glasses.

He moved slowly but confidently, without any of the fumbling I'd seen him display when the others were around.

Professor Kutsuki handed a glass to me. The bright cartoon eyes on his spectacles seemed to stare right at my face. He estimated my height well, no doubt from listening to me speak.

'Morio Goda was a vain, silly young man. He should have had a chance to grow old. No man should die because he is half-witted enough to be taken advantage of by others.'

I wondered if he had poisoned Morio Goda before sending him out into the night. He might have meant it as a joke, a payback for all the taunts Morio Goda had dished out to him, but Morio Goda had fallen and broken his neck.

Professor Kutsuki raised his glass. 'May he rest in peace,' he said, in English.

'May he rest in peace,' I said, and drank.

'You aren't afraid to die?' It took me a moment to realise he wasn't referring to the drink I had just swallowed, 'You're not afraid? Yoshio Yoshimoto refuses to drink anything I offer him.'

'I'm trying to help you. Why would you poison me?'

'If you believe that, you're more stupid than the Goda boy. You think they'll treat you well because you're useful? Pah! They'll use you up before they throw you out. All my assistants die. That's the pattern. You see that and you still want to work for me?' Professor Kutsuki shook his head, then clawed wildly at the strands of hair that had plastered themselves to his damp forehead.

'Why not? How do you know it wasn't my childhood dream to work for a nasty, smelly, foul-mouthed old blind man? Maybe this is what I always dreamed of.'

It was a risk. He seemed to be replaying my words in his brain. Then he cackled and thumped his hand on the table.

'I like you. If you're a spy sent to get secrets out of me, you're very good. Tell me, do you want to be a scientist too? Did they tell you to say that to me? Morio Goda told me he'd always wanted to be scientist. Ever since he was a boy, he said. But he couldn't tell me what kind of science he was interested in. Not interested in growing more food. Not interested in making river water safe to drink. All he was interested in was playing guns and bombs. He called me short-sighted because feeding a few more people wasn't as important as building the great Japanese Empire. He wasn't just stupid. He was boringly stupid, which is a much worse crime. You know how I know? He worshipped Yoshio Yoshimoto!'

'Yoshio Yoshimoto says the great Japanese Empire will make life better for all Asians.'

'He sees himself as the leader of the forty-seven Ronin.' Prof Kutsuki shrugged elaborately. 'I heard him talking to you. It's not my fault that I have good hearing and that man talks too loudly. He doesn't understand the forty-seven Ronin. It's not

about revenge. Oishi disarms suspicion by posing as a drunkard and womaniser to his own dishonour. That's the real sacrifice. If you cannot bear people to think you dishonourable you will only be pursuing the look of honour, not the real thing. So, girl, what would you want to do if there wasn't a war on?'

There was a war on, so it was a pointless question. But I didn't want to antagonise him when we were getting along so well. 'I wanted to be a journalist,' I said. 'Or to write stories. I thought I could use stories to help people see themselves from the outside and see other people from the inside.'

'I like *honkaku*, stories in which an amateur detective solves the riddles that the authorities cannot. Often such stories show the terrible circumstances that drive men to do terrible things. But they are entertaining. Not the propaganda they're always pushing down our throats. Do you write stories like that?'

'No, sir.'

He sighed. 'So you want to write boring love stories?' He shook his head. 'They called me a genius before I went blind. Now they say I'm crazy. But going blind was the best thing that ever happened to me. Maybe the war will be the best thing that ever happened to you as a writer. There is a war on. There is only today and now to act. Think. Tell me one thing you want to do here and now that you couldn't do if there wasn't a war on. Consider it a test, a challenge. If you pass, you can work for me. Well?'

'I want to cut your hair.'

I'd seen how irritating he found the thin dirty strands of hair clinging to his face and neck. At some point he or someone else had hacked off clumps unevenly. But it was a mess and must have been very uncomfortable.

'Pah! Don't talk rubbish.' He turned away his face. He thought I was making fun of him.

'I was apprenticed to a Japanese hairdresser before the war. I'm quite good at it, but I need to stay in practice. I don't have my razor but I keep my scissors sharp.'

The old man stayed silent till I added, 'Are you afraid of me holding scissors near you?'

When Hideki Tagawa came in later he found me standing over Professor Kutsuki with a comb and the razor he'd produced. He'd refused to take off his spectacles, so I worked around them, lifting one earpiece at a time to create the high slope he'd asked for.

Professor Kutsuki heard him and cried out, giggling, 'Help! Help! She has a knife to my throat!'

'What do you think?' I asked Hideki Tagawa. I thought I'd done a pretty good job, though it had been a long time.

'So you know how to cut hair. Is there anything you don't know how to do?'

'I know only the basics, sir. Do you want me to cut yours?'

'You should let her, so she can stay in practice. Young people are taught skills but never practise enough!' Professor Kutsuki said.

He was in a very good mood. I'd given him a neck and head massage as I'd been taught. Though he'd been tense and nervous at first, he'd finally relaxed a little, and now he was shaking his head at Hideki Tagawa, like a dog excited after a bath.

'Not bad,' Hideki Tagawa said. 'You look very smart, sir.'

'I do, don't I? Remember, the girl is supposed to be working for me. If you want her to cut your hair, I get the commission!'

Blue Coat Missing

———◆———

Mrs Maki hadn't given me much choice about coming to work at Moss House. She'd arrived at Chen Mansion in the transport driven by Captain X with Captain Y carrying a bayonet in the front seat and she'd told me to pack what I needed for a couple of days. She'd brought a letter of authorisation from Hideki Tagawa and you didn't say no to Japanese orders.

To be honest, it hadn't been that tough for me to leave. Chen Mansion was in East District, Division 221, which had been Katong before the war. It was where I'd grown up, but now my grandmother's house was crowded.

It was extra uncomfortable for me because Uncle Chen's mother-in-law had moved in to live with her surviving daughter, Shen Shen, after her husband, two sons and elder daughter had been killed. That woman had suffered a lot, but she believed most vehemently and vocally that it was my bad-luck curse that had damned my family ... and caused Shen Shen's miscarriages. Whenever she saw me, she pulled up her shirt over her nose and mouth, as though breathing in the same air as me would somehow infect her.

I tried to keep my distance from her, but several of my grandmother's tenant families who'd lost their homes had also moved in and the six of us (my grandmother, Uncle Chen, Shen Shen, their daughter Little Ling, Shen Shen's mother and me) were sleeping in various corners of my grandmother's room. So, honestly, I hadn't been that sorry to leave.

And after I left, cases of diphtheria and cholera were reported in the district and they'd been ordered to quarantine (at least Shen Shen's mother couldn't hold me responsible for that!) so I hadn't been back to visit.

That 'couple of days' had stretched to almost four months now.

I wasn't sorry to be away from there. I couldn't do much to help and would just have been another mouth to feed. But it was almost as bad here now. Tensions were rising and it was hard to be anywhere in the house without walking into someone fighting. This time it was Mrs Maki and Hideki Tagawa, who were quarrelling in my bedroom.

'I've been on the job for a long time,' Hideki Tagawa said, 'and I've seen so much that I know when someone is lying. And I can tell that you're not telling me the truth. At least, not the whole truth.'

'You're being ridiculous,' Mrs Maki said.

I wasn't (really) listening, but if people want to keep their arguments secret, they shouldn't talk so loudly in houses with thin walls and ventilation gaps.

'The losses to Japan can't be denied.'

'You have no faith. That's the problem with bureaucrats like you. The war isn't over yet. You've been listening to American propaganda. They play music and tell jokes and that's how they get inside your brain and turn you against your own people.'

'And you've fallen under Yoshio Yoshima's charismatic spell. It's time for you to wake up and see that Japan's losses are real. It's only a matter of time now.'

'Yoshio Yoshimoto has standards. It's people like you who weaken us even more than Western influence. Yoshio says that even if you were sent to learn English and the ways of the West to serve Japan, it has corrupted and morally weakened you.'

'Yoshimoto will never respect you because you are female and, also, because of the man you were married to.'

'This has nothing to do with my husband. Or Yoshio Yoshimoto.'

'You're living in denial because you don't want to accept that you allowed your husband to die for nothing.'

'How dare you? I knew you were telling everyone I betrayed him because I wanted to get rid of him. That's not true at all! I cared for him. He was good to me. He was a good father. He would have continued being good to us, providing for us.'

Even I'd heard those rumours. Her late husband had been popular in Singapore when he'd served as the unofficial Japanese ambassador. When he'd died so soon after being recalled to Japan some said it was because he'd tried to speak up for our people.

'You think I don't know people accuse me of having my husband murdered because he was against Japan going to war? Didn't you tell Yoshimoto that I passed his schedule to those young naval officers and made sure he was where he said he would be? You really don't know me, do you? You'd think someone making up stories would have made up a more dramatic part for me!'

'I've never spoken of your husband's death. Not to you, not to anyone. Certainly not to Yoshimoto.'

'Still lying to me! No one would have dared to say anything against me unless they knew they had your approval.'

The door was pulled open so suddenly that I almost fell into the room. I might have been leaning against it just a little – after all, as a cripple, I had some excuse. But Mrs Maki was in no mood for excuses. She slapped me, and shouted, 'You again! You're sneaking around everywhere. Nothing better to do except spy on people who are only trying to help you.'

'I'm sorry,' I said.

'You think you're so clever and that you know everything? Let me tell you, you don't know anything!'

Hideki Tagawa shook his head and left. I had the feeling he'd come to my room looking for me and found Mrs Maki already there. Also, that he didn't want to speak to me in front of her.

At least she didn't try to hit me again. That was an improvement.

Maybe I should just have left, but this was my room: where else was I supposed to go? Mrs Maki was walking around, opening and closing cupboard doors and drawers, muttering to herself as she went. The mutters occasionally crescendoed to questions and accusations. I was the only person there she could have been talking to, and it would have been rude to walk away.

'You've been taken in by him, like everyone else. He's such a sweet talker. Don't think you're the only one. That's his style. He's a conman. He acts difficult, then sucks you in just by being normal. That's how he gets people hooked. He makes you think there's something special about you. Actually, the only thing he thinks is special is himself!'

I assumed she was talking about Hideki Tagawa. It was true that, though I still didn't trust him, I'd stopped feeling fear and

disgust in his presence. No, let me correct that: I might have stopped feeling disgust, but I still felt fear, as I did in the presence of all Japanese. Just because they were Japanese their word was taken against yours, over yours, regardless of right or wrong. It is impossible to do your best at anything when your mind is focused less on your work than on who might be making trouble for you.

But I no longer considered Hideki Tagawa to be an emotionless killing machine as I once had. I didn't agree with what he believed in – that the Japanese were liberating us from Western colonialism – but at least he believed in something.

It might have been because, like everyone else, he shrank in Yoshio Yoshimoto's presence that he seemed less offensive. Or maybe just 'less' in general. I still thought he looked a bit like a rat, but now it was an older and very tired rat.

'You like it when he takes your side, don't you? You don't have to lie to me. I can see right through you. You're no better than your mother, always sucking up to the most important man in the room. Now he's refusing to do any work at all unless you're allowed to go to the laboratory with him. Without any top-security clearance!'

With a shock, I realised that Mrs Maki was talking about Professor Kutsuki, who was worshipped and considered the voice of science, the force that would bring victory to Japan. And just because he wanted to bring his assistant to work in his laboratory?

'"Give him whatever he wants," Yoshimoto-san tells me. Even he cannot see through that old man's tricks!'

Ah. That, then, was the rub, as Shakespeare's Hamlet (of

whom Yoshio Yoshimoto and company disapproved) says. And, as Queen Gertrude says, 'So full of artless jealousy is guilt, it spills itself in fearing to be spilt,' which summed up Mrs Maki exactly, I thought.

She was jealous because Yoshio Yoshimoto supported Professor Kutsuki in preferring me – a crippled local girl – to her as his assistant. It was clear to me that Mrs Maki would have liked Yoshio Yoshimoto to be interested in her in the way she suspected Morio Goda had been in me. Clear, too, that she cared more for him than he did for her.

It wasn't surprising. Yoshio Yoshimoto was good-looking and charming. More importantly, he knew how to talk to Mrs Maki. He teased her. She'd been used to doing things her way all her life, running her father's life and then her husband's, with everyone always saying how wonderful she was. It was new to her to have someone tell her she was old-fashioned or inefficient.

I think he was the first man she'd ever stopped to take a good look at. I remembered seeing her with her late husband. Mrs Maki had always behaved more like a hardworking secretary than a loving wife. They hadn't been a long-married couple so much as master and housekeeper.

And though she seemed so old to me, Mrs Maki must have been in her mid-forties (which seems young to me now!). She might have seemed past lust and procreation, but it is at this age that the strongest women come into their own.

But none of this was my business.

'You're just like your mother. Everything comes so easily to you. You'll never have the will or the character to see anything through, though.'

One of the (many) things that hadn't come easily to me was keeping quiet when people said stupid things. But I'd learned. Now I said, mollifying her, 'He's trying to complete the project. Yoshio Yoshimoto wants him to record his previous work, not come up with anything new.'

'You and that senile old professor are a pair. Not worth the air you breathe! I told him once, twice, three times, Kutsuki is beyond it. But if a man wants to believe something, there's nothing you can do to change his mind.'

'He told me that you arranged for him to come here.'

'Only because things are going to Hell in the Philippines. He conned me with all his big talk about science winning the war. He fooled everybody. How long has he been here already? Where's this big invention of his?'

I wondered whether she had finally snapped and gone mad. The iron control that had always been there in the old days was gone. 'He's trying to remember what was in the missing notes,' I said. 'Maybe it'll come back to him more easily in the lab.'

I hadn't taken down anything important yet. But, then, we were learning to work together. And maybe Professor Kutsuki was trying to decide whether or not to trust me. I was looking forward to working in the laboratory building by the lake – I could slip out to check on my mushroom trees.

'I want you out of the house.' Mrs Maki's words broke into my thoughts.

'But I – Professor Kutsuki—'

'Just get out. I never want to see you in here again. As if it's not bad enough already!'

Mrs Maki pushed past me and left the room. But not fast enough that I didn't see she was crying.

I didn't know what to do.

It was all the same to me, I told myself, whether I stayed or left. But could I go just because Mrs Maki couldn't stand me any more? Even if it was she who'd brought me here, Hideki Tagawa was in charge of the house, and it was Yoshio Yoshimoto's project.

And Hideki Tagawa was back. 'Don't take her too seriously. She's under a lot of strain.' He'd been listening.

The Japanese here learned more from eavesdropping on each other's conversations then from being told anything directly. It was very different from how we locals tended to tell everybody everything at the same time. But maybe it evened up to the same thing. 'I didn't mean to upset her,' I said.

'It's not you. She's just feeling guilty.'

'Guilty because she killed Morio Goda?'

'No. Of course not!' He gave me a strange look, then shook his head.

'Then what?'

'Nothing. Forget I said that.'

He looked and sounded tired to death, but I wanted to get to the bottom of this. 'You said she was feeling guilty. Guilty about what?'

'About being alive.'

All right. He had me there. I felt guilty about that too. All the time. You can't watch people being killed around you day after day without wondering what is different about you that you are still alive, and realising that there's nothing except chance. And that maybe if you'd died one of the others might still be alive.

I think that was what drove so many people to kill themselves. It wasn't the hunger, the pain, the fear. It was feeling that they didn't deserve to be alive any more than those who no longer were. I'd felt that way too, after the mass killings at the start of the Occupation. But then I'd decided that as long as I was still alive I would go on doing what I could. As Uncle Chen (was he even still alive?) always said, 'Why kill yourself when you can make them do the job?'

'Look, Su Lin. Do you want to leave here? And go home? I can have a car take you back tonight.'

The answer should have been 'Of course!' But, then, at Chen Mansion I would be doing pretty much the same as I was doing here. Foraging for food, cooking, washing, mending... I wouldn't be any more protected from Allied bombs or Japanese attacks there than I was here. In fact, I would probably be at greater risk. But that wasn't why I didn't want to go back. I remembered Mrs Maki accusing me of running away, like my mother.

'I know there's still the infection in the neighbourhood, but even so it might be safer for you there than here.'

I wasn't afraid of infection.

'I think I can help Professor Kutsuki,' I said. 'I want to.'

I couldn't leave the old blind scientist alone in a house where his hostess was ranting against him and his previous aide was dead. I didn't think Mrs Maki was going to kill him but I didn't know she wasn't, and what if she'd killed Mario Goda because he'd found out that *she* was trying to steal Professor Kutsuki's research material? 'He's not so bad when you get to know him.'

'His previous colleagues are all dead. His former assistant is dead. And you really think he's the one who needs protecting?'

'Maybe he's just been very unlucky.'

'That man is lucky. But protection has always been your strong point, hasn't it? Let's hope you mastered it.'

'So you want me to protect him?'

'I want you to protect yourself.' Hideki Tagawa stared at me. I didn't know what he was looking for. Was it the same thing Mrs Maki suspected? Was he wondering whether I had been taken in by Yoshio Yoshimoto's charm and charisma?

'Do you know what his secret project is?'

'I know it's secret. But I know I can take notes and write down whatever he remembers. And I want to wash and mend his clothes. I think there is mould in his cupboards.'

'We're not all monsters,' Hideki Tagawa said, surprising me.

'I know,' I answered, surprising myself.

I didn't believe Professor Kutsuki could do any good for the war effort, or that I could make any difference helping or hindering him. But if I could make him happy by reading him stories he wanted to listen to and comfort him by listening to the stories he wanted to tell, why not?

And if, in the course of that, I found out who'd killed Morio Goda – well, murder is murder, even if he'd been Japanese. If I learned anything I would pass it on to Prakesh Pillay and Ferdinand de Souza, so that some day his family might learn he hadn't just tripped and broken his neck for nothing. Even if it never went on the official record.

'Hitler's dead.' Hideki Tagawa cut into my thoughts without preamble. 'The war in the West is over. But that doesn't change anything here. It would be better if they acknowledged that publicly, but such decisions are made in Tokyo. Where is the *michiyuki* your cousin gave you?'

His abrupt change of subject caught me off guard. 'What? I haven't worn it for some time. She wanted me to wear it for the *47 Ronin* screening but I couldn't find it.'

Mrs Maki had invited some of the other officers to the screening and didn't want me serving them in my worn and patched *samfoo*. The *michiyuki*, whose characters translate literally as 'for travelling', was a traditional coat usually worn over a kimono. The one that Mrs Maki had given me had a pale blue pattern over a dark blue background. It had a square neckline, fastened with buttons in front and special sleeves tailored to accommodate those of a kimono: the *michiyuki* is generally worn only over a kimono. It is seldom seen in Singapore.

Mrs Maki had given the coat to me years ago, when I cleaned her house in exchange for Japanese lessons. I'd worn it only when she had important visitors who might be put off the food I'd cooked for them if I served it to them in my everyday clothes.

I'd appreciated the gesture. It was a beautiful garment that had once belonged to Mrs Maki's mother and should have passed to her daughter. I'd taken good care of it in case it ever had to be returned, and she'd reminded me to bring it with me to Moss House.

But lately I hadn't been able to find it. I hadn't worried about it because none of the officers she'd invited to the film screening had shown up. At the time I'd assumed it had been pushed to the back of some drawer. I'd been in a hurry, and looking respectable hadn't seemed as important as making sure the stewed tapioca was properly seasoned.

I glanced around and realised Hideki Tagawa must have come to my room to search for it when Mrs Maki – had she come for the same reason? – had been there too.

But it wasn't where I had left it. It wasn't anywhere in the tiny closet or folded in the laundry bag with my second bedsheet.

'You should take better care of your clothes,' Hideki Tagawa said. 'When did you last see it?'

'It must be here somewhere,' I said, searching.

But it wasn't.

Hideki Tagawa just shook his head.

'You think I went to your office?'

'Don't be ridiculous.'

'You think it was my blue coat, the blue *michiyuki* they were talking about. You think I wore it to break into your office at Headquarters?'

'I think it sounds like the coat they saw someone wearing. Did Morio Goda ever come into your room?'

'No! Of course not! You're worse than Mrs Maki!'

'Did he know where you keep your things?'

'It couldn't have been my *michiyuki*,' I said, as Hideki Tagawa rifled through the few clothes in my drawers. But why would he believe me when I didn't believe myself?

Someone had come into my room and gone through my clothes. I knew that for sure. I was much too careful with my few clothes to have misplaced the one valuable piece I had.

Also, the *kanzashi* hairpin I knew I'd wrapped in cotton and stored with the coat was still in the drawer. The delicate gold pin was a good deal more valuable than the blue *michiyuki*, if anyone had come to steal things. Not only was it rare, it carried the crest of my mother's samurai family – a chrysanthemum surrounded by leaves – and had been crafted in Kyoto more than a hundred years ago.

I was glad it hadn't been stolen.

'What was taken from your office? It wasn't really top-secret military plans, was it?'

Hideki Tagawa seemed surprised to be asked. 'Why not?'

'Because those wouldn't have been kept in a safe in your office. They would be with the commanding officers or whoever's running the operation.'

I knew Hideki Tagawa dealt with machinations and systems, making sure that everything was running smoothly.

'No. Not military plans. Some papers I was keeping safe for Professor Kutsuki are missing. I was responsible for them.'

I sensed he wasn't telling me everything. 'Papers Professor Kutsuki asked you to keep safe for him? Or that you took from him to keep safe?'

'That I was keeping safe for him.' Hideki Tagawa peered around the room. 'Nothing here.'

We both heard Professor Kutsuki calling for me.

'You'd better go. Make sure the old goat doesn't keep you working all night. And, remember, you're his assistant, not his servant. You're supposed to type out his notes, not run his bath and scrub his back.'

He scratched his neck, 'Good haircut you gave him. He should pay you.'

'Don't worry.' I felt a sudden rush of affection for him. It wouldn't occur to anyone else to worry about an old man seducing me in a bathtub. 'But there must be something else missing, something important, or you wouldn't be so concerned.'

He didn't answer straight away. I was about to leave to check on Professor Kutsuki when he said, 'There were some reports.

The surrender of Germany. Allied victories over our fleet. No one is supposed to know yet, but keeping things secret doesn't change the facts.'

'What's wrong?' Professor Kutsuki asked, when I went into his room later.

'Nothing,' I said.

The huge cartoon eyes painted on his spectacles seemed to be staring at the other side of the room. It was hard to take him seriously.

'You're lying,' he said. 'Do you know how I can tell you're lying? I can tell what people are doing and thinking from listening to their breathing patterns. If you only listen to the words you can't tell if they're speaking the truth or lying. But if you listen to their breath and their heartbeat, and smell the sweat of anxiety on them, you know them better than they know themselves.'

Professor Kutsuki was sitting cross-legged on a floor cushion, 'Don't be offended by what your cousin said. For Hideki Tagawa the ordinary is special. The ordinary life is what he wants more than anything. Poor man. Did you make any ginger tea today?'

'Why poor man?' Yes, I was carrying a mug of ginger tea for him. Some of it was now soaked into the cotton of my *samfoo*, thanks to a passing, almost absent-minded, smack from Mrs Maki.

'Those enlightened enough to want an ordinary life know too much to live it. Didn't you bring me anything to eat?'

'What would you like?'

'I have no appetite. You should move into Goda's old room. It has a lock on the door so you can keep your cousins out. And it's right here next to my room so I won't have to wait so long

when I need something and call you. Go and tell Mrs Maki that I want you here. It's a nice room,' Professor Kutsuki paused and sniffed, then sniffed again and nodded. 'And you might bring me some of those tapioca parcels you've been steaming. What kind are they?'

I knew better than to ask how he knew I'd been steaming cakes of finely grated *keledek* with coconut milk and *gula melaka* in banana-leaf packets.

'*Keledek* – orange sweet potatoes.'

'Good. Soft.'

My new room was much larger and nicer, a real room with windows instead of an amah's closet. A huge old mango tree stood just outside. There was no ripe fruit within reach but a couple of the thick old branches came so close that I would be able to lean out and pick ripe mangoes in season. Or climb out.

If Morio Goda had sneaked out that way during the night, Professor Kutsuki wouldn't have been able to hear him in the corridor and walking down the stairs. That was probably how he'd gone.

The Botanic Gardens Laboratory

———◆———

Despite the Hell we were living in, there were some good moments. Like when I first woke up the next morning in Morio Goda's room to see the dark green leaves of the mango tree dancing at the window. For a moment I didn't know where I was and thought, I'm awake – I'm alive. It was a horrible dream but it's going to be all right now.

It was a bit like I imagined how waking into whatever awaits us after death might feel.

Then, of course, I remembered where I was, that there was a war on, that we could all die at any time, and there was nothing much to eat other than tapioca and fermented fish paste.

Another plus was that, for a change, Professor Kutsuki was in a good mood. He didn't want a tray in his room, but said he would come downstairs for breakfast. 'After that we will work at the lab today. Once you come to the lab there is no backing out. This is the time to show me you have fits or faint at the sight of dead bugs,' he said, after I'd shaved him.

'Yes, sir.'

I smiled as I shook out his lap towel before folding it. I didn't have to control my facial expressions here, with no one to see.

I was coming to like grumpy old Professor Kutsuki. After years of dealing with my grandmother's tenants and business (legal and illegal) associates, I could decide very quickly whether or not someone could be trusted. It wasn't any supernatural sixth sense, but an unconscious summing-up of all the small things I observed about them. I didn't know how it worked, but in the old days my grandmother used to turn to me and ask, 'So how?' when faced with an excuse on her rent-collecting trips.

And she'd trusted my answers.

That's not to say Ah Ma wasn't shrewd, but people tended to focus on and flatter her wherever she was. It was much easier for a child to wander around and watch, unnoticed.

'Tell Mrs Maki you need a set of keys for us. Hideki Tagawa has given the order. She must give you a set of keys.'

'All right. Once you let me help you get dressed.'

'I'm not a child.'

'Sorry, sir.' I amended my tone. It was too easy to talk to him as if he was.

And that was because I was starting to relax with him.

So much of how people behave is a reaction to how they feel about the people and circumstances around them. We are only our true selves when alone and under no stress. Then some people vanish, those who can't bear to be alone when they have no one to react to. Others blossom and are happiest then.

I'd seen some ideal relationships, like that between Dr and Mrs Shankar, where the two of them had become one entity and blossomed only when they were together. I liked to think it

might have been so for my parents too. I missed and worried about the Shankars so much, but all I could do for them was keep out of trouble, thereby not adding to their problems.

'Why? Why can't you work here?'

Mrs Maki tried to stop us, especially after Professor Kutsuki deliberately provoked her at breakfast by calling the attack on Pearl Harbor the greatest miscalculation he'd ever seen. 'Of course the Pearl Harbor attack was a success! Our bombers hit all eight American battleships and destroyed more than three hundred aircraft,' she said. 'Even you can't call that a failure. And since then we've liberated Burma, Malaya and Indonesia from Western colonial rule.'

She looked at me. I didn't know what she expected me to say.

'Even you should know the facts by now. Our bombers missed oil tanks, ammunition sites and repair facilities,' Professor Kutsuki said. 'We didn't damage a single American aircraft carrier, which was how they crushed us at the battle of Midway. Which is why they are bombing us to death now.'

'I don't understand how you can say such terrible things against your own people. If you were anyone else you would be shot.'

'I'm not against Japan. Or the Emperor. I'm against pointless suffering caused by human stupidity.'

'Stop talking so much. All you do is complain and make a fuss,' Mrs Maki said.

'Stop talking so much yourself, woman. It's all your fault that Morio Goda is dead.'

Suddenly Mrs Maki seemed to realise she'd been talking to the renowned old scientist as though he was a recalcitrant

student rather than an eccentric genius. She turned to Yoshio Yoshimoto. 'I still don't see why he wants to use the laboratory. Didn't you order it to be sealed off? If he doesn't want to work in his room, he can work down here once the table is cleared.'

'Only the archive store is sealed,' Yoshio Yoshimoto said. The walls of the archive store room were reinforced with concrete that would probably survive anything other than a direct hit. It was where the British had kept records of all the plant species collected in the Botanic Gardens. The walls were guaranteed to keep out fire, floods and dry rot decay for sixty years at least.

'Look, I know you're afraid of somebody stealing his precious research. It doesn't matter what this girl sees or learns. There's nobody she can tell. Besides, it is just for now. And he needs somebody to write down all his notes. What use is it, any research he remembers, if we don't record it? She's bright enough, she's clean, and we won't find another who can speak Japanese and put up with him. So let him work with her if he wants to.'

Like Hideki Tagawa, Yoshio Yoshimoto clearly considered Professor Kutsuki's desire to go back to the laboratory a signal that he was willing to return to work.

'Just be careful in the laboratory. Don't let him close all the vents – you'll suffocate in there if he does. What's good for preserving papers and dried specimens is not so good for live humans. Anyway, there's nobody around who wants to listen to whatever he has to say. But he is paranoid about people listening in,' Hideki Tagawa said.

'See if you can find any of his other notes. He must have done more work than is in his notebooks here,' Yoshio Yoshimoto said. 'And make sure he doesn't leave anything lying

around for anyone to see. It's all top secret. If anybody asks you what you're doing there you tell them you don't know. Then you tell me who asked you.'

'If you feel the least dizziness, open the vents or get out of there. Never mind what the old man says. You may be saving his life as well as your own,' was the last thing Hideki Tagawa said to me, as we left the house.

Captain X was waiting outside and followed us when we left the house. Well, why not? They were on duty and it had to be more comfortable in the lab than sitting in the security booth by the gate.

'She's a nasty woman,' Professor Kutsuki said, as he led the way across the grounds. He tapped his stick in a semi-circle in front of him as he walked, but seemed confident of the way.

'Mrs Maki isn't always so bad,'

'Oh, of course not. When she's asleep or dead she won't be nasty. But otherwise—'

'She knew people in Hiroshima, which upset her, and so did what happened to Morio Goda.'

'That fool was my assistant. Shouldn't I be the one who's upset?'

'I think you are, sir.'

'Huh! Tadpole thinks she knows everything. As if that woman wasn't already part demon before the boy died.' He chuckled.

As he had implied, Mrs Maki had been acting strangely even before Morio Goda died. I thought it was because she was finally beginning to understand that the Japanese weren't winning the war. Even she couldn't believe they were. The signs were all around us. People don't see what they don't want to, but it takes more and more effort to deny what's more and more obvious.

Mrs Maki had always been bossy and demanding. It was only after Morio Goda's death that she'd become openly distrustful of Professor Kutsuki and me.

She'd forbidden me to leave the house without her permission, not even to fish at the lake or harvest vegetables from the garden. 'That is the houseboys' work,' she said. 'You're supposed to be busy assisting the professor.'

Of course Tanis and Ah Peng could collect the fish and vegetables we needed, but it was frustrating that I couldn't slip out to have a word with de Souza and Prakesh if they called by, and I couldn't check my mushroom trees.

'Don't worry so much,' Professor Kutsuki said. 'Whatever happens will happen whether you worry or not. And if you spend all your energy on worrying, you won't have the strength to confront it when it happens. Later you must show me how you extract spores from dried mushrooms. We might as well eat properly while advancing scientific knowledge.'

He rested his hand on my arm as we walked, though I didn't think he needed to. A cripple guiding a blind man: if that was a proverb in the making it wouldn't end well for either of us. But I felt and enjoyed the trust that was growing between Professor Kutsuki and me. It felt good to let down my guard when I was with him.

It balanced the growing distrust between me and Mrs Maki. I didn't want to believe she'd had anything to do with Morio Goda's death. But the thought kept coming back to me. She wasn't just cross or upset. She was feeling guilty about more than just being alive.

'I can find my way around,' Professor Kutsuki said. 'I already know the lab layout. I need somebody to bring me because of

all those stupid people locking doors, hiding keys and digging up the paths looking for Heaven knows what. If not for that, I could find my way around perfectly.'

Once I had unlocked the laboratory, Professor Kutsuki went inside ahead of me and walked around the small dark space easily. He touched the different walls and shelving as he went, as though reminding himself of where they were.

'You see why I like it so much here? There isn't anything to see! All you need to know right now is where the WC is, but with your nose you can probably find it yourself.' Again he chuckled. 'Just be careful. There are all kinds of snakes and bugs out there. And I don't know what else ... those mushroom trees of yours. When I smelt them on your hands I thought you were sneaking around, trying to get into my lab. Much better to grow mushrooms than spy on old men. Mushrooms – good for food, good for poisons.'

I was the one fumbling, trying to find a light switch or cord and praying it still worked.

'It's all right. Just don't move too suddenly,' he said, when I knocked into him, trying to step out of his way. 'I can tell where you are.'

'I don't want to trip you,' I said.

'You shouldn't turn on the light. Then we'll see who can find their way around better in here, eh?'

'No! Because you might trip *me!*'

That made him giggle and I had to laugh too.

'I like you, girl,' he said. 'You're smart enough not to try to be too clever. The light switch is on the right side of the door we came in. Behind the butane lamp. The lamp's empty, so don't bother with it.'

Fortunately the electric light still worked. That was one area in which the Japanese had relied on Singaporean skill. When the electricity supply was cut, local technicians had to be called in to fix the network because they were the only ones with the experience.

Once the light was on I saw that, though the air smelt stale, there was less dust than I'd expected, and no cockroaches, lizards or spiders. There was some stationery – writing paper, paper clips – but no notes. Professor Kutsuki had spent quite a lot of his time in this research lab when they'd first arrived on the island. I'd thought there would be more evidence of it here.

'I could show you around, but there really isn't anything to see.' He laughed as he systematically opened drawers and felt inside them. 'Make yourself at home, girl.'

'I thought you didn't like to work with females.'

'I don't like working with people. Females are people. Ah, I knew there would be something good in here!'

He'd found a tin box filled with Fox's Glacier Mints and sherbet lemons. Was that why we had come here?

Professor Kutsuki unwrapped and sniffed a sherbet lemon before popping it into his mouth. 'Have one? Good for working in closed spaces. Yoshio Yoshimoto and others like to summarise people so that they have a shortcut to understanding them. If you don't want them to think too much about you, you give them surface details to occupy their minds. Which are usually very shallow. My surface details are being crazy and not being able to stand women and children. He is trapped in his own fear of women so it's easy to make him see that in me. Though I might have encouraged him to think so.'

'Yoshio Yoshimoto is afraid of women?'

It struck me that the professor was much more comfortable in the dark, especially in a familiar place. Again I had to wonder whether he had had anything to do with Mario Goda's death. In the total dark caused by the blackout, the blind old man would have had the advantage.

'Of course Yoshio Yoshimoto is afraid of females. It's part of his belief system. That's the hardest thing for a man to free himself from. According to the Ketsubonkyō, Buddhist Blood Pond Sutra, women are condemned to a Blood Bowl Sutra Hell for ever. Their sin is the polluting of the world through their menstrual blood.'

His mouth, beneath the bizarre cartoon eyes on his spectacles, grinned at me.

I wondered if his sharp sense of smell and hearing had told him I'd lied when I'd told Yoshio Yoshimoto that it was my time of the month. Probably. Given the high stress and low nutrition, my period had dwindled to the mildest staining. It was as though my body wanted to conserve all the nutrients it could.

'So you mustn't believe anything Yoshio Yoshimoto says. Especially about me,' Professor Kutsuki said.

'Yoshio Yoshimoto says you're very brilliant in science,' I said. 'So I shouldn't believe that?'

'Science is the study of how the natural world works. And hopefully some day all scientific discoveries will transcend politics.' He sounded serious, but it didn't last. 'What is the most basic, most important part of science?' He didn't wait for me to answer. 'Cooking!' He held out the tin box. Inside, with the sweets, were some round flat biscuits. 'Try one. Not poisonous,

I promise you. If you want to know about poisons, you should be more careful of that cousin of yours. Mrs Maki knows a lot more about poisons than this old man. Practical chemistry – the properties of and reactions between substances – starts with poisons and cooking. How to kill and how to feed. Do you know what these are? Australian soldier biscuits.'

The golden discs looked harmless enough. 'Why are they called Australian soldier biscuits?' I hoped he wasn't going to say something about them being made of the ground-up bones of dead Australian military.

'That's where the first few biscuits came from. They were carrying them. Probably sent from home, made by their wives, mothers and sisters, who thought they would be starving, not shot to death in war.'

'How long have these been in here?'

'Don't worry. These are not the original biscuits. We tested them back in the Philippines. Just in case they contained poisons we knew nothing about.'

Of course, Japanese soldiers probably carried something to poison themselves if capture seemed imminent.

'But you didn't find any poisons?'

'None. But the biscuits were delicious. And I put my skills to analysing how they were made. Do you want my recipe? Equal amounts of flour, sugar, dried coconut, dried oats, as much butter, ghee or oil as you can get hold of, as much treacle or honey as you can spare, and a spoonful of baking soda. All you have to do is mix the dry stuff together, stir in the rest and warm gently over a fire with a bit of water until the butter or ghee melts. Then bake. The wonderful thing about these biscuits is

they can last for months without going bad or growing mould. Go on, try one.'

Against my better judgement, I did. It was delicious. But it had been so long since I'd eaten a biscuit that it probably tasted better than it really was.

'You're not keeping this place secret because you've been hiding your biscuits in here, are you?' I wouldn't have minded if that was the case.

'At a time like this, it's even more important to remember the good things about life. All the things we've left behind. Morio Goda didn't like that. He needed to have something to report back at the end of each day to feel he wasn't wasting his time with me. Oh, don't think he was just doing his job. Some people are like that even when they don't have any job to do. The only way they know how to feel good is by making other people feel bad.'

'Morio Goda didn't like your biscuits?'

'Pah! He wouldn't even try them. Probably suspected me of trying to poison him. If I'd thought of it in time I would have too. Not enough to kill him. Just enough to give him an uncomfortable night ... at both ends!'

His wicked chuckle made me laugh.

'You're thinking I'm not as bad as you imagined? Don't be taken in. I'm quite as bad.'

'I wasn't thinking anything of the sort. It's not my place.'

'You were doing so well. Don't go backwards. You may have to behave like that around the others, but don't try to take me in.'

'I don't think you're bad at all as a person,' I said honestly. 'As a scientist, I can't judge.'

'Pah! Do you even know what this project is all about?'

'I know that you're working on a poison bomb for the Japanese military.'

'I work on whatever I'm interested in.' Professor Kutsuki returned to his chair and arranged the biscuit tin beside him. 'And right now I'm interested in demonstrating to all the fools who dismissed me as useless that it's the brain, not the eyesight, that matters when it comes to science. They'll regret telling me I'm useless. They'll regret taking my position from me. They'll regret everything.'

He was so emphatic that I wondered for a moment whether I could persuade him to use his deadly inventions against the Japanese universities or whoever had made him feel useless because of his sight.

'Do you want me to write anything down?' I started to open one of the notebooks I'd brought.

'No, girl. Wait. Let me talk to you first.'

Survivors have countless rules, which cover how to dress, whom to trust, which streets are safe, which are not, and so on. They grow out of fear, superstition, nightmares and irrational hope because most of us survivors don't know which of our rules is keeping us alive. For me, one of the primary rules was to obey our Japanese masters without question. But right then my body had a more pressing need for air.

'Let me open a vent first. I can't breathe in here. If I can't breathe I won't be able to listen to you talk.'

Professor Kutsuki grunted. Then he was silent for a long moment, as though listening, before he said, 'Very well. One vent. But if I tell you to stop talking, you stop right away. Hear me?'

'Yes, sir.'

I went to one of the shuttered windows and pulled down the lever attached to the slats. I was rewarded by a light shower of dust and lizard droppings as they slid open.

'Do you know why I want the vents closed?'

'Because air and damp are bad for the important documents in here?'

'There are no more important documents in here. Only my notes. But you clearly think it's more important for a nobody like you to breathe than to preserve my notes.'

'Let me open all the vents and I promise I won't talk at all until you say so.'

He listened, sniffed, and nodded.

'Thank you.' I pulled another lever and opened another vent.

It really wasn't so bad in there when I wasn't worried about suffocating.

'You know what Morio Goda tried to do? He thought he could open all the vents without my knowing. He thinks that just because I have no eyes I also have no ears.'

I noticed that the old man's manner had changed. Here in the lab he was more relaxed – even with the window vents open. It was as though he felt safer. That made me more comfortable too.

Now I could look around I saw there was just one unshielded light-bulb in the centre of the room. That it was working showed it must be linked to the generator. I only wished they'd thought to put in a fan too.

'Don't worry, I haven't gone crazy. I know that that stupid boy is dead and maybe I should be sorry but you have to give an old man a chance. When you get to my age you will see that one less traitor in your household to watch out for is a relief,'

I knew that already. So maybe I did believe Morio Goda had deliberately stolen the blue *michiyuki* to frame me.

'We're both pretending to be less than we are. But some pretend to be more than they are. Tell me about your mushroom trees. You can show me later what you're doing. Or can't I touch them?'

'You can touch the shiitakes. They're ready to be collected. I sun-dried some on a cloth under a rattan cover so I could collect the spores.'

'Where did you get sterile cloth?'

'I boiled an old singlet I'd cut up.'

'Pah. If there are spores you won't be able to see them any more than I can. You'll need a magnifying glass. Or a microscope.'

'I can't see them, but the last time I cut up and buried scraps of the cloth I got mushrooms, so there must have been spores.'

'Hypothesis and test. That's always the best way. But you should have a control. In sterile condition. Next time, cut a scrap in the size you would plant without spores. See how the tree reacts to the cloth.'

The artificially introduced spores reflected the relationship between our occupiers and us. We, of course, being the dead tree.

'Every time you harvest you leave some. And compost. Be very careful that outside spores don't get in. They could poison you.'

'The ones I spawned most recently I won't look at for six weeks.'

'Maybe the war will be over by then and none of this will be needed,' Professor Kutsuki said.

'If they're good mushrooms they'll always be needed.'

'I already knew you were not stupid. I didn't want you working with me because Yoshio Yoshimoto said it would be good for me. I always distrust people who tell me to do things for my own good. It's usually their own good they're thinking of.'

I had to agree with him there.

'But I see why Yoshio Yoshimoto approves of you, despite your race and your sex. You have managed to make yourself useful. Useful to him. And not in the usual way that men find women useful.'

'I try to make myself useful.'

'And you try to make yourself invisible. That's your greatest strength. If you were a great beauty you'd be dead by now. Or worse. Once a beautiful woman is noticed she is in danger. But nobody is going to fight over a skinny cripple who can scavenge for food.'

Coming from anyone else, this would have been an insult. But I felt Professor Kutsuki was congratulating me. He hadn't finished.

'With luck you'll survive this. Most of the fools can understand orders given in Japanese but can't answer questions. And the greatest idiots of all think themselves so superior because they can give orders only in Japanese. They think they can make themselves better understood by shouting louder. I tell you, it is those who speak quietly and know how to listen who will get through this.'

He should have been a teacher or a philosopher, I thought. I looked around the bare, dusty room. It wouldn't be a bad place to work, once I'd got it cleaned up a bit.

'What's inside that room with a padlock?' The huge padlock

anchored a metal link chain looped through the handles of its double doors.

'It's just an archive store. Built for the Botanic Gardens records. It was designed to survive fires and floods.'

'Are your notes there now?'

'What notes?'

'Look, why don't you let me try taking some notes? Just to see whether I can keep up. It doesn't have to be anything important. Otherwise they might not let us come back here.'

'All right. Just so I can see if you're a liar like that Goda.'

I took down everything he said and read it back to him. I was impressed by his memory and saw he was impressed by my speed and accuracy. Neither of us insulted the other by showing surprise.

'I just wanted to see how much I need to slow down for you,' he said. 'None of it is new. No point sneaking copies to Yoshimoto.'

'I'm going to show this to him so he sees we can work together,' I said.

I also saw why Professor Kutsuki didn't feel the need to put down his thoughts on paper. He talked as if he was reading from a book. And maybe in his mind he was. As he spoke, I saw his fingers moving on his lap to turn a page or underscore a passage as though he was seeing it all spread out before him.

'Not too bad working for the mad old scientist, eh?'

'Very good, in fact. But I understand Yoshio Yoshimoto's frustration and why he wants you protected day and night.'

The risk of leaving such important information stored only inside the head of a capricious old man was huge.

'Pah. Nothing's going to happen to me unless I say so. Tell me, do you remember playing with origami?'

'Origami? No, sir. I never did.'

'Surely your mother must have . . .'

'I don't remember her at all. She died when I was very young.'

'Nothing at all? Not even how she smelt? That is the first sense, you know. We are animals, and animals know the smell of their mother before their eyes are open.'

'I remember she smelt nice.' I'd not thought about it until then, but it was true. When I thought of my mother, in the moment between sleep and waking when the loving arms keeping you safe in your dreams disappear into another painful day, I remembered the smell of comfort and protection. It wasn't like the smell – of food or soap or pandan leaves – that I associated with my grandmother. It was something infinitely more tender and precious.

And it was painful not just to remember but to realise how much I had forgotten.

'You have a good sense of smell as well as a good memory,' Professor Kutsuki said. 'Never regret that. Even if it causes you pain.'

Somehow I knew he was speaking for himself as well as for me. I nodded, then remembered he couldn't see me. 'I know,' I said.

'You're a good girl. Let me tell you something you may not know. Did they tell you about your mother's part in the assassination of Prime Minister Hara Takashi in 1921?'

'What?' I forgot to be polite and blurted out the question. This made him laugh and I had a feeling he'd done it on purpose.

'No. I know she ran away from her family, but–'

140

'The reason they didn't tell you was because she didn't do it. She was one of the girls they wanted to send in, disguised as geishas, to infiltrate the ceremonies. It was a gross insult to geishas as well as to the officials to presume that a few acting lessons could replace the training of years. But most impressionable young women caught up in the fervour of the cause didn't think twice. Your mother was one of several, and the best of them. But instead of going ahead with it, she saw the futility, and ran away to Singapore where she met your father. That is why no one will speak her name. And that is why you should be proud of her. Daring to go ahead is one thing, but realising you are on the wrong boat and need to get off requires even more bravery. Especially when all your family are on board, insisting that all is well.'

Professor Kutsuki had called our island 'Singapore', not 'Syonan'. That alone was enough to endear him to me. 'Thank you,' I said.

'I'm an old man, and I first knew this island as Singapore. That's how I think of you people. This is not part of Japan any more than it's part of Britain or China. The people here don't try to force their agenda on others. If you tell me the truth, I will tell you the truth. Fair enough?'

'Here we're just trying to survive. Can I ask you something? You lied to Mrs Maki about bring frightened by noises on the outside stairway, didn't you? You think she went out the night Morio Goda died and you were trying to get her to admit it.'

Professor Kutsuki shrugged, like a naughty child who knows he'll be forgiven. 'I heard her. She knew Morio Goda went out that day. She must have followed him.'

'And I think you followed her.'

'Accusing me, are you?'

'You said you would tell me the truth—'

'If only you'll let me get round to it. I followed Morio Goda outside. He was supposed to be working with me. At the very least he could have brought me my tea. But instead he just pushed me into my room, locked it from the outside and left. What would have become of me if there was a fire, eh? I would have been burned to crisp, like *chashu*. I wouldn't even smell delicious – not enough fat.'

Chashu was Japanese braised pork belly, rather like our local *char siu*. Just the mention of it made my mouth water a little. It had been so long since I'd tasted it.

'You weren't,' I said. 'There was no fire. So Mrs Maki found your door locked, then went to look for him?'

'Oh, no. I wasn't going to be locked in by some *eta*.'

Eta was an old term for 'outcast', more archaic than offensive. I got the feeling the professor had relished the challenge.

'I got out and followed him, of course. The lock is flimsy. If I wanted to keep him out I used the bolt.'

'And you told Mrs Maki that Morio Goda was going out?'

'She saw me leaving.' Professor Kutsuki's shoulders slumped a little. 'I can follow someone through the night with very little difficulty. But in the daytime, when I'm following someone, I can't tell when I'm being followed. There's a proverb in there somewhere, isn't there?'

I ignored that. 'Did you hear Morio Goda going to collect a bag from his room before he went out?'

'No. You're thinking of the briefcase that was taken from

Hideki Tagawa's office, aren't you?' Professor Kutsuki giggled. 'I guessed it was Morio Goda as soon as he tried to lie about being with you all night. But he didn't bring it back to the house, not with everyone standing around there. Even the most stupid security man would notice him carrying a missing briefcase out of the jungle, don't you think? No, he wasn't carrying anything when he left the house. He must have left it somewhere outside, meaning to collect it on the way to handing it over.'

'Handing it over to whom?'

'How would I know? I heard him insisting, "Yes, you will make time! Yes, tonight! I'll pass it to you." To be honest, I suspected he was going to meet you. And he sounded so angry that I went along just to make sure no harm was done.'

He'd been trying to protect me? That was interesting. But then, I'd believed for a while that Morio Goda was trying to protect me. It just went to show I couldn't trust myself, far less anyone else.

Allergies and Assassinations

———◆———

If there hadn't been a war on, I would have enjoyed working in the lab with Professor Kutsuki. He was very interested in my attempts to spawn my own mushrooms and lamented that the researchers who'd started the mushroom-trees project hadn't left better notes. And he had useful suggestions – like sterilising *gula melaka* by boiling it, then adding it to the decaying tree medium as additional nourishment. I meant to try that. One thing that concerned me was that I wasn't feeding the growing mushrooms. My grandmother's vegetable gardens had been constantly fed with the contents of chamber pots, goat and pig manure.

But I couldn't forget this wasn't his only work. We were talking about ways I'd tried to spawn and raise mushrooms when I said, 'Your invention could kill a lot of people.' I hadn't realised I was saying it aloud until I heard myself.

'Deaths are already occurring on a grand scale. Everybody has to die sometime.'

All right, so maybe I wouldn't be able to talk him out of it. But at least he wasn't offended.

'Do you know anything about the work I'm doing?'

'I heard it's something to do with a poison-gas bomb.'

'Pah! You expect me to believe Yoshio Yoshimoto didn't tell you to spy on me when he told you that?'

'He didn't tell me anything. I heard it from the man we get charcoal from. He'd heard it from the drain cleaner.'

'Pah.'

'The charcoal man also heard in town that you can shoot energy beams out of your eyes and that's why you have to block them with glasses. And that someone saw you take off your glasses and shoot birds out of the sky. When they landed they were fried chicken. They think you're here to shoot down the American planes.'

This pleased him. 'That would be good. Fried chicken falling out of the sky.'

'But you are working on a poison-gas bomb?'

'So you don't approve? I'm not sure I would either. It started as a scientific challenge. Anyway, it didn't start as a poison-gas bomb. It was supposed to be an energy source. I was looking for a way to grow wheat and maize faster when I discovered the explosive force. Can you imagine that?'

'It sounds dangerous.'

'Everything new is dangerous. I helped to develop the gas they used against the Chinese in the early days of the war against China. The result was as I'd expected, just that there was more energy than I'd calculated. And the gas was very flammable. All the soybean plants we were experimenting on died. And the pigs and chickens that ate the plants died, as did all the farmers who were carrying out the experiments. When the army came for me I thought they were going to arrest me, shoot me or charge

me compensation for all the dead plants, pigs and people, but they wanted me to work for them. Pah! I was so happy I would have agreed to anything.'

Professor Kutsuki scoffed at his younger self. When he continued his voice was much lower and more sober: 'That was how I ended up working on a formula for this giant poison-gas bomb that will kill all within an air range of a hundred square kilometres. Isn't it a tribute to my great scientific abilities? Why don't you tell me what you think of me?'

'I'm not thinking anything.'

'You're a liar. But at least you didn't agree with me. That shows me I can perhaps trust you. Do you think Japan has lost the war?'

The correct answer was, of course, that the war couldn't be lost, that it had already been won, and we were waiting only for the Americans and the Allied forces to admit it.

'Mrs Maki says that Japan's is a righteous war. She says that Japan will win because the Emperor and the gods say so.'

'And you still think that is possible? With all the news coming in from the West? You must have heard at least as much as I have.'

'What is happening in the West doesn't affect us here,' I quoted.

'I don't know whether you are a fool or very clever – cleverer than me – at being politic. Look at the starvation here and in Japan right now. Look at the lack of weapons and ammunition. You see all that, and you don't think the situation's hopeless for Japan? You don't think that the latest call to fight to the death of the last man, woman, child without weapons is an admission of defeat?'

I didn't think he was trying to catch me out. He really wanted to discuss this. And he was taking a risk by talking to me. It was

the closest thing to an offer of friendship that I had had since talking to Morio Goda.

And look how Morio Goda had ended up.

'I think the problem is whether to acknowledge the Emperor's desire to sue for peace or the military's call to fight to the death.'

'Which would you choose?'

'The Emperor is more powerful, but the military is running things. I would choose to stay alive.'

Professor Kutsuki roared with laughter. 'Now that's what I call wisdom,' he said. He picked up a small bottle and handed it to me. 'Do you know what's in there?'

There was no label.

'Don't open it!' Professor Kutsuki said sharply, when I made to unscrew the lid.

'I can't tell what's inside.'

'It's poison,' Professor Kutsuki said. 'Feel the lid.' My fingertips told me Prof Kutsuki had made indentations with a pin. 'So I know what's inside the bottle,' he added.

'I see.' But I couldn't distinguish what the indentations said.

'Do you? Morio Goda used to switch bottles around out of spite but I wasn't fooled.'

'He might just have got them mixed up.' But I was thinking about Morio's Goda's poison pin. 'Is it what he dipped his poison pin in?'

'You don't know anything about the poison pin. It's a very delicate mechanism. A sharp pin screwed into the waterproof poison-containing capsule of a larger, blunt screw or ladies' hairpin. A very efficient assassination device if you can get close enough. And useful for self-termination if you don't succeed. But Morio Goda? Don't make me laugh!'

He laughed anyway.

'Morio Goda was no assassin. His only job was spying on me and stealing my research, and he wasn't even good at that. No doubt that's why he's dead. That's what they want you to do, isn't it? Spy on me and steal my research?'

The huge cartoon eyes painted on his spectacles stared at me. They suddenly seemed very sinister. 'If you're not comfortable having me as an assistant I'll tell them you don't want me to—'

'Don't be in such a hurry, girl. If you'll tell them what I tell you to tell them, we'll get along very well.' His voice was low and serious. The high childlike tone and the giggle were gone. It was as though he'd suddenly been possessed by a completely different spirit.

'Did you see all the books on the shelves along the wall? You can read all these books here as long as you read them to me too.'

'What?' I had noticed the books. What I didn't understand was how he'd noticed me staring at them when all I'd done was look. Was the man really blind or had he been playing a huge joke on everyone?

'My ears are good, you know. When you're cleaning my room I hear you picking up my books, or just touching them. Like a starving child touching an empty bowl for the memory of rice. I am starving for books too. Feed me and feed yourself at the same time. When they offered me Morio Goda as an assistant, they claimed he could read English, German and Chinese. He would read to me, they said. He would read and translate for me anything I wanted. But once he moved in, he refused to read me anything other than government propaganda. He never

touched a book if he could help it. And he wasn't interested in my research.'

'I don't know anything about your research either. But I'll read you whatever you want.'

'Morio Goda could have lived to a hundred and he wouldn't have had an atom of scientific curiosity.'

'He didn't have much of a chance,' I said. 'With a war on—'

'Always trying to think the best of people! Pah! Let me tell you, girl, always think the worst of people. Then being wrong comes as a pleasant surprise. But I'm going to put a proposition to you. I have something you will like . . .'

From a tin in another drawer he drew out two cloth bags. 'Dried wild mushrooms,' he said. 'Straw mushrooms and shiitakes. Consider them payment for reading to me. We make our own deal, nothing to do with poisons and patriots. One mushroom per book?'

'One mushroom per page!' I bargained. But he was right: I liked his deal. 'Where did you get them?'

'From the ship they brought us over in. Traded a pen and a cartridge-case lighter for them. Goda's stuff, not mine. If he'd bought me some cigarettes to make up for those he stole from me, maybe I wouldn't have taken them from him, but fair's fair,'

I had to laugh.

'Wait. Stop.' He held up a hand. 'Someone is coming. He's on the trail at the bottom of the slope. From the pace, it sounds like Yoshimoto-san. It will take him almost ten minutes to get here. He is very clumsy. You were right about opening the windows. It's better to learn what others are doing than prevent them discovering what you are up to. If you want to go to the WC, this

149

may be a good time.' Professor Kutsuki giggled. 'Yoshimoto-san doesn't like thinking about women using the WC. It will give me great pleasure to tell him that's where you are.'

Far be it from me to stand between an old blind man and his pleasures. Besides, I really did need to use the bathroom, though I hoped it was just a lucky guess on his part. And while I was outside, if I hurried, I could nip around the side of the building and check my mushroom trees.

It wasn't Yoshio Yoshimoto whom Professor Kutsuki had heard coming up the slope. It was Hideki Tagawa. The old professor was not infallible.

He came around the back and side of the building rather than up the path, so I met him outside the WC and didn't see my mushroom trees because he waited to walk back with me.

'Everything going all right?'

'Yes, sir.'

Yes, I stopped to use the WC. It was clean because it was so far from the main house, and fresh because it had no roof but was open to the sky. I may seem to dwell a lot on food and the WC, but the war had made me realise that one of the greatest luxuries in life is to be able to take such things for granted.

Back in the laboratory I saw Hideki Tagawa acknowledge the open windows and my open notebook.

'Despite her race and sex,' Professor Kutsuki said grandly, 'the girl knows how to make herself useful. Where did you find her? You must never trust people who seem too helpful. They were probably trained to suit you. Or did you train her to suit me?'

'She's not here to suit you.' Hideki Tagawa was looking at my scribbled notes. He turned a page over, then another. 'Nothing new here, is there?'

That showed he could decipher my shorthand code and knew exactly what was in the professor's previous work.

'Su Lin's here to manage the household. If you don't have anything new for her to record, you should let her get back to her own work. You wouldn't be eating as well as you are if not for Su Lin. That's where she's needed.'

'So who is doing her work while she's here? Does this mean there'll be no dinner for me tonight? Or will that poisonous cousin of yours be cooking lizards' tails?'

I saw Hideki Tagawa hide a smile. I guessed it was an exchange he'd heard before and wondered what Mrs Maki had really tried to serve Professor Kutsuki.

'Now that the systems are in place they run themselves,' he said. 'Most of the locals who work for us can understand orders given in Japanese.'

'So Miss Chen can go on helping me here if she has no objections?'

'She's here, isn't she?'

'Pah. You know better than I do that that doesn't mean anything. Do you know why there's nothing new here? Because it's not safe. If I put down the assembly instructions on paper, my notes must be kept in the archive store. That's the only secure place. Away from the fleas.' Professor Kutsuki rapped on the chained doors. 'Get this opened up for me. Whatever Yoshio Yoshimoto has placed in there can't be more important. He wants the instructions, doesn't he? Give me somewhere safe to store them.'

151

He couldn't see Hideki Tagawa shaking his head wryly. He obviously thought this was just another of Professor Kutsuki's digressions. But what I'd heard had distracted me.

'Fleas?' I asked.

'Bubonic-plague fleas,' Professor Kutsuki said. 'They were developing fleas on rats and dropping the flea eggs over China. It worked too, everyone on the ground thinking we were dropping bombs that didn't work, when actually they were much deadlier and further-reaching than any "big boom" could ever be. That was why they scrapped it, not because it didn't work but because they didn't get the credit of a big boom. That's the problem with soldiers. You always forget that someone else is going to come up with a bigger boom than you. And now the Americans have.'

'That has nothing to do with anything here,' Hideki Tagawa said.

'It tells us why they moved out in such a hurry. Some of their precious, deadly fleas escaped and contaminated the research lab.'

'What?' I said involuntarily.

'No fleas here,' Hideki Tagawa said. 'I'm not worried about you, sir, but I wouldn't let my cousin work here if there was any chance of fleas carrying bubonic plague. But she has her own work to do. You shouldn't keep her here if all you're going to do is go over your old work.'

Professor Kutsuki, not the least abashed, grinned in his direction. 'Always revise, boy. Knowing your old lessons is the way to learn new ones. How about unlocking the archive store? Wouldn't it worry you, working next to a room full of goodness knows what?'

'Probably nothing in there but dust,' Hideki Tagawa tested the doors. They were locked and the chain looped between the metal hasps on the doors looked new and sound. 'Isn't there a back door? Or a window?'

'Only those air vents on either side of the doors. You think it's stuffy here? It's ten times, a hundred times worse in there! It doesn't have its own exit. The only way in is through these doors here, which are locked.'

'How do you know what the air in there is like?' I asked.

'It wasn't locked when we first got here. I went inside – empty shelves and a lot of nothing. Then, a couple of weeks later, the doors were locked. That's why I want to know what's in there.'

'Ask Mrs Maki.' Hideki Tagawa didn't seem very interested. 'She has all the keys. She's probably hoarding charcoal or something in there. So everything's good here? I'm heading to Headquarters. Probably won't be back for some time.'

'He came to make sure I wasn't bullying you,' Professor Kutsuki said, when Hideki Tagawa had gone. 'That man worries about you. He cares too much.'

'Too much?'

'Affection is always the warrior's weakest point. You should write that down. Make me sound like a wise sage, a Japanese Confucius, eh?'

'Don't you have any Japanese sages to base yourself on?'

'Pah! Insolent chit of a girl!'

It was easy to forget Professor Kutsuki was one of 'them', our Japanese overlords. Maybe that was because of his disability but I think more because he growled at me just as he growled at Mrs

Maki and Yoshio Yoshimoto. He treated me the same way he treated them.

But one thing had made me like him even before I'd come to work for him. I'd noticed he was always kind to the two little house-boys. Tanis and Ah Peng were scared of Mrs Maki, who was quick to slap and pinch them, but they didn't respect her. And they stayed a safe distance (wisely) from Yoshio Yoshimoto and Hideki Tagawa.

If Professor Kutsuki asked for a tray in his room instead of eating downstairs, he always left some of his food and insisted on one of his 'little rats' coming to collect it. Most of the time, they rushed to tackle this chore together.

'An offering for the gods or the rats,' he said, when he didn't finish what was brought to him. And when we'd managed to scrounge something special for a treat, he always left a little more. He must have known his tray would be picked clean by the time the boys had carried it down to the kitchen.

I realised I'd come to think of Professor Kutsuki as a fellow pris-oner at Moss House. I had to remind myself that he was a dangerous man. His calculations could do far more harm than any soldier with a bayonet. Until the war was over, Professor Kutsuki was an enemy.

We didn't do much work. Mostly Professor Kutsuki talked, meandering off in different directions, occasionally asking me a question or asking me to make a note of something he wanted to check later. Several times his thoughts went back to the assistant who'd died in the laboratory explosion in the Philippines. Perhaps Morio Goda's death had brought back that memory.

'You once wanted to be a writer, yes? So write what is happening here. Write and read to me what you write,' Professor Kutsuki said. 'That's what I always told Suzuki too. You remind

me a little of him. I would never have met him if not for the war, and I lost him because of it. Like you, he wanted to know the meaning of all this. I don't know why young people these days ask so many questions. And he said he was going to write his story too. But then he died. You should write your stories.'

'What if I die too?'

'Ridiculous? You won't. I have a feeling. But if you do, you won't have to worry about what you want to do with your life, will you?' He laughed. 'And I'll say the same thing to my next assistant. But I have a feeling you're going to survive. Survive working with me, at least. Come, get your notebook. We should take our places in case anyone comes to check on us.'

'Who else is coming?'

'They all will. For the first few days at least.'

We sat on different sides of the long laboratory table. With the vents open it was not unpleasant, but I missed the bustle of the house and wondered how the houseboys were getting on without me.

'It's funny how war brings people together, isn't it? It was your Mrs Maki's study of herbal poisons that led her to me. But she studied poisons as a woman, their immediate practical use. How to get rid of unwelcome household pests and unwanted relatives. It was only when she was called on to raise funds and supplies to build the big poison-gas bomb that she started reading more deeply and came across my name.'

'I thought this was Yoshio Yoshimoto's project.'

'Indeed. Which probably makes Japan's Divine Mission even more appealing to Mrs Maki.'

'Japan's Divine Mission?'

'Initially, the poison-gas bomb was to be transported to America. Hawaii, at least.'

'But how?'

'If they can't use planes, they'll use balloons. They were studying wind patterns. All of this would be fascinating if it wasn't so ridiculous.'

'Ridiculous? You don't think this can work?' I spoke without thinking.

'You think it will?' Professor Kutsuki's cartoon eyes glared at me.

'Yoshio Yoshimoto says that with the gods' help anything could work.' That was the safe, diplomatic answer.

I knew mythology claimed the Japanese were descended from the gods and destined to rule the world. I'd thought it was like the Christian crusaders massacring Jews, Muslims and anyone else who happened to be living on lands they wanted. It was something an adolescent community left behind as it matured.

'Yoshio Yoshimoto doesn't trust your cousin Mrs Maki. He thinks that, as a woman, she should not be close to something so important.'

'I thought it was Mrs Maki who brought you and Yoshio Yoshimoto together?'

'Indeed. And now she has served her purpose she irritates him by existing.'

'Poor Mrs Maki,' I said, and meant it.

'I would find it easier to feel sorry for her if she ever stopped talking. As it is, I would do anything to make her stop. It is as though she's afraid she'll cease to exist if she is silent. But for me it's an irritant. Like a mosquito I want to slap. For your own good you should keep your distance from her. She likes poisons.'

I remembered Dr Shankar saying poisons could be used to cure as well as kill. 'That's not necessarily bad.'

'True. Revenge is a poison. I feel,' Professor Kutsuki said. 'I want not revenge but justice for my dead assistant. Even if I can't put things right, I want to know exactly what happened. That's also my main reason for going on.'

There was something he wasn't telling me. I could tell he didn't entirely trust me but that was okay. Even if I liked him I didn't trust him completely either.

'Did you know Mrs Maki betrayed her husband? That woman is going to kill you one day because her feelings about you are complicated,' he added.

'I don't think they are. She's disappointed in me because I'm not my mother.'

'And her feelings towards your mother were complicated too, weren't they?'

'Yes, but—'

'Ssh!' Professor Kutsuki tilted his head to one side as though he was listening. I listened too, but I couldn't hear anything. Then, 'Come in!' he shouted. 'Don't hang around there pretending to be *kodama!*' Kodama were nature spirits thought to take refuge in trees.

But no one appeared. He picked up a couple of dried mushrooms, went to the door where he paused to consider the origin of whatever he'd heard and tossed them outside. I cried out in protest at the waste of good mushrooms.

Then we heard something that sounded like a muffled sneeze from the slope behind and above the laboratory.

A monkey? It was unlikely. There were few fruit trees in the

jungle above us, which was dense enough to deter even monkeys.

'Allergies are fascinating,' Professor Kutsuki said loudly. 'So are mushroom spores. Amazing what triggers some people. I want you to grow some more mushrooms, as many as possible.'

'Do you want to grow them too? Shall I make you some substrate? It doesn't have to be a tree trunk—'

'Oh, no, I'm not going to grow them. I want to leave them around my room as little burglar alarms!'

I'd followed him back to our stools by the laboratory table. This time even I heard the footsteps approaching the door before Yoshio Yoshimoto and Mrs Maki knocked and came in.

'We wanted to see if everything is to your liking,' Mrs Maki said, with a bright, artificial smile that was wasted on the professor. But perhaps it wasn't intended for him.

'You came to spy on me and check that I'm working,' he growled. 'You see I am, so now go away. And take that sneezing assassin with you.'

Yoshio Yoshimoto sneezed again. 'You think it's hard to be a government representative with respiratory allergies? Try being an undercover agent!' He gave me such a rueful, boyish grin that I couldn't help smiling back.

'But before you go, I want the keys to the archive store.' Professor Kutsuki thumped his stick against the locked door. 'And the key to that padlock. It's a Rabson lock, right? I can't get through it. If you don't unlock it for me I'll have to smash it.'

Mrs Maki turned to Yoshio Yoshimoto. Her face said, 'You've got the keys – give them to him.'

'Professor Kutsuki thinks his notes are so precious they cannot

be touched by air or water!' Yoshio Yoshimoto said lightly. 'No need of that. Just give us the notes and we'll take care of them.'

'How? By keeping them safe in your headquarters where people can walk in and out and help themselves to anything they want without being stopped? Pah!'

'That's uncalled-for,' Mrs Maki said. 'It wasn't Yoshimoto-san's office that was broken into. You cannot blame him for other people's carelessness.'

'There may be damp inside,' I said. 'Perhaps it would be good to check.'

'Why do you say that? Who told you about what's in there?' Yoshio Yoshimoto said.

At the same time Mrs Maki smacked the side of my head (gently for her) and said, 'Keep quiet when nobody's talking to you.'

Yoshio Yoshimoto pushed Mrs Maki aside and asked again, 'Who told you?'

'Nobody. I was wondering where that musty smell – like a wet dog – was coming from. Most of it might be Professor Kutsuki's clothes. I'll take care of that in the house. But here there's something else, a faint scent, and it's not coming from outside. It's usually because there is mould or mildew somewhere. I checked the shelves and cupboards but couldn't find the source. That's why I thought it's probably something in the archive store.'

'You have a good nose.' Professor Kutsuki didn't seem in the least offended at being compared to a wet dog. 'I see why you approve of this girl.' He waved his cane vaguely in my direction and knocked over my ink bottle. Fortunately it was tightly capped and didn't break.

'How's it going, Professor?' Yoshio Yoshimoto asked, as I set it upright, out of range of the cane. 'You need anything?' As though they hadn't been doing their utmost to get him to go back to work for the past few weeks.

'I need to get back to my work. Why are you coming here and talking nonsense?' the professor responded.

'Of course you must want to get back to your life's work,' Mrs Maki said, with a simpering smile that was painful to see. I don't know what was going on between her and Yoshio Yoshimoto, but she was clearly disappointed and trying not to show it. Whatever she had expected of him, he had not delivered. Had he been deliberately using her? Or had she just been taken in by his power and charisma and imagined the rest?

I'm sure Professor Kutsuki heard it in her voice. 'My life's work? This was thirteen years of my life's work and now it doesn't even exist. But I have nothing else to leave behind.'

'You must bring it back,' Yoshio Yoshimoto said. 'It's your greatest work, what you'll be remembered for. And we're here to do everything we can to help you.'

Everything except fulfil Professor Kutsuki's demand that he unlock the archive store.

But I was willing to believe Yoshio Yoshimoto was distracted by his reddening eyes and dripping nose, as well as Mrs Maki's attempts to fuss over him.

'Don't fuss. Allergic reaction.' He pushed her away. 'All my life I ate mushrooms without problem. Then, about five years ago, just before the war, this started. It's the revenge of the plants on a plant eater.'

'Did you see this?' Mrs Maki picked up the notebook with

my first attempts at transcription and held it out to him. 'It's gibberish. I can't understand a word of it!'

Yoshio Yoshimoto didn't take it. 'I don't know anything about science – I've made a point of not knowing about it. Leave it to the scientists, I say, and don't complicate things. But this is usable?' This to Professor Kutsuki.

'She read it back to me. Like everything else, it is if you're willing to use it,' Professor Kutsuki said. 'Think of it as a recipe. A formula is useless unless you have ingredients and heat.'

'How funny. You make science sound like cooking.' Mrs Maki laughed girlishly, her good mood restored by the evidence on paper.

'Cooking is a science,' Professor Kutsuki grumbled. 'Why are you still here? Haven't you seen enough to know we're not conspiring with the Americans in my work room?'

Mrs Maki looked offended and started for the door but Yoshio Yoshimoto turned on me. 'You! I now know why Hideki Tagawa wanted you to be part of this project.'

'It was Mrs Maki who asked for me to come to work for her, sir.'

'You don't have to lie to me. Major Dewa told me all about it.'

Major Dewa? I was confused.

'Is she a secret assassin?' Professor Kutsuki asked. 'If so, she's not very well trained. I could teach you a thing or two myself. Unless, of course, you're here to kill me, in which case I'll just have to finish you off.'

Yoshio Yoshimoto ignored him, 'Hideki Tagawa has been training this girl for the last two years. Ever since Major Dewa made him admit he meant to find out what she had been taught by the British detective Le Froy.'

What? I hadn't thought Major Dewa had such a convoluted imagination.

It was true Hideki Tagawa had asked me a lot of questions about Le Froy when we first met. I'd found it interesting, given that Le Froy had been obsessed with Japanese spies – Hideki Tagawa in particular – in the years leading up to the war.

Given that Le Froy had been mocked by his Colonial Office superiors for his 'obsession' that disguised Japanese spies were infiltrating South East Asia, there was some poetic justice in Hideki Tagawa being under scrutiny for his interest in Le Froy.

'I was working as a secretary in Le Froy's department,' I said. 'I took shorthand, typed reports and arranged the office schedule. Chief Inspector Le Froy wasn't training me for anything else.'

'You don't have to keep it secret any more. It will be good if Hideki Tagawa manages to complete the training Le Froy started, and show that Asian females can be covert investigators. I saw it for myself, remember? Your frustration when you were locked in your room the day we arrived with Professor Kutsuki. And how you climbed out of the window and edged along the ledge to the next room, so as to be downstairs to welcome us.'

He smiled. To my surprise, I saw he meant to flatter me.

'That was because I didn't realise I was supposed to be locked in. I thought there was something wrong with the door to my room. I knew Mrs Maki's guests were arriving and I wanted to make sure that everything was ready for them.'

'For security reasons the arrival of Professor Kutsuki and his assistant was to be kept secret.'

'If I'd known that, I'd have been perfectly happy to stay

locked up. You people might have told me what I wasn't supposed to know about.'

'That was what first drew Major Dewa's attention. He noted that when he met you previously, Hideki Tagawa had planted you in Colonel Fujiwara's house to spy on his daughter.'

Major Dewa was more confused about the events that had taken place beneath the cannonball tree last year than I'd realised.

'I couldn't approve of Mrs Maki's security arrangements,' Yoshio Yoshimoto went on, 'but your initiative proved that, crippled or not, you could handle yourself. And you were determined enough to find out what was happening. Were you born crippled or did Le Froy deliberately deform your leg? It's a good cover.'

'A good cover for what?' Professor Kutsuki asked. I was still processing the information just thrown at me. 'What do you want her to do?'

'A good cover for any female operative. We have to make sure they're capable and strong but at the same time not appealing to men. As bodyguards for the daughters of His Majesty the Emperor, for instance.'

I laughed. And stopped when I saw he was serious. 'Hideki Tagawa has been very kind to me because of my mother, his cousin.'

Yoshio Yoshimoto nodded, as if he was acknowledging my resolution to say nothing.

'He must think very well of your mother, eh? But don't get the idea the man likes you or sees you as a daughter. No respectable man would expose a woman to this kind of work.'

Mrs Maki's Room

———◆———

It was evening when I left the laboratory building to walk back to the house alone.

I hadn't been sorry when Mrs Maki turned up at the lab again – alone this time. It had been a long day and I was stiff from sitting still and reading to Professor Kutsuki or listening to him talk. Ah Peng and Tanis had brought us lunch at noon. It was a simple meal, steamed *ubi kayu*, or tapioca, with some green papaya pickle. Since the men were not in the house there was no point in wasting our precious rice ration. Tapioca, however, grew freely and I'd instructed the boys to plant tapioca shoots for every stalk they harvested. And I'd made the sweet papaya pickle days ago, boiling down the cubes of almost ripe papaya with *gula melaka*, lime and ginger juice.

These days, it was unlike Mrs Maki to do any housework other than organising. She'd been extremely offended when Hideki Tagawa asked her to move a chair out of Professor Kutsuki's way on his arrival and now, months later, she still muttered,

'Why ask me to move a chair? There are servants. That's what they're for.'

I'd understood she was protecting her position as one of the elite. It was especially precarious given how the elite she was most interested in impressing looked down on women as good only for serving men. So, I was very surprised when Mrs Maki insisted she was going to stay in the laboratory and wipe dust from the surfaces. I'd had a feeling she just wanted to poke around with no one there. And I was perfectly happy for her to do that. Even though I felt I'd worked hard, we hadn't produced much that was worth anything.

Professor Kutsuki made a fuss, of course. 'It's my laboratory. It's my private work space. Why should you busybody inside here? Pah!'

'All right, you stay then. I'm just going to clean. The place is filthy. Clearly some people think they're too good to clean a room once they call themselves "assistant"!'

That was for me, of course. As was 'Go and get dinner started. And you'd better give us something better than that lunch we had.'

She'd been supervising the lunch, not me, but I wasn't going to remonstrate. I left that to Professor Kutsuki who protested at my departure until 'I'll read you the story later tonight,' I'd promised.

I hoped Mrs Maki wouldn't tell Yoshio Yoshimoto I was reading stories to the old man. He'd probably disapprove of anything distracting Professor Kutsuki from his work. It might make him rethink asking me to help him. I didn't want that to happen.

Did Mrs Maki mean to grill Professor Kutsuki? I was pretty certain the old scientist could hold his own against her. I would have liked to watch her try, though.

I found the houseboys had dinner preparations well in hand, so I left them to it. There was some dried fish and they'd put together a fish dish with the curry paste we'd made with red and green chillies, garlic, ginger, shallots and the last of our cumin and turmeric. They were very proud of it – they'd taken turns to pound it in the stone mortar with the pestle. This was another of the things boys would never have done but for the war. Girls working in offices and boys in the kitchen? I didn't think it was doing them any harm.

Some day, if they ever got the chance, Tanis and Ah Peng would be great at managing households or businesses. Rather than being protected and pampered by mothers and grandmothers, they'd learned to work through difficulties with sustained effort and could assess and take risks.

I decided – recklessly, I know – to take a risk myself. I would do some cleaning. Why not? Mrs Maki was occupied in the laboratory building or trying to get something out of Professor Kutsuki. Well, good luck to her. I was going to have a quick look around her room. It was a small risk with a potentially huge pay-off. And I might never again have such a good opportunity.

I grabbed a cloth, dunked and wrung it out to take with me. Mrs Maki always cleaned her room herself, so I'd never been into it. But I was becoming more and more certain she was hiding something.

Mrs Maki would have found it so easy to remove the blue coat from my cupboard. Even if Morio Goda had been trying to give

himself an alibi by lying 'for' me, what if he hadn't been working alone? Mrs Maki could have passed the *michiyuki* to him and told him what to look for at Headquarters. She would likely have known what Hideki Tagawa had kept in a safe at Headquarters … perhaps because he'd moved it there on suspecting it wasn't safe at Moss House. And whatever Morio Goda had found, had he been killed for it? And where was it now?

I remembered finding her in my room after news of the break-in at Headquarters. Possibly she'd meant to replace the coat among my things when Hideki Tagawa had discovered her there. If I found the blue *michiyuki* hidden in Mrs Maki's room, it should clear me once and for all. And even Hideki Tagawa and Yoshio Yoshimoto would have to believe me.

Even better, I might find the briefcase that had been taken from Hideki Tagawa's office. There had been no further official search, which made me wonder if the inquiry had been called off. The news still coming in from Hiroshima two days later was so overwhelming that it was eclipsing everything else.

But Hideki Tagawa couldn't have forgotten, even if nothing of importance had been taken. Morio Goda was unlikely to have acted alone. Like Tanis and Ah Peng, he'd been a sous-chef, adept at pounding spices but not ready to choose the ingredients going into the stone mortar.

Mrs Maki and I had to be at the top of Hideki Tagawa's list of suspects. And since I knew I'd not had anything to do with it, only she remained.

More and more thoughts crowded into my head as I walked up the stairs. Mrs Maki's recent arguments with Hideki Tagawa – because Hideki Tagawa suspected her? And her cold hostility

towards me: was that because she knew she would be suspected if I cleared myself? Was that why she'd been so angry with Morio Goda for giving me an alibi?

Could she have killed Morio Goda?

After all, what did I really know about Mrs Maki?

I'd considered her an old woman when I'd first met her years ago. Old in the way you see your parents, teachers and other people you're expected to obey without question. I knew she'd been married to Consul General Yasujirō Maki, or 'Jimmy Maki', the unofficial Japanese ambassador to Singapore before the war.

I'd admired her for her cool, calm manner and for always knowing the correct thing to do in any situation.

She must have been in her late thirties then and couldn't be much over forty now. But, like almost everyone else, she looked considerably older.

I felt Mrs Maki was trying to hold on to the status she felt entitled to. Even with all the death and destruction going on in Hiroshima and around us, Mrs Maki could be petty if she felt she was not shown proper respect, whatever was due to her by birth or marriage or just for being who she was. And now she was angry with everyone – even Yoshio Yoshimoto – when she felt she wasn't given the respect she deserved. Born into the same family, my mother might have been the same, but she had left and adapted.

Unlike my mother, Mrs Maki had remained within the family and married a respectable man they approved of. Had the frustrations she'd felt at being the helpless wife of a man for whom she'd lost respect turned her into this hard, unlovable woman? I'd heard rumours that she'd been implicated in her husband's death just months after he was recalled to Japan.

Maybe my mother had made the right choice, after all.

Mrs Maki had always been super-critical of me, but in a way that you would be critical of a family member whom you were afraid was getting herself into trouble. I'd only realised this after it changed. Now Mrs Maki seemed to see me as a troublemaker who'd wormed my way into her home ... even though she had insisted I move in. And I wasn't the only one.

Mrs Maki raged constantly against her spineless family (in the person of Hideki Tagawa) and the weaklings ruining her country (also in the person of Hideki Tagawa). She might see herself as being forced to take over from someone who wasn't doing a good job.

Mrs Maki's bedroom was next to Morio Goda's old room where I was now sleeping. At worst I could say I'd got the doors mixed up.

I listened for a moment and knocked lightly just in case. No answer. The handle turned before I fully realised what I was doing and I went in. If my blue coat was here that would solve the matter. Or even the missing briefcase ...

I stopped in shock. Mrs Maki had made this room a little sanctuary of Japan. A sanctuary or a very small, very crowded museum.

Every surface was packed full of Japanese memorabilia, photographs, postcards, everything Japanese she must have loved and missed. It wasn't just clutter because it was all set up so carefully, including the cloths pinned over the windows and on the walls to provide backdrops for more items. There were paintings too. It was a microcosm of Japan, as intense and concentrated as *ton-jiro* broth boiled down for too many days into

169

a heavy sludge. Mrs Maki had always stressed the importance of appearances and first impressions. But the impression I got from this room was that something was very wrong. Even more than her manner of late, Mrs Maki's room told me her mind was off kilter.

It reminded me of her old house before the war, filled with beautiful paintings and flower arrangements on polished surfaces. Except she had tried to cram everything she'd had in that enormous house into a single room less than a tenth of the size.

I opened a cupboard, careful not to knock anything over. Inside was a mess of clean and dirty laundry all jumbled together. I threw open the wardrobe doors and found more of the same. I tried to make sense of the mess but couldn't. It wasn't at all like Mrs Maki, who was normally particular to the point of obsession about folding and neatness.

Maybe it wouldn't be as easy as I'd thought to find what I was looking for. But even clearing my name had retreated to the back of my mind as I took in what I was seeing. That cloth fixed up against the wall above the bed was probably an old shirt but folded and pinned at the edges to look square. And tacked on it were pen and pencil sketches on scrap paper, lovingly drawn lotus flowers and leaves. They looked as if they'd been the work of a child. There were so many little details, all carefully done.

I saw what looked like a family group, father, mother and two little ones. Father had spectacles and mother had a pinned bun, as Mrs Maki had worn her hair before the war.

Like the other pictures, it was drawn with more love than skill. And saved and displayed by someone who loved the figures very much.

For a moment, I felt I was seeing the real Mrs Maki for the first time. And I realised something else too. I'd seen her only as the person who'd taken me away from my family. But Mrs Maki had been taken away from her family too. If she hadn't missed her home so much she wouldn't have tried so hard to recreate it here.

What struck me most, though, was how much her life had changed. Once she'd been married to the top Japanese diplomat in Singapore, organising high-society events. Now she was a widow, possibly a traitor and a murderer.

Keeping alert for any sounds from the corridor, I searched swiftly and silently as best I could. I tried to replace everything exactly as I'd found it, but the cupboards were in such a mess I doubted she'd notice. There were some papers hidden in her underwear drawer. I reached for them, but before I had a chance to examine them I heard her voice outside, through the covered window, calling for someone.

It sounded as if she was coming back to the house fast.

I slammed the drawer shut and ran.

Accused

———◆———

I'd barely managed to get into my new room next door and pull the door shut when I heard footsteps charging up the stairs: Mrs Maki – and she wasn't alone.

I couldn't be found standing in the middle of the room doing nothing and there was nowhere to hide. The wick was already turned up on the kerosene lamp. I struck a match with trembling fingers, lit it – thank goodness it caught straight away – and threw myself onto the bed with a book just as Mrs Maki pushed open the door without knocking. She looked mad.

Captains X and Y were with her, but stayed in the corridor.

I sat up. 'What's happening?'

She looked all around the room before settling her eyes on me. 'What are you doing up here?'

The good thing about a book is you can't tell if it's just been closed or not yet opened. I held it up. 'I had a headache. Is something wrong with Professor Kutsuki?'

'He is none of your business any more,' Mrs Maki said. 'We know you're the one who broke into Tagawa-san's office in

Headquarters and stole the dispatches. Right now you're probably pinching that blind fool's samples and formulas.'

My first feeling was huge relief that she hadn't somehow found out I'd been snooping in her room. Then I saw she was trying to blame me for what I was now sure she'd done.

'Get in here!' She stood aside to let in Captain X and Captain Y, then locked the door behind them. She tossed her ring of keys onto the table by the lamp. 'You two search the room while I search the girl.'

I thought she'd gone mad. This just reinforced what I'd seen in her room. She looked mad – her normally perfectly coiffed hair was messy and sweaty and there were smears on her face and scratches on her hands. Even the two captains looked hesitant.

She was holding a bundle: my blue *michiyuki*, dirty and bunched up like a ball of rags. It was a shame what had been done to the beautiful cloth. I reached out for it without thinking. 'That's my coat! Where did you find it?'

Mrs Maki snatched it out of my reach. 'As if you don't know. You two, don't just stand there. Search the room for proof. Tagawa-san's papers must be here somewhere. I'm going to search her. And be very careful not to read anything you find.'

'Madam, what exactly are we looking for?'

'Proof! Evidence!' Mrs Maki shook the blue coat at him. 'Isn't this enough to make you believe the little traitor-slut is behind the break-in? You said yourself that you recognised it. And after all that my cousin and I have done for her!'

'Madam, I said that – we said that – it sounds like the coat they described,' Captain X appealed to me, 'because they said blue and this one is blue.'

'You are all useless! Feeble, weak half-men!'

'Mrs Maki,' I said, 'please tell me what you're looking for.'

She didn't bother to answer. It was like I was already dead and she couldn't hear me.

'If you don't find it here, go and search the kitchen and question the houseboys. She brought them in to spy for her! Arrest them and take them in for questioning immediately! Get it out of them!'

'Please explain to Tagawa-san that we must investigate all information that comes our way,' Captain X said to me.

'We're just obeying orders,' Captain Y said.

They reminded me of the contract labourers I'd seen caught between my grandmother's and Uncle Chen's instructions. The new ones, at least. More experienced workers knew Ah Ma won all the family battles. The problem was, I knew she'd not been above bending the law when necessary. Like her, Mrs Maki was playing to win. Somehow I'd become the enemy.

Had she somehow discovered I'd been in her room? But that was impossible. Was it something Professor Kutsuki had said to her after she made me leave? But that was equally unlikely. Unless he had come up with some elaborate story to tease her and she'd believed it and—

'Did I tell you to talk to her? Just do what I tell you, fools! Start searching the room and leave her to me!'

'What difference can it make to follow procedure?' Captain Y grumbled.

The difference it made was that it gave me a vital moment to see I'd nothing to lose. If Mrs Maki wanted to blame everything on me, she would. In the mood she was in, she would steamroller

everything in her path (that was me and the houseboys) and I wouldn't get a chance to find out what I was supposed to have done, let alone defend myself.

I couldn't let her take me in now.

I snatched the oil lamp off the table and threw it at Captain X. I'd meant it as a distraction and intended to miss him, but because he dodged in the wrong direction, it caught his shoulder instead of passing harmlessly by. The flame caught his shirt, following the line of oil spilled.

As both officers batted at his burning clothes, Mrs Maki lunged towards me. 'How dare you—'

It's no use theorising about the right thing to do. In a pinch, you just have to do whatever you can with whatever you have. Behind the table, I had the tree outside the open window.

I grabbed Mrs Maki's keys off the table and yanked the table away from the wall. When I shoved it hard into her, the sharp corner caught her hip with a satisfying crunch. I hoped it hurt.

Mrs Maki snarled, 'Chikushō!' I didn't have to understand the word to know that she wasn't happy.

Holding her side, she pushed away the table, but she was blocked for the instant it took me to sit on the windowsill, swing my legs over the frame and kick off, hard, against the outside wall, towards the branches of the mango tree just outside.

One advantage of being a cripple with uneven legs is you develop strong arms and are used to dealing with uneven surfaces.

Or maybe all those years of climbing trees for fruit were finally paying off.

'Go after her, you fools!' I heard Mrs Maki shout, as I started climbing down.

Captain Y's broad shoulders filled the window frame and I heard Captain X behind him: 'What's underneath?'

'There are water barrels and thick weeds. But I can't reach the branches and I don't know if they can support my weight.'

'You can't follow her that way, fools! Get downstairs and go after her!'

'The door is locked – who locked it? Where are the keys?'

If I'd had time I would have laughed. But I was glad neither man seemed seriously hurt by the fire.

'Break down the door! Are you completely useless?' I heard, as I climbed on down.

'I'm not going to let you frame me with the blue coat!' I shouted. 'I know you took it! Hideki Tagawa knew it too! He knows you stole the coat before the *47 Ronin* screening. And you meant to frame me by going to Headquarters pretending to be me. That's why you killed Morio Goda – because you knew he lied to try to help me!'

'Su Lin, stop!' I looked up and saw Mrs Maki leaning dangerously out of the window, 'Stop, you stupid girl. Wait, this is important. Why didn't you tell me someone took the coat? I found it hidden where only you could have hidden it. What am I supposed to think?'

She sounded like she meant it but I knew better than to trust her. She was just trying to delay me till they could get through that door.

It wouldn't take them long but for now I had a head start. As soon as I judged I was low enough, I let myself drop and scrambled to my feet.

Now what? Cluny Road was just beyond the driveway of

Moss House. I could turn left towards Bukit Timah Road or right towards Holland Road. Either way, there were two men, and they had a car. I headed away from both roads, across the lawn towards the scrubland that led to the rainforest. I would worry about what to do next after I got there.

Yoshio Yoshimoto to the Rescue

◆

But as I limped-ran as quickly as I could in the dim half-light, someone grabbed my arm and pulled me to a stop.

'What's happening? What's wrong? Who are you running from?' It was Yoshio Yoshimoto. He seemed to have sprung out of nowhere. But he caught me and held me steady so I didn't fall.

'Hey, hey, hey, what's happening? Who's after you?' His voice was joking, but his eyes darted all around, especially in the direction I'd come from. I knew that if he saw anything threatening he would drop me and grab his gun or knife.

But I also knew he was more likely to turn on me once Mrs Maki got to him. I had to get my story in first. 'It's Mrs Maki! She's gone mad!'

'What?' But he looked less alarmed now. I could see him thinking, Women fighting among themselves.

'She came to my room with the blue coat she gave me a long time ago. It was missing. Hideki Tagawa asked where it was and I couldn't find it. I didn't even know it was gone till he asked and came to my room to look for it. Mrs Maki must have taken it.

Now she's saying I hid it so you'll think I'm the one who wore it to Headquarters. She wants to put it back in my room and accuse me. But she took it, not me. And she got the captains to search my things and the whole house and question the houseboys—'

'The blue coat?' I couldn't read the expression on Yoshio Yoshimoto's face as he looked at the house and shook his head slowly. I could tell he was thinking, Women fighting over clothes ...

He didn't get it. My fear had turned to anger, the kind of anger that fuels both strength and confusion. I'd come to like and trust Mrs Maki and felt betrayed. 'Not just any blue coat. Remember the *kempeitai* who came about the break-in at Headquarters? They said the intruder was wearing a blue coat. Mrs Maki wants you to think this was the blue coat and it was me who wore it to the office. But it wasn't! Even if it's the same coat, I wasn't wearing it. It must have been her! And she must have killed Morio Goda because he said it couldn't have been me. Yes, he was lying about that. We weren't together that night. But it really wasn't me. And it could have been Mrs Maki. She is always sneaking out at night. Ask Prof Kutsuki!'

'Where did she find it?' Yoshio Yoshimoto cut in.

'How would I know? She wouldn't tell me anything. All I know is that I didn't hide it!' I expected Mrs Maki to appear at any moment, screaming at him to arrest or shoot me. 'You've got to tell her that I don't know anything about it.'

'I'll take care of this.' Still staring at the house, he seemed almost to have forgotten me. At least he didn't reach for his pistol as we heard the front door flung open.

The two captains came running down the path that ran round the house. They stopped when they saw Yoshio Yoshimoto, relief on their faces. They both saluted and said, 'Sir.'

'So. What's happening here? Nothing better to do than chase girls?' Yoshio Yoshimoto's tone was light and bantering. 'At ease. Tell me what's been happening. And why you can't even run as fast as a cripple.'

'We had to break down the door first, sir.'

'Mrs Maki thought she found some evidence, sir.'

'Evidence of what?'

The two captains looked at each other. Clearly they hadn't been taken into Mrs Maki's confidence.

'The break-in? At HQ?' Captain X guessed.

'Yes, sir. The break-in to Tagawa-san's office at Headquarters. Mrs Maki said she had found proof of the Headquarters break-in. And when we got here she ordered us to search Miss Chen's room.'

Yoshio Yoshimoto was shaking his head slowly.

'But after Miss Chen ran away, Mrs Maki changed her mind. She said she made a mistake. The girl didn't kill the professor's assistant. But she told us to bring her back quickly.'

'And make sure she doesn't go anywhere or talk to anyone.'

Captains X and Y clearly didn't consider Yoshio Yoshimoto 'anyone' and were relieved a senior officer was present and taking charge.

'So you just did everything she told you? If she told you to throw Miss Chen into the lake would you have done it?'

'No, sir!'

'Of course not, sir!'

'She said she had evidence that Morio Goda lied about being with Miss Chen at the time of the Headquarters break-in, sir. That was why she had to question Miss Chen.'

'So you went to search Miss Chen's room for a blue coat?'

'Sir, Mrs Maki already had the blue coat. We didn't know anything about searching Miss Chen or her room. Mrs Maki asked us whether the blue coat she showed us was the one that the intruder had been wearing.'

'But we hadn't seen it. All we could say was it was blue so it might have been.'

'That's what I said. And he said the same.'

'The blue coat?' So he had been listening to me. 'So all this fuss is women fighting over a blue coat?' The way Yoshio Yoshimoto said it made both captains laugh. Even I had to smile.

But I could tell he knew it wasn't a joke. He was clearly worried about Mrs Maki. Was he wondering if the crisis had sent her over the edge?

'Did she say whether she found anything else? The missing papers and briefcase taken from Tagawa's office?'

'No, sir.'

'No, but she wanted to search Miss Chen's room. Maybe she was looking for them there.'

I could also tell that he had read the situation and wanted to calm things down. And he was good at that. No wonder so many people trusted him. 'It wasn't me,' I said. 'It looks like my coat and maybe it is, but it wasn't me wearing it.'

Yoshio Yoshimoto silenced me with a gesture of his hand. 'Leave it to me. I'll take care of this.' To the two captains, 'Where is Mrs Maki now?'

'Still upstairs in Miss Chen's room.'

'She's still searching for some proof of something.'

Yoshio Yoshimoto looked at me, then back at the house. I thought he grimaced slightly. I didn't blame him. I wouldn't want to tackle Mrs Maki in a bad mood either.

'You two, help Miss Chen into the house and maybe she will make you some tea.' He nodded towards me. 'Don't chase her anywhere, don't climb any trees, don't talk to women about clothes. Okay?'

'Yes, sir.'

'Thank you, sir. You'll talk to Mrs Maki?'

'You mustn't believe anything she says,' I told him. 'She can't really think I had anything to do with it but she won't listen to me. It's like she's gone crazy.'

Yoshio Yoshimoto shook his head. 'Leave everything to me.'

The two captains and I walked back slowly in Yoshio Yoshimoto's wake. I didn't want to arrive until he had cleared things up with Mrs Maki. The two captains clearly felt the same. Mrs Maki might command them through sheer force of will but they had to obey a senior officer. Their relief was obvious.

They didn't apologise (they were Japanese officers, after all) but they both gave me nods that were almost bows and I returned deep bows that couldn't be mistaken for anything but the greatest respect.

'Sorry I threw the lamp at you.'

'What lamp?'

'You missed.'

And all was well between us again. I suspect the meals and snacks I'd always had the houseboys bring out to their guard post had helped.

There was, of course, no guarantee that Mrs Maki wouldn't convince Yoshio Yoshimoto to believe her, but I was relieved that at least he was there. Mrs Maki was always on her best behaviour when he was around but she had been acting so crazily and Yoshio Yoshimoto had seemed to believe me, especially with the two captains taking my side.

By mutual unspoken agreement, we delayed outside as long as we could, wanting to give him time to calm Mrs Maki down. It was already getting dark – and darker still as the few lights were extinguished in anticipation of planes with firebombs.

Suddenly there was a terrified scream followed by a loud crash at the back of the house. It sounded as if Mrs Maki had thrown something heavy out of the window of my room.

We were just at the front door and we ran in to see Yoshio Yoshimoto running down the stairs. He looked more upset than I'd ever seen him. My first thought was that Mrs Maki had said something savage to him. Damn that woman and her troublemaking!

'What did she say?' I demanded, forgetting my place and manners. 'What did Mrs Maki tell you? You mustn't believe her!'

'Mrs Maki is dead.'

'What?'

The captains moved towards the stairs but Yoshio Yoshimoto stopped them, 'She's not up there. It looks like she tried to climb out of the window and fell. She's outside, at the back of the house.'

'That was what she wanted us to do at first, climb out of the window after Miss Chen.'

She'd tried to follow me out of the window? That didn't sound like Mrs Maki, with her emphasis on ladylike behaviour.

'She might not be dead,' I said. 'Maybe just unconscious. It's not that much of a drop.' It was only one storey up. And the water barrels would have broken her fall. We all ran to the back of the house.

But Yoshio Yoshimoto was right. Mrs Maki lay on the ground outside, dead.

Looking down at her, my first thought was that she must have jumped to her death so she wouldn't be forced to confess what she had done. My second? That she'd tried to help me by providing food and shelter. It had all gone horribly wrong, but maybe if she'd never had anything to do with me or Singapore, Mrs Maki might still be alive now.

And my third and final thought? That Yoshio Yoshimoto looked really shocked.

'She jumped.' His eyes were full of tears. Had he cared for her, then? Could he have come to love her? Had I totally misjudged the relationship between them?

Mrs Maki had known my mother. I wished I'd asked her to tell me about her. It had never seemed the right time. I'd thought I could wait until things settled down – maybe when our nations were no longer at war.

'She was carrying this. We found it on her.' Captain X handed Yoshio Yoshimoto the sad bundle of blue cloth.

'It looks like Mrs Maki must have been the woman who went to Headquarters impersonating Miss Chen. She must have intended to incriminate Miss Chen as she was angry with Morio Goda for giving her an alibi.' Yoshio Yoshimoto sounded as though he was talking to himself, trying to sort out his thoughts. Then he turned away and sneezed violently.

It was hard to believe that, just hours ago, Captains X and Y had been ready to believe Mrs Maki's orders to restrain and interrogate me. Now it was as if they had suspected Mrs Maki all along and had been waiting for the chance to expose her.

'Yet you detained Miss Chen on Mrs Maki's orders?'

'Sir, we believed Mrs Maki was speaking for Hideki Tagawa and Headquarters.'

'Well, she wasn't!' Hideki Tagawa snarled. He'd returned from Headquarters earlier than usual, as though summoned by some supernatural precognition. That he'd headed straight over the bridge to the laboratory instead of to the house showed that in fact he'd been concerned with how Professor Kutsuki had handled his first day back in the laboratory.

He'd returned with the professor in tow. Or, rather, Professor Kutsuki had led him to the back of the house where we were all still standing.

'Why did you leave the professor alone in the lab on the other side of the lake?' was the first thing Hideki Tagawa said to me, though I saw his eyes darting from the crumpled body on the ground to the blue coat in Yoshio Yoshimoto's hands and back again. 'What if he, too, had ended up in the lake?'

The 'too' stung me. He was right. If I'd believed Mrs Maki had been involved with Morio Goda's death, how could I have left the old, blind and very important scientist at her mercy?

'I didn't,' I protested. 'I thought Mrs Maki was staying with him and would walk back with him. She said she wanted to clean up the lab. She ordered me to leave!'

'You shouldn't have left Professor Kutsuki. You were supposed to be responsible for him.'

'Can I touch?' Professor Kutsuki had shuffled closer. 'I can tell where the body is, but not how it's arranged. Mrs Maki didn't clean anything in the lab. As soon as you left she wanted to look at your notes but she couldn't understand what you were writing. So I told her how we were going to grow mushrooms—'

'Mushrooms?' Yoshio Yoshimoto said.

Hideki Tagawa snorted.

'That's almost exactly the sound she made,' Professor Kutsuki said. 'And then she went outside and round to the mushroom trees. I heard her pulling and throwing things around—'

'Oh, no!' I said involuntarily. They glanced at me but no one said anything.

'So, can I?' Prof Kutsuki reached out and put his hands on Mrs Maki's body without waiting for a response. Captains X and Y looked to Hideki Tagawa but he didn't respond.

'You must have moved the body already,' Professor Kutsuki said. 'She wouldn't have fallen without trying to brace her legs or use her arms to break her fall. Nobody falls and lands like that. Unless she was sleepwalking.'

'We just made sure she was really dead,' Captain X said.

'And she was,' Captain Y said. 'But we didn't move her. That's how she landed.'

'Like a *wara ningyoo*,' Professor Kutsuki said, with relish. That was a straw doll you nailed to a sacred tree to curse someone – preferably with some hair or blood of your victim mixed with the straw. Professor Kutsuki had spoken of wanting to curse Mrs Maki, but I'd thought he was joking.

'She must have known it was all going to come out,' Yoshio Yoshimoto said, 'about Morio Goda.'

'What has come out?' There was nothing in Hideki Tagawa's expression to show whether he agreed or not.

'Morio Goda?' Captain Y said. 'If the boy learned Mrs Maki was the woman who broke into your office at Headquarters, she might have killed him to prevent him telling anyone. Mrs Maki might have intended to blame his death, as well as the break-in, on Miss Chen. That was why she was able to produce the coat she meant to plant among Miss Chen's belongings. How else did she find it when you had already searched Miss Chen's things and it was not there?'

'We all had our reasons to be angry with Morio Goda,' Hideki Tagawa said, 'but there hardly seems reason enough for her to kill him.'

Captain X spoke up too, 'Remember, Mrs Maki herself gave the *michiyuki* to Miss Chen. She would have known where Miss Chen kept it and she counted on its unique design being recognised. Once the security guards at Headquarters identified Miss Chen's coat as the one they saw the intruder wearing . . .'

I couldn't help thinking that, once the Headquarters guards identified my blue *michiyuki* as the coat the intruder had worn, I wouldn't have been able to talk my way out of it. Even Hideki Tagawa wouldn't have been able to get me out of that.

'Tagawa-san?' Yoshio Yoshimoto said. He seemed very upset and barely spoke, which was most unlike him.

'It is possible Mrs Maki took the briefcase and papers from my office. But I think it extremely unlikely,' Hideki Tagawa said. 'None of that has been recovered?'

'No, sir.'

Everyone thinking Mrs Maki guilty made me wonder whether she'd been set up. I'd found myself in that position too many times.

'Not enough blood,' Professor Kutsuki said. He was being entirely too gleeful about all this.

'Let's go to your room and clean up before dinner,' I said. 'Can I take the professor upstairs?' I hoped the houseboys had started preparations for dinner. I'd assumed Mrs Maki would oversee the meal, but clearly she'd had other things - and now less than nothing - on her mind.

'Major Dewa is here,' Ah Peng called. 'It's the official car - and the flag is up so it must be the major himself.'

The death of Morio Goda hadn't deserved his personal attention. But a second death in the same place, and that of Hideki Tagawa's cousin, was to be investigated by Major Dewa in person. The best thing about that was Major Dewa didn't drive himself around. And his driver-interpreter-bodyguard winked at me when he held the door open for his superior officer. It was all I could do not to rush over to my friend Ferdinand de Souza for a hug. This was starting to feel like a nightmare within a nightmare. But first I would take Professor Kutsuki up to his room with a basin of warm water and washcloth to freshen up.

This time even the most suspicious mind (mine) couldn't suspect him of being involved in Mrs Maki's death.

'Show the major into the big dining room,' I told the houseboys, though they knew what to do. It was for the benefit of Hideki Tagawa and Yoshio Yoshimoto that I was talking. 'Make sure the windows are covered before the lights are turned on there and in the hall. Then fetch them some tea and start preparing dinner.'

Questions

———◆———

I stayed upstairs with Professor Kutsuki as long as I dared. We didn't clean him up. He insisted on sitting on the landing by the stairs so that he could hear what was being said in the dining room below.

I was quite happy to do the same. But we didn't hear much. It had started to rain again, which drowned most of their words.

When Tanis came up to tell me they wanted to talk to me, Professor Kutsuki said, 'Talk louder. And tell them to talk louder too. Tell the major you're deaf as well as crippled!'

'Come here,' Major Dewa said to me, from his place at the head of the table. De Souza, standing at attention behind his chair, didn't meet my eyes.

'I didn't kill her,' I said quickly. I was more shaken than I'd realised. I shut my mouth and bowed low to him.

'I didn't say you killed her,' Major Dewa said. 'I think you set a bad example. If you hadn't climbed out the window, Mrs Maki wouldn't have tried to follow you.'

That gave me an idea of what they'd been telling him before he'd sent for me. But I'd done a hundred things that Mrs Maki would not. And would never try now.

'But you notice things, don't you? Did you notice anything unusual about Mrs Maki before she came into your room to accuse you?'

'Unusual?'

'Was she worried about anything? Was she unhappy with the way things are going here?'

It was a strange question to ask in the middle of a war. Surely everyone was worried all the time. And was anyone 'happy'?

'I don't think so, sir. She was upset about the American bomb in Hiroshima, of course. But she said things couldn't be as bad as people were suggesting. She thought it was mostly propaganda. And that nobody would use such a terrible bomb, especially not the Americans, who talk so much about saving lives. And she said that maybe it wasn't so bad that things had got into a mess in the Philippines. She was going to make sure she knew the plan for implementing what Professor Kutsuki was doing here.'

'What exactly was the plan?'

'Major Dewa,' Hideki Tagawa said, 'can I speak with you in private? Su Lin, wait for us in the kitchen.'

Apparently 'in private' meant without me, because no one but I left the room. I hesitated outside the door and, as I'd hoped, de Souza slipped out of the room after me.

I stopped at the foot of the stairs and waited for him.

'I'll let your family know I saw you.' He spoke quickly and quietly with one eye on the door he'd closed behind him.

'They're all well. You know the district's in isolation because of the cholera, right? But Lieutenant Tsai is making sure your grandmother and family are all right.'

Lieutenant Tsai Chih-wei, or Formosa Boy as my grandmother called him, was the commanding officer of District 221 where Chen Mansion was located. He'd been conscripted in Japanese-occupied Taiwan and spoke Hokkien with my grandmother, who'd practically adopted him. Whatever her reasons, his loyalty to her (or to the meals with which she provided him) made life in Chen Mansion much easier than it might have been. That the whole family was still alive and in the family home made them luckier than most of our neighbours.

'Have you changed your mind about Formosa Boy?'

'He's okay. I'm not saying I trust him. But so far he's okay. Come on, let's go outside.'

I finally got my hug.

'You're so cold,' he said.

'You'd better go back before they miss you,' I said.

'I don't meet their security-clearance requirements either. Besides, I need to check if the major left his spectacles in the car,'

'Did he?'

De Souza showed me the tip of a spectacle case in his pocket. 'That's where I'll find them. Walk to the car with me?'

'Is he going to try to blame this on me too?'

The last time I'd encountered Major Dewa he'd accused me of everything from being a saboteur who'd blown up Colonel Fujiwara's residence to being a local witch who'd put a spell on Hideki Tagawa.

'Nah. He's just here to try to find out what's happening so that he has it on record if anyone asks. But with everyone worked up over the American bomb, nobody's going to ask.'

In a way it was a relief. I wasn't being accused of anything, and Mrs Maki's death wasn't the focus of anyone's attention. But (and, yes, I know I was making things difficult for myself) it seemed unfair to her. I hadn't been asked any more about the blue coat that had been worn as a disguise in Headquarters and had turned up in Mrs Maki's hands. Did that mean they assumed she'd been responsible for the break-in?

'Before you came down they said Mrs Maki didn't like losing and might have tried to cut her losses by switching to the winning side.'

'Who's "they"?'

'Yoshimoto-san. He said no one could say she hadn't tried to reach out to the Russians or the Americans and was afraid we would find out.'

Yoshio Yoshimoto must have been thinking of the rumour that she'd betrayed her husband. Apparently it counted against her even if she'd betrayed the late Jimmy Maki for Yoshio Yoshimoto.

'I called and told Prakesh what had happened before we left the office.'

'And?'

'He said maybe things will be easier for you from now on.'

Although – or because – Prakesh Pillay worked with the Japanese as one of their INA liaisons, he always said no living Japanese could be trusted.

But, of course, Prakesh hadn't trusted the British in the old days either. But now that Le Froy and our former British officers

from the Hill Street detective unit and police station were detained as PoWs, Prakesh was one of the most assiduous in fighting to improve conditions there.

The rain had lessened to a light drizzle and we went out to the official car on the driveway. It felt good to be outside in the night, despite the darkness. The wet gravel under our feet, the sound of the night birds and insects celebrating the rainstorm and its end, the fragrance of night jasmine and wild tree orchids were refreshing and hopeful.

'You were right about Morio Goda not drowning,' de Souza said. 'He had no water in his lungs. He must have broken his neck going down the slope. Though I don't know how the young fool managed it. A cervical sideways snap. Someone twisted his head like a chicken's.'

I winced, having done my share of chicken killing. It's kindest to do it fast, so the chicken is dead before it has time to know what's happening.

But my mind darted on to another question. 'You had someone do an autopsy? Who?' My thoughts went instantly to Dr Shankar – in prison – and Dr Leask, who I believed was somewhere in the jungle up-country if he was still alive. 'Did they let you see Dr Shankar or did–'

'A Japanese medic did it for a bag of *inai pasir* seeds.' The seeds of wild evening primrose – the plant reached up to three metres tall around marshy grounds – were a popular painkiller now medicines were no longer imported.

'You trust him?'

'No big deal to him. Everything's changing now, you know. The Japanese are realising they're no longer infallible, if they

ever were. Kind of like the British had to learn, you know?'
De Souza grimaced.

'But that's not bad, right?' I couldn't take more bad news
right now.

'It's bad. The PoWs believe the Japanese are going to kill them
and as many locals as possible if the Allies get close. They're
being made to dig tunnels and fox holes around the coast and
in the central hills for the Japanese to hide and fight if the Allies
manage to land. And there's talk that their important personnel
have already been flown out because they're planting incendiary
bombs all over the island to turn it into one big firebomb.'

'That sounds crazy. They need to keep our port open to
transport rubber and tin to Japan. I heard Tagawa-san telling
Yoshimoto-san so.' He'd said that when Yoshio Yoshimoto talked
about sabotaging the port facilities before the British and the
Americans came in.

'The warning came from the Wooden House. Mù Zhú's been
right before.'

Mù Zhú, meaning 'wooden house', was Peveril Wodehouse,
a pale, nondescript Englishman with a glass eye. He'd been a
Hong Kong-based agent of the British Secret Intelligence Service
before the war and had come to vet us all personally when the
Detective Shack was set up in Singapore.

Earlier in the Occupation, we'd been able to send him
information through the English-language Japanese paper until that
was closed down. Now working with the Pacific Allied command,
he still occasionally managed to get messages past the Japanese. It
sounded as if de Souza was plugged into the local network, though
being caught with a radio was a crime punishable by death.

'Mù Zhú says now is the most dangerous time for all for us. The Japanese win so many battles because they're not good at losing. They're like children who smash their own toys rather than let other children play with them, so other children let them have their way.'

'That sounds exactly like Mrs Maki.' I managed a small laugh.

'We're also tracking some Russian communications. I can't tell you more but there's a lot going on.'

'Aren't you going to tell me that everything will work out all right?'

'Now that that woman's dead, I'm hoping things will be better for you here. You thought she was behind Goda's death, didn't you?'

I'd been sure she was ... until she'd died.

'What's wrong?'

'I'm just surprised Mrs Maki didn't try to use her arms to break her fall.' I remembered what Professor Kutsuki had said. 'It's almost as though she was dead before she went out of the window.'

De Souza shrugged. 'Bad luck for her. I know people who've fallen further and survived with broken legs, ribs, arms ... but there are also people who trip over a root and crack their skulls. No way to tell.'

'Su Lin? Su Lin, where are you?' Old Professor Kutsuki was calling from inside the house. He knocked his cane loudly on the banisters as he made his way downstairs and called piteously, 'Where is everybody? No one brought me my dinner.'

'Please go back to your room, sir. I'll be straight up.' In all the excitement I'd completely forgotten Professor Kutsuki.

As I hurried towards the house, I wondered why he hadn't appeared sooner. Usually he was drawn to the least disturbance or altercation anywhere in the house, almost like a moth to light.

But it was too late. Professor Kutsuki, following the sound of my voice, came out to join us. How long had he been listening on the stairs?

'Who is this? Another boyfriend?'

'An old colleague, sir.'

'Sir.' De Souza bowed respectfully. 'I work for Major Dewa. I am his driver and translator,' he said in Japanese.

'That man is a clown,' Professor Kutsuki said, 'and you're a clown for working for him. Your Japanese isn't as good as mine. But I suppose you speak English.'

'Do you speak English, sir?' de Souza asked, still in Japanese.

'No. Why would I bother to learn English? Everyone here speaks Japanese.'

'Of course, sir.' De Souza bowed again respectfully.

I stepped backwards and whispered urgently in English, 'Watch out, de Souza. There's a vine snake above you.'

De Souza stayed motionless apart from glancing upwards. The green vine snake or whip snake lives in trees and bushes, camouflaged as a vine. It's pretty and harmless, hunts lizards and frogs, but people who fear snakes fear them on principle . . . like Professor Kutsuki, who was stepping cautiously away from de Souza.

De Souza looked from him to me and grinned. He didn't have to say anything in any language.

'All right, all right,' Professor Kutsuki said grumpily, 'you got me. Why don't you bribe me to answer your questions with the cigarettes you have in your pocket?'

'He doesn't smoke—' I started to say, but de Souza, still grinning, pulled an open packet of cigarettes from his pocket. 'You smelt them on him, Professor? And, de Souza, since when did you take up smoking?'

'Social interaction. I'm given packets for getting Dewa to places on time and hand them out to make sure I can go on doing so.'

'Can I use your lighter?' Professor Kutsuki asked. De Souza offered to light his cigarette but the professor pushed his hand away and grabbed his lighter.

'I'm sorry I didn't come back upstairs to read to you. You won't believe what happened,' I said.

'Pah! I know very well what happened! Locked-room mystery, like something in the tales written by my boy Suzuki.' There was glee in his voice and an excited grin on his face. He looked suddenly like a child who'd been handed a new toy and couldn't wait to pull it apart to see how it worked.

'Did those dolts apologise to you yet?'

'What?'

'Those idiot captains. And Hideki Tagawa and Yoshio Yoshimoto. For being taken in by Mrs Maki. They've all decided on Mrs Maki now, haven't they? Now they've got her marked as the traitor-burglar and murderer of Morio Goda. And they were so sure it was you. Did they apologise?'

I shook my head, then caught myself. 'No.'

'You'd think they'd have learned by now. The more evidence points towards you, the more it's not you. They should read more mystery stories. They should wait until you seem totally innocent, then arrest you.'

Professor Kutsuki wasn't upset by his hostess's death. No. He was thrilled. 'It's happening. I warned her and she didn't believe me. The people are starting to die. Just like in the story.'

'She probably thought you made it up so she would stay away from you. She knew you didn't like being around females.'

'I don't dislike being around females.'

'Yes, you do. At least, everybody thinks you do.'

'It's more a dislike of fools. I dislike being around fools. Stupidity is more infectious than smallpox.'

'And Mrs Maki was a fool?'

'Her problem was that she wasn't a fool. She thought she was clever and tried to use her cleverness, which you'd think would be better than doing nothing. So she ended up doing a lot of damage. To herself as well as those around her.'

She'd certainly damaged herself.

If only Mrs Maki had just broken an arm or a leg! Then we could have talked and exchanged our stories and theories. Maybe we could have worked out some kind of agreement. It wasn't such a great height to fall from, not like a cliff. Falling into a shallow lake didn't mean you'd drown.

Again I thought of what Professor Kutsuki had said about how her body was lying. I'd seen her. I remembered the soft, limp way she was draped over the water barrels she'd landed on. As if she hadn't even tried to block her fall with her hands. It was almost as though she'd already been dead when she fell out of the window.

'They're ready for you,' Professor Kutsuki said to de Souza. 'They're coming out of the dining room now.'

'Thanks.'

De Souza was standing properly at attention by Major Dewa's car when the front door opened. No one seemed to have expected him to return to the house. He was just the driver, after all.

'So we agree it was an accident?' Major Dewa said.

'Of course,' Yoshio Yoshimoto said. 'Obviously. What else?'

Hideki Tagawa shrugged in agreement.

'It's settled, then. Condolences to your family.'

Another accident.

After Major Dewa left, de Souza driving him, I saw Professor Kutsuki examining something with his fingers. I made him show it to me. It was a cigarette lighter.

'Where did you get that? Is it de Souza's?'

We'd remained outside, just beyond the kitchen door, for the professor to finish his cigarette.

'It's mine now. Anyway, he has no use for it. He doesn't smoke. He gives away all the cigarettes he gets.'

I knew better by now than to ask him how he knew. 'You already have a lighter.'

'I already have two lighters that you know about. That's not the point. It's just part of the game. And I'm the one playing with a handicap, remember? Would you begrudge a poor old blind man a cigarette lighter?'

'You're one of the toughest men I know, blind or not.'

I took the lighter from him. The advantage of making your own clothes is that you can put in pockets everywhere, as many as you want. I would return it to de Souza when I had the chance. And until then it would come in useful for lighting my makeshift lamp.

Professor Kutsuki accepted that with good grace. 'Thank you for the compliment. Do you think Yoshio Yoshimoto pushed her out of the window?'

'I doubt it. Why would he?'

'Honest.' He nodded to himself. 'But stupid.'

I couldn't see Yoshio Yoshimoto murdering his hostess. For one thing, he took for granted that she would be providing him and his bomb-making mad scientist with food and laundry services. 'He believes the gods are on his side and nothing can stop him. If he thinks they sent her to help him, why would he kill her?'

'Like the Westerners on their Crusades,' Professor Kutsuki said, 'believing their gods are calling them to kill everyone on their path. Except for them it was God, not gods.' He dropped his light tone. 'Don't feel bad for feeling bad. Someone you loved has been taken from you suddenly and cruelly. Of course it's a shock.'

Someone I loved? I thought of all the irritation and aggravation Mrs Maki had caused me. I felt the same about my grandmother and uncle when they were nagging me. They could be so disagreeable because they knew that I, being family, could put up with it. Mrs Maki had seen me as family too. The old scientist was right. I had loved her.

'I feel as if it's my fault. And that I need to be doing something – I just don't know what.'

Everyone accepting that Mrs Maki was guilty was making me think maybe she wasn't.

'The only thing you should do is be careful,' Professor Kutsuki said.

The Eyes of Professor Kutsuki

———◆———

With Mrs Maki gone and the project for which she'd fought so hard clearly not going anywhere, would the Japanese just end it? Didn't they have enough to deal with, now that the Americans had proved their planes could reach the Japanese mainland?

No one discussed it with me, but I heard enough to guess what was being talked about. I was only concerned with what would happen to Ah Peng and Tanis if the house was closed. I was anxious for Professor Kutsuki too, but what became of him was out of my hands. For as long as I could I would try to make him comfortable.

The morning of 9 August was bright and clear. According to the Chinese calendar, it was an auspicious day to grow plants, adopt children or buy animals. Professor Kutsuki had lost his manic excitement over Mrs Maki's death. In fact, his thoughts had moved from her death to that of Suzuki, his former assistant. When I brought him his breakfast tray he wanted to talk about how working with the young writer had changed him.

'I was so excited about my poison-gas bomb when we first started seeing its power. But I'd always seen it as – I don't know – as something necessary to defend ourselves. Like the farmers are trying to exterminate insect pests. Like processing whale oil to destroy leaf hoppers, and boiling camphor and alum to eradicate cut worms. Necessary, you know. Otherwise the crops die and people starve. And none of it works. Then while they were struggling with that, I learned what they were doing in Europe with DDT. That's how I felt – as if I could help people combat malaria, typhus, all the insect-transmitted diseases. That's all I was hoping to do. Of course I was excited. I wanted to wipe them all out. It was my own Divine Mission. My parents died of typhus, spread by lice. This was going to be my revenge on the insects!'

'Okay.' That was all I could say.

'Then Suzuki showed me it was not insects I would be killing. It was people. And he made me see killing insects and killing people weren't so different. Now, thanks to him, I can't even kill insects!'

It was true. I'd seen Professor Kutsuki sense an ant on his arm and, instead of brushing it off, rest it against a wall or table and wait till the creature crawled off unhurt.

'That boy Suzuki taught me to see.'

'You told me that losing your eyesight taught you to see,' I said.

He was silent for so long I thought he hadn't heard me. Then: 'What opened my eyes to really seeing was that story you read me. I read it myself the first time.'

'That story?'

'That story written by Suzuki, my previous assistant. I told you about him. He was only thirty-three years old when he died. When you are a child of three or thirteen, thirty-three seems ancient. But when you reach my age, thirty-three is a child. Suzuki was a child, an honest child. He tried to do a good job helping me, but it was clear that he had no interest in getting ahead in the army. He wanted to write his stories and he was good at it. If only he'd lived, he might have become a popular writer. And he would have written better stories, thanks to his time in the army. Instead he's dead and forgotten. Found with his neck broken, like one of the characters in his mine story. And now the deaths are starting here too. I can feel the curse coming down on this place.'

'No one is saying there's a curse on this place.'

'I'm saying it. Of course there is. We're all cursed because we happen to be alive here and now. And there's no escape for us.'

He pulled off his clownish spectacles and scrabbled his fingers across his face. He was crying. It was the first time he'd let me see his eyes. Terrible flattened craters in a painfully scarred face. But somehow it wasn't as bad as I'd imagined. The flesh that had suffered had also healed.

'Don't look at me!' He remembered I was there and got into a tangle trying to turn away to hide his face and replace his spectacles at the same time.

'At least your tear ducts still work.' I wiped the damp from his face with a clean corner of the good-morning towel I always carried.

This drew a reluctant snort of laughter. He let me clean away some of the dried blood and mucus encrusted there, but there was much more beneath, black, brown and grey. It must have been building up for months.

Now I was feeling angry with Morio Goda for not taking care of it, angry with Mrs Maki for not warning me that the old man couldn't clean his face, angriest of all with myself for not being aware of so much pain and discomfort so close to me.

'I'll boil some water and get a clean towel,' I said. But he grasped my wrist to keep me there.

'I can sense some difference in light quality. Even that little bit hurts, but I treasure it. It reminds me there is light in this darkness even if not for me. I don't want to lose that.'

'You won't. I'll be careful, I promise.'

I cleaned his eyes for him in the dim light of his room where the pain was least for him and I could still distinguish enough to work. Seeing Professor Kutsuki without his cartoon spectacles was like seeing him naked and vulnerable. He lay on his bed, head raised on a pillow as I dabbed and scraped and wiped. I tried to be gentle but I wanted to remove as much of the dried blood and mucus as possible. Then at least the flesh would have a chance to heal.

'It's impossible to tell if anything you do is good or bad in the long run,' Professor Kutsuki said.

'So we do whatever seems best.'

If talking distracted him from his discomfort I wanted to encourage him. Especially if it helped distract me too.

'If you stop a cart rolling over the child, are you a hero? No one will know what might have happened, not even the child. And the child may grow up to be wicked. Meaning you saved a demon – so you are responsible for his crimes. Saving him was a bad thing to do, the worst thing you could have done, right?'

'What the child does with his life is his business. But if you stand by and let a cart roll over a child, you're doing wrong. There's no other way to see it.'

'What if I was really looking the other way and didn't see the cart? Or the child? And what if I use the dead child's body for scientific tests and save the lives of other children? Wouldn't that make it the right thing to do?'

'Not if you set up the child and cart to get its body. That's murder. If you really didn't see, it's negligence. As an adult it's your responsibility to watch out for children.'

'So you think the lives of millions of children are less important than the one life of this child who might grow up to be a demon? Or grows up to be a Morio Goda who will die after achieving nothing?'

'Too many factors involved. And you can't know this child will grow up to be bad. My family was told I was bad luck and told to give me away—'

'Because you weren't a boy? Pah! Some Japanese families are like that too. Especially the farmers. They need sons to work.'

'Because I had polio. And my parents both died. They said I carried the bad luck. Like when your herbs get fungus the best thing to do is dig them up and not plant anything else there for six months.'

He was quiet under my fingers as he processed this. Then he said, 'I don't believe in bad luck. More likely they didn't want to feed a crippled girl-child they couldn't even sell as a servant or prostitute.'

'But my grandmother said, "Don't throw away firewood just because other people pissed on it. You can use it to make

charcoal!" She kept me and sent me to school to learn English when the British were running Singapore. Then, even before the war began, she apprenticed me to a Japanese hairdresser to learn Japanese.'

Professor Kutsuki laughed. 'I had a mother like that. She kept all my sisters alive. Even the one born with water in the head. She always said Fumiko was her most loving and filial child.'

Ah Ma had fed me as well as she would have fed a grandson. Despite my anger with her for indirectly causing the death of my parents, with her refusal to accept their marriage, I had to acknowledge that. And, as I'd just told Professor Kutsuki, there were too many variables involved to blame her for my parents' deaths from disease in the slums.

'But I thought Mrs Maki taught you Japanese.'

'Mrs Maki was my first Japanese teacher. I went to learn hairdressing after she and her husband were recalled to Japan.'

'Hmm.'

'It was also Mrs Maki who taught me to prepare and serve Japanese meals the way her husband liked, so if you enjoy the food you get here, it's really her doing even if I prepare it.'

'So even then she was training you to help her with her housekeeping?'

I didn't really see it like that, but talking about it had got me to the end of what I could do for his eyes. 'That's how it turned out. You'd think that being born female and the childhood polio that left me with a crippled leg were bad luck. But if I'd been born a boy and grown up healthy and strong, I would have been killed by soldiers long ago. So it's thanks to my bad luck that I'm

alive – which makes it good luck, right?'

'If you call being alive like this good.'

I dabbed his eyes gently, 'Why not leave off your spectacles for a while? Let your skin feel the fresh air.'

'I don't want to frighten people.'

'You're not that frightening.'

'Pah!' But he left off his glasses with their cartoon eyes. I gave them a good cleaning too.

'Pah! You think cleaning a blind man's spectacles can help him see?'

'I don't think so, but sometimes even a small difference is better than nothing.'

'How can you imagine you'll make a difference? You're just as much a fool as all the rest of them. A greater fool than the others, because you think you're helping me, but you don't know that someone who is about to pull the whole house down around us is eavesdropping ...'

Professor Kutsuki grabbed wildly for his spectacles and shoved them crookedly on his face.

'I wasn't eavesdropping.' Hideki Tagawa stepped into Professor Kutsuki's room. 'I was just waiting for a suitable moment to interrupt. I came to tell Miss Chen she should pack, get ready to leave.'

'But they're all sick at my grandmother's house. And Professor Kutsuki needs me here.'

'You're not going to your grandmother's house. I'm sending you back to Japan. We have family in Nagasaki who will take you under their protection for your mother's sake. Don't worry, I'll send word to your family where you've gone.'

'I've never been to Japan so I can't go "back". I don't want to leave Singapore,' I said. But I knew my eyes were shining with excitement.

No, I wasn't excited about going to Japan because I wouldn't go. The excitement was purely because Hideki Tagawa would be making plans to go back to Japan only if the Japanese were pulling out of Singapore. Whatever damage the Hiroshima bomb had done, it must have worked. Could the end really be in sight? Finally?

There was a flash of anger in Hideki Tagawa's eyes, 'You really think the British are coming back to save you? Wake up! The Brits despise Asians, like all Westerners do. Do you know, after the Great War, Japan tried to make a statement of racial equality in the League of Nations. Equality, that was all we were asking for. To be seen as equal human beings. It was vetoed by America and Great Britain because they couldn't bear the thought that any Asian could be equal to the lowest white man.'

I thought of the lovely, humble Mission ladies who'd run the school at the Mission Centre. They'd washed our scrapes and bruises and promised us that, if only we studied hard enough, we could do and be anything in the world we wanted. 'That's not true. They don't all think that way.'

He pursed his lips and raised his eyebrows in mock surprise. 'So you believe their sweet talk? You know your Australian buddies? They said they'd vote for equality with dogs before Chinamen. All they want from you is rubber and tin. And what they're most afraid of is being overrun by "Chinks" and "Nips".'

I knew too little to argue with him. I doubted I would ever see any of those countries he talked about, but the few British,

Australians and Americans I'd encountered so far had been good people.

'They don't all think that way. But the ones in charge despise all Asians as animals,' Professor Kutsuki said.

That was true too. I remembered the problems Le Froy had had with his superiors back in Britain. Perhaps because, until the war started, Singapore was a place people chose to immigrate to not emigrate from. Even the Westerners who stayed were there because they wanted to be.

'You can't really think there's a chance for Syonan,' Hideki Tagawa said. Clearly a man who didn't want to be here. 'What can you hope for on this miserable hot little island with no resources and no backing?'

I was reminded of Morio Goda, but maybe if I'd grown up anywhere else I'd find it hot and miserable here too.

But never mind Syonan. As long as there were Singaporeans alive, it was still Singapore. And they hadn't killed us all yet.

'I want to stay here and help Professor Kutsuki.'

'He will also be leaving.'

'What? Who told you that?' he exclaimed. 'Nobody told me. You people drag me out here without any warning and now you want to drag me somewhere else? Pah!'

'Sir, we've decided it's too dangerous for you to remain here. We've made arrangements for you to go to Laos—'

'Why make me go to Laos? Don't you want me dead?' Professor Kutsuki protested. 'What's wrong with us staying here? Why are you kicking me out just because that woman's dead?'

'Because I don't want anyone else to die. I want to send you somewhere safe. You'll be better off with the other scientists.

You'll have trained apprentices to take your notes.'

Hideki Tagawa glanced at the mess of damp dirty cloths, the streaks and smears of filth and dead skin that I had cleaned off Professor Kutsuki's face. 'And I'll try to arrange a proper nurse for you. Someone medically trained.'

'Pah!'

Hideki Tagawa took a deep breath and started again: 'Professor Kutsuki, the rest of the scientific team is now in Laos. But if you don't wish to go there to join them, I will arrange for you to go back to Japan.'

'Pah! First Syonan, then Laos, then Japan. I know that the only place you're trying to send me is into a hole in the ground.'

'Sir. You are much respected as a scientist. All we want is to arrange—'

'Pah! Scientists are the scum of the earth! What if I don't want to go back to Japan? What if I don't want to be shipped around like an unwanted package?'

'It would be safer for you back in Japan, sir.'

'It would have been safer for me if your cousin and her paramour had left me in the Philippines! At least it was more interesting there!'

'All I want is to do what's best for everyone,'

'Then you are the greatest fool of all.'

Hideki Tagawa nodded, a gesture wasted on the blind scientist but which I didn't miss.

Hideki Tagawa saw I was watching him. 'What are you thinking about?'

'Nothing.'

I could see he didn't believe me. Well, cousin or not, he hadn't

been honest with me either. Even before the war he'd been described as one of the most dangerous men in Asia. What might he have done to Morio Goda for breaking into his office and stealing his papers?

'Your cousin, Mrs Maki, left you these.'

He handed me a small cloth-wrapped bundle. It contained a few small pieces of jewellery I'd seen her wearing, as well as some I didn't recognise.

'I can't – she has children who should–'

'She didn't have children. Not any more. That's the only consolation of her death. That her pain in that respect has ended.'

I thought of the chaos of children's drawings and keepsakes in her room and felt a hard lump inside me. Why hadn't she said anything?

Along with her jewellery there was a note in Mrs Maki's handwriting saying I should sell whatever I could for as much as I could get to stay alive, 'Because your life is of great value, and you must understand Hideki Tagawa will have to distance himself from you to keep you safe in the event that things don't go well.'

'When did she write this? Just before she died she accused me of killing Morio Goda and stealing secret documents from your office. Why would she leave me anything if she thought I was a murderer and a thief?'

'You're still our cousin. It's settled. There's nothing to discuss.'

Hideki Tagawa left without saying more.

'But why?'

'Maybe Hideki Tagawa is going to order the destruction of

the whole of Singapore Island on the Emperor's orders,' Professor Kutsuki said, 'and wants to get all of us away first. Wrong of him, of course. But that man is soft. Too soft. That'll be his undoing.'

'That's not true,' I said. 'If Hideki Tagawa was going to order the destruction of the whole island, he wouldn't leave. And he wouldn't order us to leave. He would give us the option of staying.'

'Like in *The 47 Ronin*!' Professor Kutsuki cackled. 'Yoshio Yoshimoto's favourite show. Are we all going to get drunk? You can't be a convincingly drunken Ronin without drinking. I'm game!'

'Something's wrong,' I said. 'Not just Morio and Mrs Maki. I know what happened in Hiroshima is terrible, but it's like something is coming up on us.'

'*Kogarashi*,' Professor Kutsuki said, 'a feeling of foreboding. Winter is coming. Maybe death disguised as winter, or winter disguised as death. There's something very wrong here. I know the feeling. I've experienced it before.'

'And it came to nothing?'

'I told myself it would come to nothing. I dismissed it. I told myself I was a scientist, I had no time for stupid feelings. And because I didn't listen, my lab was blown up and I ended up blind with a dead assistant.'

What could I say to that?

'Feelings are never stupid. It's our senses warning us in ways we haven't yet learned to process logically or scientifically. But that doesn't mean instinct is not real. Dogs and small children have it. We've just forgotten how to read it, just as modern people who wear shoes outside have forgotten how to read the ground with their feet.'

'What are we going to do?'

'Wait and see.'

I hadn't trusted Professor Kutsuki when I'd started working for him. And he'd made it very clear he didn't trust me. But that had changed.

'Thanks.'

'Thank *you*. I think I'm really going to sleep. Be off with you!'

I was tired, but with so many thoughts churning in my head, I knew I wouldn't be able to sleep. I would slip out to see my mushroom trees for one last time, I decided. If I was going to be shipped off to Japan (which I intended to fight) I would never see them again.

And even if I managed to stay in Singapore I realised I'd very likely never see them again, now that I was getting a hint of what the Japanese plans for us might be. Not just my trees but my family and friends, Dr and Mrs Shankar and Le Froy: with all of their lives at risk from this undefined threat, why would I think about what had happened to Mrs Maki and Morio Goda?

I didn't know if I'd inherited these beliefs from my grandmother, the Mission School teachers or Le Froy, but I'd always tried to live by 'Every person matters' and 'That you can't do everything is no excuse to do nothing'. But what was the point of trying now? What was happening was so much bigger than I was. We were all caught up in a war so much bigger than we were.

The Mushroom Trees

———◆———

The blackout was on so everything was dark, but the walk across the overgrown lawn to the plank bridge was familiar.

I charged on, fast and angrily, trying to work off some of the pressure that had built up inside me. My worn slippers slid about as I stumbled through the tangle of weeds and dead leaves. During the monsoon season, the ground never dried completely and my steps crushed what felt like egg shells and rubber bands, which were really snails and millipedes – poor creatures – coming out of the sodden earth for air.

Mrs Maki had forbidden me to go to my mushroom trees, but she was dead and nothing was left of her but the little cache of jewellery Hideki Tagawa had given me from her.

What made me feel worse was that she'd known or suspected something was going to happen to her. And she'd thought of my future. I would have liked to get to know her better, and not just for what she could have told me about my dead mother. She had helped me so much, taught me so much. I could admit that now she was gone. But she'd always kept me at a distance. Only

now did I see it had hurt her, too, and she'd done it to keep me safe. I was angry with myself for not knowing (but how could I?) that she'd lost her children as well as her husband.

But she'd also suspected me.

I remembered Mrs Maki accusing me. She'd believed what she said, holding the blue *michiyuki* as if it was evidence that convicted me, not something she'd planned on hiding in my bedroom. The only question was, where had she found the coat?

My steps slowed. I knew now why Mrs Maki had come to search the laboratory building and sent me back to the house. And why she'd forbidden me to tend my mushroom trees. All this time she'd suspected me.

Long before I reached the mushroom trees I saw someone else had been there. Footprints led away from the site – Mrs Maki's still in the mud by the lake. She was still very much present.

I followed Mrs Maki's tracks in reverse to my mushroom trees. Even before I reached them I could tell something was very wrong. Someone had trampled all over the surrounding area and yanked off the tarpaulin. Even worse, whoever it was had clearly scrabbled around in the earth and compost. My poor baby mushrooms! Some lay around already dead and wrinkled, starting to rot. Others were trying to root themselves and adapt to the upheaval.

My improvised cough-tincture-bottle oil lamp had been tossed aside, along with the cotton squares I'd used to keep the substrate moist. Mrs Maki probably thought it was expired medicine I was hoarding. The twisted cloth wick still stuck out through the hole in the lid and I slipped it carefully into my pocket.

The footprints leading around the laboratory from its entrance showed Mrs Maki must have come out, leaving Professor Kutsuki inside, after sending me away.

I remembered the earth on the blue *michiyuki*.

A piece of cloth was caught there. Once I saw it I knew it would match the rip in the blue coat. Most likely Mrs Maki had torn it when she'd pulled it out. Because whoever had planted the blue coat to frame me would have been much more careful than her. She hadn't planted it. She had found it.

No wonder Mrs Maki had suspected me. No wonder she'd been angry. Morio Goda had said we'd been together at the mushroom trees and she must have thought I'd been in league with him, that we'd arranged it all there.

But that didn't explain how the coat had got there.

Could Morio Goda have planted it? He must have. It was the only possible answer. I was blind not to have seen it. I'd so wanted to believe he was trying to help me, so hoping for a friend that I'd forgotten we were caught up in this great movement towards death.

Morio Goda had returned to the house with me on the day of the Hiroshima bomb, so he must have come back here later. But where had he come from, when Tanis called to me across the lake?

I looked around and up the forested slope behind me. I couldn't see anything up there but trees covered with spiky rattans and thick with bird's-nest and stag's-horn ferns. The huge rattans grew till they collapsed in thorny tangles under their own weight, making it painfully difficult to pass through them. Even the wild pigs avoided the area since there were

few fruit trees up there. What had Morio Goda been doing up there?

From the tangle of tropical jungle he would have been able to watch me unseen, but I no longer believed he'd had the least interest in me. I'd been a fool to think he'd been trying to help me. He'd been trying to use me. But why me? Because I'd been in his way.

I thought about where I was right then. Within the Botanic Gardens, yes, but they covered at least two hundred acres of land, much of it conserved as 'natural habitat' with only non-invasive trails.

Moss House was nearest the Cluny Road entrance to the Botanic Gardens, just after the Holland Road junction. But you could also get into the grounds from Tyersall Avenue if you continued a little further down Holland Road. Tyersall Avenue was deserted, the few properties there abandoned when the British had left. It would be a good place to hide something like a motorised bicycle.

Morio Goda had made a fuss about getting a petrol allowance for his bike when he'd first arrived, but I'd not seen anything of it since. If he had ridden to and from Headquarters on his machine and wanted to get back to Moss House without being seen, that would be the best way. From there, if he followed a trail directly through the forest instead of going around by the roads, he'd have ended up on the embankment behind me.

I looked up. Enjoying the time stolen away from my household chores and duties, I'd never paid much attention to what was up the slope. It was too close to human habitation for wild pigs by day. I just had to watch out for snakes.

Morio Goda had been empty-handed when he came down the slope. He must have left whatever he'd taken from Headquarters somewhere else. Then, that night, he'd come back with the blue *michiyuki*. He must have pushed it under the mushroom-trees tarpaulin. The mushroom trees that I'd warned everyone else to stay away from. Of course it would incriminate me.

It had worked too: when Mrs Maki had found it she'd suspected and condemned me immediately.

Or had whoever killed him planted the coat? And had they got whatever Morio Goda took from Hideki Tagawa's office?

Hideki Tagawa would have killed him for that. For the betrayal as much as for whatever he might have found. But had he? I pushed down the thought. It wasn't relevant right now.

I climbed up the slope.

It isn't hard to climb anything if you don't worry about being ladylike and maintaining decency. I made my way to a small clearing from which I could see the tarpaulin of the mushroom trees below me. Even after two days I found signs of someone having been there. Clearly someone – or let me admit I was a lousy judge of character and say, 'Morio Goda', because who else? – had been using this spot from which to spy on me.

From this point on the slope, Morio Goda could have watched not only what I was doing but also the arrival of Captains X and Y. He must have seen it as an opportunity to use me as his alibi.

There was a bundle of clothes in a woven bag, resting on a straw hat. I poked around in it and found a half-written note: 'Given how the crazy old man was going on and on last night,

I thought I was going to crack and smack him over the head with his own slippers!'

My heart pounded in my chest. Suddenly danger seemed very close. But where was it coming from? Morio Goda was dead. And whoever he was writing to hadn't known about this spot or they would have come and taken it, wouldn't they?

Yes, they would. And they would also have taken what Morio Goda had left lying against the roots of a strangler fig, already partly covered by fallen leaves: a small rectangular shape, about eighteen inches long, eleven inches wide and five inches deep.

It had the beautiful red-brown patina of leather, with weather-dulled brass clasps and lock, perhaps one of the spoils of war our Japanese masters would either treasure or destroy, depending on the mood of the moment. I was sure this was the missing briefcase that Morio Goda had stolen from Hideki Tagawa's office. I couldn't pinpoint the moment I'd acknowledged to myself that he was the thief, but I was sure of it now.

He must have taken the blue coat from my room, as part of his disguise to wear to Headquarters. It was an old trick that even I knew: if you want to be overlooked, give people something distracting to focus on. I'd often exaggerated my limp for that purpose. Morio Goda had adopted my limp as well as my most distinctive article of clothing.

And that same night, after apparently defending me to Captains X and Y, he'd come back here to retrieve it, plant it and seal my fate. He hadn't needed to do that. No one had suspected him, and he could have left the coat up here with everything he'd collected from Headquarters.

It had been a vicious act: once the blue *michiyuki* was found hidden with the mushroom trees – which everyone knew was my project – Morio Goda had only to tell anyone who asked that I'd told him what to say and he'd lied for me. He was Japanese and he was a man. That was reason enough for them to take his word over mine.

It was only thanks to Mrs Maki confining me to the house that I hadn't found it immediately. I would have announced it, too, without thinking. That was just one more way Mrs Maki had helped me. Added, of course, to the fact that Morio Goda had died after planting the coat. Had that been Mrs Maki's doing too? Had she killed herself? Could she have thrown herself from the window head first, deliberately not allowing herself to break her fall with her arms, as penance for killing him?

But even that wasn't the main issue at the moment.

The main issue sat squatly amid the roots of the strangler fig. The wisest thing I could do was leave it there and pretend I'd never seen it. The second wisest was to take it – unopened – to Hideki Tagawa and say I'd found but not opened it.

Because I hadn't opened it. It probably contained top-secret documents, the kind of thing you could be shot for seeing under any circumstances. Even if I didn't open it, though, I had no way of proving that I hadn't. So – why not go ahead?

No. Stop. Really truly stupid, even for me, with the curiosity that had been getting me into trouble all my life.

What, then, was the alternative? Turn around, scrabble-slide back down the slope and return to the house as though nothing had changed? But everything was changing. Regardless of what I did, this part of my life was over.

Professor Kutsuki would be leaving, dispatched with the best of intentions but very little hope. I could ask to stay with him. But what good would that do? Yes, I could make him a little more comfortable. But if I succeeded in making him feel well enough to get back to work, did I really want to help him create poison bombs of mass insect and human destruction?

The only thing I would really miss from this place was my mushroom trees. My tiny growing mushrooms that had spawned but which I would never see grow to maturity. Especially now that most had been uprooted and tossed away. I only hoped the same thing wouldn't happen to Tanis and Ah Peng.

The Briefcase

I opened it, of course. Any monkey would have done the same, and I figured I could always blame the monkeys if I had to.

The interior was soft leather and still smelt expensively British, though the damp had already seeped in. Inside I found a mix of scribbled notes and carbon copies. Under the heavy shade of the forest canopy, it was difficult to make out what was written. I pulled out my little oil lamp and lit it. The tree cover that kept out the sun ought to hide its beam.

From what I could see, some of the carbons gave evidence of negotiations with the Russians. No wonder Hideki Tagawa had been worried someone would find them. There were also papers in a scrawled hand with strokes for different words combined, like a short form, using the first *kana* for compound words. I realised this was Professor Kutsuki's handwriting, meaning some of these papers dated from before the accident that had blinded him.

There was also clear evidence that he believed he had finished his giant poison-gas bomb instructions. Most of his

notes had to do with his reservations about releasing his formula: the enormous ecological damage the fallout from such a weapon would cause.

And they showed Hideki Tagawa knew (whether from being told or through spying) that Professor Kutsuki didn't trust his assistant. There were reported conversations and letters in which the professor insisted his assistant was stealing his notes and spying on him. None of that was new. What made me look again was that all of these papers dated back to before the fire in the Philippines. The assistant Professor Kutsuki had distrusted was not Morio Goda but Suzuki. This was his dead story-writing assistant of whom he spoke so fondly now. He hadn't trusted him either. Maybe he didn't trust anyone until they were dead.

There was also some 'evidence' (marked as unverified) that Mrs Maki was spying for the Allies, which didn't ring true to me, as well as other 'evidence' that pointed towards a connection with Russia. It seemed someone had been paying a lot of attention to Mrs Maki – and not just to her: there was a suspicion that Hideki Tagawa was helping her, his cousin, that they were working together. Hideki Tagawa himself was under suspicion.

Hideki Tagawa had made a note that the recommendation for his arrest had been sent to him, which meant someone was trying to be clever or was completely ignorant.

In other words, he'd been keeping an ear to the ground and tracking all the rumours going around. But it was all rumour and hearsay. I didn't see anything there worth killing or dying for. None of the material showed anything, except that Hideki Tagawa had been aware that people were watching him, but had done nothing about it.

As far as I could see, the rest of the material consisted of reports and notes compiled by Hideki Tagawa. There were reports of the Allied victories over the Japanese and the surrender of Germany, which were illegal within the bubble of optimism the Japanese had created around us. Again, it was just news, nothing worth stealing.

More interesting to me were the papers sent to Hideki Takawa stamped 'Top Secret. February 1945'. At the Yalta Conference, the Soviets had agreed to join the war against Japan. In return, Stalin would receive the southern half of Sakhalin and the Kuriles.

Yet Yoshio Yoshimoto and other local officials were still talking about Russia joining Japan against the Allies. Why hadn't Hideki Tagawa passed on this information? Or was this Western propaganda rather than fact?

Other records had a Japanese agent reaching out to the Russians offering them the plans for Professor Kutsuki's poison-gas bomb. A demonstration was offered in exchange for money and a position in the new Japanese military regime set up with Russian backing.

This, it seemed, was Hideki Tagawa's focus. There were copious notes on this case. He was clearly trying to track down the traitor, while being aware that the 'traitor' would be transformed into a 'patriotic hero' if his mission to draw in the Russians succeeded.

But Hideki Tagawa's searches and tagged results seemed almost too targeted. Did he already know who he was after? And was he carefully not stopping him and not telling his superiors in Japan who it was?

It made me wonder whether Hideki Tagawa, while ostensibly searching for the traitor, had been helping him stay under cover.

It even made me wonder whether he himself was the traitor. It was the kind of brilliant, crazy risk that no one but him would take. And that only someone like him could pull off.

I remembered Mrs Maki telling him he'd changed. I'd even heard her accuse him of being a traitor to Japan. Could she have found out about this? Given his loyalty to the Emperor and how much depended on their getting Russian support, could Hideki Tagawa have killed his cousin to stop her exposing him?

The only person I didn't think could be the traitor was Morio Goda. He didn't have the necessary connections, and he'd surely have destroyed the evidence once he'd seen it. And he had to have seen it when he put it into the briefcase.

But the same argument suggested Hideki Tagawa's innocence. If he was the traitor, why had he kept the papers pointing to him?

But was it really so naive of the Japanese to hope the Soviets would broker a peace deal with them and turn on the Allies? No doubt Stalin had encouraged them to think it possible. And then I saw what it all came down to: Japan had told Russia they had the prototype of a poison-gas bomb that would outdo in lasting destruction anything promised by the Americans. That was what Professor Kutsuki and the rest of the scientists had been working on. I thought about the fire at his lab in the Philippines. Had that been an attempt to destroy this bomb? Surely, as long as Professor Kutsuki was alive, he could reproduce his results. Which suggested that Professor Kutsuki was the real target here. Had fear stopped him working?

From what I could see of the rest of the documents, one faction in Japan was trying to negotiate a peace treaty with the Allies in which Japan would keep Malaya, including Singapore, and the rest of South East Asia. I winced, just thinking about it. Worse, it was possible. Why would America, Australia and Britain sacrifice their own men to fight for our freedom if they considered Asians inferior?

Hideki Tagawa appeared to be working more closely with a faction that wanted to talk peace terms with the Allies that guaranteed Japan remained independent and sovereign, while its Asian colonies, like Singapore and the Philippines, were granted independence from Western powers as well as from Japan. This approach received much hostility from the most nationalistic military factions. In the same folder there was a copy of the letter in which Prince Fumimaro Konoe advised Emperor Hirohito that defeat was inevitable, and urged him to abdicate.

The meeting minutes made them sound like monkeys, all those ministers and advisers going round and round saying what should be done with no idea of what was really happening. The only thing they were unanimously agreed on was rejecting the Potsdam Declaration. This had been presented as an ultimatum and stated that, without a surrender, the Allies would attack Japan, resulting in 'the inevitable and complete destruction of the Japanese armed forces and just as inevitably the utter devastation of the Japanese homeland'. 'It's a joke,' Prime Minister Kantarō Suzuki declared at a press conference. 'They don't have the air or fire power.' He added that the government intended to ignore it.

Well, after the bombing of Hiroshima, no one could doubt the Americans had the ability, but these papers had been stolen from Headquarters before the Hiroshima bomb.

Even now, days later, Emperor Hirohito had made no move to change the government position. He was still waiting for a Soviet response. Even if the Emperor wanted to negotiate for peace, the military, including Yoshio Yoshimoto, refused to allow it.

In fact, from what I could tell – Yoshio Yoshimoto becoming less concerned about secrecy than in getting his messages across – they were pushing even harder for the poison-gas bomb demonstrated in Singapore or Manila to show Russia what they had to fear from Japan if they did not agree to cooperate.

I felt cold. Colder than I'd ever felt in Singapore.

I now understood the urgency with which Hideki Tagawa was making arrangements to send me and Professor Kutsuki away. It wasn't a matter of being safer in Laos or Japan. It was simply the need to get out of Singapore. Why the urgency unless he knew Japan would go through with the poison-gas bomb? But it wasn't possible, surely. Professor Kutsuki's plans were nowhere near ready.

Then I remembered Hideki Tagawa commenting 'nothing new' on the notes I had taken down for the professor. The plans destroyed in the laboratory blaze in the Philippines had already been copied. Hideki Tagawa and others had been prepared. They might even have started the fire to throw suspicion off the final steps required to create the bomb.

Maybe I should have felt grateful that Hideki Tagawa wanted to ship me away to safety. But he couldn't get everyone out. I thought of my family at Chen Mansion, and of the people who'd

become closer to me than family – de Souza, Prakesh, Le Froy, Dr and Mrs Shankar, Ah Peng and Tanis. Of everyone and everything on our island. I wondered how it would happen. If I just went on sitting here till the poison-gas bomb was set off, would I be blown apart in the blast or choke slowly in the fumes?

Needing to move, I stood up carelessly and kicked over the briefcase. There was something below the base lining. I'd thought it was just packing material. Now I saw the rest of the briefcase was packed with folders containing ... origami mice. Flattened paper mice. Some had been unfolded and refolded wrongly, but there was nothing written inside. I undid a few and saw nothing but ink dots and dashes. I saw Professor Kutsuki's hand in this. Hideki Tagawa had clearly suspected there was a code in them but it didn't look like he'd solved it.

Le Froy had taught me all I knew about breaking and creating codes. Or, rather, he'd been training me when he set me puzzles to solve. I'd thought he was just trying to keep me occupied until he gave me a code his department was working to decipher and I'd broken it before any of the men had.

Remembering that made me smile, then want to cry. Had all that been for nothing, then? We were going to be blown up into dust or dissolved into soup, our lives and memories dissipating into nothing? And nothing was all I could do about it.

My makeshift lamp was fading. I'd unconsciously crushed the paper creature I was holding. Then, as I tried to straighten out the paper, I felt something under my thumb. The pinprick pushed through from the other side had left a raised bump, like a tiny volcano. I remembered Professor Kutsuki's bottle-cap scratches. Could it be that simple? It wasn't even a sophisticated

code, more like a game children would play, leaving messages for one another.

Which was, of course, a mark of the most successful codes. As long as I'd been trying to use only my eyes I probably wouldn't have noticed anything. It was only because it was too dark to see that I'd felt the indentation.

But now, suddenly, between the folds, I could almost make out actual words pressed into the paper. They were not made in pencil or ink, merely impressed by some instrument such as a stylus. As they were on crumpled paper, one would almost have had to know they were there in order to notice them.

Anyway it was too dark to study any writing up there, and I had no way to record what I was deciphering. What should I do now? I heard monkeys squabbling nearby and some birds, but nothing else.

I started walking, carrying the briefcase. I didn't know what I was going to do with it, but I was keeping it with me till I died or decided, as Professor Kutsuki would have put it. I made my way across the ridge, then down to Tyersall Avenue. The trail was easier to follow than I'd expected. There were path markers at intervals. Clumsy and amateur, I thought, even as I was glad to see the bits of string tied to branches. Morio Goda's doing, I suspected.

I arrived at the boundary fence hot, sweaty and scratched. Now what was I going to do? Mrs Maki was dead and I no longer trusted Hideki Tagawa, if I ever had. You can't trust the best rat exterminator in the world if you're a rat.

There was a hole cut in the fencing, right beside the giant tembusu tree. It was a well-chosen spot, hidden from the road

outside by bushes and easily located by proximity to the forty-metre tree, which had to be one of the largest in the area.

And propped up against a tree on the other side was a motorised bicycle, the ignition key looped on another string around its handlebars. Morio Goda had been a lousy agent, I decided. If he had been an agent at all. I no longer doubted he had gone to Headquarters in my blue coat and a coolie hat – the coolie hat I found tossed next to the bicycle.

In that moment I understood why some people walk – or ride – away from their complicated lives and never look back. You know you're in a very bad state when it feels safer to ride off into the unknown than return to the deadly humans you live with.

I could go back to Chen Mansion, I supposed. But the briefcase? It wasn't likely I could ride a motorised bicycle holding a briefcase, given I'd never tried riding one even without a briefcase. And I wasn't going to leave it there. But what could I do with it? No one would believe I hadn't looked in it if I brought it back to the house. What I really wanted to do was pass it on to Ferdinand de Souza or, better yet, Prakesh. If only they could somehow get this to 'Mù Zhǔ' Wodehouse and the Pacific Allied Command!

If only I could ask Le Froy what to do!

But I knew what he would say: 'First, stay alive. That's top priority. Then decide who to show the papers to.'

Professor Kutsuki, I decided. If I could catch him in one of his more reasonable moods. He knew these men and organisations better than I could. If he didn't even want to kill ants he was less likely to want to kill me.

On my way back, I collected what fungi I could salvage as I went past my mushroom trees. It would give me a good excuse for the time I'd spent outside. I noticed that whoever had caused the damage (I was sure it was Mrs Maki, but I didn't *know* it was) had been scrabbling beneath the logs, searching for anything hidden, rather than deliberately wreaking destruction. I found a good amount of termite mushrooms. We called them *cendawan busut* and had always eaten them because they were easy to grow. But after learning what they were called, Mrs Maki had refused to have them in the house. She'd had a great fear of termites, though I'd assured her mushrooms couldn't attract them. They had a symbiotic relationship, the termites farming the mushrooms, which helped them break down organic matter in their nests faster. Rather like the relationship between the colonial occupiers and us locals.

But now to the Japanese I rather thought we were more like the rotting wood the termites were feeding on.

What I couldn't use I mixed back in as mulch. Unlike humans, mushrooms could be useful even in death. This left me hot and grubby, but working with my hands helped me to decide what to do next.

I went along the marshy border of the lake to where the fish traps were set. They were all empty and I wondered if the houseboys had been checking them, and if they'd been searching the area for eggs from the jungle fowl that scraped hollows in the ground under the densest vegetation. There were usually five or six eggs per nest and I'd made sure the boys never took more than two, so there would be more chicks.

I didn't find any fresh nests, or any sign that Tanis and Ah Peng had been in the area, which was good. I didn't want to

incriminate them in any way. And I was glad for once that there were no fish in the first trap I pulled up. It wasn't fish I was after that night.

Now I had to get back inside the house without being noticed and show Professor Kutsuki what I'd found. He might be able to help me figure out what it all meant. At the very least I might be able to save his life if what I'd found persuaded him to let Hideki Tagawa ship him out to Laos or back to Japan.

The Japanese bomb wasn't the only threat right now. If the British were coming back to free us, could we stay alive till they arrived? And if it became clear the British were on the way, would the Japanese be impelled to kill us all before they came?

The Bombing of Nagasaki

———◆———

There was no chance of slipping into the house quietly. Despite the blackout orders, the lights were blazing full on in front showing three cars in the driveway. For one terrible moment I was sure they'd discovered what I was up to and were after me.

The smart thing to do was to slip back into the darkness before I was noticed. But then what? Back along the trails with pursuers coming after me? And after that, where? I couldn't go to my grandmother's house with the briefcase and information. That would bring more bad luck to the family than I'd ever been accused of previously.

I was suddenly too tired to take another step, let alone run away.

I saw Hideki Tagawa standing with one foot on the running-board of his car but he was talking urgently to Captains X and Y. None of them noticed me.

Then Yoshio Yoshimoto ran out, galvanised, still shouting into the radio he was holding, gesturing to Hideki Tagawa either

to wait or to go, it wasn't clear which. 'This cowardly attack is a provocation that must be answered! We cannot let this go! We must go ahead! This is an insult! We cannot allow this!'

Something big was going on.

'The Americans dropped another bomb. Like the one they dropped on Hiroshima.' Tanis sidled up to me out of the darkness.

'The Americans bombed Nagasaki.' Ah Peng appeared on my other side. 'Missy, we thought you ran away.'

'The Americans are always dropping bombs. The Americans are bombing everywhere now. What's the big deal?'

'Not like this one. Missy, Ah Peng thought you got killed too. He wanted to go down to the lake to look for you.'

'Not like this one,' Ah Peng echoed. His cold fingers touched and squeezed my arm gently as though making sure I was solid and not a ghost. Ah Peng's hands were always cold, no matter how much I tried to scrounge extra food for him and Tanis. He felt the weight of what I was carrying. 'You found a jackfruit? A big heavy one? Is it ripe?'

'No,' I said, deliberately vaguely. 'Why are they so upset? The Americans have been firebombing hundreds of Japanese towns and cities. Just like here.'

'And they say the Soviet Union has declared war on Japan.'

'We must wait for orders from Japan,' Hideki Tagawa said.

'It's ready!' Yoshio Yoshimoto was shouting at him. 'It's ready enough to go. It's now or never. Are you a man or a traitor? A cowardly clown?'

'We must wait to get the reports and orders from Japan,' Hideki Tagawa repeated. 'Everything is disrupted. We don't even

know the extent of the damage. We must report to Headquarters. They will give us news and orders. We must get to Headquarters.'

He saw me standing there with the boys. 'Where did you go?'

'Mushrooms.' I hefted the cloth I'd bundled them into. 'What's happening?'

'The Russians attacked the Kwantung army in Manchuria, immediately after declaring war on us.'

'Cowards!' Yoshio Yoshimoto said. 'Cowards, cheats, crooked snakes without honour!'

I didn't see the Japanese had any right to complain about the perfidy of the Russians. After all, we knew by then that Japan had only declared war on America and the British Empire almost eight hours *after* launching surprise attacks on the United States naval base at Pearl Harbor and on British forces in Malaya, Singapore and Hong Kong. They – or rather their Admiral Yamamoto and the military – considered attacking 'friends' a surprise strategy necessary for victory.

'And the Americans dropped another of their monster bombs. Nagasaki this time,' Hideki Tagawa said. I remembered he'd wanted to send me to Nagasaki because we had relations there. Well, not any more.

It seemed that the once invincible Japanese were being battered from all sides by the Russians and Americans.

'The word of the Emperor overrules what the right-wing extremists want,' Hideki Tagawa said. He started to get into the car but Yoshio Yoshimoto grabbed his arm and pulled him out. For a moment I thought Hideki Tagawa would strike him. So did Captains X and Y, who stepped forward but seemed uncertain as to which man posed the threat.

'Don't ignore me! You want to surrender! You are a coward! I tell you, the Japanese military will never permit the civilian government to surrender! We are as ready as we need to be. This is the perfect occasion. The gods have given us this chance. Don't be a fool, man! Don't!'

Yoshio Yoshimoto was ranting, like a madman desperate to convince his family there were demons under their beds.

'If you tell them to negotiate surrender based on one bomb, you are an unworthy traitor and coward! All cowardly officials must be assassinated and replaced! Reject all recommendations to surrender! Wait till we show them we have the more dangerous bomb. The Russians will have to choose to side with us! It has to be now. Russia owes her victory over Germany to Japan since Japan could have attacked Russia at the same time. Now the United States will be our shared enemy. Can't you see, you fool? I have been communicating with General Korechika Anami.'

General Korechika Anami was the war minister, a member of the Big Six, as the Supreme War Council was known, and one of the fiercest proponents of death before dishonour.

'General Anami insists diplomacy must wait until after we have dealt sustained heavy losses to the United States. It is the only way Japan can evade surrender and dishonour!'

'The true Ronin is and always was the Emperor,' Hideki Tagawa said. His voice was low but clear in the sudden quiet when Yoshio Yoshimoto stopped shouting to listen. 'Your emperor and my emperor, who has summoned us to Headquarters to hear his official announcement. If the Emperor is ready to surrender for the good of his people, as a Japanese soldier you must obey him.'

'For the good of his people!' Yoshio Yoshimoto spat. 'They summon us to sign the surrender document! Never!'

'For the good of millions of his people – our people. You know the Emperor never wanted to go to war. He was forced into it by men he was too weak to stand against. Refusing to face facts now will not make him strong.'

Even to an outsider like me, Hideki Tagawa's words came as a shock. To speak of the Emperor as a man capable of making mistakes was both treason and blasphemy.

I saw equal confusion on the faces of the others. Which of the men was the true Japanese patriot? What was the right thing to do now, when orders coming out of Japan differed so greatly, depending on which department they came from? Did a loyal patriot obey the Emperor, the Big Six or the military?

It all depended on which you valued most highly, I supposed: the lives of Japanese people or Japan's undefined 'spirit' and reputation. But who would be left to represent them if they were all dead?

'American sources predict a Japanese death toll in the millions,' Hideki Tagawa said. 'And the destruction of Singapore and Manila. This is not the time for retaliation. We must do what's best for our people.'

'It's not retaliation. It's strategy. Japan must wipe out Syonan Island. Anyone can start a fire and burn down paper and wood homes. We have the power to destroy not just the people but all the creatures on land and in the seas around it. It will frighten the American cowards and terrify the Russians, who will come round to our side.'

'It's not ready. There's nothing more to be done.'

'If the Americans and British invade, we will kill at least a million of them. Our people will fight, and the enemy will not risk their men. Remember "The Glorious Death of One Hundred Million"!'

He had referred to the propaganda campaign that called on every Japanese man, woman and child to die for the Emperor rather than surrender to the Allies.

'We will make the cost of invasion and occupation too high for the Allies to accept. We must push through. We will hold out till Japan can sign an armistice. We will never surrender in defeat!'

'Why tell me? We have orders to report to Headquarters. Come and tell them,' Hideki Tagawa said.

'Traitor!' Yoshio Yoshimoto spat.

Despite his fury, he looked in better condition than Hideki Tagawa, who looked like he'd been soaked and scrubbed in a dirty washtub, then wrung out without rinsing.

I wasn't sure I wanted him to leave either. He wasn't in any shape to drive.

'The Americans have shown their hand and it's not enough. This is the time to show them and the Russians what we've got. You think they have another bomb ready? No. If they say they do it's a bluff! Don't waste your time with talk. We need to show our hand. Just get us the transport and take us into Changi Prison. You don't have to know or do anything else.'

Hideki Tagawa got into the car and drove off after Yoshio Yoshimoto had slammed the door on him.

I'd been watching all this as though I was sitting through one of Mrs Maki's film screenings. The Japanese get angry when they see you are not paying attention to their films, but they

may become even angrier when they think you're paying too much. It was time to go.

But Yoshio Yoshimoto looked around, alerted by our movement. He saw me and started towards me. The houseboys dissolved into the darkness, like mosquitoes, present but invisible.

Yoshio Yoshimoto looked past the mushroom alibi I was carrying. He lifted the cloth over the rattan and wire fish trap and looked at the briefcase I had crammed into it.

'Good catch.'

'I found it,' I said. 'I think Morio Goda hid it. Up on the jungle slope behind the laboratory building.'

'Inside,' Yoshio Yoshimoto said, jerking his thumb towards the house.

We ended up in the dining room with the contents of the briefcase spread out on the table.

Yoshio Yoshimoto was still shaking out the origami mice to see if anything was hidden beneath them when Professor Kutsuki blundered in, singing to himself.

Yoshio Yoshimoto ignored him. 'What do you make of all this?' he asked me. 'You read them, of course.'

Of course. It would have been a waste of time and effort to protest I hadn't. But right then I was too taken aback to answer because Yoshio Yoshimoto was talking to me as though I were an equal. He spoke to me with more respect than I'd ever heard him use with Mrs Maki. He might have been speaking to another man – Morio Goda, for example.

And I guessed Morio Goda's death was the reason I was

honoured. Yoshio Yoshimoto had no one left to listen to his theories.

'The Russians,' he said, without waiting for me to say anything. 'This shows clearly the Russians are involved. Hideki Tagawa must have suspected Mrs Maki was acting for the Russians. Or she found out he was. Surely you see that. Whether he is responsible for it, or just learned about it and said nothing, he is responsible. Hideki Tagawa is the traitor. All that about a break-in at his office was just to cover his tracks.'

'What are you talking about?' Professor Kutsuki touched the papers on the table between us. He picked up one of the origami mice with a cry of surprise.

Impatiently, Yoshio Yoshimoto separated the documents from the folded papers and swept the origami further down the table. 'Stay at that end of the table.' He pushed the blind professor in the same direction.

I helped Professor Kutsuki onto a chair closer to the jumble of papers. I didn't yet know for sure if what I'd felt on them was a code he had created but I didn't want to get him into more trouble with Yoshio Yoshimoto by asking him now.

'I thought Russia was busy fighting Germany. Is it true Germany has surrendered?' I still couldn't believe that the war was over in the West.

'Germany surrendered in early May. What can you expect from Westerners? No backbone. But it doesn't make any difference to what's happening here in the East. The military cabinet called for all citizens to fight to the last man, woman and child. Death before Dishonour. Do you see now why *The 47 Ronin* is so important?'

Because the Japanese government was calling for mass suicide based on a film? 'I still don't see,' I said.

'That's because you weren't brought up with the right values. In any case, all you have to know is that this,' he waved at the papers on the table, 'clearly shows Hideki Tagawa was keeping official information and orders from the officers they were intended for. He is a traitor. Therefore disobeying his orders isn't treason.'

'You already knew about Germany and Russia and the demand for surrender?'

'There's nothing to know. The Allies issued an ultimatum. They want "unconditional surrender of the Imperial Japanese armed forces or there will be immediate and utter destruction".' He spoke in an exaggerated fake American accent, and Professor Kutsuki, who'd been unusually quiet for a while, remembered himself and giggled.

'What's Japan going to do?' I asked. 'Why did Hideki Tagawa have to go to Headquarters? Do the people there know what's in the papers that were taken from his office?'

Yoshio Yoshimoto answered only my first question: 'Japan will ignore the Allies, of course. They're whistling in the wind as usual. Once Russia comes out openly to take our side it will be all over for them. This declaration of war is just a bluff.'

'But why make a declaration of war if ...' I wanted to ask why he thought Russia would side with Japan, but that would sound as though I was asking him if he was the Russian spy Hideki Tagawa had been tracking. And maybe ...

'Look, one day you'll see that Japan standing up to the Western devils is a triumph for all Asians. You'll all thank us

once you realise the British aren't the gods they want you to worship them as.'

The last person who'd tried to convince me the British were not gods had been Chief Inspector Le Froy, which reminded me, 'What's going to happen to the PoWs in Changi Prison?'

'They should all have been shot long ago. I need to–' Yoshio Yoshimoto got up and dashed out of the room. Apparently something had to be done urgently. I just hoped it wasn't to do with the PoWs.

'The war was over for Germany once Churchill replaced Chamberlain,' Professor Kutsuki said quietly, once we were alone.

'I thought you didn't know anything about the war in Europe. And why aren't you more upset? Everyone else seems to be.'

'Because I've seen this coming for a long time. I can't be surprised any more. It's too tiring. I just take what comes.'

I didn't have to pretend not to be surprised either. I was no longer surprised by anything this man said, so maybe that part of his theory held true.

'Churchill understood Hitler and his kind better than Chamberlain could. Chamberlain was a gentleman. Churchill is not. The war was over for Japan once we bombed Pearl Harbor. That was when I knew we scientists could either choose to continue developing weapons of greater and greater destruction, or give up and admit we were no use whatsoever.'

'Weapons?' I thought about what I'd seen in the notes.

'I realised as soon as you came in that you now know about the bomb. You could have known earlier but you didn't want to think about it. I felt the same for a long time. I had all the details,

all the plans. I was so excited, and I had all the territories mapped in detail so I could target the epicentre. That was when I saw that for best effect in Singapore the bomb must be set off in the highest water catchment area. The most effective would have been Peirce Reservoir, which would connect it to Kallang River and the whole island. But, failing that, the Swan Lake here in the Botanic Gardens was a good choice.'

'Why?'

'Maybe to show that a merchant-caste boy, like I was, could do something great for the nation. And then to show them I wasn't useless even though I was blind.'

'And I've been trying to prove to everyone who notices me that a lame Chinese girl is harmless.'

'Useless because lame, because Chinese or because girl? And, by the way, "useless" and "harmless" are not the same thing.'

'Depends on who I'm talking to. But, yes, I agree.'

'You're pretty useful at a lot of things.' Professor Kutsuki was silent for a while, listening. But we could hear Yoshio Yoshimoto talking on the phone in the hall. 'For a long time my whole being was caught up with being angry. I was so angry that I lost sight of who I was angry with. I just wanted to kill and punish everyone who was still alive. But that wasn't who I was. That was just the anger talking. I was blind. Worse, Suzuki was dead. Anger was the only thing that kept me alive.'

'You did the research for the poison-gas bomb,' I said. 'Even before all that happened, you were already building the bomb.'

'They call it my poison-bomb research. When I was working on it I thought of it as energy-source research. What if, instead of taking over territories with the energy sources we needed, we

could create our own energy? It was never intended to be used as a weapon. Not until all this.'

Professor Kutsuki shook his head. But I couldn't forget that if he'd not existed, or if he'd been a mechanic working in a motorcycle factory instead of a scientist working in a laboratory, there would have been no bomb threatening us now.

Prof Kutsuki held up the origami flower he'd just folded. 'Can you really see this? This is the only art I can enjoy now. Real flowers created by nature and paper flowers created by man's fingers. Paintings and photographs are nothing to me now. What you don't understand is that it's a gift. Now the least thing means more to me than it can to you. The blind cannot use their eyes to see writing. The sighted don't know how to use their skin to read by touch. And we have more skin than we have eyes. You don't believe me, do you? Can't you feel the dot I put here between these folds? With the point of an empty pen? Ink is useless to me now.'

'I'm sorry, sir. I can't—' Would he tell me to blind myself to show I agreed with him?

'Of course not. I'm sorry. When you get to my age and you know you're running out of time, everything seems of vital importance. I feel like Hokusai begging Heaven for another five years to really understand painting. If only I had another two years – another year – maybe I could really understand what is happening.'

'Come,' I said. 'I don't have to understand now. But I can write down what you say so that everyone else will understand in the future. But not tonight.' If we could just survive tonight, if the second great bomb attack on Japan didn't provoke the

Japanese into destroying Singapore and Manila, there would be time to record and understand Professor Kutsuki's philosophy.

'We may not live to see tomorrow. Do you believe there is as much good in preventing bad things from happening as from doing good things? If nothing happens because you prevented a disaster you'll never know what might have been. You won't be remembered – not even noticed – by the unborn child whose life you saved. And in that moment you can't even be certain you're doing good. What if that child grows up to be Yoshio Yoshimoto?'

'What Yoshio Yoshimoto does is his responsibility, not yours. You are one man trying to do good, not a god.'

'You take all the fun out of being clever. Besides, Yoshio Yoshimoto thinks he's a god. A demigod, maybe. Talking to you is fun too.' Prof Kutsuki giggled.

That should have warned me. But something in his words had made me think of Mrs Maki. 'What do you do when you think you've made an awful mistake about someone? Suspected them of terrible things but you aren't sure?'

'You congratulate yourself on being human and still able to learn. Some people become calcified, take the shape of the grand masks and statues they cast themselves as. After that they cannot change their minds because it might cause cracks. So to prevent any cracks in their beautiful masks, they refuse to let in any new information. I didn't trust Mrs Maki either, until she was dead. I trust most dead people. Much more than living people. But still not entirely.'

He'd known at once that I'd been thinking of Mrs Maki. Had I been so obvious? Maybe there was something in what he'd said about the blind being more perceptive.

'That boy Suzuki, the writer of mystery stories I told you about. He had his neck broken too. Just like Mrs Maki. Just like that poor fool Goda, I'm sure.' He'd reverted to his high singsong voice.

I jumped when Yoshio Yoshimoto reached over my shoulder to grab the origami that Professor Kutsuki had folded and passed to me. 'What was the old fool talking about just now? What was that dot next to a fold supposed to mean?'

He took it for granted I knew he'd been listening to us.

I glanced at Professor Kutsuki. The anxiety coming from him was huge. He'd tried to warn me that Yoshio Yoshimoto had returned but had been distracted by what I'd said about Mrs Maki.

Now I saw he was staring at me with an apprehension that hadn't been there when he was mocking Yoshio Yoshimoto. The paper flower Yoshio Yoshimoto was holding had been a paper mouse before the professor had refolded it. It was one of the many that had been stuffed into the bottom of the suitcase, now scattered on the table.

Yoshio Yoshimoto was looking at the paper flower with its carefully placed dot, which I'd failed to understand. And suddenly I knew. It must have affected my breathing because I saw Professor Kutsuki was aware that I'd figured out his code.

When I said, 'I think I know. It's just a guess but I'll show you,' I was afraid the old man was about to faint or have a seizure.

I took the flower from Yoshio Yoshimoto. 'He was making the flower from a mouse, I can't show you exactly, but when you put that dot next to the petal of the flower, then fold it back into a mouse, the dot becomes its . . . anus.'

I'd been planning to say 'its eye' or 'its nose' but at the last minute realised neither of those was convincing as a source of Professor Kutsuki's excitement.

'Yes!' Professor Kutsuki shrieked, suddenly childish again, all his pent-up stress channelled into his act. 'Yes! Yes! Yes! You saw it! It becomes its butt hole, its shit hole! Ha-ha-ha – yes!' All the manic anxiety exploded into laughter. 'Anus! Anus! Anus!'

Heroism and absurdity. They are both closer to us than we realise. All the time.

'Paper folding is for children. Grow up!' Yoshio Yoshimoto growled.

'Look.' Professor Kutsuki held out a folded butterfly towards Yoshio Yoshimoto. 'I made this for you. You can burn it later,' he said, 'as an offering.'

Yoshio Yoshimoto crumpled and dropped it, then stormed out of the room.

'I have already given him and my country everything I can,' Professor Kutsuki said. 'It's not my fault they reject it.'

The Loyal Ronin

'You almost gave me a heart attack,' Professor Kutsuki whispered, 'but that was brilliant. Almost as good as something I might have come up with!'

We were quiet as we listened to Yoshio Yoshimoto talking to Captains X and Y in the hall. He must have summoned them both from the guard post.

'Get word to Changi. We're bringing something over. I'm giving the order. Are you challenging me?'

There was a murmur of voices, then, 'Well, go and get your bloody authorisation!'

'It's starting,' Professor Kutsuki said. 'We won't have to worry about being sent to Laos. Nobody's going anywhere.'

We sat in silence as footsteps retreated and the front door slammed.

Then Yoshio Yoshimoto's voice again: 'What is there to explain? The orders are clear. We destroy rather than surrender Singapore. The American bomb changes nothing! They've done what they can, and now they have to take the consequences,

every one of their people dead. Kill them in their cells and save the bodies to show them. It's our turn now.'

Yoshio Yoshimoto was giving instructions to kill all of the PoWs in Changi Prison.

'Radio,' Professor Kutsuki murmured. 'The Japanese right-wing fanatics grow even more fanatical. Yoshio Yoshimoto is just part of it. Mrs Maki was with them but backed away when she learned they meant to kill real people with real bombs. What did she think they were using? Flower petals? Water balloons?'

I shushed him. I wanted to hear what Yoshio Yoshimoto was saying,

'If Hideki Tagawa objects, place him under detention. These are military orders. They come directly from the Big Six. The orders to eliminate them came long ago and were buried. I have the evidence. Hideki Tagawa will be charged for suppressing the orders.'

At the beginning of the Occupation, Changi Prison had been commandeered as the principal PoW camp in South East Asia. Designed to hold around five hundred, at least five thousand prisoners were now packed into it. Captives were sleeping in the courtyards and I'd heard food was so scarce that they were scavenging for birds and rats.

'This way, even if the whole island isn't completely destroyed, the PoWs will be gone. That will show their people we're not to be disregarded,'

But the people in the Changi PoW camp weren't just foreign soldiers. They were the scholars, chemists, cooks and missionary Christians who'd come to tell us how things were supposed to be run and show us how our lives should be lived. And of the

many who'd come, the few who remained had stayed to learn as well as teach.

Some must have believed it when they told us the British Empire would protect and defend us if we trusted them. They'd been as badly let down as we had. Even if they'd arrived as overlords, they'd stayed because they'd become one with us.

Wheeled boots. Why do the oddest thoughts surface under stress? I remembered Le Froy suggesting I try wearing a wheeled boot on my polio-crippled leg. Like Dr Shankar, he'd never been resigned to 'the way things are'. If we got through this, I was going to tell Le Froy he ought to try a wheeled boot in place of his amputated foot. If we both survived this war, I was going to do so many things so differently ... even though I longed for things to go back to exactly how they once were.

It was ridiculous to think I could do anything to save them. And it was impossible that I wouldn't try.

Le Froy had been in there, as had Dr and Mrs Shankar and all the Mission School teachers ... I didn't know why I was talking about them in the past tense. Parshanti's parents weren't dead as far as I knew. And I knew I had to keep Yoshio Yoshimoto's people away from the PoWs in Changi Prison.

'Make sure the message gets through to Japanese intelligence. Inform the Russians Syonan will be destroyed by the Japanese super poison-gas bomb. And make clear that the bomb that destroys Singapore is just a warning. It's far worse than anything the Americans have got. And we have another in Laos ready to set off if they don't listen. After seeing our force, the Russians will break with the Americans and side with Japan or face the consequences,' we heard Yoshio Yoshimoto say.

'What's the difference between a crusading saviour and a savage invader? Which side of the sword you're on,' Professor Kutsuki murmured happily to himself. 'We don't have a bomb ready. Not here, not in Laos, not anywhere.'

'Doesn't matter. Don't you hear what he's saying? He's going to blow up the island! With your bomb! For a demonstration of strength to the Russians!'

'Yoshio Yoshimoto is trying to make the Japanese Empire save the rest of Asia, even if it doesn't want to be saved. Hideki Tagawa is old-school, obeying orders whether or not he agrees with them, even to dying for the Emperor.'

All that might be very deep and philosophical but it wasn't doing anything for me right then.

It's one thing to commit suicide rather than surrender. It's a totally different matter to make that death decision on behalf of hundreds of thousands of people who might prefer to live a little longer, even if under the yoke of imperialism. That was something Le Froy had said, although he'd been talking about his own government, not the Japanese. Le Froy, who was always telling me to stay quiet and say nothing if it would do no good: 'Don't get involved. Live to fight another day.'

Well, that might be what Le Froy would tell me but it wasn't what he would do. He would have spoken up for what he thought right, even if it was detrimental to himself. He'd got into trouble standing up for us locals so many times that we'd known he was speaking from experience even if he never listened to his own advice.

Maybe that was the most important lesson the British had taught us. It wasn't in anything they'd told us to do but in how the best of them had tried to live.

And if I didn't do something now, Le Froy and all the other PoWs in prison with him were going to die.

But how could I do anything? Me with my crippled leg.

'They'll get him,' I heard Yoshio Yoshimoto say, with great satisfaction. He'd started another call. 'Nothing to worry about. Tagawa is not the sort of man to be prepared. No lighter, no poison pin. Get what you can out of him, then finish him off quietly.'

Yoshio Yoshimoto had mentioned a lighter and a poison pin just like Morio Goda.

Well, maybe they'd studied with the same master of racial superiority or whatever.

Or maybe Yoshio Yoshimoto was Morio Goda's master. He'd sent Morio Goda to break into Hideki Tagawa's office at Headquarters, and then?

Morio Goda's neck had been broken, 'like a chicken's', de Souza had told me. I assumed he'd been thinking of the sideways snap of the cervical vertebra. But I knew who most chickens were killed by – the people who'd reared and fed and sheltered them up to that last moment.

'Didn't you say your assistant Suzuki's neck was broken too?'

'What has Suzuki got to do with anything?'

'Morio Goda was found in the lake, but not drowned. He'd broken his neck first, falling down the slope, or something. And then Mrs Maki fell out of a window on the first floor and broke her neck. Falling out of a window onto rain barrels doesn't mean breaking your neck. Unless her neck was already broken before she was thrown out of the window. What exactly happened to your assistant Suzuki?'

'He went out to meet someone. His master, I thought. Whoever was getting him to spy on me. The next thing I knew, he was dead. But that was the night of the explosion in my laboratory. Everything's mixed up in my head. All I know is, he wasn't there and then he was dead.'

I remembered the urgency with which Morio Goda had asked Yoshio Yoshimoto to meet him in private the day before he disappeared. I'd come to believe he'd wanted to turn over evidence he'd found on Hideki Tagawa. I'd deliberately avoided thinking about it because if Tagawa was betraying the Japanese it might be good for us in the long term but meant big trouble whenever it came out.

Then there were Yoshio Yoshimoto's tears after Mrs Maki's death. What if that wasn't grief? What if they'd been triggered by the mushroom spores on the blue *michiyuki*?

Professor Kutsuki was studying me. Or, rather, he was frozen with one hand cupped behind an ear turned in my direction.

'If Mrs Maki had already fallen from the upstairs window with the coat, when Yoshio Yoshimoto reached the room would there have enough spores left to trigger his allergy? I've served him in the house often enough after working at my mushroom trees and his eyes have never bothered him. The problem is, I don't know what it takes to trigger an allergy.'

'That's something you need scientists and experiments to find out about,' Professor Kutsuki said. 'But it seems that scientists these days are more interested in creating bombs than solving hunger or allergies. Still, I'd say activity and excitement can either promote or suppress allergies. For instance, if the man had just killed someone. No matter how calm and controlled he

was during the killing, afterwards he might have been more vulnerable to any spores still in the air or that had rubbed off on him.'

The professor was thinking along the same lines as I was.

I'd always been so proud that, thanks to my family's black-market dealings, I'd learned to assess people and investments from an early age. I was good at it too. I'd been able to tell that Hideki Tagawa was hiding information from his own people. So why hadn't I sensed the terrible things that Yoshio Yoshimoto had done? Why had I always seen him as almost absurdly proper and honour-bound? I still couldn't believe the suspicions now rising in me.

The answer was obvious as his voice came through the closed door. Yoshio Yoshimoto was certain that he was on the side of the gods and all that was right, holy and honourable. I could sense people's doubts and uncertainty, but this man was completely confident in himself and his mission.

Now he was berating Captains X and Y again. They must have returned with bad news because Yoshio Yoshimoto sounded angry. Why couldn't they do such a simple thing as hunt down Hideki Tagawa? The guards were clearly hesitant, making the excuse they didn't know where Hideki Tagawa was and they'd been ordered to remain at the house to watch and protect Professor Kutsuki. He had severely reprimanded them for leaving Professor Kutsuki alone when obeying Mrs Maki's orders to go after me. Maybe they were getting back at him a little for that.

'I really need to do something,' I said. 'Without being seen by . . . anyone.'

There's a kind of courage that comes out under extreme stress. Or maybe it's just the realisation that you've nothing to lose.

'Sir. Professor Kutsuki. Will you help me?'

'Tell him I want to talk about my poison-gas bomb,' Professor Kutsuki understood immediately. 'I should be able to give you thirty minutes.'

'Thank you, sir.'

I bowed to him, a long and low bow. I wanted to give him my deepest respect, even if he couldn't see it. I didn't know if I would ever see him again.

Yoshio Yoshimoto stopped shouting at the captains when he saw me. 'What do you want now?'

'Sir, Professor Kutsuki says he wants to talk about his . . .' I hesitated as though I wanted to get the words right '. . . his poison-gas bomb.'

'Ah!'

Yoshio Yoshimoto pushed past me into the dining room, pulling the door shut behind him. We heard Professor Kutsuki's high, childish voice raised as he chattered in excitement. Bless the brave old man. I would do the best I could with the time he was giving me.

I turned to Captains X and Y. 'Go and find Hideki Tagawa and bring him back here. Tell him it's urgent. Give him this note I'm writing.'

I could hear Yoshio Yoshimoto trying to reason with Professor Kutsuki, who was being very difficult, yet with enough talk of 'components' and 'detonation' to keep Yoshio Yoshimoto hooked.

I tore off a corner of a propaganda poster and scribbled on the back: *Yoshio Yoshimoto killed Mrs Maki and Morio Goda, Professor Kutsuki's former assistant and probably will kill Professor Kutsuki and me.* I handed it to them. I didn't care if they read it, as long as they delivered it for me.

'Give him this too.' I passed them the origami mouse, now refolded from the flower Professor Kutsuki had made, hoping he would understand it had come from the briefcase and that I'd found it.

For a moment I was afraid they were going to argue with me, as they had with Yoshio Yoshimoto, or insist on taking Professor Kutsuki with them. But instead they looked at each other. Then, without a word, they turned to bow to me and slip silently out of the front door.

Their covert movements, so unlike their usual noisy clumsiness, made me realise Captains X and Y probably hadn't spent all their time down at the security post. They must have been lurking in the house to spy on us. Well, whatever they'd seen had led them to trust me more than Yoshio Yoshimoto.

'Missy?'

Tanis and Ah Peng were watching me from the darkness beyond the stairs. I hurried to them, praying Professor Kutsuki would give me a little more time.

'You know my friends Prakesh Pillay and Ferdinand de Souza? You've seen them here before.'

They nodded.

'I want you to find them. Go to Ferdinand de Souza first. He will be somewhere in the Hill Street police station. If you can

find him he should be able to tell you where to find Prakesh or he'll reach him himself. Tell Major Dewa if you can't find de Souza.'

They looked confused, but nodded.

'When you find him, give him this,' I scribbled the same message on another scrap of poster: *Yoshio Yoshimoto killed Mrs Maki and Morio Goda and probably will kill Professor Kutsuki and me. Trust Hideki Tagawa.*

'Missy, come with us,' Ah Peng pleaded.

'I can't. Does either of you know how to ride a motorised bicycle?'

To my surprise they nodded. Clearly their inattendance at school hadn't stopped them picking up skills.

'You know the boundary fence along Tyersall Avenue? Near the old tembusu tree there's a hole cut in the fencing. Go through it. On the other side there's a motorised bicycle – here's the key for it.'

I'd taken the key, of course. As Morio Goda had tried to set me up I figured it was fair play.

Tanis took the key. Ah Peng reached out to touch it, as though to verify it was real.

'Don't take any risks. If anyone catches you, say that Yoshio Yoshimoto sent you with a message because the phone line is down at the Botanic Gardens. Say he wants a repairman.'

'What are you going to do, Missy?'

I didn't know. 'Whatever I have to.'

'We'll come back to help,' Tanis said. 'After we find them we'll come back and help you,'

'We'll come back and help,' Ah Peng agreed.

'No. Once you've found them go to your families and stay

there. Don't come back. You hear me? No, Ah Peng can go to your house, Tanis.' They nodded.

'Don't come back. Don't die for nothing. You are not to come here no matter what. Promise!'

'Missy, are you going to be all right?' Ah Peng's voice was thick with tears he was struggling not to release. 'I don't want you to die too.' He'd already lost most of his family.

'I need you to do this. Please?'

I hugged their thin bodies to me. Then they ran out into the night, both dashing tears from their faces.

Resourcefulness and survival: that's what makes you human. Or, rather, that's what determines the kind of human you are. I hoped they would survive. At least I'd given them a chance.

It doesn't matter what caste you were born into or what religion your parents followed. Everything you truly are is the total of every small or big choice you make. Sometimes being a true hero is not about fighting and confrontation but about surviving in any way you can. Those terrified children were the real heroes.

Through the dining-room door, I could hear Professor Kutsuki singing:

> 'A tanuki is in the Senba mountains.
> A hunter shoots it with a gun:
> Boils it –
> Roasts it –
> Eats it.
> Let's hide it in the leaves!'

Even in the stress of the moment I couldn't help smiling.

The old man had guts. And he'd already bought me more time than I'd hoped for.

I went outside through the kitchen. First I cut the phone wires with the pruning shears. Yoshio Yoshimoto had a radio, but he'd been communicating with his contacts about Changi Prison by phone. Then I sabotaged the tyres of the single armoured car left in the driveway.

It was one of those prepared by the British for their troops and used by the Japanese. I couldn't cut through the tyres even with the cleaver so I took my precious cache of bent nails waiting to be straightened and scattered them around all four wheels. It might take a little longer but it should stop him.

Just to be safe – and why not? – I cut the power lines too.

There was a shout from inside the house as the lights went out.

I couldn't think of anything else to do. It was hugely frustrating. There were people all around me oblivious to what might be coming down on them and I couldn't think of anything else to do to keep them alive.

Necessary Murders

'What happened to the lights?' Yoshio Yoshimoto threw open the door I'd knocked on. 'Where are you? Send the boys out to check. Must be a damn tree down somewhere.'

I'd brought the oil lamp from the kitchen and he took it from me as he went into the corridor. Maybe I was crazy to go back in there but I couldn't abandon Professor Kutsuki.

'I try to avoid passions myself. Obsession is passion carried to extreme lengths,' said Professor Kutsuki. 'I want my tea. Miss Chen, will you make me some tea? I'm thirsty.'

'And the damned phone lines are down too!'

Yoshio Yoshimoto was slamming the receiver against the wall between trying to reach an operator. Unfortunately for him, this tactic didn't work as well on inanimate objects as men's skulls.

'Where are those damned boys? Get them here, will you? Tell them to report the phones are down. I want them here now.'

And I wanted to delay him finding out they weren't there as long as possible. 'Is it true that Mrs Maki's neck was broken before she was pushed out of the window?'

'The fool woman is dead. It makes no difference how.'

But the look on his face told me I'd distracted him from the phone and the boys at least.

Poor Mrs Maki, I was using her death, but I hoped in a way she would have approved of. I was sure she'd been hysterical the night Morio Goda had died because she'd just killed him. I saw now she'd thought I'd killed Morio Goda – for taking advantage of me? – and she was trying to figure out how to get me away before anyone else realised it. At least she hadn't died believing that.

'I was remembering what she called to me just before she fell to her death. She shouted that she knew I didn't do it, but that she knew who did. Do you know who she meant?'

Yoshio Yoshimoto hooked the useless phone receiver back on its stand.

'You killed Mrs Maki, didn't you?' I said. 'And Morio Goda.'

It seemed the natural thing to say. The worst he could do was kill me, and I was dead anyway. If I could just gain more time for the captains and the boys to deliver their messages …

'Of course he did,' Professor Kutsuki called from the dining room. 'She was foolish. She was so angry it never occurred to her to protect herself to save others. Sometimes self-sacrifice is just selfishness on a grand scale. You knew that Mrs Maki would not stop till she understood how Morio Goda had acquired the information on how to get into the main offices. You could not allow her to do so. She had to die.'

'Her lack of moral strength made it necessary.' Yoshio Yoshimoto glanced quickly around, then ushered me back into the dining room, pushing Professor Kutsuki out of the way. This time he locked the door.

'Mrs Maki would have destroyed my poison-gas notes. That was why you had to get Morio Goda to steal them – isn't that right? She never thought you were going to use them. Once she realised Miss Chen had not stolen the plans from Tagawa's office, she realised it had to be Morio Goda, acting under your instructions, or he would not have known how to get to the office.'

'He wasn't acting on my instructions. Morio Goda was a fool. Breaking into Headquarters was the act of a fool.'

Professor Kutsuki looked pleased. 'I guessed as much! In stealing Hideki Tagawa's papers Morio Goda saw evidence that you'd been recorded making contact with the Russian agents. He knew that Hideki Tagawa was framing you or you were the traitor, collaborating with the Russians. That's what he confronted you with, didn't he?'

'He came running to tell me he'd found evidence that Hideki Tagawa was fabricating evidence to frame me as a traitor! Too much of a fool to be useful but not enough of a fool to be safe. I reached out to the Russians on behalf of Japan. Nothing traitorous about that. While Hideki Tagawa is trying to preserve the standing of a weak emperor we are planning for the future. Anyway, those deaths are officially recorded as accidents. There's no point in speculating about what happened.'

'I don't have to speculate. I know what happened. Mrs Maki became too weak for you. And she was dropping all those clues … her film screenings, for instance.' Professor Kutsuki turned to address the empty room as though he was delivering a lecture. 'Like Oishi in *The 47 Ronin*, Yoshio Yoshimoto managed to antagonise Hideki Tagawa and his bosses by making them see him as a limited guy following instructions during "on" time,

otherwise drinking and womanising. Mrs Maki knew what he was doing. That was why she loved the film so much. But after a while he got tired of playing the part. He was never very good at sustaining any kind of effort.'

Yoshio Yoshimoto growled at him. Professor Kutsuki bowed slightly, as though acknowledging a question from the audience,

'Especially as Japan's fight became about not losing rather than winning. Especially not losing face to the Westerners and inferior Asian races.'

'Look, old man,' Yoshio Yoshimoto said, 'the unofficial official version we're going with is this. Mrs Maki killed your young aide Morio Goda. Then she killed herself out of guilt but was clever enough to make it look as if she was murdered. Isn't that smart enough for one of your stupid stories?'

Prof Kutsuki shook his head. 'It's too complicated. Besides, where is her motive? And even if she had one, why did she wait so long? Why not kill herself the same night she killed him? I think it makes a better story if Yoshio Yoshima murdered them all. Yoshimoto, don't you agree?'

I waited for his high-pitched giggle, but it didn't come. Professor Kutsuki was done with playing the feeble-minded idiot – even if what he was saying now sounded even more far-fetched than his fantasy stories.

'When Mrs Maki realised it wasn't Su Lin who'd gone to Headquarters in that coat, it must have been clear to her that it had been Morio Goda. Because it must have been someone from the house. Hideki Tagawa and Yoshio Yoshimoto were familiar faces at Headquarters and would have been recognised – besides, neither of you could be mistaken for a woman. And, most

importantly, she knew it wasn't her. That was what threw us off track at first. We were too busy thinking she was the one.'

He was being kind. I was the one who'd been so sure it was Mrs Maki because of the sudden change in her behaviour towards me. But even that was totally understandable if she'd been equally sure that I had sneaked into Headquarters and killed Morio Goda.

'But why would the fool of a boy do something like that? Morio Goda couldn't even carry a bucket of water upstairs without calling for a servant. He must have been acting under someone's orders. Someone whose instructions he took more seriously than hers or mine. Tell me, why did you kill Morio Goda if he was working for you?'

'No one is saying I killed him,' Yoshio Yoshimoto said. 'Who else have you said this rubbish to?'

Professor Kutsuki laughed softly. 'If anyone was going to kill Morio Goda it should have been me. He was sneaking out at night and stealing things. This started even before we left the Philippines. My assistant stealing my work! That was why I stopped dictating to him. But I didn't stop working.'

I didn't think it was anything to laugh about. 'You knew Morio Goda was under orders to steal your work? Why didn't you say something sooner?'

Yoshio Yoshimoto said, 'He didn't do that on my orders. I would never have allowed it. I'm not so stupid. His only instructions from me were to make copies of all the notes Kutsuki made. He said the old man kept most of his formulas in his head. He thought he was so clever and couldn't keep his mouth shut. He was a constant threat. It was reckless and stupid

of him to break into Headquarters. Morio Goda was too impatient and he could have ended up jeopardising top-secret information.'

'That's what you were going to say if it came out? That you killed him because he was a traitor?' I demanded.

'Use the story that works, girl. But nobody's going to care what happened to him. He didn't even get me anything useful! But even if he had, it couldn't have been used without the connection between us coming out. Morio Goda had to die. I thought at first of killing the two of you together. It would have made a great story and people love to believe stories. "Double suicide of young lovers", something like that.'

'I should have known at once you killed Mrs Maki too.' Poor Mrs Maki. 'Your eyes were watering because of the spores on the blue coat she was holding. Because she found it under the mushroom trees where Morio Goda hid it. They made you sneeze. It was an allergic reaction. If she'd fallen out of the window before you reached her, you wouldn't have touched the coat. You had to have come into close contact with her. Did she attack you? Confront you?'

'I never intended to do it so clumsily,' Yoshio Yoshimoto said. 'I had been so patient. I was content to wait for my friend, for she was my friend, to do things her way. I wished that for her. It was her own weakness that brought her down. Mrs Maki was weak. Like all women. She believed once in "death before dishonour", but changed her mind when she saw the reality of war on children. As though it makes any difference whether you kill them as puppies or as dogs!'

'Yoshio Yoshimoto's greatest problem may be that he despises

everyone,' Professor Kutsuki said thoughtfully. 'His enemies, yes, but even more those on his side.'

I was the opposite, I supposed, because I'd always looked for good even in my enemies. I could see now I'd been stupid. But I wasn't sorry.

'You knew all along, didn't you, sir? Why didn't you tell me?'

'What for? Because there was nothing you could do about it. Like there's nothing you can do about it now. If you try to turn on Yoshio Yoshimoto, he'll just kill you too. Like he killed my previous assistant. With his knife-hand strike and twist to the third vertebra, the anchor of the spinal column. All these deaths because of my super poison bomb. And I was only trying to create energy.'

'The bomb is the only worthwhile thing you'll ever come up with,' Yoshio Yoshimoto said. 'I want the detailed final sequencing instructions. The only deaths it will bring are necessary. I promise your memory will be honoured.'

'Yoshio Yoshimoto is a hereditary Shinto priest who clawed his way out of poverty by working for the Japanese Yakuza. But he's still uncomfortable with talk about killing,' Professor Kutsuki said. 'He doesn't mind doing it, just talking about it.'

This gentle statement made Yoshio Yoshimoto pull out his radio and leave the room, locking the door behind him.

'I'm scared,' I said.

'Pah! It's good to be scared. That means you're still alive!'

I had to laugh. I was impressed by how calm he seemed.

'On the other hand, at least we know what happened to Morio Goda and Mrs Maki.' Professor Kutsuki wrestled a bundled handkerchief out of his pocket and started shaking it out.

I moved to help him, thinking he was looking for something in it, but he pushed me aside and moved to the door, still shaking the cloth vigorously.

'We must not trust our feelings because we're human, and most of the time human beings don't think. We react, respond, are influenced by pollen that's blown on us by the wind. We are the substrate that ideas land on and grow. Like mushrooms. Pollen, spores, they get everywhere and stick to everything...'

He returned to his seat just as a huge sneeze came from the other side of the door.

'It's so hard to be a secret agent when you have allergies,' Professor Kutsuki said. 'Why don't you come back in, Yoshimoto-san? I think it's about time we got everything out in the open.'

As Yoshio Yoshimoto unlocked the door and entered, Professor Kutsuki added, 'Interesting, isn't it? That all your samurai and ninja training cannot compete against my superior hearing and sense of smell.'

'Enough of your nonsense. I want the final assembly instructions you wouldn't let Morio Goda see.'

'And I want revenge for my dead assistant.'

Yoshio Yoshimoto laughed. 'Morio Goda was working for me, not for you.'

'I'm talking about my previous assistant, Fukutarō Suzuki. The boy who wrote mystery stories and changed my mind about science and war. And who confessed to me he was supposed to steal my work and learn to set the bomb. He said he was going to tell you he couldn't betray me. He begged me to take my papers and flee. When he did not return from meeting you, I knew the boy was dead.'

'If he'd stayed with you he'd likely have been killed by that bomb the rebels set off in your lab. I had nothing to do with that. I would never have risked research we had so much invested in.'

'I started the fire,' Professor Kutsuki said. 'I set off the bomb in my laboratory. I deliberately destroyed my work to prevent it falling into your hands. I knew you killed him. He was innocent. You should have killed me. You don't know how that felt. It was like killing my own children. But better dead than twisted and used by evil men. I meant to kill myself but ended up blind. I thought then that it was my punishment. I see now that it was to give me the chance to avenge him.'

'I already saw enough of your experiment results to know it works.'

'You are out of touch with reality, you and your nostalgic longings for feudal Japan. Things weren't that great then, you know. We were all fighting each other and, worse, getting whipped by the Mongols. Primitives on ships. You killed Suzuki, didn't you? I know you did. Admit it.'

Yoshio Yoshimoto didn't deny it. 'He deserved it. He was weak and useless, a traitor.'

'He was a good boy. He could have been a great man.'

'You may know some science tricks, but you don't know anything about the real world,' Yoshio Yoshimoto sneered.

'Young man, I know the real world. I know Imperial Japan lost this war three years ago when we were defeated at the battle of the Coral Sea, even though our numbers were greater. Then, the following month, the Imperial Japanese Navy lost aircraft carriers at the battle of Midway. The *Akagi* was scuttled when it

became clear she could not be saved. My sister's grandson was on board. He was the last we had to lose.'

'You are the last.'

'I died long before this.'

'You were all for serving the Japanese Empire once. Why did you decide to betray the cause?'

'Reading made me less convinced of Japanese superiority. Of the superiority of any race. Young Suzuki influenced me as much as I influenced him.

'You read his story.' Professor Kutsuki turned to me. 'What if the foreman had not been the kind of character to kill his men to keep them quiet? The most wicked and greedy of bosses could have had no power over what happened underground in the mine.'

'What are you talking about?' Yoshio Yoshimoto demanded.

'A story by Keikichi Ōsaka, real name Fukutarō Suzuki, died July the second 1945 in Luzon,' said Professor Kutsuki. 'But I'd received the message he was sending me.'

'Your useless assistant Suzuki? Just because he wrote some stories and died you think the war is lost?'

'In the story the engineer Kikuchi says, "There's no way we can fight the sea." That may be true, but it is not the sea he fights. He exposes Foreman Asakawa, who murdered his colleagues. That's where you are now. You're trying to fight the sea. There's no way you can win.'

'You're mad. Who fights the sea?' Yoshio Yoshimoto said. 'In any case you blew up your lab and blinded yourself for nothing. I already had enough information to assemble the components. I want the secret assembly instructions you wouldn't let Morio Goda see.'

'There are no instructions. I destroyed them. It was too dangerous. One wrong move and the person working on it dies.'

'That doesn't matter now.' Yoshio Yoshimoto raised his pistol. 'We are all going to die anyway. Now, I want the bomb-assembly instructions. If you can't remember them, you're useless to me. Where do you want me to put the first bullet?'

He moved the gun downwards between Professor Kutsuki's knees. The old man clenched his fists, steeling himself.

'Wait,' I said. 'His assembly instructions are in the briefcase. I saw them.'

'What?' The gun shifted to me.

'Hideki Tagawa must have figured it out. That was why he put the origami in his safe. The origami Professor Kutsuki folded. Morio Goda took them because they were in the safe, even though he didn't know what they meant. The secret formula is already there.'

Professor Kutsuki's mouth gaped. Even the grotesque cartoon eyes on his spectacles were looking at me as if I'd betrayed him.

'No!' Professor Kutsuki said, in an agonised whisper. 'Not in the origami!'

I think that, more than anything else, convinced Yoshio Yoshimoto.

Origami Secrets

———◆———

'I knew you would never have destroyed your life's work,' Yoshio Yoshimoto said. He put away his gun. 'The only conclusion I can draw is that you intended to try to use it to bargain with the Allies. That means I have no choice but to treat you as a traitor.'

Yoshio Yoshimoto swept the origami towards him. 'You couldn't bear to waste all the work you've already done? Because you couldn't be bothered to record it? I knew better than that. You wouldn't want to be forgotten.' He started sifting through them.

'Maybe better to be forgotten than remembered as a monster,' Professor Kutsuki said. His arms were crossed and he was facing resolutely away from me.

'Why would you choose to die for nothing and be forgotten, when you could die for the cause and be celebrated as a hero for ever? You're going to die either way. You think you'll be remembered as a hero? You'll be completely forgotten. You won't even have a grave for me to piss on!'

Yoshio Yoshimoto unfolded a piece of origami, squinted at it and cast it aside.

'It's dangerous to leave things on paper, as your spies and thieves have shown,' Professor Kutsuki said. 'The girl is lying. My formulas are safe only in my head!'

I could see he was rattled and wished I could comfort him. But there were more important things at stake right now. I only hoped Tanis and Ah Peng were safely on their way.

'All their lies about the American bomb will be forgotten once they see what our great poison bomb can do. Not just human deaths but the land, the seas around will be dead for generations. That is the price of daring to humiliate Japan!'

Yoshio Yoshimoto still hadn't found anything. I could see he wasn't familiar with handling paper. He had the thickly calloused hands of a martial artist, and the way he moved the documents close to his eyes suggested he needed reading glasses. Perhaps he thought them unmanly or too Western.

'What I don't understand is why you would sabotage your own invention. This might have been your finest moment. You could have been the father of the bomb that saved the Japanese Empire!'

'I judge based on the facts. When the facts changed, I changed my mind. You should know that Tagawa's orders came directly from Prince Higashikuni Naruhiko. It is the Emperor's wish that there be an orderly and peaceful transition. Prince Higashikuni Naruhiko has been asked to form new cabinet.'

'He told you that?' Yoshio Yoshimoto looked disbelieving. 'You are as big a liar as he is!'

'He didn't have to. I can hear what people say on the phone. And sometimes I can even hear what people are thinking.

For instance, you are thinking surrender would dishonour you, regardless of all the lives – all the Japanese lives – a peace treaty would save.'

'A peace-treaty negotiation must wait until after we give the Emperor a *tennozan*, a great victory that he can use to start negotiations from a stronger bargaining point with the Allies. That is what we are going to give him. A striking victory. It is a glorious privilege to die for the holy Emperor of Japan, and every Japanese man, woman and child should be glad to die for him!'

Yoshio Yoshimoto sounded like one of the Christian revival preachers who used to turn up regularly before the war, railing against the marks of Satan they saw on us heathens (mostly protective bead bracelets and forehead bindis, though they also railed at women in *samfoo* trousers and men in sarongs, and thought that anything other than English was the language of the devil).

Like Yoshio Yoshimoto, they'd also called on us to embrace the glorious privilege of dying for their Church on earth. Or at least to donate funds to support them and finance their good works. Mostly we thought them mad, but as mad white men they had to be humoured and kept happy. In the same way and even more urgently, Yoshio Yoshimoto must now be humoured and kept from killing anybody else.

'His Majesty is a pacifist. As such and as the state Shinto leader, he wished to avoid war from the start. And now that the army and navy are feuding with the state, Japan is headed for disaster,' Professor Kutsuki said. I could see he was still trying to distract him.

'The samurai know the most effective weapon is the man unafraid to die. The Americans have nothing that can stand against

us! And you – you aren't even a samurai. You never wanted anything to do with a bomb. You think it's more important to invent fertiliser! As though any cow in any field doesn't know how to produce it! There's nothing written here!' Yoshio Yoshimoto pushed away the papers, then leaned across the corner of the table and smacked Professor Kutsuki on the side of his head. 'I should kill you for wasting my time and making a fool of me.'

Professor Kutsuki fell back with a little cry and Yoshio Yoshimoto raised his gun. 'Give me the plans in your head or I will blow them out of it!'

'Wait! Please!' I cried. 'It isn't just what's written on the paper. There's a code!'

'What?' At least he turned away from Professor Kutsuki. 'What does a girl like you know about codes?'

'Hideki Tagawa must have guessed – that's why he took the papers. But he couldn't figure out what they said. It's only because my eyesight is so poor that I managed to feel it with my fingers.'

I didn't mention I'd also had the advantage of having worked with Uncle Chen's instructions to his men, most of whom couldn't read, which involved diagrams and the tying of knots.

'You're lying,' Yoshio Yoshimoto said. Coming from him, this was encouragement to go on.

'It's how he recorded the formulas – the information is in the origami. If you look at the lines from the folds as well as the points pricked around them …'

Yoshio Yoshimoto shuffled the pile of origami and picked one out. 'Tell me what this says.'

It was a bird. I unfolded it. 'If you look here, this is where he wrote his formulas – on the underside of the papers. The folds

of paper separate the characters as well as form the strokes.'
I pointed out the lines and dots.

'Read it out to me. Show me.'

'No!' said Professor Kutsuki.

I charged on, not wanting him to say anything. I read or
translated or invented a warning about the importance of
keeping the components separate until ready to combine.
Keeping them dry but—

'They're dry,' Yoshio Yoshimoto said. 'All the poison-bomb
components have been transported to the laboratory archive.'

I was counting on Yoshio Yoshimoto not wanting to admit
he didn't see anything ... In any case, there was nothing to see
because I was making it up as I went along. Either I was wrong
about the instructions being encoded in the origami or this was
one of the birds I'd folded because I didn't see anything that
made sense. There were words, yes. But it read more like a
farewell poem to a loved one than instructions ...

But Yoshio Yoshimoto was nodding as though he understood
so I went on 'reading': '"To build up pressure it must be assembled
in a sealed chamber safely away from water."'

'Away from water? It was Professor Kutsuki who chose the
Swan Lake as a possible detonation point. That's why I chose
the archive room as the closest storage area. Let me see that.'

I didn't dare look at Professor Kutsuki as I went on making
up scientific gobbledygook. Thank goodness for the long hours
I'd put into translating the dullest news for the Japanese
propaganda papers.

'Stop it! Girl, keep your mouth shut!' Professor Kutsuki's
shriek of exaggerated alarm reassured Yoshio Yoshimoto.

He didn't notice the professor's shrill, high-pitched tone had returned. If I ever got the opportunity, I would have to tell him he was giving himself away when he overplayed it.

'Earlier he said it was best set off near water.' Yoshio Yoshimoto looked doubtful. He squinted at the paper I was holding and touched it with his fingertip. 'Is that the symbol for water?'

I reminded myself not to underestimate his eyesight and squinted at the note. 'Best stored near enough water that there's humidity so that it doesn't spontaneously combust. You need to be near water, that's what it says – and not seawater.'

'Why?'

'I don't know. It's what it says. You must have water in the atmosphere. See here? Because it's close enough to water for the air to be humid and keep the components stable. But not too close to the water, which would dissolve and deactivate them.'

He waved away the paper I held out to him. If it was something I was willing to show him, he wasn't interested. 'I remember something about that. That's why we chose this spot. Because of the Swan Lake. I thought the old fool was following some *fusui* superstition.'

Like our *feng shui*, Japanese *fusui* was more about creating harmony and balance in the environment than superstition. But I wasn't going to argue with Yoshio Yoshimoto. I felt him assess me as he studied me. Across a mahjong table I'd say he was weighing up the help I could give against the likelihood I would try to sabotage him.

I made a show of rubbing my hip and wincing, as though I was having trouble standing. Then, as though I suddenly realised

what I was doing, I stood as straight as I could and plastered an obviously fake, but brave, smile on my face.

It worked.

'You're hopeless!' Yoshio Yoshimoto said. 'Go through those and see if there's anything else useful.'

He stepped away to watch me work as he used his radio. It was the perfect distance. I heard him demanding why Hideki Tagawa hadn't been detained and questioned. He wanted to know why the power and phones were down at Moss House. Was it bombs? Sabotage? Weather? He couldn't see what I was scribbling as I paused, apparently squinting and holding up the intricate papers to the oil lamp as I tried to figure out what they said.

'I have all the bomb components ready and waiting. We're doing this tonight. You're going to help me move them out to the lakeside and figure out the steps. That's the nearest body of water. According to his instructions, the bomb must be detonated near a body of water for greatest effect. If he won't give us the instructions, we'll just pile it all by the lake and set it off with a stick of dynamite ... Dynamite. I need the dynamite ...'

'Fool!' Professor Kutsuki cackled, 'You great fool. You think that will do it? Without any build-up of pressure? Hah! That just goes to show you don't have the whole plan. You don't have the secret that makes it a super-bomb. All you'll get is a bunch of dead fish!'

'Think, girl, use your head! Isn't there anything inside your skull?' I heard Miss Briggs's voice loud and clear. I would have thought it was a spirit speaking to me except, as far as I knew, Miss Briggs was still alive somewhere in the women's PoW detention centre, marked as a dangerous enemy alien.

(Over twenty years later we learned her cousin Ruth had been part of the team that decrypted the Germans' Enigma machine, so she'd had dangerous connections. But at the time Miss Briggs's greatest threat lay in her being a British lady who believed girls were worth educating.)

At the Mission School Miss Briggs had taught us domestic science and arithmetic, often at the same time. She'd been strict, but told us she was preparing us to manage our future homes and husbands' businesses. She'd always told us to collect all the facts, then assess them. Not impartially: we were to try to judge our assets and arrange them to please our mothers-in-law, no matter how demanding they might be – but always keep aside a little nest egg for ourselves, just in case. If we never needed it, it would be a nice present to leave to any daughters we had.

Had there really been a time when the worst we could imagine for our lives was being controlled by a demanding mother-in-law?

Well, now Yoshio Yoshimoto was the person in control. My goal was to make him think I would help him detonate the poison-gas bomb that could wipe out our island. My asset? That the British-built archive store had been constructed to withstand a direct bomb hit from outside. With any luck, it would withstand the same force from within.

'You want to kill me? Why don't you just shoot me! I'll never help a traitor like you!'

Professor Kutsuki was trying to goad Yoshio Yoshimoto into killing him. I knew why: he couldn't bear to kill himself any more than he could destroy his deadly calculations. He loved those

equations as a work of art as well as of science. And he didn't want to see his art destroying lives.

And maybe, also, because he'd guessed I'd sent for help and was stalling till anyone who might stop Yoshio Yoshimoto could get there.

'Maybe I should,' Yoshio Yoshimoto said. He was playing with his radio, clearly not getting the responses he wanted.

I wished I knew what was going on outside. 'You may need his input later,' I said.

'He's only useful as a computing machine. He was set to work out how a bomb can do the most damage with the least trouble. Now we've got his calculations, he's redundant.'

He looked up from his radio at me. 'Why are you helping me? What do you want?'

'I think it's what my mother and her people would want me to do.'

I'd no idea what my late mother would have wanted, but it seemed like a good idea to remind him that at least half of me carried his valued samurai heritage.

'I think she would agree it is better to die than live underfoot.' I tried to look like I desperately wanted his approval – was totally sincere: I wanted to keep him focused on his cause and justifications rather than any threat I might pose to him.

Luckily for me, others had prepared him to believe women would fall out of the sky for him.

'Put all the origami birds and mice back in the briefcase and come with me. Never mind the rest of the papers. Hurry up.'

I purposely set aside the paper I'd already 'read' to him with my fingers.

Now I wanted to hurry Yoshio Yoshimoto to the archive store where his bomb components were. If I couldn't stop him setting off the bomb, I could at least try to make sure it did the least harm possible. I hoped the reinforced archive store was as impermeable as the British had believed.

Yoshio Yoshimoto swore at the phone lines again. Luckily a thunderstorm was in progress and got the blame for that. But it was unlucky, too, because the rainwater would spread the effects of the poison-gas bomb further and faster than anything else.

He was trying his radio again – this time there was only static.

'Sir? We don't have much time. We should hurry.'

'Come with me,' he said. 'Bring the paper instructions.'

'But it will take time to read them all.'

'All the components are ready. How difficult can it be? I have dynamite, which should be enough to trigger the blast. We don't have to follow all his precious procedures.'

I handed the unfolded origami paper to Professor Kutsuki. 'It's already clear what this one says, so we won't need it.'

Professor Kutsuki had stopped protesting. He looked stunned.

Yoshio Yoshimoto glanced at him and seemed satisfied. 'Come on. Now! Bring the old fool!'

'Sir, you don't need him if we already have the origami—'

'And leave him here to wander off and make trouble?'

He yanked Professor Kutsuki to his feet. The old man fell heavily against him and whimpered. 'I want my origami,' he said. 'I don't want to go out in the thunderstorm.'

'Hurry up,' Yoshio Yoshimoto said.

The Archive Store

———◆———

'**C**ome on!'

It was dark outside the house because of the blackout and the heavily clouded sky. Only Yoshio Yoshimoto had a small flashlight. He marched Professor Kutsuki and me out across the driveway. He hadn't looked in the direction of his car, which meant I'd wasted my time and those nails – and also that I'd sabotaged my only chance of driving Professor Kutsuki away from here if I'd somehow managed to separate us from Yoshio Yoshimoto.

Well, given that I couldn't drive, that had been a pretty long shot. If I got out of this alive, I told myself, I would find a way to learn. Though the probability of us surviving was so low I might as well have promised myself I'd learn to fly an aeroplane, like Amelia Earhart.

But that was all moot.

I already knew I wasn't going to survive this. That wasn't even on the table. The only thing I could hope to do was stop Yoshio Yoshimoto from destroying everything and everyone else on the island.

And if he had already assembled the components, the only chance for that was to find a way to get the poison-gas bomb neutralised quickly. Before he calmed down enough to study the instructions more thoroughly. And before any of his co-conspirators who understood either science or origami script better than he did arrived to translate them.

Now the best I could hope was that the reinforced archive store would contain the explosion for sixty years at least. Wasn't that what the builder had promised? After that time even Professor Kutsuki's poisons should have decayed or dissipated or whatever deadly poisons did.

Oh, if only I'd paid more attention to Dr Shankar and his plant poisons!

'Hurry up!'

Because of my poor eyesight and uneven legs I was very aware of uneven terrain. I walked carefully. But Professor Kutsuki wasn't helping. In fact, he was slowing us down. He usually took pride in how surefooted he was on familiar paths but now he was struggling to keep his footing. He kept stumbling and falling and dropping things. I picked up a pen and a handkerchief and returned them to him. But when he promptly dropped them again I left them. If he was having a tantrum at least it was a quiet one.

'Will you read to me again? If we get out of this alive?' He clutched at my arm. 'You're not angry with me?'

He reminded me of the children asking for stories to distract them from hunger because they knew it was no good asking for food.

'Of course,' I said. 'I'm not angry with you. Not at all. I hope you're not angry with me.'

'Never, girl.' Professor Kutsuki stumbled and fell again. I knew he was acting because he could move around perfectly well when he wanted to. Or maybe he had lost all hope.

We ended up inside the laboratory building, at the locked door to the archive store.

Yoshio Yoshimoto produced a ring of keys and unlocked the chain padlock as well as the two locks on the door with a smug flourish.

Nothing I'd seen up till then had prepared me for the contents of that store room. I'd expected filing cabinets. Instead it was filled with metal containers. Dull red canisters three deep against one wall and packing cases along another. These had been prised open and I saw inside them sacks of some powdery substance.

The cement-lined bunker was as long as the laboratory Professor Kutsuki used but just half its width. There were signs all around saying that the ventilation shafts must be left open when anyone was inside the space. It had clearly been designed for long-term rather than top-secret storage.

The air was stuffy, even worse than the air in the lab had been. Not surprising as the air vents were still closed. And it smelt bad, as if a lizard or a small bat had got trapped in there and died.

'It's all here.' Yoshio Yoshimoto pointed his torch around the rows and rows of canisters, some red, some white, but mostly a dull metallic grey with a red biohazard danger warning.

'These are the bomb materials?' They looked like canisters of milk or petrol.

'Simple sheet-metal but designed to hold white phosphorus

or liquid mustard gas.' Professor Kutsuki sounded proud and excited now. 'Blow it up and mustard gas will be released into the atmosphere. But even that won't do as much damage as it could. All you'd get is short-term effect. Anyone within range, their lungs are ruined and they die in about two weeks. Same as what happened in the Great War. But that's where we've improved on it with our superior intellects. You have to blow it up under contained pressure. You've collected the ingredients, but where's your oven?' He walked forward and touched a canister. 'I knew it,' he said, 'I knew you were hiding something in here all along. And I was right.'

He ran his fingers down it lightly, then down the next one. 'Remember when the Portuguese introduced castella cake to Nagasaki? Nagasaki was the only port open to foreigners, the only place you could get sugar from China, in those days. But even with sugar, flour and eggs, there were no ovens. So we invented the *hiki gama*, cooking castella cake on the brazier with hot charcoal on the lid as well as beneath. Such ingenuity, the housewives of Nagasaki. And all dead now ... all blown up ... lucky to be killed instantly by the blast. Because the alternative would have been infinitely worse, if their bomb is what I think it is.'

The professor's fear had disappeared with his manic childishness. In fact, he seemed enormously relieved. As if all the pressure we'd been enduring had suddenly dissipated.

'I'm going outside to sit down,' he said. 'I can't breathe in here.'

To my surprise, Yoshio Yoshimoto followed him out instead of stopping him.

'Wait! Aren't you going to lock up the archive store and set

off the bomb?' Hadn't he taken in what the professor said about building pressure? Did I have to give the man a chemistry lesson before he realised what he had to do to kill us in there?

Frustrated, I followed them out.

Professor Kutsuki had taken his usual seat in the laboratory. He'd been listening for me, I realised. When I came to stand beside Yoshio Yoshimoto, he spoke as though he'd been interrupted in the middle of a lecture.

'As you may or may not know, this all began in the Philippines. The support for my plant-based energy-generation research project. It could be the solution to all our energy needs for generations. But how many people knew I was given the war department's nerve-gas research and asked to see what I could do with it? It was research that had been officially banned for fear that the Americans would retaliate. In other words, I wasn't developing a clean energy generator, I was creating a bomb.'

'You were working for the future of the Japanese Empire. For the good of your people!' Yoshio Yoshimoto said.

'Sir, do you have your dynamite ready?' I said, in case he'd forgotten he was supposed to be detonating a bomb. But they ignored me.

I realised Yoshio Yoshimoto might be getting cold feet... as though he hadn't already let me down enough! That would be good, unless one of his fellow conspirators with more guts – or scientific knowhow – showed up.

'It was only later I realised that research hadn't come from the war department,' Professor Kutsuki said, 'or, rather than being issued by the war department, it had been stolen from

the war department. Why else would you instruct me not to mention it to the prime minister?'

Yoshio Yoshimoto stared at him. 'I hope you're not suggesting that I—'

'I'm not suggesting anything. I'm telling you I know that you and your ultra right-wing nationalists were working on your own, directly contrary to instructions given by the Emperor at the Imperial Conferences. Going further even than the Big Six could imagine.'

'Because they are stupid old men. A bunch of cowards. Their time is over and they can't even see it!'

'But why? That's what I want to understand. I won't insult you by asking what you are getting out of it. I've seen enough to know you aren't doing anything for personal gain or glory. But something must be driving you to all this destruction.'

Yoshio Yoshimoto looked at Professor Kutsuki as though he was seeing him for the first time. Maybe he was.

'You probably won't understand, but I was doing it for Japan. For the honour of the true Japan.'

'You're right. I don't see how directly disobeying imperial and military commands could be for the good of Japan.'

'Of course you don't see. You're blind!' Yoshio Yoshimoto laughed. 'The Emperor, the government, the supreme war council, they're just old men behaving like cowardly children. There are huge issues facing Japan. The whole world is watching us and waiting to shame us in our disgrace. This is the time for us to break through and deliver the death blow to them!'

'And you think you could do what the Emperor and his best men could not?'

'Because I'm not a coward like them. I'm not afraid of dying. And I'm not taken in by your delaying tactics. It won't do you any good. No one is coming to save you.'

Delaying tactics? As far as I could tell, Yoshio Yoshimoto was the one doing the delaying.

'We had all the components ready. The first bomb was planned for the Philippines, but the Americans moved in before we could assemble everything so we came to Singapore. That was Mrs Maki's idea. She thought the threat would be enough to deter the Americans.'

'But it wasn't enough for you,' Professor Kutsuki said. 'You want to die gloriously and you don't care who you have to crush on your way to Hell.'

'It wasn't enough because the bomb's devastating effects have to be seen to be believed. Any country can claim they have the greatest powers, but talk is worth nothing.'

'Why Singapore?' I asked.

'Destroying their precious gem will hurt Britain and Mr Churchill most. And all the bomb components are already here,' Yoshio Yoshimoto said. He gave Professor Kutsuki a mock bow, as though congratulating him.

'Sir, you still have to set off the bomb,' I reminded him.

He brushed me off as if I was an irritating fly.

'The problem is sunk costs,' Professor Kutsuki said. 'Effort already put in, money already spent that can never be recovered. That's why many people won't change their minds even if they know they're wrong – because they've spent so much time being wrong that they don't want to admit it. So they go on walking deeper and deeper into the swamp. They close their eyes, they

cover their ears, so they don't have to see or hear that they're going the wrong way. I prefer the cynics. The mercenaries who are out to make money from these fools. They at least know what they're doing. And then there's people like Yoshio Yoshimoto.'

Yoshio Yoshimoto looked superior. 'I've been ahead of you all the time. Suzuki managed to give us a pretty good idea of what was needed before you decided to stop working – and I had all the bomb components moved here. Close to water to do the most damage, as your instructions said, right?'

'So what if you have all the components lined up in the archive store? Hydrogen and oxygen are the components of water. There's hydrogen and oxygen in the air you breathe. Does that mean your lungs fill with water every time you take a breath? Pah! You're a fool! You're all ignorant fools! No education and no common sense!'

Quite calmly, Yoshio Yoshimoto pulled out his gun and shot Professor Kutsuki in the thigh. 'You're the fool. You don't know how long I've wanted to do that.'

Professor Kutsuki crashed backwards into the desk, then toppled sideways onto the floor. A dark red circle appeared on his trousers. I screamed and ran over to him, but he pushed me away. 'Pah! Call yourself a soldier?' he said to Yoshio Yoshimoto. 'You can't even shoot straight.'

I batted his arm away, squatted beside him and pressed down on the wound. Through the thick cloth I couldn't tell how bad the bleeding was.

Yoshio Yoshimoto raised the gun again.

'How many bullets do you have left?' I asked innocently. 'Should you reload?'

'Come here, and bring the origami with you.' Yoshio Yoshimoto lowered his gun. I'd been right in guessing he would value ammunition over Professor Kutsuki's life.

He kicked him as he passed and the old man moaned, which made Yoshio Yoshimoto snort and say he was no samurai.

Collecting the scattered origami, I crouched by Professor Kutsuki. 'I'm sorry,' I said. I didn't have time to explain why I was glad he wouldn't be joining us inside the archive store.

'I'm sorry too, my child.'

'And thank you. Thank you for everything.'

'Come on!' Yoshio Yoshimoto said.

'Go. Just go. Do whatever Yoshio Yoshimoto wants. Give him whatever he wants. Just try to survive as long as you can. I don't want to lose another young friend. You have much work to do with your life.'

'I'm going to die. No more work for me.'

I'd meant it as a joke, but Professor Kutsuki answered seriously, 'Everyone dies. How you die can be the most important work of all. But, believe me, it isn't your time yet. As long as you just stretch it out, take your time.'

If he still didn't want to admit there was no hope for me, I wasn't going to take that away from him.

'You too. Hold on. Not for yourself but for those like Suzuki whose strengths lie in other fields. Try to give them a chance to fight for themselves.'

I didn't know if Professor Kutsuki would be safe in the laboratory from the gas. I only hoped the British engineering designed to keep contamination out would also keep it in.

'Try to get others to read his stories. Don't let him be forgotten.'

I might only be giving the old man a slower and more painful

death. But I was also increasing his chance of surviving by a minuscule amount. When you reached the stage we were at, you had to cling to anything you could find.

I followed Yoshio Yoshimoto into the archive store with the origami.

At least Professor Kutsuki was still alive for now. At least my family in Katong, Le Froy and Dr Shankar in Changi Prison were at a good distance. If the reinforced archive store could somehow limit the force of this bomb, they might yet survive this.

Maybe going on without any real hope is the truest definition of hope. Some might call it faith, others madness. But in the moment it's just one small choice on top of all the other small choices that led you to this point.

Yoshio Yoshimoto was holding a stick of dynamite. 'Go through those papers and tell me what to do.'

I wouldn't be able to stop him but I could make sure it did as little harm as possible.

'We have to set it off in here,' I said. 'Close the ventilation shaft and set off the explosive.'

'In here?' He looked dubious. But he wasn't suspicious. Yet.

'It's to build up pressure,' I said. I've never been very good at lying. But I did my best. 'That's why Professor Kutsuki was so particular about getting a sealed chamber, with no chance of water getting in. If the pressure is contained at the time of the first explosion it will build up that much more, forcing the components to combine and resulting in a much greater effect.'

'Like gunpowder in a closed capsule,' Yoshio Yoshimoto said. 'This whole room is the capsule. It will be huge! The old fool knows his stuff.'

He unfolded a faded carbon copy from a folder stuck behind one of the canisters and jabbed at it. 'Here – that's the sign for water, isn't it? And doesn't that mean danger? Next to the water sign?'

I looked at the paper. This note was quite clear. The poison-gas bomb would have the greatest and swiftest effect if it was detonated out of doors preferably near a large body of water during a heavy rainstorm. We were in the height of the south-west monsoon season. A thundering rainstorm was going on outside now, though inside the insulated walls of the archive store we could barely hear it. Sometimes these storms lasted days and nights without stopping. The thought of how much damage the poison could do, spread by those waters, was horrifying.

'It says to keep away from water or other chemicals may lose effect,' I said. Apart from the tremor in my voice I thought I sounded convincing. And it was natural to be scared in such a situation. 'That's why Professor Kutsuki wanted them stored so safely. He said they could not go anywhere near water or damp. They had to be kept here and dry, so that they would not lose their potency.'

Close enough to the water, the deadly gas would access the whole island's connected river and canal network, and the precious water in the reservoirs. And once it reached the Kallang River, it would be deadly to the whole island and the seas around it.

'Don't worry,' Professor Kutsuki called from the laboratory. 'Don't be frightened, girl. There is no bomb. Nothing's going to happen. I took care of it.'

'You lie, old man!'

Yoshio Yoshimoto went out to the laboratory and smacked him across the back of the head with the butt of his gun.

Maybe he wanted to cause pain just once more before he died. Or maybe he was trying to put it off because the brave patriot was a little afraid of dying.

'Sir, your dynamite.' I reminded him. 'You must seal the room and set off your dynamite.'

'You women! You never stop nagging!'

'Distant mountains move when a woman speaks. Better watch out!' Professor Kutsuki's high-pitched giggle (I would never get the chance to warn him about it now) told me I was missing something yet again. But what?

Then I realised that he and Yoshio Yoshimoto weren't the only ones in the laboratory.

Dying Together

———◆———

I saw Professor Kutsuki sitting on the floor with a pool of blood beneath him and a beatific grin on his face. 'Welcome, one, welcome, all! Come in, come in, come in!' he was shouting.

A quick glance round the space showed Hideki Tagawa, Captains X and Y and several other uniformed officers I didn't recognise. I also saw de Souza, but not Prakesh.

The reinforcements had arrived faster than I'd thought possible. Too soon, in fact. I'd hoped they would be in time to keep the chamber and its contents locked down after we'd blown ourselves up but—

'How'd you get here so fast?'

'I was on standby,' de Souza grinned, 'so when your kids showed up I was all set.'

Even Tanis and Ah Peng were there. Hadn't they promised not to come back? I was glad to see them alive but I gave them the evil eye. It wasn't over yet. If we survived the night I was going to *hantam* them. A Singlish word, *hantam* covers a range of meanings from slapping or whacking someone, through

criticising and finding fault with them, to squeezing them so hard with affection that it hurts. Right then all of those applied.

'How'd you know to come out here?'

'There was a trail from the house.' Captain X showed what he was holding: the bits of paper Professor Kutsuki had dropped along the way, as well as a handkerchief and an ink stamp. Captain Y had several keys and the professor's comb. 'We are here to arrest Yoshio Yoshimoto for opposing the Emperor's orders and for attacking Professor Kutsuki with the intention to steal and sell the poison-gas bomb plans to rival factions. And, most of all, for destroying Japanese property, and for illicit communications with the Russians,' Captain X said.

Yoshio Yoshimoto was silent for once. His eyes, fixed on Hideki Tagawa, asked the question.

'Their bomb over Hiroshima triggered intense firestorms that destroyed everything within a radius of two kilometres,' Hideki Tagawa said.

'The firebreaks? Hiroshima is in an earthquake zone. The buildings are reinforced concrete and very strongly constructed,' Yoshio Yoshimoto said.

'Even if the buildings survived, everyone in them is dead. More than fifty thousand people so far and they haven't found them all yet. The firebreaks were ineffective. And from the early reports, the bomb over Nagasaki did even worse damage.'

'The Emperor is calling for the Big Six to discuss terms,' Hideki Tagawa said. 'It's not that your plan was a bad one, just that it came too late. The Americans wanted to impress the Russians and they have. Russia has signed an agreement with the Allies. It's over.'

'You lie,' Yoshio Yoshimoto said, his lips barely moving. 'Traitor. Traitors, all of you. Nothing has changed. Prime Minister Suzuki made the announcement himself. The Japanese government orders are to ignore the Allies' demands and fight on.'

'It's no use, whatever you've got,' Hideki Tagawa said. 'Russia has already signed an agreement with America. They were deceiving us all along.'

I yelped as Yoshio Yoshimoto grabbed me and put his gun to my head.

'Careful,' Professor Kutsuki said. 'That man thinks he has a bomb!'

'Don't shoot!' I said to Captains X and Y and de Souza, who'd all dropped the trail trinkets left by Professor Kutsuki and pulled out guns. The door to the archive store was open. I didn't know what it would take to detonate the poison-bomb components within. I didn't want anything set off by a stray bullet.

'Let her go,' Hideki Tagawa said. 'Let her go and you can do what you want.'

'Not so brave now, hah?' Yoshio Yoshimoto said. 'Where's all your big talk?'

This wasn't *The 47 Ronin*. Yoshio Yoshimoto was the demon foreman in Suzuki's 'The Demon in the Cave' story. He wasn't sacrificing himself for his master's honour. He was sacrificing everyone else to get what he wanted. Now he was planning to go out with a bang while the others were still trying to scrape small grains of victory from the jaws of defeat.

I thought fast. One lesson I'd learned from my British teachers at the Mission School (who'd struggled against colonial diktats as much as anyone local): you can do as you're told, or you can do as you must and ask forgiveness later.

The worst thing that could happen right now was shots fired into the archive store cracking and igniting the bomb components. With the door and the vents open, the gases would get into the air and the water of the lake and poison the whole island. And I didn't trust Yoshio Yoshimoto to close all the vents. The man was already so tightly wound up I could feel him shaking with nerves as he held me.

'Get us inside the archive store!' I shouted. 'Yoshimoto-san, wake up! Get us in there and barricade the door! The bomb is what is important!'

Yoshio Yoshimoto stiffened, then muttered, 'Yes!' and dragged me inside the archive store, slamming me painfully into the wall as he leaped to slide the inside bolt across the doors.

'We must shut all the vents, then set off the explosive. The powders will mix as they burn as long as you build up enough pressure in here. Do you have the dynamite?'

I was checking the vents, like a crazy woman. Yes, all shut tight. We were in business.

'I have the dynamite!' He believed he'd convinced me.

'Then light it!'

With luck, the components wouldn't come together in Professor Kutsuki's formula. And they would all dissipate without coming into contact with water and becoming more lethal.

I closed my eyes. I knew the dynamite alone would kill us. I just hoped it would be fast. And I prayed the gas wouldn't leave the archive store.

Dynamite is set off by lighting a simple cord fuse. What could be simpler? Why was it taking so long?

'Have you any matches?'

I opened one eye. 'What?'

'My lighter is missing,' Yoshio Yoshimoto said. He was holding his poison pin box and digging wildly in his pockets. 'It's gone!'

I remembered Professor Kutsuki falling heavily against him and groaned. That must have been when he'd pinched Yoshio Yoshimoto's lighter. It had been very clever of him, but it didn't help me defuse his poison-gas bomb. Well, it wasn't a bomb yet, but I hadn't seen all the instructions. I was afraid it was some kind of British one-bowl cake bomb where, once everything was in one room, all you had to do to destroy the island was trigger it with dynamite. And even if not, how much damage would the individual poisons do? 'You must have dropped it coming up the path just now.'

Yoshio Yoshimoto dashed the pin box to the ground and swore.

I slid open one of the vents and called through it, 'Hideki Tagawa!'

Yoshio Yoshimoto smacked me roughly away. 'Shut your mouth! Did you steal my lighter? Where is it?'

'I haven't got it. Let me do this.' I turned back to the vent. 'Tagawa-san! Do you have your Bettini lighter with you?'

'My lighter?'

'Yes!'

Yoshio Yoshimoto came to stand beside me at the vent. Wiping the blood from my lip I shouted, 'Push your lighter through the vent hole. But carefully. I don't want chemicals to catch fire before combining into the poison gas.'

The light dimmed as Hideki Tagawa came up close to the other side of the vent.

Then I whisper-hissed, 'Leave the area. Leave us sealed up in here till the poison gas dissipates. Very important: don't let the gas contaminate the Swan Lake or it will ruin the whole island's water supply.'

Over Hideki Tagawa's sucked-in breath, Yoshio Yoshimoto shouted, 'I don't trust him. That man is a traitor to Japan!'

'Traitor or not, I have a lighter,' Hideki Tagawa bellowed. 'What for? You're taking up smoking?'

'Yes,' I said. 'A last cigarette before dying.'

Yoshio Yoshimoto nodded his approval.

There were some scraping sounds. 'It won't go through. It's too big.'

'Can you break one of the filter frames?' Surely any leakage would be minimal as long as the vent was closed.

But Yoshio Yoshimoto was already lifting the bolt across the doors to open them. 'Tell him to throw it in and to keep his distance. I have a gun on you.'

Hideki Tagawa's hand appeared, holding the lighter. I'd meant to grab it and slam the door once the lighter was in, but Hideki Tagawa jammed his boot in the door.

'You told the children not to die for nothing. Why not practise that yourself?'

'I was planning to die for something, not nothing,' I said. 'Give that to me and get out of here!'

'Here.' Hideki Tagawa lowered his arm and tossed the lighter into the archive store, high in the air. Instinctively Yoshio Yoshimoto raised his hands to grab it. Then Hideki Tagawa was in the room. He punched Yoshio Yoshimoto and threw him across the room. Yoshio Yoshimoto crashed into the barrels of chemicals against the reinforced wall and slumped there, stunned.

'Go away!' I shouted at him. Japanese or Singaporean, enough people had already died. 'We have to sabotage the bomb! You don't understand!'

'No, you don't understand, Su Lin. It's all right – listen to me. It's really all right–'

'Ha!' Yoshio Yoshimoto held up his stick of dynamite. The cord wick was alight and burning.

Hideki Tagawa swore at himself.

'Get out of here!' I tried to push him out. 'Shut the doors!'

'Prepare to die, traitor!' Yoshio Yoshimoto shouted, and rushed towards us.

Hideki Tagawa picked me up like a sack of rice and flung me out of the room. I heard the bolt slam into place even as I was still rolling. And then the pop of the blasting cap and the heavier ground-shaking explosion.

It was huge. We all waited in silence. A moment later, there was a series of small pops. The poison-gas bomb was a huge anticlimax.

I sniffed. I smelt smoke and . . . bananas? No poison gases. 'The vent wasn't closed. The poison gases?'

Now that I looked around, I saw Captains X and Y and the other soldiers squatting around Professor Kutsuki, who was rocking gently from side to side as he sat on the floor refusing to let them attend to him. 'It's all right,' he said. 'Don't worry. You'd better go and see what's left of them.'

'But what about the gases leaking out? And the lake? Can we block the run-off just in case?'

'It's all right, child. Even if he followed the instructions that were stolen from me, all he would get is some very smelly fertiliser.'

'What?' I sniffed. He was right about the smell. 'Fertiliser?'

Professor Kutsuki nodded. 'After I lost the assistant I'd always made fun of, I found I'd taken on his beliefs. When you lose a person, what you really lose is who you were when you were with that person. I had come round to Suzuki's way of thinking before he died. We corrected the components in the formulas together. Anything that Morio Goda stole would be nothing but our concoctions. Did you think I'd allow a rat like him to get away with stealing my actual bomb plans? I'm impressed by you, girl. You tried to destroy the madman's plan of destruction by containing the bomb blast. But there was no bomb to contain.'

Tanis and Ah Peng sidled up to me, looking guilty. 'I'm so angry with you two!' I said, hugging them. I was so glad to see them alive.

'Are you all right?' De Souza had come to me too.

'What happened at Changi Prison?' I demanded. 'He was going to kill all the prisoners – he ordered them all to be shot.'

'Once they heard Emperor Hirohito's announcement, the Japanese soldiers guarding Changi simply handed over the keys and control to the locals. Someone you might know, actually. One Sergeant Pillay of the INA.'

'What? Shouldn't they all have fought to the death or killed themselves?' I couldn't help asking. 'Wait – you mean Prakesh?'

'They were obeying an Imperial order. Obeying orders is no disgrace to family or country.'

'That depends where the order comes from,' I said, thinking of Yoshio Yoshimoto.

'I got the impression no one else wanted to take charge. Neither did Prakesh, but he stepped up. Just for the handover. The men are staying there till we know what's what.'

'But the PoW officers?'

'Will probably take over in time. Right now they're not in any condition. They're getting what food and medication is available to those most in need. The locals are rallying around, sharing whatever they can.'

'Did you see Le Froy?' I just wanted to know.

'Not myself. But if anything had happened to him I'm sure I would have been informed. Glad you're all right, Su Lin.'

'Why are all of you just standing around? Open it quick,' Professor Kutsuki said. 'Blast it open!'

'Wait,' I said. 'Are you sure about the poison gas? Something smells really bad. Should we give it some time – a couple of months? Days? Hours at least?' I still had trouble in accepting that there was nothing dangerous in there.

'No!' Professor Kutsuki said, 'There is no bomb. The blast was just the dynamite. They may still be alive.'

'So all that was for nothing?' I couldn't believe it. 'Wait—'

'The components are inert. I made sure of that before I let Morio Goda steal my notes.'

They started working on trying to get the archive-store door open.

'So it was all for nothing.'

'For what it's worth, you saved our lives. Yours and mine. Yoshio Yoshimoto would have killed us as soon as he knew there was no bomb. Us and as many others as he could. Even if that doesn't mean anything to you, it means something to this old man. I believed I was ready to die. But in that moment when things could have gone either way, I realised I wouldn't mind living on. So thank you.'

'Excuse Me. I Must Go Now.'

———◆———

It's a human instinct to want to fit in. If you can't fit in with the majority, you try to persuade others (but mostly yourself) that you are superior to them. If you try hard enough, you may actually become superior. But you will find you still don't fit in.

The British looked different enough to feel superior just from the colour of their sunburned skin.

The Japanese looked more like us so had to work harder to put us down.

'You saved our lives. If he believed there was no bomb, he would have killed us. I was so afraid you were going to give everything away when you figured out my origami code. That was clever of you, by the way.'

'You did tell Yoshimoto-san,' I remembered, 'but you told him in a way that he wouldn't believe you.'

Yoshio Yoshimoto had called him a liar. But then 'You lie!' was his standard answer to anything he didn't like.

"What did the forty-seven Ronin do? They killed and they

died. Was that honourable?" That was what was written in the origami bird he made me read to him.

'They were my farewell poems to science,' Professor Kutsuki explained. 'And to young Suzuki. That was what I wrote in the origami birds that Hideki Tagawa was keeping for me, explaining why I was leaving science, because it was not meant to be, not now and not ever. After Yoshio Yoshimoto killed Suzuki I realised my love for science had created something lovely but greatly destructive.'

'So you destroyed the records, your life's work,' I murmured.

The poison-gas bomb didn't happen because this man and probably other Japanese scientists couldn't bring themselves to submit something so destructive to their nation's military. The American scientists hadn't had the same qualms.

But it was hard to judge them. Like the American firebombers, they'd done it to save us.

'For a long time I wanted to be remembered for the poison-gas bomb. My greatest creation. The bomb that won the war for Japan. And then I realised being remembered didn't matter if the most important someone was not alive to remember. Once Suzuki confessed to me and went to tell Yoshio Yoshimoto, I knew it was all over. I knew Yoshimoto would kill him. But I wanted to give the boy that one chance to redeem himself, so that I could remember him as good. I was already smarter than all of them then, even if I hadn't yet lost my eyesight. I knew he was spying on me long before he confessed. So the information about the materials needed for the great bomb was already lies. That was what made Suzuki suspect I knew. He was enough of a scientist to see that it was all wrong. If Yoshimoto had known

or cared the least thing about science he would have known too.'

My main reason for suspecting Professor Kutsuki was that his previous assistant had also died under strange circumstances. I hadn't known it was that death that had saved all our lives.

Professor Kutsuki might have started out as the man with the power to kill us all but he ended up sacrificing his invention.

We were interrupted by a cry of triumph. They'd managed to get the door open.

The dynamite blast had killed Yoshio Yoshimoto immediately. Most of his face and chest were blown away, as well as the arm that gripped the dynamite.

Hideki Tagawa was still alive.

I knelt beside him. Burns, lacerations, blast injuries, neck injuries, and who knew what was going on inside? His lungs were damaged. He could only manage the shallowest breaths.

There was blood on the floor beneath him and I smelt burning flesh.

'Get me a knife. I have to—'

'No.'

'I have to do it my way. Please.'

I didn't have a knife. I gave him Yoshio Yoshimoto's poison pin. At least the poison would work faster and less painfully – I hoped. 'I don't know how it works or even if it works—'

He clearly did, though.

'Don't forget your mother. You're very like Ryoko. Always a rebel. Never listening to any advice. You must stay strong. Don't forget you come from noble samurai lineage.'

Hideki Tagawa had loved my mother. She'd not taken him seriously but he had been in love with her all his life.

'If you see my mother before I do, tell her you saved my life.'

'I will tell her you are beautiful. And you know what she'll say?'

He didn't continue, but I heard the words as clearly as if he'd spoken. *I already know.*

'Carefully unscrew the head of the pin. Very carefully. The poison tip is within.'

The head of the blunt nail unscrewed to reveal a very tiny, wickedly sharp point that was still wet from the liquid that had been in the compartment.

I slid the head of the sharp-pointed pin between his thumb and index finger and he nodded his thanks.

I felt tears on my face. For this enemy who'd saved my life, this cousin who was my last connection with my dead mother's family. 'You're my only connection to her.'

'No, I'm not,' Hideki Tagawa said gently. 'The connection is still in you. Excuse me. I must go now.'

'Excuse me. I must go now' is what Oishi says in *The 47 Ronin* before he goes to commit *seppuku.*

I stayed with him till he died.

If anyone asks, my cousin Hideki Tagawa died a noble death.

After the men had secured the archive store and made certain nothing in there could explode, and I had secured a pressure tie over Professor Kutsuki's wound, de Souza carried him back to Moss House.

'My lighters are all down there,' Professor Kutsuki said sadly, as we crossed the plank bridge.

'My lighter, too?' de Souza said, mock serious.

'All my lighters,' Professor Kutsuki said. 'Yours, Yoshimoto-san's. I didn't want to take any risks. Men can do such stupid things when they have a stick of dynamite to play with.'

De Souza's surprised bark of laughter made him smile. 'I'll get you another lighter, sir. But no dynamite.'

At the house I sent the boys to bed and started preparing the tapioca for breakfast. De Souza would be spending the night in Professor Kutsuki's room, in case his condition worsened.

I was so tired but also too tightly wound up to lie down, let alone sleep.

I was sick of tapioca, but we would starve without it. Sometimes what looks like a choice is really no choice at all.

But as long as you're alive there's hope, the British used to say.

And as long as you're alive there's work, as we locals say.

All goals are temporary, whether we succeed or fail. We need something to aim for.

My small goal had been to make it through one more day.

My big goal had been to survive the war and live to make other goals.

For a long time these had seemed impossible but now, for the first time, I felt a stirring of hope that I might make it through the war. And Le Froy was alive: he might come through too.

Epilogue: The Mushroom Trees

Despite what Yoshio Yoshimoto said would happen, the war ended in August, after that day's terrible bombing of Nagasaki, and the Soviet Union's official declaration of war against Japan.

Without that second bomb, the Japanese military would likely have fought on at the cost of not only hundreds of thousands of American casualties but also the death by starvation of many millions of Japanese civilians and the virtual destruction of the Japanese nation.

Kyoto had been the next target after Hiroshima and Nagasaki.

Professor Kutsuki elected to stay on in Singapore after the Japanese surrender and was placed under arrest for war crimes. But while the Japanese didn't know he hadn't done as commanded, I told Le Froy that he'd destroyed his own invention to make sure the poison-gas bomb was never activated.

With that on (confidential) record Professor Kutsuki received the best medical care available and spent most of his 'detention'

time in a hospital ward, where he complained non-stop about the heat. When I went to see him and asked if he would rather be moved to the up-country highlands, he said, 'Spare me. I need to have something to complain about so that the gods don't get jealous and strike me down. May all my problems be this small. And may all my assistants smell as intelligent as you. And may you someday write your articles and maybe even make an English translation of Suzuki's writing.'

Professor Kutsuki went back to his fertiliser investigations. He ended up in an American agricultural university. The last I heard he was working on processing waste products and very excited about the rich quality of waste the Americans produced.

We all went to the Municipal Building of Singapore to watch Lord Louis Mountbatten accept the official Japanese surrender. Yes, we were Singapore again. Syonan was gone for ever.

I spotted Chief Inspector Le Froy among the other released PoWs. He looked smaller, thinner, shrunken, frighteningly emaciated and tens of years older. Like they all did.

The Shankars didn't go to the ceremony. Dr Shankar still spent most of his time attending to patients who'd been his fellow prisoners, but now he had the help of Dr Leask. And Mrs Shankar would hardly let Parshanti out of her sight now she was back. I was surprised how well Parshanti had borne it. She'd changed so much. We all had. Le Froy hardly spoke when we met. And when he did, there was something in his manner that reminded me of Professor Kutsuki playing at being a madman.

'He'll get back his strength,' de Souza said, seeing my eyes on Le Froy.

'He'll never get back his foot,' Prakesh said glumly. 'Goodbye, interdepartmental tug-of-war cup!'

But it wasn't just the recently released prisoners who'd changed. Even the British officers who came in after the Japanese surrender no longer carried the aura of God-given supremacy.

They'd won this war, but only just. And only because American scientists had done what at least one Japanese scientist had refused to do.

Now we had to find new gods. Things would never go back to the way they had been.

I'd thought that all I could hope for was the British to rescue us and restore order. Now I was realising that maybe what we actually needed to do was grow up and take responsibility for our own lives.

The surrender ceremony ended with the hoisting of the Union Flag, the same flag that had flown over Government House before the war. Civil servant Mervyn Sheppard had rescued and kept it hidden in his pillow throughout his captivity in Changi Prison. It was stories like this that would help us build our new lives.

Tanis and Ah Peng, small boys again, were cheering wildly too. They didn't remember a time when they could walk down the street without fear and identification passes.

The darkest period Singapore had gone through was over, even if the dawn had not yet come.

Months later, I went back to the mushroom trees at the Botanic Gardens. I was amazed and delighted to find a profusion of

dancing maitake mushrooms. Being tossed around had somehow stimulated the spores to grow better than my careful tending. Sometimes we need disorder before we can go on to a better life.

I harvested them – not quite legally given I no longer lived there, but I felt I'd earned one crop at least.

I would use them to make maitake rice. It would be an offering to Mrs Maki, who had loved the rich umami flavour of maitake mushrooms, so delicious and virtuously vegetarian.

Mrs Maki must once have had dreams and good intentions. How different would her life have been if my mother had taken her with her to Singapore all those years ago? Maybe it would have made no difference at all. Maybe nothing we do makes any difference.

Much later I learned I'd inherited the estate of Hideki Tagawa. Doesn't seem likely I'll find out what it is, or that there'll be anything left. But I treasured the connection to my mother's family. And we treasure – for a while – this fragile peace.

Acknowledgements

I must thank all the wonderful, patient people responsible for this book, like my agent Priya Doraswamy, editorial director Krystyna Green, managing editor Amanda Keats, copy-editor Hazel Orme, Japanese fact-checker Yumiko Matsudaira, cover designer Andy Bridge and the wonderful team at Constable/ Little, Brown, especially Eleanor Russell, Sarah Murphy, Hannah Wann, Kim Bishop, Chris Sturtivant, Simon McArt, Beth Wright and Francesca Banks. I learned so much from putting this story together, but it's these good people who turned it into a book.

And thank you for picking it up. May you read it in good health and please look me up on Facebook or my webpage at https://www.ovidiayu.com if you'd like to share any thoughts or comments.